Calvin and the consolidation of the Genevan Reformation presents a complete re-evaluation of Calvin's rise to power in Geneva.

Calvin's consolidation of his position and particular brand of Protestantism was of paramount importance to the wider Reformation movement, especially in France, Scotland and England. Extensive research in Geneva's archives has produced this new in-depth view of Geneva's politics, ruling elite, and socio-economic milieu. The book effectively widens the previously known interpretation of Geneva beyond Calvin and a few prominent Genevans to include the entire political ruling class, the other ministers, the French refugees, and Calvin's local Genevan supporters on the Consistory, Geneva's ecclesiastical court.

William G. Naphy is a lecturer in history at the University of Manchester

WILLIAM G. NAPHY

Calvin and the consolidation of the Genevan Reformation

Manchester University Press

Manchester and New York

distributed exclusively in the USA and Canada by St. Martin's Press

Copyright © William G. Naphy 1994

Published by Manchester University Press
Oxford Road, Manchester M13 9NR, UK
and Room 400, 175 Fifth Avenue, New York, NY 10010, USA

Distributed exclusively in the USA and Canada by
St. Martin's Press, Inc., 175 Fifth Avenue, New York, NY 10010, USA

British Library Cataloguing-in-Publication Data
A catalogue record is available from the British Library

Library of Congress Cataloguing-in-Publication Data

Naphy, William G., 1960–
    Calvin and the consolidation of the Genevan Reformation / William
G. Naphy
        p.   cm.
    Includes bibliographical references.
    ISBN 0-7190-4141-4 (cl.)
    1. Calvin, Jean, 1509–1564. 2. Reformation—Switzerland—Geneva.
3. Geneva (Switzerland)—Church history—16th century. 4. Geneva
(Switzerland)—History—1536–1603. 5. Reformed Church—Switzerland
—Geneva—Clergy—Biography. I. Title.
    BX9418.N27   1994
    274.94′5106—dc20   93-50554

ISBN 0 7190 4141 4 *hardback*

Typeset in Adobe Garamond
by Koinonia, Manchester
Printed in Great Britain
by Bookcraft Ltd, Midsomer Norton

CONTENTS

FIGURES

TABLES

APPENDICES

ACKNOWLEDGEMENTS

It is an impossible task to attempt to thank all those people whose assistance helped bring a project to completion. Nevertheless, I feel compelled to express my thanks to those whose special help, advice, and direction made this work possible.

I am indebted to the financial aid which I received from the Russell Trust and the Steven Watson Memorial Trust. Without their assistance, I would not have been able to have spent the necessary hours in the Archives d'Etat de Genève. I am also deeply grateful to the University of St Andrews for the generous Studentship which they gave me and the other helps which they extended to me through such sources as the Travel Fund. I must also make mention of the generosity of my department, Modern History, which proved to be of value on so many occasions.

I cannot begin to thank all of those individuals who aided me in the research and completion of this volume. Special thanks must be given to Ms Christine Gascoigne and Mr Robert Smart in the University Library Muniments for their patience and generous help. Also, I thank Mr William Kay, Ms Karin Maag, and Mr Peter Maxwell-Stuart for enduring the difficult but essential task of proof-reading. I would also make mention of the constant encouragement I received from Dr Jane Dawson, Professor Bruce Lenman, and Dr Hamish Scott. I am greatly indebted as well to Professor James Cameron and Professor Robert Kingdon for their advice and support. Nor can I fail to express my gratitude to all those individuals in Geneva who helped me as I researched there, especially Mlle Barbara Roth-Lochner, of the Archives d'Etat, and Professor Francis Higman, of the Institut d'Histoire de la Réformation. Of course, sincere thanks are owed to Manchester University Press and its editor, Ms Jane Thorniley-Walker, for their assistance and trust in publishing this volume.

Finally, my deepest expression of gratitude is reserved for the three people whose efforts at every stage of the way made this volume a reality. First, I will never be able to repay the debt which I owe to my supervisor, Dr Andrew Pettegree. It would be impossible, I believe, for anyone to have had a better mentor or advisor. And last, but most definitely not least, I extend my sincerest thanks to my parents, Paul and Arlene Naphy, for all the love and support they have always shown me; it is to them that I dedicate this work.

William G. Naphy
St Andrews, 1993

ABBREVIATIONS

Advis	François Bonivard. *Advis et Devis sur l'Ancienne et Nouvelle Police de Genève* (Geneva: 1865).
AEG	Archives d'Etat de Genève.
ARG	*Archiv für Reformationsgeschichte.*
Bourg.	Alfred Covelle. *Le Livre des Bourgeois* (Geneva:1897).
BN	Bibliothèque Nationale, Paris.
Chroniques	François Bonivard. *Les Chroniques de Genève* (Geneva: 1831).
CO	E. Cunitz and E. Baum, eds. *Joannis Calvini Opera.* (*Corpus Reformatorum,* 29–87, 1863–1900).
Consist.	Registres de Consistoire.
DBF	*Dictionnaire de Biographie Français.*
Froment	Antoine Froment. *Les Actes et Gestes Merveilleux* [Geneva: Jean Girard, 1554] (modern edition, Geneva: 1854).
Habit.	P. F. Geisendorf. *Livre des Habitants de Genève* (Geneva: 1957).
MDG	*Mémoires et documents publiés par la Société d'Histoire et d'Archéologie de Genève.*
Min	Minutes des Notaires.
NAK	*Nederlands Archief voor Kerkgeschiedenis*
PC	Procès Criminels.
RC	Registres du Conseil.
RCP	J. F. Bergier *et al.,* eds. *Registres de la Compagnie des Pasteurs de Genève au Temps de Calvin* (Geneva: 1962).
Roset	Michel Roset. *Les Chroniques de Genève* (modern edition, Geneva: 1894).
SC	R. Peter, J. Benoit *et al.,* eds. *Supplementa Calviniana.* (Neurkirchen-Vluyn: 1971).

INTRODUCTION

Calvin's defeat of his opponents in 1555 represented a triumph over various political, social, and ecclesiastical problems which had hindered the consolidation of the Reformation in Geneva as Calvin envisioned it, and had kept him in a precarious and troublesome position for nearly the whole of the decade and a half after his return from exile to Geneva in 1541. The ministry of Calvin in Geneva prior to 1555 had been marked by almost continuous debate, dissension, and outright opposition. After his singular victory Calvin became what could fairly be described as the most powerful person in Geneva and, with the aid of his supporters, the virtual ruler of the city. With most of his opponents expelled from the city, Calvin's local troubles ceased. The central question to be addressed in this volume is how this came about: how a foreign pastor, a paid civil servant with no official political powers or rights managed to resist and ultimately defeat so completely a large, powerful faction of native Genevans.

The secondary literature on the Genevan Reformation presents broad variations in interpretations which are often contradictory in nature. In part, this stems from the fact that the available, published primary source evidence is contradictory and confusing; too often it presents biased, personal interpretations of Geneva's history. The principal explanation for this situation, though, is that insufficient evidence has been used to make definitive conclusions and so the variant analyses are the result of conjecture. Thus, the sources consulted to date have provided an incomplete picture of the situation in Geneva. The obvious contradictions in the secondary literature demand a thorough re-examination of the sources normally used as well as all the unpublished primary source documents from the period of Calvin's ministry in Geneva. Only this return to original documentation can hope to unravel the web of supposition and prejudice found in the present historical literature.

What one finds in the secondary literature is that the primary sources used are extremely limited and, because of their very nature, of dubious quality when used on their own. Only the historians Robert M. Kingdon and William Monter have shown a real zeal for researching behind the readily accessible works and, as a result, their publications have already had a great impact in reshaping the prevailing understanding of Geneva in this period.[1] Further, research at the state archives in Geneva has shown that the sources commonly used represent only a small fraction of the total amount of material available for studying the social and political context of Calvin's situation in Geneva. It seems reasonable to explain this assertion at some length. As this volume will present information gathered from unpublished and almost wholly unused sources, it may also be beneficial to discuss these documents. For practical reasons it is best to divide the materials used to study Geneva into three groups: secondary literature, published primary sources, and manuscript documents. As the latter group has provided the bulk of the material in this work, the documents contained in this area will be discussed at greater length.

It would be unrealistic and pointless to begin a critique of the entire body of secondary literature. Suffice it to say that an examination of the works used by most scholars shows an almost total reliance, for secondary sources, on the works of nineteenth-century historians such as Roget and Galiffe. The primary sources used are those published at about the same time these earlier historians were working. It is true that recent years have seen works on specific aspects of Geneva utilising unpublished materials, but the general works on Calvin and his Genevan ministry still rely heavily on the earlier historians' works.[2] As noted above, Kingdon and Monter are notable exceptions, as are Olson, Innes, and somewhat earlier, Naef, though the former two deal only with very specialised topics, while Naef remains the best available source for the study of the beginnings of the Reformation in Geneva.[3] Nevertheless, when current discussions of Calvin and Geneva are taken together one can see the extent to which almost all of them rest upon these twin pillars, the earlier Genevan historians and the primary documents compiled and published nearly a century ago.[4]

This is not, of course, to deny the value of those early scholarly works. They provide the researcher with an excellent window into the wealth of original sources which exist in Geneva. Roget, Galiffe, and Gautier, for example, have given to subsequent historians invaluable extracts and set a very high standard for later research. Their works are a point of departure for a fuller understanding of Calvin and Geneva, challenging researchers to study, in detail, the veritable mountain of material at which they hint. Yet the foretaste which they provide, the result of years of labour, ought not to be changed into something they themselves would not have recognised. They provide selections from and interpretations of the original documents; surely they would never have envisioned that their works might all but replace the primary materials.

The problem with the use of these earlier works has been that later historians have mined them for their anecdotes and relied on them for their analytical conclusions. That these earlier scholars chose to select different facts to buttress their views, explains, to a large degree, if not entirely, the wide variations one finds in later authors. Often bibliographies and footnotes in modern works show that these sources have been used as though they were primary sources.[5] Pursuing the trail of evidence presented in later works also shows that even when these documents are not used directly they normally lie at the end of the search through various mediating authors.[6]

An excellent example of the use of these earlier secondary sources in place of primary documents and the effect of such mediation can be found in McGrath. He commented that a 'prototype (Consistory) had actually been established' in Geneva prior to Calvin's return.[7] In saying this he cited Höpfl, who implied that a Consistory had been established.[8] Höpfl, in turn, was relying on Kampschulte, who said that an attempt (*Versuch*) was made to establish a 'besondere Behörde'. Kampschulte relied on the Council Records for his material.[9] Obviously the matter has been moved from an attempt to a certainty. In reality the Council Records show that after discussion the decision 'sus l'erection du Consistoyre' was postponed until a later date.[10] No more was heard on the matter. Not only has Kampschulte been used in place of the original material, but the story has changed in the telling. What Kampschulte said was not a problem; what he has since been understood to have said is a different matter. Moreover, because of the goals and methods used by these early historians their works must be used with caution. They cannot, and should not, be used in place of detailed research into the primary, manuscript materials which lie behind them. This is especially true when one realises that the mountain of material, yet unpublished, which they used is still available to scholars. This fact alone would seem to suggest that it is time for a serious re-examination of Calvin's political struggles through a return to these original documents.

Where the established, earlier literature provides no clear guidelines, modern works have too often relied on pure conjecture. For example, when one looks at the way in which various authors have treated the basic and crucial matter of the effect of Calvin's preaching on the local populace, a wide range of opinions and assumptions present themselves. T. H. L. Parker said that Calvin's 'language was clear and easy. He spoke in a way that the Genevese could understand, even, it would seem, to the point of using some of their idiosyncracies of French.'[11] This view stands in marked contrast to McGrath's assertion that 'French remained a language alien to most Genevans during the sixteenth century.'[12] Höpfl took a more guarded, but equally contradictory view, when he said that 'the official language of Geneva was French' but that it was not clear 'how well ordinary Genevans understood the entirely French and francophone ministry' and that 'Calvin certainly did not preach in patois, and there is no evidence that he understood more than a few words of it.'[13] Since none of these comments has a reference it is impossible to evaluate these assertions from their sources. Nevertheless it is clear than any attempt to discuss the role and importance of Calvin's ministry in Geneva must resolve this basic question of language. That such contradictory and unsupported conjectures exist on so crucial a matter is itself proof of the need for a serious re-evaluation of Calvin's place in Genevan society and politics.

The other major source of historical material commonly examined in studies of Calvin's Genevan ministry is the published primary documents. Generally, however, these are not all used equally or given the same value. Indeed, some of them are almost always overlooked; the selectivity which one finds in the utilisation of these sources explains the problems in interpreting the events. This very obvious selectivity led this author to wonder whether there might not be more to the story of Geneva and Calvin than has been described up till now. Once subsequent research proved the extent to which the present understanding of Geneva during Calvin's years rests on so few original sources it became necessary to undertake an entirely new study.

The group of published primary materials most often used includes two basic sets of documents: Calvin's letters in the *Calvini Opera* of the *Corpus Reformatorum* and the *Registres de la Compagnie des Pasteurs au Temps de Calvin*. The *Registres* cover the period after 1549 only and is thus of less value. In the *Opera*, as said above, the most used materials are Calvin's letters; these give little detailed systematic information as they were not intended to give specific data on the internal machinations of Genevan politics and society. More importantly, both these sources represent what can fairly be described as Calvin's view of the situation in Geneva. At this point one realises that modern students of Geneva are almost wholly dependent upon Calvin for their understanding of the social and political problems which he faced in Geneva. Invaluable as his letters are in many ways, however, it should be obvious that any uncritical reliance on these sources is a very dubious course. The unquestioned acceptance of Calvin's presentation of the facts coupled with his interpretation of them adds yet another reason for a new examination of the Genevan records to discover whether a more detailed, less biased, understanding of the Geneva of the period can be achieved.

What is more, there are three works which are given only cursory use:

the chronicles of Michel Roset, Antoine Froment, and François Bonivard, all of whom were contemporaries of Calvin.[14] Obviously their works provide an account as personal as those which communicate Calvin's viewpoint; for the most part they are extremely sympathetic to Calvin. But no attempt is made by modern scholars to allow these sources to correct or refine Calvin's perspective; rather, they are scoured for anecdotal material.[15] It is truly amazing that three eyewitness accounts are so often overlooked in favour of the uncritical acceptance of Calvin's presentation, and interpretation of the events in Geneva.

Finally, there is a group of primary documents which have been allowed to languish in relative obscurity. These are Calvin's sermons, the *Livre des Bourgeois* and the *Livre des Habitants*. Calvin's sermons, if nothing else, hold out the possibility of presenting Calvin's unguarded, extemporaneous statements relating to Genevan events.[16] The sad truth is that his sermons are so often ignored that there is no discussion of their content as it relates to the political, social, and ecclesiastical situation in Geneva.[17] When one recalls that Calvin was, first and foremost, a local pastor it is especially surprising that historians have tended to overlook the uses to which Calvin put his unique platform in Geneva as chief minister. As this book will show, as a local leader Calvin did not stay above the mundane events of Geneva's factional fighting; rather, he threw himself into the midst of them. Unfortunately, up till now, no one has thought of discussing, at length, the importance of Calvin's control of the only effective means of mass communication in Geneva.

The *Livre des Bourgeois* and *Livre des Habitants*, on the other hand, provide interesting and useful statistical evidence relating to demographic and hence social pressures present in Genevan society during the period before Calvin's triumph in 1555. Obviously though, these latter two works are only of real use, except for purely demographic studies, when combined with many other more detailed and relevant sources. When studied along with the notarial records, for example, as will appear later, they provide invaluable information on the refugees who fled to Geneva, the extent of their involvement with one another and in Genevan society in general. The prominent role played by the French refugees in the events surrounding Calvin's political triumph has long been recognised; it is all the more extraordinary, therefore, that these sources are all but unused.

Thus, what one sees in the published primary documents and the use made of them is a general bias in favour of those works which present Calvin's interpretation of the events in Geneva. On the other hand there is a tendency to ignore or downplay those sources which might present an alternative view or those which give raw factual data with little or no interpretive commentary. This consideration, when combined with the earlier comments on the secondary sources, demonstrates that the over-whelming bulk of the historical literature on Calvin and Geneva arises either from the obviously partial writings of Calvin himself or the rather selective works of earlier historians. It becomes readily apparent, therefore, that there is a crucial need for a new study encompassing as much of the primary material as possible.

The earlier historical works seem to imply that there are sufficient additional documents to warrant a detailed re-examination of Calvin and the political, social, and ecclesiastical troubles which preceded his consolidation of power in 1555. The question, though, is whether these documents could do more than simply add more anecdotal material. This work will attempt to show that such a study is possible and indeed necessary. What is more difficult to explain is the equally obvious question of why such an examination has not already taken place. The apparent answer is that Calvin's importance as a great theologian and international figure has so overshadowed his role as a minister in Geneva that this aspect of his life has been allowed to remain in an obscurity illuminated only by his own interpretation of Geneva and his difficulties there. Perhaps it is time to rescue Geneva and Calvin's work there from Calvin's all-pervasive grasp and examine them for their own sake, thereby providing the historical context for Calvin's work as a theologian and leader of the wider Reform movement.

This work will attempt such a re-evaluation based upon a more balanced use of the printed primary materials; but in addition conclusions will be based upon an examination of the copious body of documentation which survives in the Genevan state archives. Thus, the records of the Councils, the Criminal Courts, the Notaries, and the Consistory will play a crucial role in this examination of Calvin's consolidation of the Reformation in Geneva. Together these sources provide a highly detailed, indeed almost daily, account of the social, political, and ecclesiastical situation in Geneva: and as they are mostly legal documents or minutes of meetings they allow one to examine an account of the events in Geneva which has been left relatively uninterpreted. Thus they represent a vast wealth of raw data on nearly every aspect of life in Geneva in the period before the consolidation of Calvin's Reformation in 1555.

The *Registres du Conseil* are the minute books of the governing councils of Geneva. For the period of Calvin's ministry they have been preserved intact. These copious volumes contain the details of all the business discussed by Geneva's political rulers. In many cases the particulars of a given discussion have been preserved at some length. As the councils, especially the Petit Conseil (or Senate), met almost every day, the *Registres* provide a wealth of information about the political activities of Geneva's magistrates. Finally, as the ministers were paid employees of these same magistrates, one can find a vivid account of the interplay between the pastors and the elected rulers of Geneva.

The main uses of these minutes are threefold. First, by charting the membership of each council and the names of various office-holders it should be possible to gauge the relative strength of Geneva's factions. Second, the preservation of vote totals in a number of elections should allow one to assess the position of some individual leaders of the factions in Geneva. Thirdly, Geneva was a city famous for factionalism. At almost every stage of Genevan history, from the first moves to oust Savoy until Calvin's victory in the mid-1550s, factions arising from Geneva's internal social and political situation played a major role; the collapse of every triumphant faction into competing groups hastened the advent of each subsequent crisis. By collating the entries found in this source with the information gathered from other documents one can collect the largest possible amount of detail relating to any given event, thereby producing a fuller, more reliable picture of what actually took place.

The second large source of material is the *Procès Criminels*, or the records of the criminal courts. These, when compared with the data in the Consistory records, provide a full understanding of many individual cases. There are two ways to approach these documents. First, there exists a fairly detailed analysis of each surviving dossier, prepared in the last century. This provides the date, charge, sentence and the name of one or more of the defendants as well as a concise synopsis of the case. These analyses allow Geneva's criminal justice system to be studied statistically over the entire period of Calvin's ministry in Geneva. However, the analyses are very brief and therefore, by nature, selective. While the analyses are a useful guide to individual cases they must not be used in place of the primary source materials themselves.

A more fruitful way is to examine the original dossiers. The quality and quantity of material here is very diverse indeed. Some consist merely of the official letter declaring the court's decision. Other cases preserve the testimony, sometimes in the witness's own hand, and depositions relevant to the case. In these latter examples, for instance, one can often find an account of the very words which sparked a riot. Also, in the originals one can discover, at times, what event or actions led a person to blaspheme God or slander someone else. This is of great importance, as the analyses will normally report only that a person was accused of blasphemy or slander without relating the specific details behind the accusation. Again, while of inherent value on their own, these documents are best used in combination with parallel accounts of a particular case found in other sources. When these are compared with first-hand accounts, such as Calvin's, one can discern the bias of the eyewitness by examining what has been emphasised in relating the details of a case and what has been passed over.

The records of the notaries also provide a rich source of information. Volume after volume contain the personal legal transactions of the Genevans. These manuscripts include wills, deeds of sale, loan agreements, leases, business partnerships, and even some inventories of belongings. Obviously, these materials would be of greatest use to an economic historian. Nevertheless, they are not without interest to the student of Genevan society and politics. Time and again these records not only give details of the various ties which linked individual Genevans, but also fairly detailed information on the financial and social status of individuals. Clearly this can be of great use, for example, in attempting to assess the impact of the French religious refugees on Genevan society.

On its own, the material in the notary records might seem to be of scant use for the purposes of this book. But that is just the point of discussing all of these sources of manuscript records. Alone they are of varied importance; taken together these documents may allow one to reconstruct with a high degree of accuracy the social, political, economic, and religious state of Geneva. If one wishes, the notary records can often serve to supply the missing pieces of a puzzle. Thus, one might wonder why certain people supported each other in various situations only to discover that they were business partners, connected by a distant marriage, or renting parts of the same house. Likewise, the account of an arbitration settlement of a dispute could explain why two people seemed to have parted company. Thus the notary records can provide invaluable clues to the personal and commercial ties which linked individuals together but which are so rarely mentioned in other sources.

As with the criminal court records, the Genevan archives contain analyses of these notarial records. The analyses date from the last century but unfortunately they suffer from some serious defects. First, the folio numbers given as references for the original records are often incorrect, for example, the designation 'verso' is rarely used. Second, in only a few cases are the dates of individual documents recorded in the analyses—a serious fault from the historian's point of view as the originals are not always in chronological order. Finally, and perhaps worst of all, over two-thirds of the original documents are simply ignored. Thus the analyses can never replace a detailed examination of the original notarial records. Nevertheless, with the exception of the pagination, the analyses are usually accurate in the material they contain, and serve as a useful aid in the speed with which one can examine the originals.

The last two groups of documents are the records of the Genevan Consistory and the historical extracts contained in the *Corpus Reformatorum*. Because of the overlap between this court and the criminal courts the Consistory records often give another look at individual cases. As the Consistory records contain minutes of the sessions rather than depositions, they often give a livelier account. It must be said, however, that any significant case would have gone to the criminal courts and those which did not would involve the domestic troubles and minor morality offences so often seen before the Consistory. Robert Kingdon is owed a great debt of gratitude for the generous way in which he made available to this author his, as yet unpublished, transcription of the Consistory records. Finally, the *Annales* in the *Calvini Opera* of the *Corpus Reformatorum* contain a wealth of extracts from many of the sources just discussed. Unfortunately, though, the principal interest of this work was to find specific references to Calvin himself. Thus many things were overlooked and, most importantly, the whole context of the extracts lost. For the most part, the *Annales* simply reinforce the bias towards Calvin's interpretations of events already found in his letters.

It is to be hoped that the foregoing discussion will have shown the truth of the initial assertion that there are sufficient unused documentary materials to warrant a fresh examination of the political, social, and religious conflicts which marked Calvin's ministry in Geneva prior to 1555. What should be apparent is the extent to which the current historical picture of Calvin and Geneva is, for the most part, a construct which largely accepts Calvin's interpretation of the events and issues. The subsequent chapters will attempt to prove that a fresh examination of all of the available sources can and does present one with a markedly different understanding of Calvin and Geneva than has been received hitherto from the secondary literature or from Calvin himself.

NOTES

1 For example, Kingdon, *Geneva and the Coming of the Wars of Religion in France* (Geneva: 1956), 'Calvin and "Presbytery": The Genevan Company of Pastors', in the *Pacific Theological Review*, 18: 2 (Winter, 1985), pp. 43–55 and 'The Economic Behavior of Ministers in Geneva in the Middle of the Sixteenth Century', in *ARG*, 50: 1, pp. 33–9. Kingdon is overseeing the transcription of the Consistory records and he kindly made his, as yet unpublished, transcription available for this volume. Also, Monter, *Calvin's Geneva* (London: 1967), *Enforcing Morality in Early Modern Europe* (London: 1987) and

'Historical Demography and Religious History in Sixteenth Century Geneva', in the *Journal of Interdisciplinary History*, 9: 3 (Winter, 1979), pp. 399–427.

2   For example, J. Olson, *Calvin and Social Welfare: Deacons and the* Bourse Française (Sellingsgrove, Penn.: 1989), W. Innes, *Social Concerns in Calvin's Geneva* (Allison Park, Penn.: 1983) and earlier, A. Babel, *Histoire Economique de Genève des Origines au Début du XVIe Siècle* (Geneva: 1963).

3   H. Naef, *Les Origines de la Réforme à Genève* (Geneva: 1936).

4   For example, an examination of the bibliographies and notes of the following books shows an almost total reliance on Calvin's letters for primary material about his ministry in Geneva: J. Bohatec, *Calvin und das Recht* (Graz: 1934); W. J. Bouwsma, *John Calvin: A Sixteenth-Century Portrait* (Oxford: 1988); Q. Breen, *John Calvin: A Study in French Humanism* (Hamden: 1968); E. Doumergue, *Jean Calvin: Les Hommes et les Choses de son Temps*, 7 vols. (Lausanne: 1899–1917); A. Ganoczy, *The Young Calvin* (Philadelphia: 1987); A. McGrath, *A Life of John Calvin* (Oxford: 1990); and F. Wendel, *John Calvin* (London: 1963). Limited use of other sources (e.g. Froment, Roset, Bonivard, Calvin's Sermons) can be found in these additional works, although Calvin's letters still form the basic pool of primary material: W. Balke, *Calvin and the Anabaptist Radicals* (Grand Rapids: 1981); A. Bieler, *Pensée Economique et Sociale de Calvin* (Geneva: 1961), H. Höpfl, *The Christian Polity of John Calvin* (Cambridge: 1982); U. Plath, *Calvin und Basel in den Jahren 1552–1556* (Zürich: 1974); and T. H. L. Parker, *John Calvin: A Biography* (London: 1975). Indeed, Parker lists Froment, Roset and Bonivard in his bibliography and yet never cites them, and Balke uses them only a few times. Moreover, it is essential to grasp that the later works accept and build upon the earlier ones, thereby reinforcing this reliance upon Calvin's interpretation through the almost exclusive use of his letters for primary material. Finally, while it may seem of less importance, it is illuminating none the less that there is even, at times, confusion over what the published primary sources actually contain. Thus, R. N. Caswell, 'Calvin's View of Ecclesiastical Discipline', in E. Duffield, ed., *John Calvin* (Abingdon: 1966), p. 222f., refers to the disturbing nature of the Consistory records but his footnote shows that he was actually referring to the records of the Company of Pastors.

5   For example, J. Gaberel, *Histoire de l'Eglise de Genève* (Geneva: 1858), vol. 1, pp. 265, 270f., suggested that the Articulants were a party composed of Catholic sympathisers. This view is then presented as fact by Wendel, *Calvin*, p. 53. Cf., McGrath, *Calvin*, p. 101, where he also mentions the threat of Catholic resurgence.

6   It might be useful to give a rather lengthy quotation from Monter where he complains of a specific symptom of the same problem:

> Over a century ago, Jules Michelet, in his famous essay, *La Sorcière*, briefly mentioned 500 witches put to death in only three months by the bishop of Geneva in 1513, listing this among the worst examples of judicial cruelty he had found. Recently, Hugh Trevor-Roper has argued that 'in Geneva, which before had been free from witch-craft trials, Calvin introduced a new reign of terror: in the sixty years after his coming, one hundred and fifty witches were burned'. Both statements were made by these distinguished scholars without fear and without research. Their remarks are contradictory but psychologically complementary insofar as both have contributed toward shaping a Black Legend about sixteenth-century Geneva. It is high time to replace such affirmations by investigation and to bring enough evidence to bear on the issue of witchcraft persecution in Geneva to dissolve this kind of legend once and for all. It may even be possible to replace it by something more interesting: the authentic history of witchcraft in post-Reformation Geneva, the history of the encounter between the Calvinist system and a tenacious network of

indigenous witchcraft beliefs.

'Witchcraft in Geneva, 1537–1662', in the *Journal of Modern History*, 43: 2 (June 1971), p. 179.

7 McGrath, *Calvin*, p. 112.

8 Höpfl, *Polity*, p. 95.

9 F. W. Kampschulte, *Johann Calvin, seine Kirche und sein Staat in Genf* (Leipzig: 1869–99), p. 377.

10 AEG/RC/[volume] 35, fol. 207 (17 May 1541).

11 Parker, *Calvin*, p. 93.

12 McGrath, *Calvin*, p. 88.

13 Höpfl, *Polity*, p. 134f. This issue will be discussed later in this work during an examination of Calvin's sermons themselves.

14 *Advis*, Roset, and Froment.

15 An example is Balke, *Anabaptist*, p. 80, who cites Roset for the comment that some citizens were Anabaptists. This is used to support his contention that Anabaptism was a major part of the Articulant faction. This overlooks the extent to which Roset tends to emphasise the importance of politics and personal factionalism in the problem. Indeed, the comment on Anabaptism is not repeated, and surely if it had been a great problem there would have been substantial discussion of the matter.

16 See below, pp. 153–62.

17 However, brilliant use has been made of Calvin's sermons to study his attitude on the later religious crisis in France. See W. Nijenhuis, 'De Grenzen der Burgerlijke Gehoorzaanheid in Calvijns Laatstbekende Preken: Ontwikkeling van Zijn Opvaltingen Aangaande het Veretsrecht', in *Historisch Bewogen, Bundel opstellen voor Prof. dr. A. F. Mellink* (Groningen: 1984), pp. 67–97.

I   *Factionalism: the Genevan Disease*

Intestinum semen disidii

> When our Lord has executed the sort of judgement that ought to make men's ears redden there is no need to speak of it: because these defenders of the honour of Geneva complain about it. What I mean is that here is a man who has made a horrible spectacle of himself. He is a source of fear and trembling for everyone as a result. This blasphemer spited God and the faith. His own mother thinks he has come from the Devil. But if someone uses him as an example, these defenders of Geneva protest that the city is being dishonoured. Right there are those good zealots of the honour of the city, who would have Geneva sink into a pit. Everyone knows who they are. No one needs to point them out with his finger or to call them by name. They are known well enough. And yet they pretend that they want to defend the honour of the city. But one can see from what sort of heart their actions proceed.[1]

When Calvin preached this sermon in the third week of August 1554 he was not simply offering some general reflections on the state of Genevan society in the manner of popular preachers everywhere. Rather, he was directly attacking leading citizens of Geneva in their very presence: and what was his charge? He was pointing out that a group of influential citizens was supporting someone whom he believed 'despitoit Dieu et toute religion'. He further alleged that these men committed this offence under the hypocritical excuse of defending 'l'honneur de la ville'. Here, in a nutshell, Calvin held up for examination two contradictory views of the faction which was contesting his authority. Calvin asserted that, in his view, these men were irreligious blasphemers bent on disobeying the Church, but portrayed themselves falsely, he argued, as the defenders of Geneva's honour, liberty, and civic rights.

In fact, Calvin was pointing his finger, perhaps literally, at a recognised faction in Genevan society. The city was famous for its divisions, which formed and re-formed throughout the period of Calvin's ministry. The immediate origins of this process of factionalism can be discovered at the beginning of the Revolution. Thus, to understand Calvin's opponents in 1554, one must turn to the very birth of the Republic and the subsequent crises which brought Genevan politics to the nadir against which Calvin railed. This chapter will not attempt any comprehensive analysis of the origins of the Reformation in Geneva. Rather, it will sketch the intensity and character of the various crises and divisions in Genevan society and their resolution prior to 1541.[2] From this examination will be drawn an understanding of the tensions and issues which continued to concern Genevans. It is essential to comprehend the history and role of factionalism in Geneva for, as Calvin wrote, 'in urbe, ut iam dixi, habemus intestinum semen dissidii'.[3]

In the medieval period, Geneva was a city ruled by a Prince-Bishop through his appointed representative, the Vidôme.[4] Ultimately, the city owed its allegiance to the Dukes of Savoy and the Bishop was normally a member of the House of Savoy. Problems began to develop between the Bishop and the Genevans at the end of the fifteenth century. The city, a market and fair town in the medieval period, was in marked economic decline, having lost most of its business to the fairs at Lyon. The Genevan political situation began to deteriorate rapidly in the 1510s and by 1519, eighty-six citizens, led by François Bonivard, accepted citizenship with Fribourg; this formed a combourgeoisie, an alliance, and was seen as a means of linking Geneva to the Swiss towns. But Savoyard pressure and power was exerted in Geneva, Fribourg and other Swiss towns and the pact was annulled. A general amnesty was declared and the Swiss army raised to aid Geneva was dismissed after Geneva agreed to pay them around 30,000 ff.; temporarily, this settled the affair.

By August 1519, though, the Bishop had broken the amnesty and executed Philibert Berthelier, the leader of the opposition. He also dismissed the four Syndics who had been legitimately elected and appointed four of his own. Further, he declared that future Syndics could hold office only with episcopal consent. But the political jousting between Geneva's overlord, the Duke of Savoy, and its direct master, the Bishop, kept the situation confused. Although Geneva's last Prince–Bishop, Pierre de la Baume, was an exceptionally talented man, a scion of a prominent international family, he was to prove politically inept. He was always complicating a situation more than was necessary or beneficial; this flaw was catastrophically apparent in his political machinations. His downfall came as a result of his inability to side with either of the two dominant political groupings in the city, the Savoyards or the nationalists. Rather, he tried to please both and play them off against each other for his own benefit.

Calm was restored to an increasingly volatile situation by the residence of the Duke of Savoy in Geneva from August 1523 to March 1524. With tensions building, Charles III, Duke of Savoy, had entered the city; his opponents took to the forests and the Swiss cities. He convoked a general assembly over the protests of the Bishop's vicar who rightly complained that such power belonged to the Bishop alone. Charles demanded a veto over the syndical elections and forbade any alliances with the Swiss. Faced with the Duke's armed retinue the Genevans consented, and the Duke departed secure in the knowledge that his sovereignty had been restored intact. Meanwhile, the fugitives were busily trying to convince Berne and Fribourg to join Geneva in an alliance against Savoy. At length they were successful. The Bishop actually aided them in their attempt by sending two letters to Berne; one supported the alliance, the other rejected it. Two days later he sent another letter which forcefully denounced the pact; he was simply ignored. Amid scenes of jubilation the fugitives returned to Geneva. This new alliance held and formed the basis for the successful military revolt against Savoy which freed Geneva by 1535. Moreover, it set in motion the final disintegration of Genevan society into rival factions which would continue to trouble Geneva until 1541 and which would again flare up, for the last time, in 1550–55.

In his eyewitness account of events, François Bonivard, the former prior of St-Victor, listed three political clashes before 1541, all of which resulted in substantial numbers of citizens being forced into exile. The defeated parties were known as the Mammelus, the Peneysans, and the Articulants.[5] The first two groups were involved in the complex struggle to oust Savoyard control and break the power of the Prince–Bishop in the years leading up to the establishment of the Republic in 1535. Thus, although these two crises may reasonably be discussed together, it is nevertheless essential to remember that these two factions, the Peneysans and the Mammelus, were not the same, although they are often treated as identical. It is necessary to delineate the differences between the goals of the Peneysans and the Mammelus. The Mammelus were Genevans who wanted to be ruled by the Duke of Savoy and strove to keep Geneva in his domain. They were, to use Gaberel's somewhat prejudicial description, the 'fauteurs de la servitude étrangère'.[6] Their title was a derisive term given to them by their opponents and referred to those who had sold themselves as slaves to the rulers of Egypt.[7] For their part they referred to themselves as Monseigneuristes, asserting their loyalty to the rulers of Savoy, their legal overlords.[8]

In this contest the Mammelus were opposed by a faction which is known to historians as the Eidgenots, from the Swiss word Eidgnossen, or confederates, a reference to the desire of this faction for Geneva to have closer ties with the free cities of the Swiss confederation. As Gaberel said, they desired to protect their freedom under the rule of the Prince–Bishop. These were 'les Eidgnos ou Alliés' who defended their liberties by relying on the support of the Swiss.[9] However, this name, too, was originally applied to them in derision by their opponents. They called themselves 'Les Enfants de Genève' and took as their symbol 'une croix marquée sur leur pourpoint'.[10]

The first leader of the Enfants was Philibert Berthelier who was executed by the Savoyards in 1519.[11] In the case against him it becomes clear that his faction was already well established and recognised as a group of companions commonly called 'les Enfans' of the city.[12] Although Berthelier's death provided his supporters with a martyr the movement languished for nearly a decade. His last words, spoken to his kinsman, Bonivard, were later held up as examples of the sacrifice necessary to win, and then maintain Geneva's liberties. 'Pour amour de la liberté de Genève vous pergaz votre Benefice, et moi la teste.'[13] These words would continue to ring in the ears of all those who would dedicate themselves to the preservation of the rights, privileges, and liberties of Geneva. Berthelier's martyrdom galvanised resistance to Savoy and bound the Enfants into a dedicated, though temporarily subdued, faction. As Naef pointed out, the Genevan nationalists, under their leader, the Capitaine Général (or Abbé, occasionally), were striving to better Geneva, honour God and maintain justice. They pledged to answer all alarms and to defend one another with the arms they kept close at hand ('estre garnys d'armoys et d'aultre bastons deffensables'). Their programme of mutual support was to form the basis for the future motto of the Enfants: 'qui touche l'un touch l'aultre.'[14]

This group, united by the common threat that they might suffer the same fate as Berthelier, engaged in a long struggle to oust the Mammelus. By this point the Enfants were led by Bezanson Hugues who proved able to lead a renewed Enfants faction against the Mammelus.[15] Finally, with assistance from Fribourg and Berne they were successful. By 1527 the Enfants were able to condemn and banish nearly forty of their opponents including ten former Syndics.[16] This effectively broke direct Savoyard control over Geneva. It did not, however, remove the threat of a Savoyard attack or reconquest, nor did it eliminate Savoy's indirect means of control through the Prince–Bishop.[17]

With the initial problem of direct Savoyard rule seemingly resolved, Hugues faced four areas of potential problems. The task before him was simple in principle but very difficult to implement. He tried to maintain the episcopal power but more for the benefit of the city than the Bishop. He had to retain the support of Fribourg and Berne and the benefits accorded under the Triple Combourgeoisie with these two cities. Further,

FIGURE I *Geneva and its environs*
Source: Binz, *Vie Religieuse*

Hugues strove to keep the forms of the Church intact while removing those clergy hostile to the new situation. Finally, he had to control radical elements released by the revolt and strengthen the power of the magistracy, especially the Syndics.[18] At best this would have been a difficult balancing act; in reality, it was an impossible task.

The problem for Hugues was that there was an obvious desire on the part of many Genevan citizens to profit at the Church's expense. Part of the desire was motivated by the wish to punish the ecclesiastics, most of whom were of Savoyard extraction, for refusing to assist the city financially during the struggle for independence.[19] But attempts to curtail the power and privilege of the Church necessarily meant limiting the authority of the Prince–Bishop. Unfortunately for the Bishop, his only external

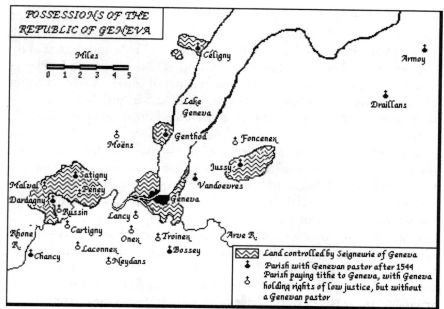

POSSESSIONS OF THE REPUBLIC OF GENEVA

Miles
0 1 2 3 4 5

Céligny

Armoy

Lake Geneva

Draillans

Genthod

Moëns

Foncenex

Jussy

Satigny

Vandoeuvres

Malval

Peney

Dardagny

Geneva

Russin

Lancy

Rhone R.

Cartigny

Onex

Troinex

Arve R.

Chancy

Laconnex

Meydans

Bossey

Land controlled by Seigneurie of Geneva
Parish with Genevan pastor after 1544
Parish paying tithe to Geneva, with Geneva holding rights of low justice, but without a Genevan pastor

FIGURE 2 *Possessions of the Republic of Geneva*
Source: Monter, *Geneva*

source of support was Savoy. What this meant in practical terms was that support for the Church and the Bishop implied reliance on Savoy. Such reliance would always appear treasonable to those desirous of defending the newly-freed Republic.

It is crucial to realise that moves against the ecclesiastical structure predate any real evidence of the Reformation. Thus, in December 1527 and January 1528, the Petit Conseil, or Senate, began a careful examination of the Church's position with a special emphasis upon its sources of revenue.[20] Nor was this any small matter. The Church was extremely wealthy by this period, with most of the rural revenues going directly to various sections of the Church's structure: the chapter, confraternities, monasteries, and parish churches. Thus, from the perspective of many Genevans, control of ecclesiastical power, and the inherent threat that the Church structure posed to their hard-won liberties, would have been seen as a political matter of the greatest concern.

Figures 1 and 2 are useful in comprehending the extent of the Church's landed possessions.[21] The Bishop held sovereignty in the city and three rural mandements, or districts.[22] These latter were Peney, including Burdigny, Choully, Satigny, Peissy, Dardagny, Russin, etc., the mandement of Jussy, and part of the mandement of Ternier. Control of the city itself also included the nearby areas of Petit-Sacconex, Chêne and Cologny. The cathedral chapter of St-Pierre had control over Designy, Droisy, Valliery, Onex, Lancras, Bossey, Crevin, Charly and the rest of the mandement of Ternier and the mandements of Chaumont and La Planaz. The priory of St-Victor possessed the revenues of Moëns, Collex, Pregny, Feuillasse, Meyrin, Vernier, Bernex and Troinex. In addition, there were thiry-seven named confraternities as well as those administered by the chapter.[23]

The methods Geneva's lay rulers used to solve the problems with which the ecclesiastical structure presented them are illustrative of certain attitudes towards the Church which were to plague Calvin later. The concentration of judicial, social and economic power in the hands of foreign clerics was a serious threat to Genevan independence. It was left to the magistrates to discover ways to curtail or destroy this power. Moreover, as Geneva was in serious need of money to finance its new-found freedom, the city had a further reason to move against the entrenched privileges of the Church. That the State was able to resolve most of these issues without reference to the clergy would have lasting implications for the future.

It is not surprising if, in the view of many Genevans, the Church was seen as a potentially dangerous fifth column for Savoy, and for other foreign powers as well. The Church was dominated by foreigners and when defending itself looked to Savoy for assistance, as did the Bishop. Further, without the control of the rural revenues Geneva's magistrates would have had only a superficial show of power with no real economic substance behind it; power would have remained in the hands of the clergy. Finally, the city, in desperate need of funds to defend itself against Savoy, was denied access to the largest source of native wealth by the stubbornness of the clerics. Obviously, all of this led to an intolerable situation only exacerbated by the vacillating behaviour of the Bishop, who seemed unable to decide whether to throw in his lot with Savoy or Geneva.

The magistrates' primary concern was to limit the power which the Church had as a result of its economic strength. This becomes clear when one considers the use to which they put the Church's revenues once these had been confiscated. In the end the magistrates designated the former ecclesiastical revenues to the hospital which they established in 1535 to replace the plethora of ecclesiastical hospitals which had hitherto existed. Further, they began a free education system for children in the city.[24] Such altruism, however, was not entirely successful in overcoming the temptation to spend the money elsewhere, for the funds went directly into the city budget and were often diverted to other uses, such as defence.[25] In the main, it was the question of ecclesiastical power and privilege that sparked the second major crisis. This later struggle might be seen as a part of the Enfant/Mammelus conflict but is, in reality, a dispute over the position of the Bishop and the clerics and involved Savoy only indirectly. The problem which faced the Bishop was that he had to look to Savoy to protect his privileges, and this automatically made him suspect in the eyes of the Enfants. During this period the Bishop professed loyalty to his subjects, but it was obvious that his continued dealings with the Duke evidenced a desire for a reconciliation with Savoy. The contradictory forces which pulled at him proved, in the end, to be mutually exclusive.[26] As a result a second struggle began at Geneva which was a contest 'des Evesquains et des Communaires'.[27]

This is the first example of a situation which will be shown to repeat itself in subsequent crises. Until 1555 every victorious political faction splintered into rival groups which competed until one side was defeated. In this particular case the broad group of 'les républicains genevois' broke into two opposing camps. In the view of Gaberel, those Genevans who adhered to the theory of divine right felt that the city was the lawful possession of the Bishop and they strove to retain their ruler. The other citizens held to the 'droit des nations'. These men wanted to limit the episcopal power which they saw as debased by its former representatives. In the end, opinion against the Bishop centred around the ideas of the Reformation.[28] While Gaberel's analysis is correct to some extent, his conviction that the catalyst of the trouble was the preaching of the Reformation is weakened by the fact that many of the anti-ecclesiastical moves had already begun for political and economic reasons. Moreover, the actions taken to limit episcopal authority were inseparably entwined with the Bishop's ambivalence towards Savoy.[29]

Indeed, when one considers the vacillating actions of the Bishop it is quite easy to see why many would support any move which would weaken the ecclesiastical structure. He remained the most obvious source of danger to the new Republic internally while Savoy, the Church's main prop, was Geneva's greatest external threat. Under the circumstances it appears highly probable that those preaching the Reform in Geneva must have found a sympathetic ear among those members of the Genevan ruling elite who already had reason to resent the position of the Church. The only means of breaking the Church was to cut off its money, but it was necessary to find a reasonable excuse to move against the Church's holdings. An exchange between a clerical and civic leader of the time highlights the problem and the solution:

> Sire Jaques, à qui doit-on payer, sinon à l'Eglise?
> Et Bel de répondre tout de go: «aux pauvres!»

Mot magique, que se répétait le populaire. La révolte sociale précédait la Réforme; et les «possédants» eux-mêmes semaient la tempête.[30]

Thus at this point, the desires of the political rulers of Geneva and the Reformers coincided; the politicians and preachers were agreed.

Geneva also found support for these moves against the Church from her strongest military ally, Berne, which had already embraced the Reform. In the face of the city's dependence on Bernese military support it is no wonder that a 'politico-confessionel' party took shape at the same time as the promulgation of the Reformed edicts in Berne.[31] This religious situation forced Geneva to risk the loss of the support of Catholic Fribourg, the lesser of Geneva's allies. Berne enthusiastically encouraged the adoption of its faith at Geneva and Lausanne; religion would follow the lead of politics.[32] The final impetus for Geneva's religious change came from the continuing mismanagement of the political situation by the Bishop.

Events had begun to move very rapidly in the crisis. In October 1534 the Bishop, who was still trying to support Savoy, was deposed by a vote of the Petit Conseil. The magistrates clearly viewed themselves as competent to act in this manner and considered their authority paramount in delineating the correct relationship between Geneva's Church and State.[33] The Bishop retaliated by excommunicating 250 Genevans.[34] The Bishop's political incompetence is apparent in this action; the move was more likely to unite these Genevans than to induce them to submit to the Bishop. By August 1535 the Mass had been suspended and in May of the following year the citizens and bourgeois of Geneva voted unanimously to establish the Reformation in their city.[35]

Thus, one comes to the conclusion of Geneva's struggles against Savoy and the Prince–Bishop. A number of trends is already apparent in Genevan politics. The break with Savoy and Geneva's international situation made the city very wary of foreign domination. Geneva, to protect its liberty, had striven to break the power of the ecclesiastical establishment which was dominated by foreigners with allegiances and concerns beyond those of the city.[36] The overthrow of the Bishop meant that Geneva's rulers had made an irrevocable break with the old faith. Not only were they excommunicated but they had committed treason against their temporal lord, the Bishop. There was no going back to Savoy or to the Bishop. Finally, the fractured nature of Genevan society which saw the victorious faction turn in on itself almost immediately after triumphing set a pattern which was to repeat itself in later crises. In 1535, although the Revolution had triumphed, the situation remained highly unstable. An observer of

Genevan politics at this time would have found a newly-established, but already faction-ridden, ruling elite extremely wary of foreigners and foreign domination, jealous of its liberties, surrounded by implacable foes and allies of dubious quality.

Although only two (Berne, Savoy) of Geneva's three neighbours (France, the third) have been mentioned, it is perhaps useful at this point to comment at some length on Geneva's international situation. All three of these states shared, or claimed, control of territory which Geneva considered its own. Savoy laid claim to the entirety of the new Republic. Berne and France had lesser direct claims but also had discreet designs on most of Geneva's territory. Geneva's awareness, and wariness, of its neighbours' desires were certainly justified and played an important role (especially with regard to Berne) in Geneva's domestic political considerations. These three states, therefore, and their competing ambitions in and around Geneva are worthy of some detailed attention.

Geneva found itself at the apex of a clash of two expansionist powers (France and Berne) who were increasing their power at the expense of Savoy. Geographically and economically Geneva was the linchpin of Northern Savoy.[37] The city straddled one of the three routes between Imperial possessions in Italy and the Low Countries.[38] Consequently, the area was of strategic military importance in the struggle between France and the Hapsburg countries.[39] Finally, it is worth noting that Geneva was a large city by the standards of neighbouring Switzerland and thus likely to attract the avarice of others. Its normal population of around 10,000 inhabitants (which swelled to around 17,000 under the pressure of refugee immigration) made it the equal of Basle, the Swiss Confederation's largest city with 9,000–10,000 people.[40]

However, the immediate causes of the French and Swiss expansion (led by Berne) into Savoy were twofold. First, Savoy was internally weak as the result of a period of dynastic instability. In the last quarter of the fifteenth century (1478–1504) Savoy had five separate rulers: three youths and two female regencies.[41] The Burgundian wars and the incessant turmoil in Italy had devastated much of the Duchy.[42] Secondly, Savoy had abandoned, by 1524, its historic alliance with France and the Swiss and sided with the Emperor, Charles V.[43] Thus France, which was concerned to secure the Alpine passes through Savoy into Northern Italy, and the Swiss, especially Berne, Fribourg, and the Vallais, had a pretext to expand at Savoy's expense and avenge the perceived betrayal.[44]

Before detailing the various circumstances which brought Savoy to this deplorable state, it might be worthwhile describing the Duchy itself.

Savoy, at its north-western limit, reached to Bourg-en-Bresse, Lyon and Burgundy and included Chambéry. Its northern frontier then passed north of Geneva and Lake Leman (Geneva), incorporating Yverdon, Lausanne and Neuchâtel. The eastern border turned south to the Mediterranean passing to the east of Genoa. Savoy's western boundary went south from near Lyon to the coast west of Nice and Monaco. Thus, Savoy straddled the present Franco-Italian border and included much of western, Francophone Switzerland. The Duchy commanded the all-important Alpine passes which allowed access, for France's armies, into the northern Italian plain. Conversely, in Imperial hands, these same passes would have rendered Provence vulnerable to attack.[45]

French interest in Savoy is easily understood. While Savoy remained loyal to France and Francis I, the approaches to Italy were secure. The alliance should have remained the centre of the Duchy's foreign policy' while Duke Charles III, uncle of Francis I, ruled.[46] But Charles's marriage to Beatrice of Portugal, sister-in-law to Emperor Charles V, and politico-military realities increasingly drew Savoy into the Imperial orbit.[47] Francis I was thus given an excuse for making the Alpine passes his own to counter the Duke's perceived duplicity and the threat to French security; in addition, France took the opportunity to annex the regions around Bourg-en-Bresse and Chambéry.[48] The Duchy was so powerless before the French onslaught that it was effectively occupied and subsequently governed by a French-style Parliament established by Francis I at Chambéry from 1536 to 1559.[49] Charles III died in exile in 1551 and not until the Treaty of Cateau-Cambrésis was the Duchy restored to full independence under Emmanuel-Philibert.[50] This temporary reduction of Savoy to the status of a French protectorate, however, in no way lessened Savoyard desire to regain lands lost to the Swiss and Geneva. Indeed, Savoy's impotence before the French as well as religious issues meant that Savoy would naturally seek to recapture those areas to restore national pride and the ducal patrimony. Thus, unable to move against France, Catholic Savoy was even more of a zealous threat to the independence of Protestant Geneva.

The Swiss interest and expansion in Northern Savoy is somewhat more difficult to explain, especially as the Swiss religious divide increasingly complicated the situation. Primarily, Berne led the drive to the west.[51] In part this was the result of Berne's inability to grow in any other directions. Berne's moves were helped by the fact that the internal Swiss religious debate meant that the natural rivalries which existed among Berne, Zürich, and Basle began to fade.[52] These powerful Protestant cities became much more concerned with their Catholic neighbours.[53] This gave Berne the freedom to direct its attention westwards. Berne was fully aware that any attempt to strengthen its position in the Valais required control of the Pays de Vaud. However, 'le clé du Pays de Vaud' was Geneva.[54] The other Savoyard possessions, Neuchâtel, Valdengin, Gruyère, Chablais, Evian, and the Prince–Bishopric of Lausanne, in and around the Vaud were also necessary and logical targets for Bernese aggrandisement.[55] Nor were Fribourg and other Swiss areas, regardless of their religion, slow to seize lands made available by the precipitous collapse of Savoyard power.[56]

It is salutary to recall that in this period the Swiss were at the height of their power, controlling their largest territorial expanse; many of these areas would be lost by the end of the century. Swiss power, militarily and politically, was a force to be reckoned with. In 1513, the Swiss advanced to Dijon and forced a humiliating peace (later repudiated) on the French.[57] Despite their singular defeat at Marignano (1515), the Swiss were a dominant force in the northern Italian theatre.[58] By 1512–13, the Swiss had secured a virtual protectorate over parts of the Piedmont (Savoy), Lombardy, and Milan (where they maintained a garrison).[59] Swiss political power was able to play a major part in denying Francis I the Imperial throne.[60] This brief flirtation with the new Emperor, Charles V, encouraged a conciliatory policy from France resulting in the Treaties of Geneva (7 November 1515) and Fribourg (29 November 1516) on terms favourable to the Swiss. This process culminated in the signing of 'alliance perpetuelle' on 5 May 1521 which was renewed by subsequent French monarchs for centuries.[61]

As can be seen, Geneva was at the epicentre of these competing forces. Geographically, militarily, and economically, Geneva was situated at a crucial European crossroads. However, the balance in the relations between France and Switzerland meant that both powers were determined to keep Geneva from becoming a direct possession of the other. Both were the great threats, and guarantors, of Genevan freedom—Savoyard pretensions remained stymied by Bernese power.[62] Thus Geneva was trapped between, and protected by, the proverbial 'rock and a hard place'. The danger, however, was that some passing Imperial army, bound for the Low Countries, might turn aside and sack the city. As will be shown, with the outbreak of religious war in Germany, this possibility constantly terrified Geneva's rulers and populace.[63]

Before leaving the discussion of Geneva's struggle for independence in the face of the competing aims and ambitions of its neighbours it may be useful to give some consideration to the effect that these first two, interrelated crises had had on Geneva. Inevitably, drastic political changes of this nature must have disrupted Genevan society in diverse ways. First, in

TABLE I: *Bourgeois admissions 1526–46*

Year	No.	Year	No.	Year	No.
1526	6	1533	3	1540	31
1527	2	1534	25	1541	21
1528	0	1535	61	1542	17
1529	0	1536	11	1543	28
1530	19	1537	20	1544	8
1531	26	1538	20	1545	7
1532	16	1539	14	1546	9

Total bourgeois admitted   434   *Average admissions per annum*   20.7

addition to the economic, religious, and political changes already mentioned, these crises dramatically altered Geneva demographically and socially. Almost fifty Genevans, with their families, were expelled as Mammelus. To these were added another forty men banished for supporting the Bishop, the so called Peneysans, named after the castle at Peney from which the Bishop tried to rule during the crisis. The Peneysans seem to have been drawn from those moderate Genevans who were never ardent supporters of the revolutionaries or of the Savoyard loyalists; only two Peneysans could be classified as dedicated Enfants. In all, between eighty and ninety men and their families were forced out of Geneva.[64] In addition, most of the clerics left. Finally the suburbs, the Faubourgs, were levelled in 1531 to clear the land around the city walls which made the city easier to defend from attack. This meant that Geneva was drastically reduced in size while the population within the walls was increased.[65] It has been estimated that as many as 1,300 persons were forced into the city from the suburbs alone.[66] This left Geneva full of refugees from its suburbs and, at the same time, bereft of many of the members of its former ruling class and much of their wealth and expertise.[67]

These momentous changes had a considerable effect upon economic relations within the city. Obviously, the confiscation of church revenues and properties and the mass exodus of the clerics left Geneva with a net increase in wealth.[68] The property of the exiles was of less value because the city could profit from them only if it could find buyers, and the loss of population caused by the various exiles left the citizenry substantially reduced. In this situation one sees that Geneva turned to the sale of bourgeois rights; a good source of revenue and the obvious means of replenishing the body politic. In 1535 alone Geneva sold civic rights to at least sixty-one men. The years after 1530 (see Table 1) all show a marked increase in admissions, except for 1533 when tensions and the dangerous crisis with the Bishop seem to have slowed the process. It is essential to recall that bourgeois status opened every right to an individual as a citizen except the right to serve on the Petit Conseil.[69] Moreover, children born in Geneva to bourgeois parents automatically became citizens. As will be shown later, because of the use of this method to raise money, replenish the population, and attract persons of merit and value, the preservation of bourgeois rights and privileges would be of interest and importance to a large segment of Geneva's electorate. This was to have serious repercussions during the later crisis between Calvin and his political opponents in the 1550s.[70]

Concentration on internal problems has led some to underplay the role external relations had on Genevan politics. But Geneva's situation (detailed above), surrounded by hostile powers, inevitably had an effect on Geneva internally. In the first crisis Geneva had been supported by Berne and Fribourg but the latter broke its alliance as a result of the subsequent changes which Geneva made to the Church.[71] This left Geneva in a precarious position indeed. The city faced a Savoy determined to regain control over Geneva and a Fribourg opposed to Geneva on religious grounds and desirous of securing the return of the Bishop. France, meanwhile, was also looking to increase its influence over the city. Its relations with Geneva were further complicated by a serious territorial dispute with Geneva. Geneva's lone ally was Berne, which wanted greater control over Geneva and hoped to force the city to conform its religious practices to those of Berne. The relationship with Berne was further complicated by the fact that the two cities had serious territorial disputes involving overlapping jurisdictions.[72]

Concern over Geneva's international situation and its precarious relationship with Berne was to dominate Genevan political discussions until 1541. Thus the double crisis of Savoyard and episcopal rule was over but now Geneva had to find some way of fending off the attempts of others to dominate the city. The Genevans had refused to submit to the 'protection' offered by the French King. They had also rejected Berne's demand to be given the powers and privileges of the former Bishop. They remained as princes in their own realm: the city had substituted its own sovereignty for that of the Bishop.[73] Geneva found itself forced to base its independence from Savoyard overlordship upon a Bernese protectorate. It was essential that the city find a balance which would preserve Geneva's freedoms and the alliance while avoiding Bernese ambitions; maintaining this political *via media* was not only to prove difficult but also extremely divisive.

It is necessary to examine those options which were actually available to Geneva in this period and the various arguments advanced in support of each. This is, of course, the period of Calvin's first arrival, expulsion, and triumphant return. An examination of these events is necessary if one is to determine what role, if any, religion and Calvin, in particular, played in the events of 1536–41. It is much easier to understand Calvin's return in 1541 if one sees that the crisis surrounding his exile was a political matter and his part purely incidental.

As already briefly noted, Geneva had jurisdictional disputes over territory with France and Berne, the city's likeliest allies against Savoy. Thus Geneva found it necessary to balance its desire for independence with the expansionist goals of these two nations; the disputed areas made this balance very difficult to maintain. In fact, it was in Geneva's interests to cement the alliance with Berne in every way, short of accepting direct Bernese rule. To that end it might well have appeared advisable to yield to many of the Bernese demands in return for a strengthening of the relationship between the two states. Opposed to this course were those who urged the city not to give anything away regardless of the consequences. The problem with this latter course was that it always ran the risk of producing a rupture in the alliance with Berne which would have left Geneva dangerously exposed to a Savoyard attack. Finally, and of no small consequence, Berne presented a model of a Protestant ecclesiastical structure firmly under magisterial control which was appealing to many in Geneva, a city newly freed from clerical domination.[74] A religious settlement after the Bernese pattern would also remove one additional area of possible friction between the two cities sharing, as they did, religious jurisdiction in a number of parishes. Therefore, it was in the interests of Geneva to appease and conform to Berne in as many ways as possible in order to guarantee Bernese military support and to remove or reduce possible points of conflict while maintaining a maximum amount of internal independence.

Unfortunately, there was no consensus on the best course to follow and once again factionalism and personal animosity divided the Genevan electorate. Two factions then organised to dispute the control and direction of Geneva's revolution. They were centred around Ami Porral and Jean Philippe.[75] Froment, however, has written that the animosity lay between Philippe and Michel Sept, another leading figure allied with Porral. In either case it was personal competition which began the hatred and division in Geneva. This animosity sparked the renewed factionalism whence came, as Froment said, 'beaucoup de maulx dans Geneve, assavoir, mortz, bannissementz, pertes de biens, d'honneur, et de personnes'.[76] It would seem that the root cause of this was the manner in which Sept, Porral, and Jean Goulaz were conducting affairs. They were so imperious that Pierre Vandel, an opponent in the coming crisis, accused them of the treasonable aim of wanting to be princes in Geneva; the matter was taken seriously and resulted in charges being brought against him, as a result of which he was forced to apologise.[77]

It was into this unsettled and contentious environment that Calvin came when, as a young scholar, he was persuaded to remain as a preacher in Geneva by the fiery admonitions of Farel. Obviously, he was not aware of the origins of the divisions in Genevan society, much less the tensions placed upon the body politic by the external pressures facing the city. Indeed, the chaotic nature of the Genevan situation would have made it nearly impossible for any contemporary observer, let alone participant, to understand all of the problems facing the nascent Republic or to forsee the future consequences of these issues and cross-currents which were then buffeting the city. Most importantly though, he could hardly be expected to understand the native Genevan distrust of clerics and foreigners. While some scholars might suggest that the subsequent crisis which erupted around the ministers was primarily the result of religious issues, it is much easier to see this next crisis as a continuation of the struggles which had gone before. Closer analysis seems to suggest that Calvin was not the epicentre of the contest but was, in fact, almost incidental to the crisis.

Initially, the internal crisis seemed to revolve around the need to enforce the new religious settlement. The ministers had presented for approval a new Confession of Faith, and asked that everyone be ordered to swear to it personally. The Petit Conseil had agreed but had also decreed that excommunication was not to be used to enforce the order.[78] This left only persuasion and the threat of secular punishment to get the population to take the oath.[79] Berne made the situation worse when its ambassadors said that such an oath, too difficult to keep, would result in perjury and this led many to resist this attempt to impose an ecclesiastical authority on them. Many resisted the idea that the rights and privileges of citizenship were to be made dependent upon signing some document devised by foreign theologians. Already aroused by the Revolution, the citizens of Geneva were not about to tolerate such outrageous pretensions on the part of their preachers.[80]

This internal crisis developed at the same time as the city found itself embroiled in a dispute with Berne over control of the lands of St Victor and the Chapter.[81] Moreover, Berne now began to interest itself in the religious situation in Geneva. The government of Berne seemed to feel that it had some sort of control over the Genevan Church because the city had been actively involved in its establishment. It had no intention of watching Farel and Calvin make changes to the government of the Church which Berne considered ill-advised, especially as Berne had not been consulted in advance.[82] Not only did Berne take a great interest in Geneva but, no doubt, many Genevans were very concerned about the possible Bernese reaction to the internal situation in their city. Thus, for various reasons, the Confession of Faith alienated diverse groups in Geneva. It is not unreasonable to suggest that the main reason many influential Genevans resisted this Confession was because they saw it as a threat to their relationship with Berne. Since the very existence of the Republic depended upon Bernese military might it is not surprising to find that many Genevans would strive to avoid anything which could cause offence to their benefactors.[83]

By February 1538 tensions were so high that the Petit Conseil would not allow any discussions to take place at the elections, only the vote itself. The result was that four new Syndics were elected: Claude Richardet, Jean Philippe, Jean Lullin and Aimé Chapeaurouge. The last three had been staunch supporters of the early reform but were now openly opposed to the ministers' position.[84] The question which arises is, what motive lay behind this political switch? Clearly, it is essential to this investigation to decide whether these men had become enemies of the Reform or whether they were opposed only to the possible consequences of the ministers' present proceedings.

The secondary literature is rife with completely contradictory explanations of these events. Those historians who wish to stress that the crisis of 1538–41 was a religious struggle present a number of possible interpretations. It has been variously suggested that the new leaders were Catholic sympathisers who longed to restore the old faith, that they were men of loose morals who wanted only a superficial form of Protestantism, or more bizarrely still, that the ministers' opponents were actually Anabaptists who wanted to lead Geneva into an even more radical Reformation, or some combination of all three.[85] That religious matters were, to some degree, a factor in the political crisis over the relationship with Berne is not really the question. It would be easy to dismiss all of these various interpretations by pointing out that Geneva's politicians wanted even closer ties with Protestant Berne and were hardly likely to approve of, or support any of the three groups just mentioned. Berne's negative reaction to the subsequent expulsion of the ministers is less a comment upon the religious affections of Genevans, than the overriding importance Berne placed upon stability in Geneva.[86] Indeed, one could argue that by sacking the ministers, the Genevans had gone well beyond the expectations of the Bernese.[87]

The former view that these politicians were Catholics and men of loose morals can be traced back to Gaberel. In this view a small faction of Catholics sided with those who had chased out the priests and condemned Papal abuses and who expressed the desire that their ministers confine themselves to an intellectual explication of the Bible. Moreover, the ecclesiastical rules held no sway over the men with whom the Catholics chose to ally themselves. They were free of auricular confession but they had not brought themselves to praying directly to God for mercy. They rejected indulgences but would not submit to the rule of the Supreme Judge. Likewise, they had freed themselves from the cost of masses for the dead but did not desire to make living sacrifices to obtain eternity. Finally, they no longer bowed themselves down before images but neither would they worship God in spirit and in truth.[88]

One might find it difficult to imagine any situation in which such a group would ally itself with people desirous of a return to Catholicism and by implication, the rule of the Prince–Bishop. This last fact alone makes this interpretation very dubious indeed. Too many people had profited by the destruction of the supporters of Savoy and the Bishop. Thus, while some might still argue for a role for a Catholic faction, Ganoczy is more correct in asserting that the only person reliably identifiable as a Catholic to remain in Geneva was the elder Jean Balard. While he argued for liberty of conscience, he relented when faced with the threat of banishment and in no way can be seen as part of a larger Catholic reaction.[91] A glance at Table 2 should convince anyone that Geneva's rulers were hardly likely to want to risk the consequences of the return of the Bishop and the ecclesiastical structure, as so many of them had purchased the Church's lands and goods. Moreover, as noted above, around 250 men had been excommunicated and were less than likely to expect leniency should the Bishop ever return to Geneva.

The accusation that these new rulers were motivated by some desire for immorality is a much subtler argument and therefore more difficult to evaluate or refute. The sources of this interpretation, apart from Calvin himself, are Roset and Beza, both supporters of Calvin.[92] Gaberel, as noted above, followed in this tradition which saw these men, to use Martin's phrase, as the 'parti anti-disciplinaire'.[93] Parker is perhaps the best exponent of this position in the English historical literature on Geneva. He wrote that the members of this faction 'concerned for their personal liberty, both disliked and feared this authority (ecclesiastical discipline) as a threat against their existence'.[94] One ought not to assume that this

TABLE 2   *Purchase of Church lands (C)/revenues and goods of exiles (E),*
Apr 1536–Nov 1537

Individuals (faction[89])	Purchase (owner[90])	Amount (florins)	Reference (AEG)
Pierre Tissot (A)	land (E)	385	RC/29, fol. 81
Pernet des Fosses (G)	land (E)	117	RC/29, fol. 93
	land (C)	c. 1,000	RC/30, fol. 246
Michel Sept (G)	house (E)	1,150	RC/29, fol. 102
Mye Dunant (A?)	house (E)	190	RC/29, fol. 102
François Favre (G)	land (E)	140	RC/29, fol. 140f
	goods (E)	1,000	RC/30, fol. 5v
	goods (C)	c. 2,300	RC/30, fol. 207v
Claude de Pain (?)	land (E)	70	RC/30, fol. 120v
Amblard Corne (G)	land (E)	c. 250	RC/30, fol. 121v
Jean Coquet (A)	revenues (C)	c. 2,300	RC/30, fol. 225
Jean Lambert (G)	goods at St Victor (C)	620	RC/30, fol. 60
Jean Lambert (G) and Aimé Chambouz (G)	goods (C)	520	RC/30, fol. 63v
Jean Lambert (G) and Jean Sourd (?)	tithes (C)	300	RC/30, fol. 226v
Jean Pertemps (G) and Claude Pertemps	goods (E)	1,045	RC/30, fol. 60
Claude Pertemps (G)	goods at Jussy (C/E)	545	RC/30, fol. 60
Jean Pertemps (G) and Jean de Bonis (?)	goods at St Gervais (C)	900	RC/30, fol. 60
Claude Bernard (G)	goods at Thiez (C)	1,900	RC/30, fol. 60
Jean Goulaz (G)	goods at Piney, Satigny (C/E)	1,800	RC/30, fol. 60
François Forel (A)	goods at Rive (C)	800	RC/30, fol. 60
Claude Roset (G)	goods at St Victor (C)	300	RC/31, fol. 88v

represents the whole range of historical interpretation. Roget asserted that the new rulers were not less moral and that they started their new reign by supporting ministerial calls for stricter controls on morals.[95] Indeed, as will be shown later, the only difference between the control of morality by these politicians and the ministers was, as Höpfl argued, that the former wanted the authority in controlling morals to reside in the magistracy while the latter felt the ministers should have a greater degree of freedom and power in censuring immoral behaviour.[96]

Legislation against immorality predated the Reformation but specific laws were passed in February 1534 against blasphemy, two years later against blasphemy and card-playing, and by 1537 shops were ordered to

TABLE 3   *Prosecutions for moral/religious offences, Jan 1536–Jan 1540*

Crime	Punishment	Date	Reference (AEG)
January 1536-11 February 1538[98]			
Fornication	unknown	1 Feb 1537	PC/2e Ser. 372
Witchcraft	tortured	7 Jul 1537	PC/1re Ser. 314
Adultery	banished	26 Jul 1537	PC/2e Ser. 383
Fornication	banished	11 Aug 1537	PC/1re Ser. 315
Anabaptism	unknown	11 Sep 1537	PC/2e Ser. 385
Gambling	unknown	21 Sep 1537	PC/2e Ser. 386
Fornication	banished/beaten	12 Jan 1538	PC/1re Ser. 317
Adultery	unknown	4 Feb 1538	PC/2e Ser. 394
11 February-January 1540:			
Superstition	unknown	29 Jun 1538	PC/2e Ser. 414
Bigamy	unknown	11 Jul 1538	PC/2e Ser. 416
Fornication	unknown	14 Nov 1538	PC/2e Ser. 428
Fornication	unknown	1538	PC/2e Ser. 435
Fornication with fiancée	warned/released	6 Feb 1539	PC/2e Ser. 442
Dancing on the Sabbath	warned	20 Feb 1539	PC/2e Ser. 443
Catholic views	unknown	17 Apr 1539	PC/2e Ser. 447
Fornication	unknown	31 May 1539	PC/2e Ser. 451
Blasphemy	jailed	4 Jun 1539	PC/2e Ser. 452
Adultery	unknown	27 Jun 1539	PC/2e Ser. 456
Witchcraft	tortured	6 Jul 1539	PC/2e Ser. 458
Witchcraft	unknown	11 Aug 1539	PC/2e Ser. 463
Witchcraft	beheaded	8 Sep 1539	PC/2e Ser. 464
Apostasy	warned/fined	8 Sep 1539	PC/2e Ser. 465
Fornication	unknown	19 Sep 1539	PC/2e Ser. 466
Fornication	unknown	15 Dec 1539	PC/2e Ser. 474
Fornication	unknown	Dec 1539	PC/2e Ser. 475
Fornication	banished	13 Jan 1540	PC/1re Ser. 334

close during the sermon hours.[97] But what must be stressed is that the change in government in 1538 did not alter this pattern, nor did the loss of Farel and Calvin mean that fewer complaints were brought by the ministers against immorality in Geneva.[99] The ministers still demanded that the city compel people to attend the sermons and the city was quick to comply.[100] In 1538 strict laws against immorality with heavy fines were passed, connecting, for the first time, morality offences with automatic, secular punishments.[101]

Moreover, an examination of the criminal cases preserved from the period 1536–38 with 1538–40 will show that, if anything, there was an increase in prosecutions, if not penalties in the latter period. Table 3 shows that prior to the elections of 1538 the records of eight cases survive relating to morality or religion, including one each for witchcraft, gambling and Anabaptism. The other five cases concern sexual offences. In these cases banishment was used as the punishment four times, once after a beating was administered, and torture was used in the witch trial. However, after the election there are eighteen such cases preserved. Ten cases are for sexual offences, and this corresponds closely to the proportion (five to eight) in the previous period. There were three witch trials and one each for superstition, apostasy and Catholicism, dancing on the Sabbath, and blasphemy. Punishments included banishments, warnings, fines, torture and one execution. It is almost impossible to see how these cases could imply any other conclusion except that morality continued to be controlled with at least the same enthusiasm and rigour after 1538 as it had been before.

Therefore, one must wonder whether it is reasonable to interpret the crisis of 1538–41 as a dispute over religion and morals. If by that one means a Catholic resurgence, the prosecutions for superstition, apostasy and Catholicism are sufficient to call this view into doubt. The theory that the political victors of 1538 were men who longed for a Geneva free from the control of morals seems difficult to support. As for Bouwsma's assertion that they might have been Anabaptists, this appears to be equally untenable, especially as there is no evidence of widespread Anabaptist sympathy in Geneva and the cases brought against Anabaptists, with one exception, involved foreigners.[102] The obvious conclusion, then, is that one must look elsewhere to explain the political crisis which gripped Geneva in 1538–41.

Here, the reaction of Calvin himself is very illuminating. Had his opponents been Catholics, Libertines, or Anabaptists one would expect him to raise the issue loudly and violently. Yet his advice to his Genevan supporters time and again implies that he felt the matter was of another nature.[103] He stated clearly that the true marks of the Church were still to be found in the Genevan Church although 'some points of doctrine are not quite so pure'.[104] Likewise, as the situation resolved itself and the affairs in Geneva took on 'a more settled and composed state', he exhorted his adherents to be reconciled to their enemies and especially the new ministers.[105] It would be hard to imagine Calvin recommending, let alone commanding, such a course of action were the rulers of Geneva motivated by such extreme religious views as suggested above.

A more plausible explanation might be to see the crisis as a continuation of the divisions arising from the disputes in Geneva over authority and who was to exercise it. The issue was an extension of the struggle for ministerial independence against magisterial control, or rather, a debate growing out of the question of whether the freedom of the pulpit ought to be supreme or whether it should be limited by the magistrates. For the Genevan magistrates the issue was whether they were to have and use the same rights and powers which the other Swiss republics exercised over their ministers, including the right to control the content of sermons.[106] The problem is that opposition to ministerial freedom can often be interpreted as resistance to morality, which would seem to explain the attitude of Calvin and his supporters to their opponents.[107] The previous discussion though would seem to imply that Calvin's interpretation is not wholly accurate. Is there, indeed, sufficient evidence to support the proposition that the dispute was a struggle for authority between the ministers and the magistrates?

Before examining this issue in detail no one should infer that Calvin is accused of intentionally misrepresenting the events in Geneva in this period. Rather, his unfamiliarity with Geneva's immediate history and the complexities of the city's domestic and international political situation make it unrealistic to expect Calvin to see any other explanation for the crisis than one which immediately touched himself. Calvin saw the crisis as a struggle for ministerial freedom. What is being asserted here is that this is not the interpretation which best explains the events nor the one which directed the actions of Geneva's rulers. They felt the issue at stake was Geneva's independence from Bernese control and interference. As will be shown subsequently, these divergent interpretations of the crisis and, more importantly, its subsequent resolution, meant that there existed a fundamental difference of opinion and aims (especially in relation to ministerial freedom from magisterial control) between Calvin and his apparent supporters. Thus, the subsequent break with leading Guillermins was not the result of a change in their views but rather the logical consequence of the realisation by Calvin and many of the city's elite that they were not, nor had they ever been, of one mind.

The central disputed issue at the beginning of the crisis in 1538 was whether or not the magistracy had the power to order changes to the religious practices of Geneva without consulting the ministers or getting their approval, as they did when they ordered the ministers to conform to Bernese practices in April 1538.[108] The ministers protested but were warned not to meddle in political matters.[109] This act, though provocative from the ministers' viewpoint, was not inconsistent with the earlier actions of the magistrates in establishing the Reformation.[110] It is useful to recall that even the previous governing group, dominated by future Guillermins, had refused to allow excommunication to be used as a tool for coercing citizens into signing the Confession.[111] The magistrates' goal, consistent throughout, was to provide Geneva with internal and external stability to secure Geneva's new freedoms; the retention of the school regent and the teachers, who supported Calvin and Farel, for almost a year after the ministers' expulsion demonstrated the magistrates' reluctance to disrupt Geneva further.[112]

The actions of the magistrates after the expulsion of Calvin and Farel, in fact, provide further evidence of their desire to limit the independence of the ministry. Thus, for the first time the ministers were to be salaried employees of the State. This change coincided with the switch in the records from the use of the term 'prédicant' to 'ministre évangelique'. This seems to show an assumption that the ministers of the Genevan Church were, in effect, simply employees of the State.[113] Obviously, they were moving to a situation in which there would be less chance for the sort of disputed jurisdiction of authority which led to the clash with the ministers in 1538.[114] Their primary goal, in this view, becomes the strengthening and preservation of magisterial authority.[115] In the light of what had happened, one can well understand why the magistracy found the actions of the ministers unacceptable. Surely they would not have been expected to tolerate Corault, Calvin's and Farel's elder colleague, preaching that Geneva was like 'le royaume des grenoilles at les rats parmy la paille'?[116] Nor were they likely to overlook the flagrant disobedience of Calvin and Farel in refusing to conduct the Easter Eucharist as ordered.[117]

Nevertheless, this still fails to explain the crisis of 1538–41. The 1538 disruption over the changing of Genevan ecclesiastical rites to conform to those of Berne was followed by the disastrous negotiation of a treaty, or Articles, with Berne. These Articles became the source of the name Articulant (later corrupted to Artichaux) which was applied to the political victors of 1538.[118] This treaty was rejected by the Guillermins, so called because of their support for Guillaume Farel. They were derisively called Farets, or burnt-out candles.[119] Two of their leaders, Ami Perrin and Claude Bonna (alias Pertemps), denounced the treaty as 'contre nous libertes'.[120] Eight months later, after the electoral defeat of the Articulants, the magistrates told Berne that the 'Articles son contraries aut mode de vivre Bourgeoysie nous Libertes & franchises aussy les Instructions des Ambassadeurs'.[121]

This highlights the last interpretation usually given to the events of 1538–41 and the one which is most persuasive. All the evidence points to the fact that the Articulants were working from a desire to cement the alliance with Berne by removing all possible barriers to good relations.

Thus, one can see the reconciliation of Genevan ecclesiastical practices to those of Berne and the cession of almost all disputed territories and jurisdictions as the means to an overall goal of securing the Bernese alliance and thereby safeguarding Genevan independence. To begin with, Geneva had every reason to fear that Berne might use any excuse to assert its authority over Geneva. Berne had come to Geneva's aid in the war with Savoy only because she felt that she could defeat Savoy and feared the possibility that France might move into the area and dominate Geneva.[122] Further, once in Geneva, Berne had demanded all the powers once reserved for the Bishop and his representative and had left only when it became clear that the Genevan rulers had no intention of surrendering their hard-won liberty so easily or quickly.[123]

Thus the territorial disputes which Geneva had with Berne, and to a lesser degree with France, produced a constant source of friction and provided a potential flashpoint for conflict. The dispute with France over Thiez has already been mentioned, but it may be useful to detail the situation with Berne. In 1536 four Genevan ambassadors, Estienne Chapeaurouge, Michel Sept, George Les Clefs, and Jean Lullin signed a treaty with Berne.[124] As a result Geneva was to become a city open to Berne and it was forbidden from negotiating or concluding any alliances without Berne's prior consent.[125] Further, Geneva gave to Berne some of the properties confiscated from the supporters of Savoy and the Bishop. Berne was allowed to retain the revenues of the ecclesiastical lands it had actually occupied. For its part, Berne relinquished any claim to the revenues of the Prior of St Victor, but reserved 'les appellations, les devoirs d'hommes et les maléfices', that is, the administration of criminal justice. Moreover Geneva was granted the goods and lands of the Chapter and the initial exercise of justice but appeals were to go to Berne. Finally, Geneva gained complete control over Peney, Jussy, Thiez (which was also claimed by France), Gex and Gailliard.[126]

Moreover, Berne had a great deal of interest in Geneva as the city was heavily indebted to Berne and because Berne continued to fear any extension of French influence.[127] Geneva had borrowed over 20,000 ff from Berne and Basle in the decade before 1540 which gave Berne a vested interest in Genevan affairs.[128] This shows the positive side of the relationship with Berne; the negative aspect is apparent in the cost of the embassies necessary to maintain the relationship, many of which dealt with the disputed territories and shared jurisdictions. In the period 1537–39 Geneva spent over 10,000 ff on these embassies alone at a time when city revenues were around 22,000 ff per annum. The dispute with France would later consume (in 1544) over 3,600 ff.[129] Together these provide evidence of the financial drain which these territorial problems imposed upon Geneva, in addition to the danger of a deterioration of the alliance.

One should not leave this discussion without some reflection on the personal motives of the protagonists. The discussion thus far has been presented in terms of principle and high policy; but, as with all such events, members of the ruling elite had something to gain or lose by the policies they were promoting. At an obvious level the loss of territorial rights and privileges to Berne would have less of an impact on the Articulants. Table 2 shows the extent to which the Guillermins had invested capital into the ecclesiastical lands; they were likely to be more affected if Geneva lessened its hold over these areas. Guillermin objections were as much a defence of their personal wealth as of any principles. Their debates with the Articulants, as the crisis developed, would have had a very strong element of individual animosity as they began to realise that their opponents were quite willing to concede to Bernese authority large properties which they had purchased.

This raises the question of the role that personal disputes played in the crisis. This latter area has been left totally unexplored except that some people have discussed, and dismissed, the possibility that the dispute was the result of an ethnic battle between Genevans of French and German ancestry.[130] Having dismissed an ethnic element, though, is it fair to assume that personality played no part at all? Although it is impossible to give a definitive answer, sufficient evidence does survive in the Genevan records to allow for some general comments. Table 4 shows that of the twenty-nine disputes recorded in the Genevan council records from 1535 to 1540, over half (sixteen) involve members of the Guillermin faction against Articulants. This ratio is only slightly lower in the period before the Articulant victory (nine out of twenty-one). What is interesting is that after the 1538 elections there is no record of a dispute amongst individuals of the same faction. Indeed, all but one of the disputes occuring after 1538 involves a Guillermin. This would seem to imply an increasing belligerence on the part of the Guillermins and a closing of the factional ranks. But the most obvious and important conclusion which can be drawn is that these two groups not only had political differences as factions but also individual personal disputes which predated the 1538 crisis.

It is hardly surprising that in a city as small as Geneva in this period (around 10,000 inhabitants) one finds such a degree of interaction amongst the ruling elite.[133] Appendix 1 shows the extent to which these people did have connections with one another. The contractural evidence which survives does show some areas of interaction between the

TABLE 4 *Personal disputes, 1535–40*

Person (faction[132]) vs	*Person* (faction)	*Reference* (AEG)
1535-11 February 1538[31]		
George Dentand (?)	Jaques (G) & Aimé (G) des Arts	RC/28, fol. 4
Jean Cuendoz (?)	Jaques (G) & Aimé (G) des Arts	RC/28, fol. 31
Antoine Testu (A)	François Favre (G)	RC/28, fol. 35
Claude Richardet (A)	Jean Philippe (A)	RC/28, fol. 42v
Antoine Gervais (?)	Aimé Chapeaurouge (A)	RC/28, fol. 116v
Pierre Vandel (A)	Baudichon de la Maisonneuve (G)	RC/29, fol. 5
Thomas Genod (?)	Domaine d'Arlod (G)	RC/29, fol. 55v
Claude Savoye (G), Baudichon de la Maisonneuve (G), and Jean Levet (A)	Jean Balard, elder (A) and Bartholomie Messeri (A)	RC/29, fol. 56v
Michel Sept (G)	Aimé Chapeaurouge (A)	RC/29, fol. 63
François Perrisod (?)	Aimé Chapeaurouge (A)	RC/30, fols. 87v, 140v
Jaques des Arts (G)	François Rosset (A)	RC/30, fol. 119v
Jean Pecollat (G)	Jean Goulaz (G)	RC/30, fol. 150v
Pierre Vandel (A)	Ami Porral (G)	RC/30, fol. 154
Domaine d'Arlod (G)	Jean Coquet (A)	RC/30, fol. 161
Amblard Corne (G)	François Chamois (A)	RC/30, fols. 186v, 193
Jean-Ami Curtet (G) and Amblard Corne (G)	Pierre Vandel (A)	RC/30, fol. 237
Jaques des Arts (G)	François Rosset (A)	RC/31, fol. 15v
Jean Philippe (A)	Jean Goulaz (G)	RC/31, fol. 135v
Jean Levet (A)	Ami Bandière (G)	RC/31, fol. 171v
11 February 1538-January 1540		
Aimé Chapeaurouge (A)	Michel Sept (G)	RC/32, fol. 7
Pierre Vandel (A)	Jean-Ami Curtet (G)	RC/32, fol. 14
Claude Savoye (G)	Jean Levet (A)	RC/32, fol. 38
François Chamois (A)	Thomas Genod (?)	RC/32, fol. 41
Girardin de la Rive (A)	Henry Goulaz (G)	RC/32, fol. 81
Ami Bandière (G)	Jean Levet (A)	RC/32, fol. 194
Domaine d'Arlod (G)	Claude Clement (?)	RC/32, fol. 227v
Pierre Verna (?)	Jean Pecollat (G)	RC/33, fol. 323v

Guillermins and the Articulants. For example, Bezanson, Dadaz and Maisonneuve were involved in a property deal.[134] Also, the loan involving Jaques des Arts and Pierre Bertillion would seem to imply some ties between the two groups.[135] But it is of interest to note that the Guillermins do seem to have had a tendency to group together. Thus one sees a large number of Guillermins witnessing the marriage of François Paquet and the daughter of Jean Balard the younger.[136] Also, Guillermin business ties are obvious, for example between Aubert and Favre[137] or between

Maisonneuve and Goulaz.[138] The conclusion seems to be that the Guillermins were more likely to share exclusive ties with one another. This would obviously provide this faction with greater internal cohesion and could well explain its ability to remain intact in the early phase of the crisis. In any case, these men shared more than a political viewpoint.

The crucial period for the Articulants came after the Genevan populace became aware of the treaty, or Articles, which had been negotiated with Berne. Up to this point the bulk of the population seems to have supported the general Articulant goal of cementing the relationship with Berne. However, when the price which the Articulants were willing to pay to guarantee Bernese protection became known, the citizenry deserted them. The records of votes cast in the elections of 1540 and 1541 survive and give an idea of the relative strength of the two groups and show the massive swing in Genevan popular opinion as a result of the dispute over the treaty with Berne and the subsequent removal of many Articulants in the summer of 1540. Before one discusses these elections in detail, however, it may be useful to give a brief explanation of the Genevan governmental system.

The Petit Conseil, or Senate, consisted of the four Syndics and twenty-one Conseillers. Eight men were nominated for the Syndic seats and the Conseil des Deux Cents then elected four; the Conseillers of the previous year were given an individual vote of confidence by the Deux Cents and replaced if they failed to get a majority. The Conseil des Soixante was an extension of about thirty-five men to the Petit Conseil, drawn from the Deux Cents. They were involved in some important decisions, especially those of a diplomatic nature. The Deux Cents was appointed by the Petit Conseil after its election by the Deux Cents of the previous year. The Conseil Général, made up of all citoyens and bourgeois, elected the treasurer and Lieutenant and was called upon to approve all new laws.[146]

Eventually, the four Syndics were each given charge of one area of Genevan administration. The first Syndic was president of the court of Secondes Appellations, or the civil appeals court. Another Syndic presided over the court of Premières Appellations, or lower civil court.[147] The third Syndic headed the Chambre des Comptes and, after 1543, the fourth Syndic presided over the Consistoire. The various other offices were appointed by either the Deux Cents or the Petit Conseil. The Deux Cents named the two secretaries of state, the auditors, the Contrôlleur, the Capitaine Général, the Banderet Général, the Maître de l'Artillerie, the gaoler, the Sautier, and the heralds. The Petit Conseil was responsible for electing the captains of the city districts, the other banderets, the dizeniers, the gatekeepers, the notaries, the guets, the messeliers, the inspectors of

TABLE 5   *Genevan election results, 1540-41*

February 1540

Syndic[139]

Upper city		Lower city	
Person (party)	Votes	Person (party)	Votes
Ant. Gerbel (?)	36	Est. Chapeaurouge (A)	46
J. Philippin (?)	38	Est. Dadaz (A)	32
J. Chappuis (?)	9	Ami Bandière (G)	23
P. Tissot (A)	17	Fr. Lullin (A)	1
J.-G. Monathon (A)	2		102 *Total*
P. Ameaux (G)	1		
P. Vandel (A)	1		
Fr. Beguin (G)	1		
	105 *Total*		

February 1541

Syndic[140]

J.-A. Curtet (G)	78	A. Bandière (G)	67
P. Des Fosses (G)	87	Dom. d'Arlod (G)	82
P. Tissot (A)	15	Cl. Pertemps (G)	43
Cl. Roset (G)	24	Amb. Corne (G)	16
	204 *Total*	A. Perrin (G)	4
		J. Lambert (?)	1
		J.-P. Donzel (G)	1
			214 *Total*

Treasurer[141]   *Contrôleur*[142]

A. Corne (G)	41	A. Corne (G)	34
P. Tissot (A)	47	Cl du Pan (?)	22
P. Bonna (G)	4	L. Chabbod (G)	15
J.-P. Donzel (G)	3	J.-P. Donzel (G)	1
Cl. Roset (G)	2	H. du Mollard (?)	2
	97 *Total*	Jaq. des Arts (G)	1
			75 *Total*

Secrétaire de la Chambre des Comptes[143]

Cl. Roset (G)	51
Fr. Beguin (G)	32
	83 *Total*

A = Articulant
G = Guillermin

TABLE 6   *Negotiators with Berne, 1540*

May 1540[144]

Juges		Procureurs (no votes recorded)
Person (party)	Votes	Person (party)
J. Philippin (?)	1	Michel Sept (G)
Ant. Gerbel (?)	0	P. Vandel (A)
J. Coquet (A)	7	
Gir. de la Rive (A)	34	Secrétaire (no votes recorded)
Dom. d'Arlod (G)	26	
A. Bandière (G)	3	Cl. Roset (G)
M. Sept (G)	2	
	73 Total	Conseillers (no votes recorded)
		Cl. Pertemps (G)
		J.-P. Donzel (G)

Sep 1540 (no votes recorded)[145]

Juges	Secrétaire
Gir. de la Rive (A)	P. Ruffi (?)
J.-A. Curtet (G)	

Procureurs	Conseillers
Cl. Pertemps (G)	J. Lambert (?)
Cl. Roset (G)	A. Porral (G)
Fr. Beguin (G)	Gme. Vellut (?)
	L. du Four (G)
	Jaq. des Arts (G)

A = Articulant
G = Guillermin

weights and measures, the inspector of fish, the masons and the judges. This gives some idea not only of the large number of individuals involved in the Genevan government but also of the importance of the elections.[148]

The elections of 1540 (see Table 5) show the strength of the Articulant party. In the lower city the Articulant candidates attracted seventy-nine votes against twenty-three for Ami Bandière, the lone Guillermin candidate. In the upper city, Gerbel and Philippin, who cannot be assigned to either faction, took both Syndic seats with seventy-four votes with Chappuis, also of neither group, getting an additional nine votes. Articulants took twenty votes with only two votes going to any Guillermins. But, as can be seen in Table 6, a shift in popular strength is apparent by May 1540 when negotiators were elected to meet with Berne. The non-partisan Syndics Gerbel and Philippin are reduced to only one vote between them. The Guillermins capture thirty-one votes against forty-one cast for Articulant candidates. A similar swing to the Guillermins is even more apparent in the other members of the embassy, for whom the votes are not preserved. Here, all but one position goes to a Guillermin. The negotiators for September 1540 show the same situation. By then the embassy included only one person, Girardin de la Rive, who could be identified, in any way, with the Articulants. All the others are either Guillermins or men who cannot be associated with either faction.

The votes cast in February 1541 (see Table 5) show the extent to which the tide had turned in the course of the year. Only one Articulant, Pierre Tissot, received any votes at all and he was able to win the post of Treasurer. In this election the Articulants were completely routed. The 1540 elections show the real strength of the Articulants long after the expulsion of the ministers and the changes to the ecclesiastical structure in Geneva. Their support collapsed only after Geneva became aware of the full scope of the concessions made to Berne which clearly went far beyond the expectations or wishes of the Genevans. Indeed, in the overall position of the two factions it is hard to see that the actions against the ministers played any significant part at all.

In conclusion, it should be possible to comment upon those aspects of Genevan society and politics which continued throughout all the crises prior to 1541. First, personal morality or a desire for lax morals seems to have played no part in the events. If nothing else, it is hard to consider the Guillermins to be paragons of virtue when two of them, Jean Ami Curtet and Pierre Malligniod and a later long-serving member of the Consistory and staunch Calvinist, Pierre Dorsière, were all convicted of sexual immorality before 1538.[149] In any case there is no evidence to suggest any relaxation in the control of morals in the period 1538–40 when the Articulants were in power. What does appear is a lively debate over the role of the ministers and the degree of freedom and authority they were to have in the context of a much wider political dispute. To some, especially Calvin and Farel, this attempt to assert magisterial authority may have been perceived as an attempt to dilute the power of the ministers to control morality. Obviously, there was a dispute over the relative position of the magistrates *vis-à-vis* the ministers. The question is not why the ministers opposed these moves but why, and whether, so many Genevans did.

However, the question of the relationship between Geneva and Berne seems to be at the heart of the 1538 crisis. For those Genevans opposed to the actions of the Articulants, fearful of an extension of Bernese influence and the subsequent loss of Genevan independence, the actions against the ministers would have served as an excellent rallying-point for opposition to the Articulants. The fact that none of the acts was repealed seems to imply that the ecclesiastical changes were not, in themselves, the main point of contention. Further, the lack of enthusiasm for Calvin's recall is another indication that the ecclesiastical aspects of the crisis were of secondary importance. When the Guillermins regained control in the summer of 1540 they made no attempt to contact Calvin about his possible return.

Indeed it was not until after Morand and Marcourt, the ministers hired by the Articulants to replace Calvin and Farel, had abandoned their posts that Geneva acted to recall Calvin. 'Pource que le sus nomme maystre anthone marcour predicant sen est alle Resolu de donnez charge aut sgr Amy perrin de trouve moyeant si pouveray fere venyr maystre Caulvin.'[150] The most obvious reason for Calvin's recall, then, was not nostalgic sentiment but the need to shore up the deplorable state of the Church, bereft of its two best ministers.[151] Thus, for three months after the defeat of the Articulants the city failed to recall Calvin. It was only the disastrous state of the Church, brought about by the resignations of Marcourt and Morand, which led the city to turn to their former minister.[152] Clearly, one cannot say that Calvin was central to the 1538 crisis.

All this simply reinforces the view that the crisis was first and foremost political in nature. Just as the Church played a part in the fight against the Bishop so here it was a rallying-point for those opposed to any increase in Bernese power. This is not to imply that the Guillermins were supporters of the Church for purely cynical reasons but rather that they had no real complaint about what had been done, (namely, the changes to the rites) or even how (by magisterial decree), but that they opposed the reason which lay behind these actions. They were opposed to any attempt to place Geneva in a closer, more dependent relationship with Berne. To stop this encroachment by Berne they were willing to seize upon any issue and indeed to risk war.[153] Once the situation was resolved and Berne forced to accept the status quo whereby Geneva was left relatively free in internal matters, Geneva and its rulers were willing to rehabilitate the exiled Articulants, a unique amnesty, and showed a decided lack of interest in the ecclesiastical issues which had signalled the start of the crisis.[154]

This analysis should also have demonstrated that there were distinct similarities between the 1538 crisis and the previous crises involving Savoy and the Bishop. All these events manifested those tendencies which can be discerned in Genevan society and politics which would be of importance in the later 1555 conflict. A number of factors are apparent. First, many Genevans were almost fanatically devoted to preserving the city's independence and the privileges which accompanied it. This is particularily obvious in that to preserve their understanding of Geneva's freedom they were not only willing to risk Bernese support but came perilously close to war with Berne. Second, there seems to have been a general acceptance of the idea of magisterial control over ecclesiastical affairs. The magistrates' deposition of the Bishop and the moves against the Church before the advent of Protestant preaching is clear evidence of this. Next, the magistracy was quite willing to control morality in Geneva but showed a clear reluctance to use excommunication as a means of coercion. This is apparent in the conduct of both the Guillermins and the Articulants. Moreover, there was a deep-seated fear of foreign domination which was connected with the desire to protect Geneva's liberties.

Finally, it must be borne in mind that Geneva was a city in which politics and personal relationships were of great importance because of the high level of involvement in civic affairs. As Höpfl astutely pointed out,

> What needs to be stressed in this connection is that all Genevan public offices and councils were in some manner and measure elective. While a persistent drift in an oligarchical direction is discernible, habits of popular activism, or at any rate assembly-politics, had been contracted by the citizenry. These centred as often as not on the taverns, and drunken and noisy demonstrations in the streets were by no means unknown. But however much choice at elections might be guided and constrained, it was real choice.[155]

It might also be added that this political situation could be affected by personal disputes as well, especially when one considers the size of the city, its relative openness to debate, and the obvious tendency of the Genevans to factionalism. It was certainly no understatement on Calvin's part when he would later comment on this 'intestinum semen disidii' in Geneva. What is questionable is his interpretation of the causes of this factionalism.[156]

It remains to be seen which of these factors was to play the greatest part in the future crises of Calvin's ministry, leading to the decisive showdown in 1555. What may appear reasonable, though, is to expect that all these tensions in Genevan society and politics would be involved. In any case one must constantly remember that Geneva was a volatile city, with an unsettled constitution, full of tensions and competing social, political and economic forces, surrounded by dangerous, avaricious states. The following years saw many of these issues being played out as Geneva, newly independent, freshly Protestant, became a settled Republic.

NOTES

1 CO, vol. 34, col. 213f. (Sermon on Job 21: 1–6, August 1554).
2 The best discussion of the establishment of the reformation in Geneva remains Naef, *Origines*.
3 CO, col. 11, col. 376–81 (to Myconius, 14 May 1542).
4 This brief overview generally follows, and is indebted to, Monter's discussion. Cf. Monter, *Geneva*, pp. 36–43.
5 *Advis*, pp. 45f.
6 Gaberel, *Histoire*, vol. 1, p. 180; J. Balard, *Journal*, J. J. Chaponnière, ed.(Geneva: 1854), p. 72.
7 Originally the Mamelukes, from the Arabic for slave, were a military band of slaves recruited by Saladin from the Turks in the Caucasus. In the 1200s they usurped authority in Egypt where they ruled until they were massacred in 1811. Since those called Mammelus in Geneva were claiming that they were supporters of the legitimate rulers of Geneva, this epithet had the double effect of portraying them as men who had sold themselves to foreign rulers and as usurpers of power from the rightful rulers.
8 Roset, p. 87; *Advis*, p. 19 and *Chroniques*, p. 331; P. E. Martin, 'L'Emancipation Politique de Genèva 1519–1536', in the *Almanach Paroissial* (Geneva: 1925), p. 28. Cf., also, A. Gautier, *Familles Genevoises d'Origine Italienne* (Bari: 1893), p. 3. The large number of immigrants to Geneva before the Revolution is clearly noted in J. F. Bergier, 'Marchands Italiens de Genève au Début du XVIe Siècle', in *Mélanges d'Histoire du XVIe Siècle offerts à Henri Meylan,* in *Bibliothèque Historique Vaudoise*, vol. 43 (Lausanne: 1970).
9 Gaberel, *Histoire*, vol. 1, p. 180.
10 See Naef, *Origines*, vol. 2, pp. 13, 50 where Bezanson Hugues is described as the 'capitaine (sometimes abbé) des enffans de Genève'. The militia which developed into the 'enfants' had its roots in a Genevan youth society, the 'abbaye des Enfants'. Cf., N. Davis, 'The Reasons of Misrule: Youth Groups and Charivaris in Sixteenth-Century France', in *P&P*, 1971 (50), p. 61. See p. 86. Also *Chroniques*, vol. 2, p. 56 (marginal note). For Eidgenots as a derisive term see Roset, p. 87 and *Advis*, p. 21. Cf., P. Charpenne, *Histoire de la Réforme et des Réformateurs de Genève* (Paris: 1861), p. 64; A. Roget, *Les Suisses et Genève* (Geneva: 1864), vol. 1, p. 105. Other symbols were used as well; the Mammelus wore holly in their hats, the Enfants, cock feathers. McGrath, *Calvin*, p. 89.
11 Gaberel, *Histoire*, vol. 1, pp. 83f.
12 AEG/PC/1re Ser., 190 (16 Mar 1518). Cf., J. B. G. Galiffe, *Matériaux pour l'Histoire de Genève*, vol. 2 (Geneva: 1830), pp. 93–154 for a transcription of the Berthelier case.
13 *Chroniques*, vol. 2, p. 238.
14 Naef, *Origines*, vol. 1, pp. 113f. Also, P. Vaucher, *Luttes de Genève contre la Savoie: 1517–1530* (Geneva: 1889), pp. 4f., J. B. G. Galiffe, 'Bezanson Hugues', in *MDG*, vol. 11 (Geneva: 1859), pp. 210–13, 227. The 'enfants de la ville' in Lyon were also noted for their defence of one another's honour and person. Davis, 'Misrule', p. 63.
15 Hugues was Sieur de Perolles near Fribourg. He was elected to the Petit Conseil for the first time in 1518, Syndic in 1528 and died in 1532. His father was a Senator and Syndic (1508, 1510). He married Clauda de Fernex and produced a son, Denis (châtelain of Jussy in 1551) and two daughters, Jeanne (wife of Jean du Molard) and Antoina (wife of Louis Franc). Cf., J. A. Galiffe, *Notices Généalogiques de Genève* (Paris: 1829–95), vol. 1, pp. 1–7.
16 Naef, *Origines*, vol. 2, pp. 15, 112. *Chroniques*, vol. 2, pp. 277f., gives a list of those proscribed. Gaberel, *Histoire*, vol. 1, pp. 404f. lists the leading Enfants. Cf., also, Vaucher, *Luttes*, p. 28.

17 Gaberel, *Histoire*, vol. 1, pp. 182f.

18 Naef, *Origines*, vol. 2, p. 107.

19 Naef, *Origines*, vol. 2, pp. 270f.

20 Naef, *Origines*, vol. 2, pp. 60f. For more information on Geneva's governmental system see pp. 38–40.

21 Figure 1 is adapted from Binz, *Vie Religieuse*, Figure 2 from Monter, *Geneva*.

22 Martin, 'L'Emancipation', p. 27.

23 A. L. Head-König and B. Veyrasset-Herren, 'Les Revenus Décimaux à Genève de 1540 à 1783', in J. Goy and E. Ladurie, eds., *Les Fluctuations du Produit de la Dîme* (Paris: 1972), p. 166; Naef, *Origines*, vol. 1, p. 5; F. Fleury, *Les Confréries de Genève* (Geneva: 1869), pp. 1f.

24 Gaberel, *Histoire*, vol. 1, pp. 249–51. The Protestant church structure was much less of a financial burden on the Genevans than the previous Catholic structure had been. Cf., E. W. Monter, *Studies in Genevan Government* (Geneva: 1964), p. 20; Innes, *Social Concerns*, pp. 146f. The enormous size of the pre-Reformation Genevan church is well documented in Binz, *Vie Religieuse*, pp. 489–503. In 1443 alone, there were 990 clerics tonsured in Geneva's diocese as well as eighty-eight lower clergy.

25 Martin, 'L'Emancipation', p. 30. Also, B. Lescaze, *Sauver l'Ame Nourrir le Corps* (Geneva: 1958), pp. 56f. Cf., Monter, *Geneva*, p. 156. Secularisation, when combined with the massive decrease in the clergy, meant a large net increase in revenues for the city. Thus in 1544 Geneva spent 4,000ff. on the ministers and 1,500ff. on the hospital while taking in nearly 12,000ff. in former ecclesiastical revenues. Florins (ff) were the Genevan unit of account and in the period five florins were roughly equal to one écu.

26 Naef, *Origines*, vol. 2, p. 51.

27 *Chroniques*, vol. 2, p. 287.

28 Gaberel, *Histoire*, vol. 1, p. 181.

29 Naef, *Origines*, vol. 2, p. 174, does stress some individual early support for Bernese Protestantism at Geneva. A. Girard promised to lead men to aid Berne after Fribourg threatened to attack if Bernese peasants who wanted the Mass were not granted toleration.

30 Naef, *Origines*, vol. 2, p. 177; Roget, *Suisses*, vol. 2, p. 151.

31 Naef, *Origines*, vol. 2, p. 145.

32 Naef, *Origines*, vol. 2, p. 215; Martin, 'L'Emancipation', p. 30. A helpful discussion on cities and the Reformation is S. Ozment, *Reformation in the Cities* (London: 1975) while details on Geneva's nearest neighbour, Berne, can be found in K. Guggisberg, *Bernische Kirchengeschichte* (Berne: 1958).

33 Gaberel, *Histoire*, vol. 1, p. 191; Roset, pp. 190f.

34 Gaberel, *Histoire*, vol. 1, p. 194; Vaucher, *Luttes*, p. 5.

35 Gaberel, *Histoire*, vol. 1, pp. 221, 262; Roset, pp. 201, 233. By the end of 1535 Geneva was exercising every power of a sovereign state and, in addition to controlling all of the revenues in its domains, had begun minting its own money, cf., E. Demole, *Histoire Monétaire de Genève de 1535 à 1848* (Geneva: 1978), p. 7.

36 Indeed, many of the orders, e.g. the Frères Mineurs, had been established directly by the House of Savoy, cf., l'Abbé Tremey, 'Obituaire des Cordeliers de Genève', in *Mémoires et Documents publiés par l'Académie Salésienne*, vol. 28 (Annecy: 1904), p. 235. Cf., R. M. Kingdon, 'Presbytery', p. 44, who also stresses the Genevan fear of ecclesiastical and foreign domination.

37 W. Martin, *Histoire de la Suisse* (Lausanne: 1959), p. 110.

38 The other two ran through Switzerland proper. The pass at St Gotthard so closely identified with its geographic protector that the Venetians referred to it as 'Basel Street'.

Cf., M. Körner, 'Réformes, Ruptures, Croissances', in J. Favez, *et al.*, eds, *Nouvelle Histoire de la Suisse et des Suisses* (Lausanne: 1983), p. 26 and W Oechsli, *History of Switzerland*, E. and C. Paul, trans. (Cambridge: 1922), p. 15.

39 Cf., H. Ménabréa, *Histoire de la Suisse* (Chambéry: 1960), p. 127; Oechsli, *Switzerland*, p. 23; J. Major, *The Monarchy, the Estates and the Aristocracy in Renaissance France* (London: 1988), essay I, p. 113.

40 Körner, 'Réformes', p. 11. Zürich had 5,000–8,000 people, Berne around 5,000.

41 R. Paquier, *Le Pays de Vaud des Origines à la Conquête Bernoise* (Lausanne: 1942), p. 228 and Ménabréa, *Histoire*, p. 119. For details on the early Duchy, its laws, customs, polity, and internal organisation see R. Mariotte-Löber, *Ville et Seigneurie, Les Chartes de Franchises des Comtes de Savoie* (Geneva: 1973).

42 Paquier, *Vaud*, pp. 225f. For details on the importance of geography on the politico-military decisions of the region see L. Roulet, 'L'Obstacle de la Montagne dans les Guerres de Bourgogne', in *Revue Internationale d'Histoire Militaire*, 1988 (65), pp. 91–104.

43 Oechsli, *Switzerland*, p. 134; Ménabréa, *Histoire*, pp. 123f.

44 Ménabréa, *Histoire*, p. 120; Oechsli, *Switzerland*, p. 40. The region's value to France is obvious in the investment France consistently made in Lyon, including the court's residence there (1494–1551) throughout the period. L. Bourgeois, *Quand la Cour de France vivait à Lyon* (Paris: 1980), pp. 23–44.

45 See the map inserted at the end of Ménabréa, *Histoire*. This French interest continued until the Treaty of Cateau-Cambrésis (1559) when domestic concerns distracted France from external affairs. Major, *Monarchy*, essay IV, p. 461.

46 Ménabréa, *Histoire*, p. 127

47 Ménabréa, *Histoire*, pp. 123f.

48 Savoyard power in the north was already weakened by the effective cessation of the area to Charles's relative Philippe (1514), Ménabréa, *Histoire*, pp. 120–5.

49 Ménabréa, *Histoire*, pp. 128–30.

50 Ménabréa, *Histoire*, pp. 133–5. Emmanuel-Philibert cemented the new arrangement with France by marrying Marguerite, daughter of Francis I.

51 Martin, *Suisse*, p. 78.

52 H. Wackernagel, *Die Politik der Stadt Basel während die Jahre 1524–1528* (Basel: 1922), pp. 39–42. Zürich traditionally opposed Bernese expansionism, cf., Martin, *Suisse*, p. 80.

53 See Wackernagel, *Basel*, pp. 22–6 on Basel's aims in southern Germany. Also, for details on Basel's relations with Geneva, primarily as the city's financier, see Plath, *Basel*. Zürich was interested in expanding into southern Germany also, cf., Martin, *Suisse*, pp. 107–9.

54 Martin, *Suisse*, p. 110. Naguely, commanding the Bernese army with troops drawn from Neuchâtel, Payerne, and Gruyère, swept across the Vaud, seizing Lausanne and relieving Geneva. He withdrew from his positions beyond Geneva to allow France a clear road to move against Chambéry. Oechsli, *Switzerland*, pp. 146–8.

55 Lausanne, ruled by Savoy in a fashion to that used in Geneva, was much smaller than Geneva with a less developed sense of 'national' spirit and was not able to maintain its independence from the Bernese 'liberators'. L. Junod, 'De la Ville Episcopale au Chef-Lieu de Bailliage', in J. Biaudet *et al.*, *Histoire de Lausanne* (Lausanne: 1982), pp. 152f, 155, 160. Oechsli, *Switzerland*, pp. 127f., Neuchâtel and Gruyère had already fallen under the 'protection' of Berne and Fribourg.

56 These advances marked Switzerland's greatest territorial limit. Körner, 'Réformes', p. 8.

57 G. Thürer, *Free and Swiss, the Story of Switzerland*, R. Heller and E. Long, trans. (London: 1970), pp. 49f.

58 Berne, Fribourg and Solothurn refused to heed calls to avenge the defeat inflicted on the Swiss at Marignano by France despite the rise in anti-French sentiment in western Switzerland which had already manifested itself (in 1513) in popular uprisings against pro-French magistrates (some were executed) in the three states. Oechsli, *Switzerland*, pp. 46f, 55–7. Despite a lessening of pro-French sentiment, Switzerland still needed France's support to resist Imperial incursions. Cf., Oechsli, *Switzerland*, pp. 27–9 and S. de Zeigler, 'L'Alliance Perpétuelle entre les Confédérés Suisses et le Roi de France', in *Revue des Deux Mondes*, 1984 (6), p. 553.

59 Oechsli, *Switzerland*, pp. 40f.

60 Oechsli, *Switzerland*, pp. 60f.

61 Oechsli, *Switzerland*, pp. 57, 59, 62; Zeigler, 'Alliance', pp. 554f.

62 The withdrawal of Fribourg's protection left Geneva wholly dependent upon Berne. Oechsli, *Switzerland*, p. 143.

63 Berne remained the most powerful Canton and, therefore, a sure defence for Geneva. Oechsli, *Switzerland*, p. 107; Körner, 'Réformes', p. 76. Berne was determined to keep Geneva from France's grasp and, to secure Geneva's reliance upon Protestant Berne rather than Catholic France, Farel and Froment were dispatched to Geneva with the 'recommandation expresse des autorités bernoises'. Martin, *Suisse*, p. 11. The importance of the Bernese use of Protestantism to consolidate its position in the Francophone area is clear in its actions in the Vaud. Cf., H. Vuilleumier, *Histoire de l'Eglise Réformée du Pays de Vaud* (Lausanne: 1927).

64 AEG/RC/28, fol. 89 (13 Jul 1535) lists thirty-eight condemned with fines totalling around ff.1.5 million. For a lively account of the general civic tumult accompanying the Reformation in Geneva and, especially, the iconoclasm and the clerics' reaction to the deteriorating position of the Church see Roset, pp. 185–195.

65 P. E. Martin, *Histoire de Genève des Origines à 1798* (Geneva: 1951), p. 222; A. Perrenoud, *La Population de Genève* (Geneva: 1979), p. 11.

66 Perrenoud, *Population*, p. 31. About 5,000 persons were dispossessed as a result of the Faubourgs' destruction and the war. Cf., Gaberel, *Histoire*, vol. 1, p. 223.

67 For the names of the Peneysans, the excommunicated Genevans, the leading Protestants and Catholics see Gaberel, *Histoire*, vol. 1, pp. 58–61, and vol. 1, pp. 404f., for the names of the Enfants. Also, see *Chroniques*, vol. 2, pp. 277f., and Naef, *Origines*, vol. 2, p. 15, for the names of the Mammelus.

68 Cf., Tremey, 'Obituaire', p. 237. Not all of the clerics left. Jaques Bernard, a Franciscan, and F. Bonivard, Prior of St-Victor, are leading examples of those who stayed. Gaberel, *Histoire*, vol. 1, p. 256, lists nine former clerics who stayed, but only Bernard remained a minister in the city. Extensive research in notarial records has produced evidence that over sixty former clerics remained in Geneva, cf., G. Cahier-Buccelli, 'Dans l'Ombre de la Réforme: les Membres de l'Ancien Clergé demeurés à Généve', in *Bulletin de la Société d'Histoire et d'Archéologie de Genève*, 18 (4), pp. 367–89.

69 Höpfl, *Polity*, p. 133f. A *citoyen* was a person born in Geneva to citoyen or bourgeois parents. A *bourgeois* was someone who had purchased, or been granted, the rights and responsibilities of a citoyen (except the ability to serve in the Petit Conseil). An *habitant* was an alien granted rights of residence in the city in return for some form of allegiance to the city and a promise to obey Geneva's laws. Although anyone in these groups was a *sujet* of the city the term would more appropriately describe the city's rural population or the urban natives who did not possess citoyen or bourgeois status. Complete details on Geneva's laws during Calvin's ministry can be found in E. Rivoire and V. van

Berchem, eds., *Les Sources du Droit du Canton de Genève* (Aarau: 1927–35), vol. 2 (1461–1550) and vol. 3 (1551–1620).

70 Roget, *Suisses*, vol. 2, p. 192. The totals in the figure are compiled from *Bourg.* The individual cost of bourgeois status was low and the city made substantial revenues only when it admitted a large number of new bourgeois. Cf., *Monter,* 'Demography', p. 407.

71 Martin, 'L'Emancipation', p. 30. As early as February 1533 Fribourg threatened to quit the alliance over Geneva's toleration of 'la foy Lutherienne', J. Flournois, *Extraits Contenus de Tout ce qu'il y a d'Important dans les Registres Publics de Geneve* (Geneva: 1832), p. 14.

72 Höpfl, *Polity,* p. 129.

73 Martin, 'L'Emancipation', p. 31.

74 This model remained popular with many Genevans throughout the period before 1555 and Calvin's final triumph over this view. Cf., M. E. Chenevière, *La Pensée Politique de Calvin* (Geneva: 1970), p. 253.

75 A. Roget, *Histoire du Peuple de Genève* (Geneva: 1870–87), vol. 1, pp. 29f. The rivalry can be traced back to a dispute in the 1535–36 war. Monter, *Geneva*, pp. 65f. Cf., T. Beza, 'Life of Calvin', in H. Beveridge, trans., *Tracts Relating to the Reformation by John Calvin* (Edinburgh: 1844), p. 32. Porral became a severe critic of the ministers who remained after Calvin's departure, A. Roget, *Etrennes Genevoises* (Geneva: 1877), vol. 5, pp. 172f.

76 Froment, p. 182.

77 Roget, *Histoire,* vol. 1, pp. 37f.

78 But they could be banished by the secular authorities. Cf., R. W. Collins, *Calvin and the Libertines* (Vancouver: 1968) p. 103.

79 A. D. Ainsworth, *The Relations between the Church and State in the City and Canton of Geneva* (Atlanta: 1965), p. 15; Gaberel, *Histoire,* vol. 1, p. 286.

80 Roget, *Histoire,* vol. 1, p. 48. Berne's pre-emptive and presumptious attack on the Confession would have implied that the document posed a threat to the alliance, an additional reason to resists its imposition.

81 Roget, *Histoire,* vol. 1, p. 49.

82 Roget, *Histoire,* vol. 1, p. 56.

83 Roget, *Histoire,* vol. 1, p. 56. Cf., AEG/RC/30, fol. 212 (Apr 1537); RC/31, fol. 61v (Sep 1537), where decrees were made to force persons to swear to the Confession and AEG/RC/31, fol. 90 (Nov 1537) where lack of response, including no one from the Rue des Allemans, is mentioned.

84 Roget, *Histoire,* vol. 1, pp. 62f., 69.

85 Balke, *Anabaptist,* p. 84, is a particularily enthusiastic proponent of this interpretation. He relies rather heavily on Beza's and Colladon's accounts of the disputes with the Anabaptists and a single case involving a number of local Genevans. Balke does admit that this view, and the reliance upon Beza and Colladon, were not favoured by Kampschulte or Roget (*Anabaptist,* p. 83).

86 Even though Berne never cared for Calvin and Farel and their combative approach to problems, the Bernese put a premium on Genevan stability. Cf., Roget, *Histoire,* vol. 1, pp. 76–8.

87 Roget, *Histoire,* vol. 1, p. 96.

88 See Gaberel, *Histoire,* vol. 1, pp. 265, 270f., for his view of the various groups within the Articulants (the faction which supported compromise and conciliation as the best means of securing the Bernese alliance; they were opposed by the Guillermins). Also compare his views on the 'libertine' elements with his comment (vol. 1, p. 303) that Richardet *et al.*, were stricter in controlling rural mores than Calvin and Farel had ever been.

89 G = Guillermin, A = Articulant.

90 E = Property of exile, C = Church property.

91 Ganoczy, *Calvin*, p. 107. Cf., Collins, *Libertines*, pp. 102f. An excellent example of the contradictory nature of the secondary literature is evidenced by W. Walker, *John Calvin* (London: 1906), p. 250, who wrote that 'the revolution of 1538 ... had been in no sense a Romanising movement, the new ministers and the government were thoroughly Protestant', and Wendel's comment that the 'Catholic party and the waverers were surprised to find themselves so numerous', *Calvin*, p. 53.

92 Roset, pp. 255, 262, 265; Beza, 'Calvin', p. 32. Roset's account is reproduced in P. Geisendorf, 'Les Annalistes', *MDG*, vol 37, pp. 481–94.

93 Martin, *Histoire*, p. 235.

94 Parker, *Calvin*, p. 97. Cf., Collins, *Libertines*, pp. 105, 113, where a similar assertion is made but the Articulants are confused with the later Perrinists/Libertines, most of whom were in fact Guillermins. A similar error is made by Innes, *Social Concerns*, p. 210, where he identifies Perrin as an Articulant.

95 Roget, *Histoire*, vol. 1, p. 71. See AEG/RC/31, fol. 195 (13 Feb 1538) where the new Petit Conseil took the ministers' advice and passed laws against blasphemy and hired three new French ministers.

96 Höpfl, *Polity*, p. 115, n. 31 (on p. 262).

97 AEG/RC/28, fol. 4 (12 Feb 1534); RC/29, fol. 33 (28 Feb 1538); RC/30, fols. 152, 152v (16 Jan 1537). For additional comments on pre-Reformation legislation see Innes, *Social Concerns*, pp. 272–74 and Collins, *Libertines*, pp. 98f.

98 Date of the election which brought the Articulants to power. Geneva's criminal cases compare well with those found in other areas. Indeed, they show a lower degree of violence in the city than one might have expected to find. Cf., H. Kamen, *European Society 1500–1700* (London: 1984), pp., 173–177, 198f, as well as specific studies on the subject such as, Y. M. Bercé, 'Aspects de la Criminalité au XVIIe Siècle', in *Revue Historique* (1968); P. Clark and P. Slack, *Crisis and Order in English Towns 1500–1700* (London: 1972); J. S. Cockburn, ed., *Crime in England 1550–1800* (London: 1977); V. A. C. Gartrell, *et al.*, *Crime and the Law. The Social History of Crime in Western Europe since 1500* (London: 1980); B. Geremek, 'Criminalité, Vagabondage, Paupérisme: la Marginalité à l'Aube des Temps Moderne', in *Revue d'Histoire Moderne et Contemporaine*, 21 (1974); J. A. Sharpe, 'The History of Crime in Late Medieval and Early Modern England: A Review of the Field', in *Social History*, 7: 2 (1982); N. Z. Davies, *Society and Culture in Early Modern France* (London: 1975); J. Delumeau, *Le Péché et la Peur. La Culpabilisation en Occident, XIIIe–XVIIIe Siècles* (Paris: 1983); H. Kamen, *Inquisition and Society in Spain* (London: 1985); as well as the somewhat later study, H. Kamen, 'Public Authority and Popular Crime: Banditry in Valencia 1660–1714', in *Journal of European Economic History*, 3 (1974).

99 See AEG/RC/32, fol. 52 (10 May 1538) where Jaques Bernard complained about adultery. Also, AEG/RC/32, fol. 149 (17 Sep 1538); RC/34, fols. 219 (30 Apr 1540), 334v (16 Jul 1540), where all the ministers complained of slanders against them. And also, AEG/RC/33, fol. 19 (19 Feb 1539) for another ministerial complaint about immorality.

100 AEG/RC/32, fol. 129v (23 Aug 1538).

101 AEG/RC/32, fol. 105 (19 Jul 1538). A first offender was to be fined 60 sols and subsequent offences were 'destre pugnys az rigeur du droyct'.

102 Cf., Bouwsma, *Calvin*, p. 20, where he follows the view of Balke, *Anabaptist*, pp. 73–96. The case mentioned, AEG/PC/2e Ser., 385 (11–14 Sep 1537), involved Jaques Merauld from Lyon.

103 Cf., CO, vol. 10, col. 250–5 (to the Genevan church, 1 Oct 1548) where the stress is laid on factionalism.

104 CO, vol. 10, col. 273–6 (to Farel, 24 Oct 1538).

105 CO, vol. 10, col. 350–5 (to the Genevan church, 25 Jun 1539).

106 Höpfl, *Polity*, p. 77; Roget, *Histoire*, vol. 1, p. 78 and p. 78, n. 1. Cf., Collins, *Libertines*, p. 105, who, while stressing the Catholic–Libertine alliance, posited a third strand in the Articulant faction of men who wished to limit ecclesiastical power under magisterial authority.

107 Cf., Gaberel, *Histoire*, vol. 1, pp. 287f., where he seems to imply, contrary to his previous views (vol. 1, p. 265) that the magisterial opposition was to unlimited ministerial power not the actual control of morals.

108 AEG/RC/32, fol. 35v (6 Mar 1539).

109 F. T. L. Grenus-Saladin, *Fragments Biographiques et Historiques* (Geneva: 1815), p. 5; W. F. Graham, *The Constructive Revolutionary: John Calvin & His Socio-Economic Impact* (Atlanta: 1978), p. 36.

110 Monter, *Geneva*, p. 49; Höpfl, *Polity*, pp. 77, 102, 133.

111 See pp. 23f.

112 AEG/RC/32, fol. 248 (26 Dec 1538). Their expulsion came when they and many Guillermins refused to receive Communion according to the new rite. In all thirty-six men were prosecuted as a result, AEG/PC/2e Ser., 437 (26 Dec 1538). Cf., Roset, p. 262.

113 J. F. Bergier, 'Salaires des Pasteurs de Genève au XVIe Siècle', in *Mélanges d'Histoire du XVIe Siècle offerts à Henri Meylan*, in *Bibliothèque Historique Vaudoise*, vol. 43 (Lausanne: 1970), pp. 165f.

114 Cf., Innes, *Social Concerns*, p. 121.

115 Martin, *Histoire*, pp. 232f.

116 Roset, p. 251; AEG/RC/32, fol. 23v. (8 Apr 1538).

117 Cf., Parker, *Calvin*, p. 97, 'he (Calvin) always obeyed the Seigneurie, and I do not suppose he ever broke a Genevan law in his life'. The ministers' conduct on this occasion also calls into question the view that Calvin was always careful to maintain a distinction between the spiritual government ('inner man, eternal life') and the secular state ('civil justice, outward morality') which was expressed by R. C. Hancock, *Calvin and the Foundations of Modern Politics* (London: 1989), p. 25.

118 Roset, p. 270. Some, notably, McGrath, *Calvin*, p. 103, have taken the view that the Genevan negotiators, Girardin de la Rive, Aimé Chapeaurouge, and, especially, Jean Lullin, were duped by the Bernese because of their inability to understand Bernese German. This explanation collapses, though, when one realises that Chapeaurouge's father was from Strasbourg, Lullin's mother, Catherine, was also German, and Lullin's brother, François, was later (see p. 216) used by Geneva to translate Bernese communications to the city.

119 Roset, p. 255. The relative strength of the two factions can be gauged from Appendix 2 which lists all the men who can be clearly identified with either faction. It is also worth noting the ties between the members of each faction obvious in the predominance of certain surnames in each faction.

120 AEG/RC/33, fol. 259v (25 Aug 1539).

121 AEG/RC/34, fol. 185 (16 Apr 1540); Roset, p. 266.

122 Graham, *Calvin*, p. 33; Monter, *Geneva*, p. 55.

123 Walker, *Calvin*, pp. 175f.

124 Of the negotiators only M. Sept was to be a Guillermin; the other three were Articulants. It is of special interest to note that G. Les Clefs did not receive bourgeois status until 25 February 1539 (Grenus-Saladin, *Fragments*, p. 5; he is not noted in *Bourg.*).

125 E. Dunant, *Les Relations Politiques de Genève avec Berne et les Suisses* (Geneva: 1894), p. 22.

126 Dunant, *Relations Politiques*, pp. 22–4.
127 Höpfl, *Polity*, p. 131.
128 Cf., Monter, *Government*, p. 12; Innes, *Social Concerns*, p. 254.
129 J. F. Bergier, 'La Démission de Trésorier Amblard Corne', in *Mélanges offerts à M. Paul-E. Martin*, from *MDG*, vol. 40 (Geneva: 1961), p. 460.
130 Roget, *Histoire*, vol. 1, pp. 71, 252f.; Monter, *Geneva*, pp. 8f.; Parker, *Calvin*, p. 65.
131 See note 98 Table 3.
132 See note 98 Table 3.
133 Perrenoud, *Population*, p. 44.
134 AEG/Min/C. de Compois, vol. 10, fol. 232v (4 Sep 1537).
135 AEG/RC/30, fol. 51 (5 Sep 1536).
136 AEG/Min/C. de Compois, vol. 13, fol. 102 (10 Jan 1540).
137 AEG/Min/C. de Compois, vol. 11, fol. 160 (21 May 1538).
138 AEG/Min/J. du Verney, vol. 8, fol. 439 (17 Nov 1544).
139 AEG/RC/34, fols. 82v–83.
140 AEG/RC/35, fols. 52v–53; Monter, *Government*, p. 87, n. 4
141 AEG/RC/35, fols. 52v–53; Monter, *Government*, p. 87, n. 4.
142 AEG/RC/35, fol. 67.
143 AEG/RC/35, fol. 67.
144 AEG/RC/34, fol. 247v.
145 AEG/RC/34, fol. 464.
146 The Lieutenant ran the lower courts, collected fines, and summoned people to testify. Cf., Innes, *Social Concerns*, p. 166.
147 For an explanation of the Genevan appellate system and the proceedings and later development of the Genevan justice system see Monter, *Government*, pp. 64f and, especially, B. Roth-Lochner, *Messieurs de la Justice et leur Greffe* in *MDG*, 54 (Geneva: 1992).
148 Martin, *Histoire*, pp. 240–2.
149 P. Malligniod was charged with fornication, AEG/RC/29, fol. 63 (31 Mar 1536). P. Dorsière was convicted of fornication, AEG/RC/31, fol. 27 (20 Jul 1537). Jean Ami Curtet was arrested for adultery, AEG/RC/30, fol. 39 (11 Aug 1536) and later fined 50ff for debauching a servant girl, Grenus-Saladin, *Fragments*, p. 6 (11 Mar 1538).
150 Morand departed on 10 August 1540 (AEG/RC/34, fol. 376), and Marcourt left on 20 September 1540 (AEG/RC/34, fol. 452) and the Petit Conseil acted the next day to recall Calvin (AEG/RC/34, fol. 452v). This would also call into question the assertion that the Guillermins were actually partisans of Calvin and Farel from 1538; a view expressed in R. Guerdin, *Histoire de Genève* (Paris: 1981), p. 80.
151 Wendel, *Calvin* (London: 1963), p. 67; Walker, *Calvin*, p. 258.
152 Roget, *Histoire*, vol. 1, p. 291. This contrasts with the misleading interpretation which Beza, 'Calvin', p. 37, later gave to the crisis. He presented the entire crisis as the result of the Articulants 'misconducting themselves on a certain embassy' and stressed that the Genevans longed for the return of Calvin and Farel.
153 Dunant, *Relations Politiques*, pp. 69f.
154 Dunant, *Relations Politiques*, pp. 69f.
155 Höpfl, *Polity*, p. 133. A majority of the households in Geneva would have been enfranchised, cf., Monter, *Government*, p. 88; Barbara Roth of the Archives d'Etat de Genève thinks the figure may have been as high as 80 per cent of the adult male population. The limitations of the Genevan system are ably delineated by Chenevière, *Pensée*, pp. 204f.
156 It is worth noting that an inability to interpret the actions of opponents clearly was not

limited to Calvin or Geneva. In Toulouse, the Catholic leaders often found it impossible to see any difference between the Huguenot (religiously motivated) and the Dampvillistes (purely political) faction. Cf., J. Davies, 'Persecution and Protestantism: Toulouse, 1562–1575', in *Historical Journal*, 1979, 22(1), pp. 46f.

Calvin and his colleagues

Scis quales habeam commilitiones [1]

When Calvin returned to Geneva in September 1541 the Petit Conseil immediately constituted a committee to meet Calvin to prepare a draft of the Ecclesiastical Ordinances which would regulate the Church and religious aspects of Genevan society, including the establishment of a Consistory. The committee was comprised of leading Guillermins: Claude Pertemps, Ami Perrin, Claude Roset, Jean Lambert, Jean Goulaz, and Jean Porral.[2] Calvin found the Church seriously demoralised and in turmoil as a result of the previous years of controversy. Moreover, Calvin was expected to work with two men who had refused to share his exile, Jaques Bernard and Henry de la Mare, and another, Aimé Champereau, who had been hired by the Articulants to serve at the rural parish of Satigny.[3] Not surprisingly under the circumstances, Calvin expressed some qualms about his colleagues. Nor could he have failed to realise that the actions taken against him and Farel had been made easier by the lack of unity among the ministers and the tacit approval of those moves provided by the ministers who remained in Geneva.

The situation in Geneva in 1541 was, however, ideal for Calvin in a number of ways. The Guillermins wanted order in the Church and Geneva. The city was short of ministers and Calvin was naturally given a great deal of latitude in hiring new men. Geneva's rulers had shown a tendency to allow their senior minister a fair degree of freedom in this regard, as was evidenced in the hiring of Calvin by Farel. So little importance was attached to the man and the event that the magisterial records simply noted Calvin as 'ille gallus'.[4] In any event, as will be shown, Calvin certainly felt that his position and power as chief minister was, for the moment, secure. The first task facing Calvin upon his return was the quick establishment of a sound and ordered structure for the Church. This, however, raised a number of problems. First, Calvin required suitable colleagues, and more of them. Second, he needed a settled and supportive Consistory. If the Company of Pastors and the Consistory could be well founded, and unified around Calvin, then his authority would be strengthened immeasurably. This chapter will show the extent to which, by 1546, Calvin had been successful in gathering together a competent, powerful Company of Pastors as well as collecting a united body of lay elders in the Consistory. Eventually, Calvin would succeed in most of his endeavours to establish a qualified and competent ministry, but not without a great deal of arduous toil. Initially, though, the return to Geneva brought something of a rude awakening and he soon became aware of the mountainous problems which he would face in building an adequate Church.

In introducing a discussion of these problems, one can hardly do better than to allow Calvin to speak for himself. Whether his analysis of the situation is correct remains to be seen; that he believed it, and that his interpretation directed his actions, ought not to be doubted.

> Our colleagues are rather a hindrance than a help to us: they are rude and self-conceited, have no zeal, and less learning. But what is worst of all, I cannot trust them, even although I very much wish that I could: for by many evidences they shew they are estranged from us, and give scarcely any indication of a sincere and trustworthy disposition. I bear with them, however, or rather I humour them, with the utmost leniency.... I shall do my utmost ... to avoid disturbing the peace of the Church with our quarrels; for I dread the factions which must always necessarily arise from the dissension of ministers. On my first arrival I might have driven them away had I wished to do so, and that is also even now in my power. I shall never, however, repent the degree of moderation which I have observed; since no one can justly complain that I have been too severe.... What you observe, from the example of our Church, of the great injury which is inflicted by the noisome plague of discord among the ministry, I can confirm, from my own experience, to the fullest extent, in the calamity which has befallen this Church. No persons could be on closer terms of intimacy than we were here with one another. But when Satan had stirred up that deplorable misunderstanding between these brethren and ourselves, you know yourself what followed thereupon. My determination was therefore made at once, that unless with the evidence of an entire reconciliation, I would never undertake this charge, because I despaired of any benefit from my ministry here, unless they held out a helping hand to me. Meanwhile, many in their assembly are not over friendly, others are openly hostile to me. But this I carefully provide against, that the spirit of contention may not arise among us. We have an intestine seed of discord in the city, as I have already mentioned; but we take special care, by our patient and mild deportment, that the Church may not suffer any inconvenience from that circumstance, and that nothing of that kind may reach the common people. They all know very well, by experience, the pleasant and humane disposition of Viret: I am in no way more harsh, at least in this matter. Perhaps you will scarcely believe this.... Indeed, I value the public peace and cordial agreement among ourselves so highly, that I lay restraint upon myself: those who are opposed to us

are themselves compelled to award this praise to me. This feeling prevails to such an extent, that from day to day those who were once open enemies have become friends; others I conciliate by courtesy, and I feel that I have been in some measure successful, although not everywhere and on all occasions.

On my arrival, it was in my power to have disconcerted our enemies most triumphantly, entering with full sail among the whole of that tribe who had done the mischief. I have abstained: if I had liked, I could daily, not merely with impunity, but with the approval of very many, have used sharp reproof. I forbear; even with the most scrupulous care do I avoid everything of the kind, lest even by some slight word I should appear to persecute any individual, much less all of them at once... . It happens, however, sometimes, that it is necessary to withstand our colleagues; but we never do so unless they either compel us by the unseasonable importunity, or some weightier consideration demands our interference. I will relate an instance to you... When we were considering about the introduction of ecclesiastical censure, and the Senate had given us a commission to that effect, these worthy persons appeared in public to assent; doubtless because they were ashamed to offer direct opposition in a matter that was so plain and evident. Afterwards, however, they were to be seen going about secretly, dealing separately with each of the senators, exhorting them not to lay at our feet the power which was in their own hands, (as they said,) not to abdicate the authority which God had intrusted to them, and not to give occasion to sedition, with many other arguments of a like nature. We dared not close our eyes to such perfidious conduct. We endeavoured, however, to arrange the matter in such a way as not to stir up strife among us. We at length possess a Presbyterial Court, such as it is, and a form of discipline, such as these disjointed times permit ... those troops of unclean spirits break forth in all directions, who, in order that they may escape from healthy discipline, which they can in no way submit to, seek every sort of pretext for slipping from the authority of the Church.[5]

This extended quotation from Calvin gives a frank picture not only of his view of his fellow-ministers but also of Geneva, its populace, and the 1538 crisis. Perhaps most interestingly, he also provided his own perception of his conduct. Since so much of the comment about Calvin's ministry rests upon an acceptance of his understanding of the events there and of his own actions, a comparison of this exemplary passage with other contemporary sources can provide an early guide to the relative reliability of Calvin's interpretation. This is not to imply that Calvin was intentionally misleading; rather, that his perceptions might differ radically from the reality of a situation because of his personal beliefs and presuppositions. Thus, there is no error in using Calvin's understanding of events. There may well be a problem, though, when one relies wholly and uncritically on his interpretation.

At the very start it is necessary to comment upon his interesting interpretation of the 1538 crisis. He saw the break amongst the ministers as a 'deplorable misunderstanding'. Further, he commented on a residue of hostility towards him in the magistracy; some were 'openly hostile' to him. As most of the Articulants were in disgrace or exile one must assume that he is referring to members of the Guillermin group. If one views, as the previous chapter argued, the Guillermins as a party primarily motivated by political, not religious considerations, and note the reluctance to recall Calvin, then one might assume that he did face some opposition from the very moment of his return; he certainly was convinced that this was so.

The most difficult problem Calvin encountered upon his return was the state of the ministry in general; he described his colleagues as truly deplorable. They were impediments, 'rude and self-conceited', and having 'no zeal, and less learning'. They were estranged from Calvin and Viret, lacking any sign of a 'faithful and sincere spirit'. But Calvin's most damning comment about them was that he could not trust them. It would be hard to imagine that one could find the Genevan ministry in a worse condition. But Calvin claimed that he could bear with all of this. His first and greatest concern was that no sign of disharmony or contention would be apparent to the masses. Nevertheless, he realised that the establishment of an ecclesiastical court had already stirred up additional opposition to him. Of course, the question which arises is why there was such opposition. In Calvin's view, it was the result of 'profane spirits' wishing, in any way possible, 'to escape the authority of the Church'. But this is not necessarily the only possible explanation.

Indeed, Calvin alluded to other reasons for opposing his system of discipline which in no way required any dislike for morality and its enforcement. Maddeningly for Calvin, his fellow ministers articulated these views. Worse yet, they put their case secretly after making a public show of agreement with Calvin and Viret. Their arguments were not the result of some desire to prohibit too strict a control on morals; rather, these ministers said that the Petit Conseil should beware lest it give to the ministers a power which the magistrates should reserve for themselves. This authority had been given to the magistracy by God and ought not to be surrendered. It was argued that such a transfer of power would result in disorder and revolt. Thus, they presented socio-political arguments against Calvin's system, not religious or moral ones.

In the context of a city only recently freed from foreign and clerical domination this position would have been very persuasive. From this episode, and their actions in 1538, it would also seem that these ministers had a very different understanding of the relationship between the Church and State, the ministers and the magistrates from that of Calvin. Such dissent would have been intolerable to Calvin as it would only breed the factionalism which he felt always arose from divisions amongst the ministers. It may well be that this desire for stability motivated the magistrates to accept Calvin's proposal, though it is worth noting that the final Ecclesiastical Ordinances are noticeably more ambiguous than those initially proposed about the exercising of church authority and discipline.[6] But for Calvin, the principal lesson of this, as he himself stressed, was the crucial importance of ministerial unity.

Thus, according to Calvin's understanding, one finds him in an uneasy truce with his colleagues six months after his return. Calvin seems to have adopted a somewhat guarded, indeed patronising approach to his fellow-ministers. Hence he could say that he tolerated, 'or rather, humoured them'. He was restrained by his own leniency and moderation. Calvin claimed that he had had the power to expel all of them but had refrained from doing so because he did not want any one to be able to accuse him of being too severe. Not surprisingly, he felt that Myconius might find this difficult to believe. One might well be led to opine that moderation was in reality no more than a course of action which Calvin, very astutely, chose to follow in the light of the political reality of the situation which he found upon his return to Geneva.

One can believe that Calvin behaved this way to prevent additional turmoil in the Church. What is harder to accept is his assertion that he had the power to remove these men but chose not to. Indeed, it is difficult to decide which is the more incredible assertion, that Calvin decided to keep such men when he did not have to, or that the magistrates might actually have been willing to reduce the city's ministerial staff to Calvin alone. One is then led to wonder whether Calvin's claim of moderation is reliable, and, if so, how long it continued. It is reasonable to presume that Calvin's subsequent relationship with his colleagues may shed light on this problem.

The emphasis which Calvin placed upon his reasonableness and moderation is belied by the actual events. In the next few years many of these early ministers would find themselves pushed aside as Calvin worked to create a unified, qualified Company of Pastors. An examination of the ministers as a group (Table 7) shows an obvious change in the pattern of tenure at 1546. In the eight years from Calvin's expulsion in 1538 until the end of 1546, thiry-one ministers worked in Geneva. Over half were assigned to rural parishes at some point which highlights the extent to which Geneva wanted to secure its country regions. More important, though, is the fact that only one, Jaques Bernard, served throughout this

TABLE 7   *Genevan ministers 1538-54*

Person	1538	39	40	41	42	43	44	45	46	47	48	49	50	51	52	53	54
Farel	dep																
Corault	dep																
Calvin	dep			G	G	G	G	G	G	G	G	G	G	G	G	G	G
Mare	G	G	G	G	G	R	R	R	dep								
Bernard	G	G	G	G	R	R	R	R	R	R	R	R	R	R	R	R	R
A. Rabier	R	R	R	res													
P. Denise	R	res															
Fr. du Pont	R	R	R	R	res												
Morand	G	G	res														
Marcourt	G	G	res														
Champereau			G	G	G	G	G	dep									
Viret				T	T												
Vandert				R	dep												
Blanchet					G	dec											
Geneston					G	G	G	dec									
Treppereaux					G	G	R	R	R	R	R	R	R	R	R	res	
Ecclesia					G	G	R	R	R	R	R	R	R	R	R	R	dep
Baud						dep											
Poupin						G	G	G	G	G	G	G	G	G	G	G	G
Regalis						R	dec										
Ninaud						G	R	R	R	R	R	R	R	R	R	R	R
Cugniez						R	R	R	R	R	R	R	R	dec			
Moreau						R	dep										
Megret						R	R	dep									
des Gallars							G	G	G	G	G	G	G	G	G	R	R
Ferron							G	G	G	G	G	dep					
Delecluse							R	dep									
Petit							R	R	R	R	R	R	R	R	R	R	R
Chauvet								G	G	G	G	G	G	G	G	G	G
Bourgoing								G	G	G	G	G	G	G	R	R	R
Perier								R	R	R	R	R	R	R	R	R	R
Cop								G	G	G	G	G	G	G	G	G	G
St-André									R	R	R	R	R	R	G	G	G
Balduin									R	R	R	R	R	R	R	R	R
Chappuis									R	R	R	R	R	R	R	R	R
Macar											G	G	G	G	G	R	R
Fabri												G	G	G	G	G	G
Colladon																G	G

G= city minister
R= rural minister
T=temporary
res= resigned
dep= deposed
dec= deceased

period. Nine ministers were deposed, five resigned and another two died; the Church's leadership was wracked by instability. By 1545, the average tenure of ministers at Geneva was somewhat less than three years. Many of these men were shifted from city to country in an apparent attempt to find the best ministers for Geneva but with the result that it must have seemed as though Geneva had nothing more than temporary ministers.

These changes were the result of Geneva's inordinate haste in making new ministerial appointments; the city had no choice but to hire ministers as quickly as possible. But Calvin was extremely dissatisfied with the quality of the men hired soon after his return as well as those who had remained during the period of Articulant ascendancy. Nor could he have been pleased with Geneva's continued reliance in the rural parishes upon former priests, a situation which was to continue until 1544.[7] The low calibre of the early replacements was a result of Geneva's overwhelming need for ministers. It was only in 1545–46 that Calvin was able to collect a cadre of trusted colleagues of the quality required.

What was needed was a programme of recruitment to fill all these vacancies and to provide Geneva with the ministers necessary to fulfil the pastoral duties required of a state Church. This, of course, meant that not only did the former ministers need to be replaced but that many additional ministers needed to be hired. The last thing Calvin or the magistrates needed was a group of men who would not last. But what one sees upon examination is that those men hired in 1541–45 were not, as a group, of the best calibre or character. Of the nineteen men hired in this period, twelve would be gone by 1554, of whom four died; the rest were deposed or resigned. Thus, around 40 per cent of those initially hired under Calvin's leadership would not stay the course. The obvious conclusion is that upon his return Calvin and Geneva were so desperate to fill the ministerial vacancies that men of lesser ability were hired and would be replaced as better men became available. There is no evidence that this was an intentional course of action but it does seem to have been the reality none the less.

Therefore, the initial years after Calvin's return were a period of turmoil; Calvin was never satisfied. He was discontented with the low quality of his colleagues and filled with resentment towards those who had broken ranks with him and remained to serve the Articulants. This latter group was to feel the full weight of Calvin's opprobrium; the case of Henri de la Mare is the clearest example of this. Calvin's hostility to De la Mare comes through quite clearly in his correspondence, regardless of his protestations of moderation and leniency, and serves as the best case-study of Calvin's relationship with his ministerial colleagues before 1546. But the full extent of the persecution which De la Mare faced becomes apparent only when one examines the other contemporary records.

The antipathy of Calvin and Farel towards De la Mare was evident even before the Articulants' defeat. In a letter to Farel, Calvin described De la Mare as a coward.[8] Moreover, he was suspected of immorality. Although he was cleared, the possibility that De la Mare might have committed adultery could only have served to confirm Calvin in his suspicions.[9] Calvin dripped sarcasm from his pen soon after his return when he commented to Viret that Viret would be amazed at De la Mare's insistence upon the honour of the ministry, 'especially when he presented such a distinguished example of firmness and constancy of principle in his own action'.[10] De la Mare had also clashed with Ami Porral, a leading Guillermin, before Calvin's return.[11] Thus De la Mare found himself in the unenviable position of being disliked by Calvin and leading magistrates alike: and yet he was able to stay at his post, uncomfortable and precarious though it must have been. The next reference to De la Mare is in a general complaint by Calvin of a dispute amongst the ministers. Calvin complained that two of the ministers, supported by a former monk, perhaps Trolliet, were involved in a disagreement which could not be resolved; it was not even possible to discover who was actually at fault. It was also apparent, Calvin claimed, that this monk and some of the ministers were involved in a plot to undermine his position in the city.[12] De la Mare was also mentioned as a participant in the troubles which accompanied the Ameaux case and the dancing at Antoine Lect's house. Calvin accused De la Mare of always hating him and of working to stir up others against him; he was pleased to note that Henri had finally been deposed.[13]

The validity of Calvin's understanding of the situation in Geneva is even more questionable after an examination of his relationship with Henri de la Mare. His actions with regards to De la Mare are of such interest that they are worthy of detailed comment. First, though, one must understand why De la Mare was able to resist Calvin's actions for so long but ultimately failed to keep his post, as his fellow-minister Bernard was able to do. Unlike the citizen Bernard, De la Mare, a foreigner from Rouen, was hardly likely to have had any local political support and therefore little chance of maintaining his position against a concerted move on Calvin's part. De la Mare's tenacity in retaining his office until 1546 is thus primarily the result of the magistrates' unwillingness to disturb the Church unnecessarily.

However, it would appear that De la Mare was not entirely without local support. There is some dispute as to De la Mare's origins. Roget stated that De la Mare was a native Genevan and related to a prominent local family.[14] Claparède, following Herminjard, took the view that he was from Rouen.[15] There does exist a notary document which mentions De la Mare's wife and his brothers as participants in a local dispute.[16] This evidence would seem to support Roget's conclusion, unless one assumes that his brothers had also moved to Geneva. What is apparent from the notary records (see Appendix 3), however, is that De la Mare, native or not, was involved with local Genevans and was certainly married to one.[17] The lack of protest by members of the prominent De la Mare (or Mar) family at the minister's imprisonment and dismissal would seem to suggest that they were not in fact related and that the similarity in names was purely coincidental; this would also support the supposition that De la Mare was foreign and that his brothers had joined him in Geneva.

Moves against De la Mare began soon after Calvin's return; De la Mare followed Bernard into a rural parish and the new minister, Poupin, took his place. Henri did not accept this transfer to Jussy complacently; rather, he complained very strongly not only about the move itself but also the horrid conditions he found when he got to his new house and church. The Senate responded to his complaints by dispatching a committee to look into the affair. The committee was comprised of Jean Philippin, a Syndic, Jean Lambert, the local châtelain, or representative of Genevan authority at Jussy, and Jean Calvin.[18] The two magistrates, staunch Guillermins, were hardly likely to provide De la Mare with a fair and impartial hearing. Nevertheless, the city responded with haste; less than four days after De la Mare's complaints (on 23 April) the committee was constituted and it returned its report after three days of deliberation and investigation. The committee said that it had been able 'to convince' De la Mare to accept the new post and recommended that his house and church be repaired; the Senate accepted the recommendation.[19] But, as will be shown, there was a vast difference between the speed of the committee's report and the implementation of its recommendations.

De la Mare is next heard of a month later in a complaint brought against him by Calvin and Poupin before the Senate. They accused him of not obeying the Ecclesiastical Ordinances on marriage. It is not clear what his exact fault was but apparently he had blessed the union of two children, aged eleven and seven.[20] The magistrates instituted an investigation and sternly admonished De la Mare to obey the regulations in the future.[21] This was undoubtedly just one more black mark against his name as far as Calvin was concerned. The civil authorities showed less concern; three days later they ordered the disbursement of 50ff to cover the cost of repairs to De la Mare's house and the church at Jussy.[22] In reality this failed to provide all the assistance which De la Mare required. In fact, one sees a decided bias against De la Mare, as well as Bernard, in the provision of aid.

All the ministers, except Calvin, were in constant financial need because of their low salaries; the State was notoriously slow to respond to the need. In one case the litany of complaints brought the response that the Senate 'resolu de leur (the ministers) fere bonnes Remonstrances des grandes charges que la ville supporter & quil ayen ung peu de patience'.[23]

The state did have a valid point; it had hired an additional four ministers in 1542.[24] The total salary of ministers had climbed from around 1,800ff a year to 2,700ff, a 50 per cent increase.[25] This remained the constant amount until 1544, as the one minister who died of plague and the two sacked for immorality were quickly replaced.[26] Nevertheless, while an increase in personnel might have lessened the individual workload of the ministers it did not solve their immediate financial problems. By August 1544, Calvin was forced to complain that the ministers were all 'in a state of abject poverty'.[27] The actions of the Senate confirmed the general validity of the assertion made by Calvin. In January 1544, the magistrates had given 20ff each to three ministers to help them with their winter needs.[28] Not surprisingly, De la Mare and Bernard were excluded. In fact, for De la Mare, the situation was made even worse. Three months later, in March, he was given the parish of Foncenex as well; his work increased but his salary did not.[29] Bernard, the citizen, fared better; in 1543 he had been given the additional charge of Dardigny but he had been granted some extra money to support a horse and a place to stable it free of charge.[30] As can be seen from Figure 2 the distances involved are the same, but De la Mare got little extra assistance; the State disbursed some food and about 5ff to meet the needs of the poor in his parish.[31]

As if to rub salt in the wound, almost all the other ministers, except De la Mare, Bernard and one of the newer ministers Treppereaux, were given bonuses. The three excluded were 'advised' to be content with their wages.[32] Treppereaux had no grounds for complaint; he had been in jail the previous month for calling the magistrates 'usuriers, papistes et buvieurs de sang'.[33] The magistrates' refusal to raise their ministers' salaries and remove this cause of complaint may have been the result, as the case of Treppereaux shows, of a desire to maintain a measure of control over the ministers by keeping them dependent on the bonuses given them. The situation seems to have been too much for De la Mare; his banishment to a rural parish, the extra work, the distances involved, were more than enough. Moreover, he was also always passed over in favour of new ministers in the assignment of city parishes. Worst of all, his house and the church were still in need of major repairs. Not surprisingly, the local châtelain, Pierre Somareta, an ardent supporter of Calvin, had occasion to bring a charge of insolence against De la Mare.[34] Pierre Somareta, who would later serve as a consistorial elder, hôpitalier, and senator after Calvin's victory in 1555, was the last person De la Mare needed to antagonise.

De la Mare's position was increasingly precarious; there can be little doubt that Calvin still remained personally hostile to him. Calvin's earlier comments show that he viewed De la Mare with disgust and contempt. Nothing that had happened since 1541 seemed to have altered that attitude, indeed the situation had deteriorated. Further, De la Mare seems to have been unable to repair his relationships with the magistrates, that is, the Guillermins who still controlled Geneva. His treatment whenever he complained, as well as the manner in which newcomers were always preferred to him, leads one to believe that Calvin and the magistrates viewed him with disdain, if not outright hostility. His plight, however, could still get worse, though he was persistent if nothing else, perhaps of necessity. He came before the Senate again, on 16 September 1544. He said that his house and church still needed repairs as they had since his arrival in May 1543. The Senate considered his requests and voted an additional sum of 30ff to effect the repairs.[35] It is not clear whether the original sum of 50ff, ordered in 1543, had ever been disbursed. However, as will become clear, both sums were woefully insufficient and the situation had worsened.

Despite his obvious needs, De la Mare was noticeably absent from the records for the next three months; Calvin, however, was not. Indeed, Calvin was very active in this same period on behalf of the other ministers, which leads one to believe that De la Mare was being overlooked on purpose. In October, Calvin begged the Senate to aid Treppereaux and another minister. Treppereaux was given 10ff and a temporary house to live in while repairs were made to his residence.[36] The other minister, Simon Moreau, was reported ill and in need according to Calvin.[37] In the latter case the Senate failed to act but Calvin returned again in November to beseech the magistrates on Moreau's behalf. As a result of this second request Calvin was able to persuade the Senate to give Moreau a bonus of 10ff and permission to gather firewood from the city forests.[38] November was an especially bad month for ministers, it seems. With the exception of De la Mare, everyone who requested assistance that autumn and winter of 1544 was eventually given help. Megret, a rural minister, was given an extra 20ff.[39] Bernard complained of the insufficiency of his wages and got 20ff to help him out.[40] Finally, Poupin, who had the plague, had his wages advanced.[41]

On 1 December 1544, De la Mare returned to the Senate. Finally, the records contain a full account of his complaints. He said that no one was coming to church because the building was a ruin and the châtelain, Somareta, was doing nothing to compel the people to attend or to repair the building. By ruin he meant that the church had neither doors nor windows. Obviously, it would have been difficult to get the poor peasants to attend church in the winter, under those circumstances. What is most surprising is that De la Mare said that this had been the situation since he had arrived in May 1543. Also, as if that were not enough, there was not even a pulpit for him at the front of the church. Further, the condition of his house, in desperate need of repairs for a year and a half, had become worse; a wall had collapsed. This was the source of the initial complaint in September; by December, the wall was still missing. Of course, it is not possible to tell how serious the situation was but the report would imply something more than a hole; indeed it appears that the whole structure may have become unsound.

The charges did not stop there; De la Mare complained that the châtelain, Somareta, had done nothing, and he mentioned that the châtelain had made substantial repairs to one of his own outbuildings. De la Mare's implication was clear; the 30ff had been diverted to Somareta's personal use.[42] Nor is this the lone stain attached to Somareta's character; this ardent Calvinist had been convicted of fornication in 1543 and charged with insolence and disobedience when he objected to his sentence before the Senate.[43] At long last the Senate was moved to act. The matter must not have been too surprising, though, as the investigation was completed and the report made by that same evening; all De la Mare's charges were substantiated. It would even appear that his hints of embezzlement were valid or so the Senate's decree would imply; the magistrates ordered Somareta to make all the repairs, to compel people to attend the sermons and, most damning of all, to repay the original 30ff.[44]

Sadly for De la Mare, this does not appear to have brought any immediate action. On 22 December, De la Mare complained that the Christmas Communion service was approaching but the church was still in a ruined state. He pointed out that there was little hope of having people attend when the place still lacked doors and windows; and he still wanted a pulpit.[45] One might wonder why Calvin failed to come to De la Mare's defence; a church left with neither doors nor windows could only have brought disrepute to the ministry. Moreover, one would expect Calvin to have complained about Somareta's malfeasance. Whatever Calvin was doing, he was not helping De la Mare, although he made supplication for the other ministers in their difficulties. The fact that the Jussy church was an empty husk of a building brought forth not a word. Apparently, he did not have enough compassion for De la Mare to be moved by the image of him huddled through the winter in his three-walled house. When the Senate was moved to consider De la Mare's plight it would appear that Calvin did not even accompany him to the Senate chamber.

Calvin's silence in the affair is such that one might wonder whether he was actually in Geneva at the time: and yet twice in that same month he interceded for other ministers. A week after De la Mare's appearance on 1 December, Calvin asked for assistance for the ministers and the poor people of the city.[46] The city responded to his request by giving some relief to the poor but postponed any action on behalf of the ministers.[47] Calvin returned on New Year's Day 1545 to seek money for the ministers again; once more he was put off.[48] But the next day the Senate relented in the face of Calvin's third appearance. To the joy of most, but not all, the Senate granted an extra 40ff to each city minister and 30ff to every rural cleric. Some were overlooked: Ecclesia who was then out of Calvin's favour, Jaques Bernard and, of course, De la Mare, the minister in the ruins. The Senate gave no explanation and said only that the three 'should be content with their wages'.[49]

How Henri was to be content, paid less than half of what Calvin was, sitting in a house with only three walls in midwinter is a mystery. Most galling of all must have been the Senate decision to send bonuses to seven citizens in Basle. This 'gift' of 900ff was paid out to thank these men for their help in mediating the territorial disputes with Berne, and yet only three days later De la Mare and the others were told to be content.[50] There must have been some reason for De la Mare to receive such treatment; perhaps Somareta was a particularily poor châtelain or De la Mare had committed some grievous fault. The parish was poor and Geneva was not blind to its needs. In April 1544, the magistrates had given money to help the needy there. In February 1545, Somareta, who could not be bothered to help De la Mare, requested, and was given money to help the poor of Jussy.[51] However, the main cause for De la Mare's neglect seems undeniably to have been the antipathy of Calvin and his supporters. Somareta's later career shows him solidly in the Calvinist camp and therefore likely to share Calvin's feelings. There seems to be no other way to reconcile the fact that three months after he was found to have embezzled money rather than help De la Mare he returned to seek help for the other poor of the parish. This antipathy alone would seem to explain Calvin's deafening silence throughout. Perhaps it was hoped that he would simply give up and abandon his post as Marcourt and Morand had done earlier in the face of personal opposition.

The rest of 1545 was no better for De la Mare. Twice he had to complain about the state of his house, first in May and then again in July.[52] In both cases Somareta was ordered to take care of the situation. Lest anyone think that the magistrates were universally ineffective in helping the ministers it must be pointed out that on the same day that De la Mare complained in May, a Syndic and the city controller were dispatched to the rural parish of Draillans to oversee, personally, the repairs needed there.[53] The only apparent difference appears to be that the minister at Draillans, Jean Regalis, was not disliked by Calvin or the magistrates. It was also in 1545 that De la Mare finally went beyond the pale in his relationship with Calvin and the other ministers. In April, he was linked with Jean Trolliet. Trolliet, a citizen, had been a monk in Burgundy and had returned to Geneva after embracing the Reform to obtain a ministerial post. The Senate supported Trolliet but Calvin remained implacably opposed to him. Forced to accept the fact that he could not be a minister, Trolliet became a notary, but he remained one of Calvin's fiercest opponents and was eventually censured for supporting the views of Calvin's theological opponent Bolsec, on the doctrine of predestination.[54] After this dispute over Trolliet, the ministers seem to have set their faces against De la Mare.

It is useful to speculate at this point whether part of the trouble between Calvin and De la Mare might not have been theological in nature. Calvin had been personally angered by De la Mare's refusal to accompany him into exile in 1538, but here in 1545 De la Mare is linked to an opponent of Calvin's doctrine of predestination. Nor would this be the only such occasion; De la Mare's end would finally come as a result of his personal association with Pierre Ameaux. Ameaux, also a citizen, was a cardmaker whose career had been ended by the enforcement of the regulations against cards passed in 1536. After a plea to the Senate he had been hired to oversee the storing of Geneva's gunpowder supply. He first clashed with Calvin when he asked for a divorce from his adulterous wife and was ordered to take her back. Ameaux, already angered over the loss of his livelihood and Calvin's insistence that he take back his adulterous wife, became embroiled in a theological dispute with Calvin. Ameaux was arrested for comments he made at a dinner party at his home. He was reported to have said that

> Calvin is nothing but a wicked man, cursed by God. He and his colleagues have been preaching false doctrine for seven years here. It is we who have the true doctrine, and I can prove it. For example, this seducer refuses to teach the children Latin lest they be able to discover his false beliefs, which he fears. He is a sinful Frenchman, he and his supporters want to be like bishops of Geneva. The magistrates don't do anything without consulting him.[55]

Ameaux also attacked Calvin's views on predestination, which, he said, made God the author of sin, and he attacked the *Institutes* as full of false doctrine. Calvin demanded harsh and immediate action. The magistrates were inclined to give Ameaux an 'honourable fine'; he would have to apologise, in private, to the Senate and Calvin. This was wholly unacceptable to Calvin. He and the other ministers demanded that Ameaux be humiliated in public and, under intense pressure, the Senate agreed. Ameaux was forced to parade through the city dressed only in a shirt, carrying a torch. He had to kneel and kiss the ground in front of the main church and beg mercy from God, Calvin, and the magistrates in a loud voice. Popular fury at the public humiliation of a citizen led the magistrates to erect a gibbet in Ameaux's district to prevent his neighbours from rioting. It is clear that this is one of the events of 1546 which finally destroyed the coalition which had ruled Geneva since the 1541 defeat of the Articulants.[56]

This also proved to be the end of De la Mare's ministerial career in Geneva. If Calvin was able, and willing, to degrade publicly a citizen despite popular protest there was little hope for De la Mare, a foreigner, serving a distant rural parish. He was jailed for his support of the theological views of his friend Ameaux on 15 March 1546.[57] He remained in prison until 13 April 1546 when he met the other ministers.[58] The ministers, for their part, had demanded his dismissal as early as 22 March but the magistrates had refused and advised reconciliation instead.[59] But the result of the meeting was that it became apparent the ministers had no intention of accepting De la Mare back into their company. The Senate had no choice but to sack him on 15 April 1546.[60] Two weeks later his post was filled by a new French minister, Jean Balduin.[61] De la Mare made one final appearance in the city records in June 1546 when he requested that he be compensated for the repairs which he had been forced to make on his house. He also asked for a letter of attestation so that he could accept a post on the Bernese territory of Gex; both requests were granted.[62] He later used his pulpit in Gex to thunder against Calvin, personally and theologically. After six years of facing Calvin's opposition he was to remain a problem for Calvin for a few more years. De la Mare added his voice to Champereau's, for the latter had been deposed ten months earlier for indecencies in the public baths and had also taken a post across the border in Bernese territory.[63]

It is difficult to see any other interpretation of the events surrounding De la Mare than that he was the object of a concerted attempt to make his life miserable. Geneva needed him in as much as he filled a post which required a minister. In this he was also of use to Calvin who could hardly have lamented the lack of ministers while pressing for De la Mare's expulsion. At the same time, Calvin's lack of concern for De la Mare's obvious need is truly striking. It is all the more remarkable considering how tirelessly Calvin worked to help other ministers. The fact that the pattern repeated itself with regard to Bernard and Champereau, and those who later fell foul of Calvin, only strengthens the perception that Calvin had a particularly unforgiving side to his character. Amazingly, Calvin expressed surprise at the time that he was accused of always seeking to avenge himself on his enemies.[64]

This rather lengthy telling of De la Mare's tale serves as a useful counterbalance in assessing Calvin's interpretation of the situation. Calvin's basic charge against his fellow ministers was that they were opposed to him and the establishment of church discipline. Further, Calvin saw himself as the long-suffering, ever tolerant victim of their cold-hearted recalcitrance; this is the same view which Calvin expressed about his magisterial opponents in 1555. The De la Mare case shows the extent to which Calvin's view of a situation must be filtered through other sources to discover the actual chain of events; the motives which Calvin ascribes to himself and others must be treated with extreme caution. Also, Calvin's tolerance can be seen to have been little more than barely controlled, scarcely concealed antipathy, especially for De la Mare. The actions of Calvin and some of his supporters bordered on outright persecution of De la Mare. This question of the validity of Calvin's perspective will again be posed in the context of the later secular crisis of 1555.

By 1546 a new situation was beginning to develop; the new ministers, hired in 1545–46, were a different sort. The Company of Pastors became marked by stability and an ever-increasing pool of experience in Genevan ministry. Only three were deposed in the next eight years and all of those sacked had been hired in the earlier period. Another, also hired earlier, resigned and one minister died. In this second period, thirteen ministers remained throughout and thus the rural and city parishes finally experienced stability and continuity. Indeed by 1554, the members of the Company of Pastors had averaged ten years apiece in Geneva's ministry. This new group of ministers were markedly different from their predecessors, a group beset by serious problems.

It will be useful to examine briefly the earlier ministers. One might be inclined to dismiss the two who died, but even their deaths ministering in the Plague Hospital provide insight into the character of their colleagues. Geneva experienced a severe outbreak of plague in 1543 lasting three years during which time the magistrates found it extremely difficult to persuade any of the ministers to work with the sick; most simply refused. Only two of the newest ministers could be convinced to accept the dangerous charge.[65] By 1546, this source of tension was alleviated when the magistrates hired a minister, Mathieu Malisie, especially to work with the plague victims. This not only calmed a situation rife with anxiety, but it also showed a greater organisational stability in the Genevan ministry which allowed for a specialisation of posts to meet the whole pastoral needs of the city. The unwillingness of the ministers to work with the plague victims annoyed the magistrates and illustrates a certain timidity in these earlier ministers.

The resignations which occurred were of less interest; they were almost entirely the result of the denouement of the 1538 crisis. Calvin resented those men who had worked in Geneva during his absence and the pressures brought to bear on them by him and many of the Guillermins, to whom they would have appeared as Articulant tools, must have been great. Morand and Marcourt abandoned their posts as a direct result of popular dislike, despite magisterial objections. The other three, Denise, Rabier, and Dupont had been recommended by Calvin and Farel and hired by the Articulants right before the break with the ministers.[66] Denise left quickly and the other two did not long survive the Articulant defeat. This, of course, left Geneva with only some of the former priests, Bernard, and De la Mare, as established ministers; Calvin returned to a lukewarm welcome from these ministers and some magistrates.[67] Geneva's ministry was woefully understaffed; the city could scarcely afford any more defections.

All these men, successful or otherwise, had one thing in common; they were all French. It is also important to realise that many of these new men were found wanting by Calvin very early on. This is obviously the case with those who were deposed quickly but a similar attitude can be found towards others as well. Both Blanchet and Geneston, who died working where others would not serve, were disappointing to Calvin. Of Blanchet, Calvin wrote to Viret that he had 'shown some signs which are not pleasing', while Geneston 'as I always feared, has more levity and incontinence in his words and deeds than is decent for one of our ministers'.[68] This does indeed seem a harsh judgement for men who died ministering to plague victims. Of the other two who died, Cugniez and Regalis, nothing can be said other than that their origins are obscure; Regalis's wife also succumbed to the plague.

The treatment of the other ministers highlights the unsettled nature of the Genevan Church in the years immediately after Calvin's return. Vandert and Baud went quickly. Baud was removed from his parish after his wife, Bernarde, was banished for adultery. The scandal was such that

Baud was deemed 'n'est capable de anuncer le st evangele'.[69] He was not
wholly ruined however, as he was allowed to minister to the poor in the
hospital. Vandert was deposed because he refused to visit the sick and 'ne
fayct les aultres choses necesseres' for his office.[70] It is not clear what
exactly he was failing to do, and although he was not deposed for another
four months he was first warned of his behaviour in August 1542.[71] There
appears to have been no doubt about his lack of ability but Calvin reported
to Viret that the Company of Pastors were opposed to his hasty removal so
that 'the precedent of an easy removal of a minister might not be established'.[72] This ministerial opposition would seem to explain why it took so
long for the magistrates to remove him. This stands in marked contrast to
the manner in which De la Mare seems to have been hounded; in his case
the ministers were much more enthusiastic than the magistrates.

The greatest loss of ministers was suffered between April 1545 and
February 1546. Four ministers were deposed in this period, which must
have unsettled the Church greatly. Three, Moreau, Delecluse and Megret,
were sacked for immorality while Champereau was removed for insolence
arising out of a charge of scandalous behaviour. It is worth noting that
these men left just as Chauvet, Cop, and Bourgoing arrived. As will be
shown, this represented a dramatic change in the nature, calibre, and
character of the Genevan Company of Pastors. Moreau was removed first.
On 6 April 1545, he was accused of fornication with two women at the
Plague Hospital.[73] He was arrested the next day.[74] Four days later, after
consultations with the ministers, he was released, deposed and banished.[75]
Similar short shrift was given to Delecluse. But in his case it was much
easier for the city. He had abandoned his family and fled with 40ff which
he had embezzled.[76] He was deposed and provision was made for his
family at the Hospital.[77]

The expulsions of Champereau and Megret were somewhat more
complex. Champereau's problems began in June 1545 when he refused a
transfer to the rural parish of Bossey.[78] There was a stalemate at first until
the ministers suggested that he might take the post at Draillans.[79] Within a
month he was involved in a dispute with Calvin. The causes were twofold.
First, it would appear that he had refused the Draillans post, saying that
his wife was ill and he did not want to leave the city.[80] This is not at all
surprising since Draillans is even further from Geneva than Bossey (see
Figure 1). Also, he was accused of immoral behaviour in spending the
night in one room with his wife, two of her female relations and two other
ministers Megret and Veyron. At this point it seemed as though nothing
untoward had happened.[81] He was persuaded to take the new post when
the city advanced him part of his salary.[82] Apparently he was still unhappy

as his behaviour was questioned in August.[83] By September, he was demanding that he be returned to the city because of his wife's condition. At this point it appears that the ministers and magistrates despaired of the impasse and he was dismissed.[84] Champereau continued his dispute with Calvin, whom he blamed for his removal, and he demanded a letter of attestation from the magistrates.[85] The situation is so confused that it is almost impossible to assess blame but Champereau certainly developed a lasting dislike for Calvin as a result. For his part, Calvin made no comments about Champereau's wife and could only express regret that 'no one got an advantage' as a result of his removal.[86]

Aimé Megret suffered a similar fate; in the end, he was removed for a specific act of immorality. In November 1545 he was involved in a dispute with the other ministers led by Calvin.[87] Unfortunately, the cause is not clear. Within a fortnight of the initial complaint, Poupin, Des Gallars and Cop were all charging him with insolence to the other ministers.[88] The magistrates were so disturbed by the intensity of the dispute that they deputed a senator to settle the problem; his success was only temporary.[89] In January, the Consistory at Ternier accused a minister, Claude Veyron, in the Bernese-controlled parish of Compesière, of fornication. This would seem to be a continuation of the earlier case mentioned above. Champereau, by then serving Berne at Gex, and Megret were also implicated.[90] Veyron was acquitted but Poupin requested more information.[91] As a result of the investigation Megret was charged with fornication and deposed in February 1546.[92]

It might be useful to look at the one apparent success story from this period, Jaques Bernard. He alone remained in office throughout all the events after 1535. Bernard had been the guardian of the Franciscan convent and a leader of the Reformation in Geneva. Farel acknowledged that it was Bernard who was primarily responsible for obtaining the Senate's approval for the disputation which swept the old faith aside. It would appear, though, that Bernard's unique position as a citizen was the only thing which saved him from sharing the fate of so many of his colleagues and secured his post. Bernard was a formidable person. His brother, Louis, and nephew, Jean François, would both serve as senators. Also, Jaques had been a member of the Conseil des Deux Cents, unique among the ministers of the period, in 1539 at the height of Articulant power. His political associations with the Articulants may explain the haste with which he was sent back to the countryside where he had served before, in 1538; he was transferred soon after Calvin's return. A measure of Bernard's position can also be seen in the fact that he was allowed to keep his city salary, which was a full 20 per cent higher than the usual rural wage.[93]

There can be little doubt, though, that he was a special object of Calvin's displeasure. Calvin strongly disapproved of Bernard's remaining behind in 1538 and his repugnance is clear in a letter to Farel. Calvin related the arrival of a penitent letter from Bernard which he said was 'nauseating with adoration'. Nor can it be said that Calvin was content with Bernard's relegation to a rural parish. He confessed to Farel that he had been hesitant about recommending him but felt sure that the matter would work out in the long run. Calvin's dealings with Bernard would also seem to call into question Calvin's assertion that he had the power to sweep aside his colleagues had he so wished. One must wonder whether Calvin's claim of leniency and moderation can be taken at face value or whether Bernard's position was such that Calvin had little choice but to tolerate him.

What one sees is a process by which the Company of Pastors was remade during the years before 1546. The removal of so many ministers resulted in a significant change to the Company of Pastors but in one crucial area the ministers remained the same; except for Bernard, they were all French. The hallmark of those men who left by 1546 was their relative obscurity and apparent lack of education or expertise. Only Morand and Marcourt were educated and relatively well known. The rest came and went leaving few traces behind to mark their stay in Geneva. The other striking feature of the Company of Pastors prior to 1546 was the degree of dissension and instability in the group as well as the shockingly high level of scandalous behaviour. Clearly what Geneva needed and Calvin wanted was a stable, unified group of colleagues of good character and exceptional quality. By 1546 just such a body of ministers had been gathered.

The new men brought in by Calvin differed substantially from those who composed the Company of Pastors in the years immediately after Calvin's return to Geneva. It is essential to grasp the unique nature of this new Company of Pastors and the high level of learning, expertise and quality united in it. Not only was such a group able to provide a good-quality ministry for Geneva but it would prove to be a formidable force, rallied around Calvin, in the later struggles with some of the magistrates. The respect such qualified men must have commanded among the Genevans could well explain the apparent unwillingness or inability of their magisterial opponents to move against them ruthlessly in the later dispute. As Table 7 shows, prior to the admission of Poupin in 1543, no minister would survive until 1554 except Calvin and Bernard. The latter seems to have been able to remain largely because of his unique position as a member of a powerful family. Poupin was similar to the earlier ministers in that he came from obscurity, in Seiches, and is not known to have had any specialised training or education. His one great strength seems to have been his complete loyalty to Calvin who had nothing but praise for him.

As seen above, the ministers hired in 1544 were not particularily good: Moreau, Megret and Delecluse went swiftly, Ferron would be removed later for fornication.[94] Cugniez and Regalis both died, though they seem to have been in good favour with Calvin throughout their brief ministries. Nothing is known of them except that they were of French origin. Petit and Ninaud were also little known, though they survived in their posts.[95] But with the arrival of Des Gallars one begins to see the first of a new sort of minister in Geneva. He was of noble birth and would later serve in many prominent posts, including minister to the Queen of Navarre.[96]

The ministers called in 1545, Chauvet, Bourgoing, and Cop, show that Des Gallars was not a unique choice but a harbinger of things to come. Chauvet was already known as a prominent French Protestant and had been imprisoned for his faith. A forceful preacher, he would find himself detained by the Bernese authorities for a sermon they found especially offensive.[97] Cop was even better known; his father was Guillaume Cop, doctor to Louis XII and Francis I and his brother, Nicolas, was the famous rector of the University of Paris. He was also a fiery preacher who was nearly deposed for one of his sermons less than a year after his arrival in Geneva.[98] Bourgoing, like Des Gallars, was of aristocratic birth. Moreover, the advanced level of learning which these new men possessed is apparent in that Des Gallars, Cop, Bourgoing and Chauvet all published respected religious works.[99]

The three men hired for rural work in 1546, St André, Balduin and Chappuis, were men of more humble origins, which might explain their long stay in the countryside. It may well be that, as with Perier in 1545, the less renowned ministers were to be tested in the relative safety and obscurity of the rural parishes before possible promotion to a Genevan pulpit. It is interesting to note that the one eventually moved to Geneva before 1554, St André, was, like Chauvet, detained by Berne because of one of his sermons. Indeed, he was promoted that very same year.[100] It is also of some significance that Petit and Perier had fled religious persecution in France as a result of their religious convictions.[101]

There was not only a change in the quality of the ministers but also in their economic status. As exemplified by De la Mare, the ministers had always had to struggle to survive and were entirely dependent on the periodic donations from the magistrates.[102] But just as the ministers who arrived in 1546 were often of a higher social standing, it would also appear that they were in a more secure financial position as well. Indeed, in

TABLE 8   *Ministers before the Petit Conseil (1541-50) causes and complaints*

Year	Complaints on morals	Admonished[106]	Internal trouble[107]	Other	Total
1541	1	2	2	3	8
1542	4	0	11	2	17
1543	0	4[108]	4	3	11
1544	6	1	29	4	40
1545	3	2	17	6	28
1546	7[109]	6[110]	9	2	24
1547	18	4[111]	9[112]	4	35
1548	15	4	1	5	25
1549	13	1	8[113]	2	24
1550	27	0	5[114]	2	34

addition to Calvin, three ministers, Bourgoing, Cop and St André, were to be contributors to the *Bourse Française* which, after 1550, provided financial assistance to the poorer French religious refugees.[103] An examination of the notarial records gives the clearest proof of this changed status. The first thing that is apparent is the almost total lack of active business involvement on the part of the earlier ministers (see Appendix 3). The most noticeable exception is Marcourt, who was owed 500ff, a sum equal to Calvin's yearly wage.[104] It is surely not a coincidence that of the earlier ministers, Marcourt is the only one who would have fitted into the same social and educational group as the later ministers.

In general, though, Marcourt as well as Bernard, Ecclesia, Mare and Megret was involved in only a few contracts in any role other than that of witness. It is also interesting to note the fact that many ministers remained involved in the lives of other Genevans even after their deposition or resignation. This is especially true of Megret but perhaps understandable when one notices his marriage into the Rosets, one of Geneva's more prominent families. This level of continued contact could well explain the constant complaints of the other ministers about the activities and sermons of the former Genevan ministers who had found new posts just inside Bernese territory. It was not only the sermons of the dissident ministers which were a problem but their participation in the lives of prominent Genevans after their expulsion as ministers; Geneva's new ministers could not tolerate a continued pastoral role for their exiled predecessors.[105]

When one examines the economic activity of the later ministers (Appendix 4), the contrast is striking. Clearly Bougoing and Cop possessed funds well above their yearly salary of 240ff; the sums they offered the state for their Genevan houses were substantial. Moreover, even Petit, a rural minister, was active economically. The obvious difference is that these ministers ceased being primarily passive witnesses and became actively involved in the business life of Geneva. What is more, their economic power, as a group, freed them from the almost beggarly dependence on the magistrates which had been the lot of the earlier ministers.[115] This change is especially obvious in Table 8 where one sees the shift in the complaints brought by the ministers to the Petit Conseil away from issues related to their salaries and working conditions and to a more direct involvement in Genevan politics and society.

It is also worth noting the absence of the later ministers as witnesses to wills and marriages. One might normally expect to see them in this role. While only a handful of wills were ever witnessed by ministers the earlier ministers seem to have been more active in this area. Thus, one sees four ministers, Calvin, Mare, Viret and Champereau, witnessing Antoine Rey's will in 1542. It is possible that the marriage contracts were signed before the ceremony and that a reluctance on the part of a minister to appear at the deathbed in a role not unlike that of a last confessor may have inclined the ministers to stay away. Of course, it is possible that the social standing of the newer ministers separated them from their parishioners even more than their ethnic differences did. This would make it less likely that they would have such intimate contact with the local Genevans. This conclusion is strengthened by the fact that of the three cases in which the later ministers witnessed wills, only the one involving Petit may have been for a Genevan. The others were wills for prominent religious refugees.

What one sees, then, is a distinct tendency to hire better qualified, more experienced men of prominent backgrounds after 1544. There was also a clear bias towards Frenchmen; no native Genevan, apart from Trolliet, ever seems to have been considered. The result of this process was that by 1546 Geneva was equipped with what would prove to be a stable, unified Company of Pastors. These pastors were marked by education, proven religious zeal, noble birth, fiery preaching, and economic activity.[116] No single person exemplified all these characteristics but it is clear that as a body, the Company of Pastors noticeably differed in these areas from the earlier ministers.

Nevertheless, this did not complete the reformation of the Genevan ecclesiastical structure. The Company of Pastors, while influential through their position and control of the pulpits, was also part of the Consistory. This latter body was composed of all the ministers and twelve

TABLE 9   *Consistorial membership 1543-52*

Person	Year 1543	44	45	46	47	48	49	50	51	52
Mich. Morel	Cons			Cons	Cons	Cons		Cons	Synd	
Cl. du Pan	Cons	Cons	Cons							
P. Verna	x	x								
J. Pensabin	x	x								
L. Syman	x									
P. d'Orsieres	x			x	x	x	x	x	x	x
B. de la Maisonneuve	x									
J. du Molard	x	x	x	x	x	x	x	x	x	x
P. Veyrier	x	x								
M. Blondin	x	x	x	x	x	x	x	x	x	x
J. de Leurmoz	x	x	x							
A. Chiccand	Synd	Cons	Cons							Synd
J. Philippin		Synd								Synd
Gme. Vellut		x	x	x						
J. Donzel		x	x		x	x	x			
J. Permet		x	x	x						
Jaq. des Arts			Synd							
J. Fontannaz				x						
P. Bertillion		x		x	x	x	x	x	x	x
Fr. Symon/Sernavd		x		x	x	x	x	x	x	x
Amb. Corne				Synd						
L. Bernard				Cons						
J. Chappuis				x	x	x	x	x	x	x
Gme. Chiccand				x	x	x	x	x	x	x
Hud. du Molard					Synd					
Est. Chapeaurouge					Cons	Synd				
J. Genod					x	x	x	x	x	x
P. Bonna						Cons		Synd		
P. Tissot							Synd			
A. Gervais							Cons	Cons		
J. Chautemps							Cons	x	x	
Gme. Beney									Cons	Cons
Cl. Deletra									Cons	Cons
J.P. Bonna										x

Cons = Conseiller
Synd = Syndic

elders, who were the representatives of the magistracy.[117] For obvious
geographical reasons the city ministers would have found it easier to
attend the weekly meetings. This would have favoured the more prestigious ministers such as Chauvet, Bourgoing and Cop. But it was also
essential that this body become as stable and as unified as the Company of
Pastors.

The Consistory's magisterial members were composed of one presiding
Syndic and two other senators, as well as nine members drawn from the
Conseils des Soixante and Deux Cents. As Table 9 shows, to a large extent
the Syndic and Senatorial representatives did not function as long-term
members and in only a few cases served for consecutive years. Indeed no

one served for more than three years in this capacity. However, this is obviously not the case when one examines the other nine elders. By 1546 the Consistory had managed to attract a core of seven elders who would serve for the next seven years. An eighth, Jehanton Genod, was added to this number in 1547. Thus, after 1546–47 the Consistory included ministers and elders who continued to serve in a stable, unified body for at least the next six years. This gave a stability to the Genevan ecclesiastical structure, in marked contrast to the chaotic situation which had been the hallmark of the previous eleven years.

It will be useful to study these eight men in some detail to see whether they have any characteristics in common. The first thing which is apparent is that many of them had ties with the defeated Articulants. Bertillion was himself a member of that party while Dorsière, Chappuis, Du Molard, and Genod were all related to leading Articulants. Moreover, Chiccand's brother, Antoine, was one of the few men who had been able to please both the Articulants and the Guillermins and serve as a senator throughout the period.[118] It may be interesting to speculate why these Articulant supporters were in the Consistory. First, it is important to recall that all the Articulants had been pardoned by 1544 and were generally rehabilitated. Further, the Articulant ties of these men would seem to strengthen the earlier conclusion that the 1538–41 crisis was not really a religious dispute. The relative obscurity of these men and their past party affiliations might well imply that the Consistorial duty was seen as a post of little importance. If the Consistory had been seen as a potential source of power, social or political, it might well have attracted men of Geneva's ruling elite. Instead, the mundane nature of its function and the frequency of its meetings may have inclined Geneva's leaders to leave it to men of lesser rank. Time would show that such an underestimation of the potential power of the Consistory in Genevan society was a serious miscalculation.

Also, only a few came from prominent families, for example the Chiccand family. Pierre Dorsière's family had supplied Geneva with syndics for the previous four generations but was in a reduced state at this time. Two men, Mermet Blandin (Blondin) and François Symon (Servand) were of obscure families and never gained any prominence. Moreover, the relative lack of economic activity as seen in the notary records seems to support the view that these men were relatively unimportant. Other than as witnesses to a handful of documents, only Dorsière, Bertillion and Blondin appeared (the latter two as minor debtors in the will of François Bron in 1540).[119] Dorsière was slightly more active; most notably, he loaned 500ff to Christofle Favon in 1554.[120] One can say that their near total absence from the notary records is indicative of their obscure position in society prior to Calvin's victory in 1555.

This leads one to the next most obvious characteristic of these men. Five of them, Dorsière, Bertillion, Chappuis, Chiccand and Genod, would all reach senatorial rank only after Calvin's triumph in 1555. As will be shown below, these men would prove to be a substantial part of the core of Calvin's local supporters and they would personally profit as a result of the overthrow of Perrin and his supporters. In this light it is interesting to note that none of them had strong family connections with the Perrin–Favre–Sept–Berthelier group. Finally, on a more practical level, all but Mermet Blandin also served at some point on the Genevan civil courts. This seems to imply a certain expertise or predilection for judging civil disputes.[121] Such disputes formed the bulk of the Consistory's cases. Thus, in the first instance, they may have been made elders because of their special qualifications or personal interests and only later came under the strong influence of the ministers. There is nothing to imply that these men came to this court as ardent supporters of Calvin. Indeed the rivalry between the Articulants and Guillermins and Calvin's attachment to the latter party leads one to expect the exact opposite. Nor were they of such a spotless character that they were naturally suited for the Consistory. Dorsière had fathered an illegitimate child and Bertillion had once been accused of favouring the Mass.[122]

What appears, then, is that these eight men were from backgrounds which meant they were out of power and likely to remain so. Further they were, as a group, very active in the administration of civil justice in Geneva which involved the same areas of concern as the Consistory. They were outside the family connections of those men who would prove to be Calvin's staunchest opponents and they would eventually owe their rise to power to the success of Calvin's actions in Geneva. For the purposes of the discussion to this point, however, the most significant fact is that these men represented, by 1546, the establishment of a unified and stable magisterial element in the Consistory. To this was added the coalescing of a similar group of pastors. Together these men, in regular contact with one another, provided Geneva with a united and secure ecclesiastical structure.

The establishment of a Company of Pastors united around Calvin must have presented his later opponents with a difficult problem. It would be hard to imagine that they would willingly accept the destruction of the entire Company. Geneva's ecclesiastical structure relied on an extremely small band of pastors (between nine and twelve, throughout the period) and any moves which might have resulted in a mass resignation would have been very dangerous. Geneva's religious stability demanded a unified

Company of Pastors; the need to preserve that stability would serve to insulate Calvin and the other ministers from the threat of removal. Also, the existence of an equally stable lay element to the Consistory must have been of great importance. Any attempt to alter that group radically would have had serious consequences for the maintenance of good order in Geneva. Thus, as long as these men remained unified they posed a serious threat to anyone who might attempt to assail Calvin's position in Geneva for, borrowing the motto of the Enfants, touching one would be touching all of them.

Geneva's church in 1535–46 was marked by constant instability, dissension and chaotic changes in personnel. In practical terms this meant that Genevan society was very visibly out of control. Changes in the Senate were as obvious but the constant fighting among the ministers provided Genevans with quite a public spectacle. It is impossible to estimate the extent to which this previous period of instability had instilled in all Genevans a·desire for permanence in their pastorate and stability in their church structure. Clearly though, the maintenance of order in this institution was of great importance to Geneva's rulers. The events prior to 1541 must have convinced many Genevans of the dangers of uncontrolled factionalism. The effects this had on the Church would have made many unwilling to support a direct attack on the ministers. Also, the quality of the ministry provided by the Company, after 1546, as well as the prominence socially and internationally of many of its members, protected the ministers. Finally, one must consider the psychological consequences of these men, ministers and elders, remaining at their public posts for so long. By 1555 they would have secured for themselves a prominent place in Genevan society and religious life which was a powerful platform from which to assail their magisterial opponents.

NOTES

1 CO, vol. II, col. 321f. (to Farel, II Nov 1541).
2 AEG/RC/35, fol. 324 (13 Sep 1541). Goulaz, ousted by the Articulants in 1538, had renounced his bourgeoisie but then returned when the situation began to improve. Grenus-Saladin, *Fragments*, p. 6 (4, 5 Mar 1538).
3 AEG/RC/34, fol. 244 (22 May 1540).
4 AEG/RC/34, fol. 244 (22 May 1540).
5 CO, vol. II, col. 378f (to Myconius, 14 Mar 1542); J. Calvin, *Letters*, J. Bonnet, trans. (Edinburgh: 1855), vol. I, pp. 290–2.
6 The magistrates continued to resist Calvin's desire to celebrate Communion more often; in Strasbourg, Calvin had been able to have a monthly Eucharist. R. Bornert, *La Réforme Protestante du Culte à Strasbourg au XVIe Siècle* (Leiden: 1981), p. 195. It is worth noting, though, that Strasbourg had rejected, in 1534, the use of excommunication and

forced sermon attendance, requiring only baptism; Calvin desired all of these. T. Brady, *Ruling Class, Regime and Reformation at Strasbourg* (Leiden: 1978), p. 247.

7   The full extent of Geneva's reliance upon these former priests is discussed in my 'The Renovation of the Genevan Ministry', in A. Pettegree, ed., *The Reformation of the Parishes. The Ministry and the Reformation in Town and Country* (Manchester: 1993).

8   CO, vol. 10, col. 310–14 (to Farel, 28 Jul 1542).

9   AEG/RC/34, fol. 244 (22 May 1540).

10   CO, vol. 11, col. 431f. (to Viret, 23 Aug 1542).

11   CO, vol. 11, col. 431f. (to Viret, 23 Aug 1542).

12   CO, vol. 11, col. 719–22 (to Farel, 30 May 1544).

13   CO, vol. 12, col. 334–7 (to Farel, Apr 1546).

14   Roget, *Histoire*, vol. 1, p. 94.

15   T. Claparède, 'Les Collaborateurs de Calvin à Genève', in *Histoire de Genève Varia*, AEG, 2012 (14). His lecture of 23 February 1882 followed the view of Herminjard. H. Heyer, *L'Eglise de Genève* (Geneva: 1909), p. 449, lists no place of origin for Mare.

16   AEG/Min/J. du Verney, vol. 5, fol. 43 (23 Nov 1542).

17   This is hardly surprising as De la Mare had been in Geneva since 1534 and had been involved in the establishment of the Reformation at Geneva. Cf., J. B. G. Galiffe, *Le Procès de Pierre Ameaux*, in *Mémoires de l'Institut National Genevois* (Geneva: 1863), vol. 9, pp. 38f.

18   AEG/RC/37, fol. 74v (27 Apr 1543).

19   AEG/RC/37, fol. 80v (1 May 1543).

20   Gaberel, *Histoire* , vol. 1, p. 361.

21   AEG/RC/37, fol. 117v (5 Jun 1543).

22   AEG/RC/37, fol. 124 (8 Jun 1543).

23   AEG/RC/37, fol. 226v (24 Sep 1543). J. A. Gautier, *Histoire de Genève* (Geneva: 1898), vol. 3, p. 282, stressed that Calvin was very concerned about the meagre salaries of his colleagues.

24   AEG/RC/36, fol. 72 (16 Jul 1542).

25   AEG/RC/36, fol. 76 (22 Jul 1542).

26   AEG/RC/38, fols. 118, 203v (10 Mar, 16 May 1544).

27   AEG/RC/38, fol. 309 (1 Aug 1544).

28   AEG/RC/38, fol. 30v (14 Jan 1544).

29   AEG/RC/38, fol. 128 (18 Mar 1544).

30   AEG/RC/37, fol. 25 (2 Mar 1543).

31   AEG/RC/38, fol. 146 (1 Apr 1544).

32   AEG/RC/38, fol. 328 (14 Aug 1544).

33   AEG/RC/38, fol. 264 (26 Jun 1544). Gaberel, *Histoire*, vol. 1, p. 360.

34   AEG/RC/38, fol. 348v (2 Sep 1544).

35   AEG/RC/38, fol. 374v (16 Sep 1544).

36   AEG/RC/38, fol. 399 (6 Oct 1544).

37   AEG/RC/38, fol. 398v (6 Oct 1544).

38   AEG/RC/39, fol. 47 (21 Nov 1544).

39   AEG/RC/39, fols. 27–27v (4 Nov 1544).

40   AEG/RC/39, fol. 46 (20 Nov 1544).

41   AEG/RC/39, fol. 51 (25 Nov 1544).

42   AEG/RC/39, fol. 53v (1 Dec 1544).

43   AEG/PC/2e Ser., 579 (6 Apr 1543); 2e Ser., 586 (27 Jan 1543).

44   AEG/RC/39, fols. 53v–54 (1 Dec 1544).

45   AEG/RC/39, fol. 76 (22 Dec 1544).

46 AEG/RC/39, fol. 83 (29 Dec 1544).
47 AEG/RC/39, fol. 84v (31 Dec 1544).
48 AEG/RC/39, fol. 85v (1 Jan 1545)
49 AEG/RC/39, fol. 87v (2 Jan 1545).
50 AEG/RC/39, fol. 90v (5 Jan 1545).
51 AEG/RC/40, fol. 28 (19 Feb 1545).
52 AEG/RC/40, fol. 123 (22 May 1545); RC/40, fol. 168 (1 Jul 1545).
53 AEG/RC/40, fol. 125 (22 May 1545).
54 Roset, pp. 311f, 315; *RCP*, vol. 1, pp. 143f (7 Nov 1552).
55 Gaberel, *Histoire*, vol. 1, pp. 374f. Gautier, *Histoire*, vol. 3, pp. 260f. Cf., also, Galiffe,
    Ameaux, for full details on the original documentation. Calvin apparently supported
    the divorce until the Senate demanded reconciliation. The clash with Ameaux,
    therefore, would seem to be the result, primarily, of theological differences.
56 AEG/RC/41, fol. 47 (11 Mar 1546). See pp. 83–5.
57 AEG/PC/2e Ser, 684 (26 Jan–8 Apr 1546); Gaberel, *Histoire*, vol. 1, p. 375; Roget,
    Histoire, pp. 209–23, *passim*.
58 AEG/RC/41, fol. 72 (13 Apr 1546).
59 AEG/PC/1re Ser, 423 (22 Mar 1546).
60 AEG/PC/2e Ser, 702 (15 Apr 1546).
61 AEG/RC/41, fol. 85v (4 May 1546).
62 AEG/RC/41, fols. 111, 112 (10, 11 Jun 1546).
63 *RCP*, vol. 1, p. 20, n. 2 (3 Jun 1547); Heyer, *L'Eglise*, p. 437; Gaberel, *Histoire*, vol. 1, p.
    360.
64 CO, vol. 12, col. 284 (to Farel, 13 Feb 1546). This complaint against Calvin also appeared
    in 1548 when it was said that 'Monsieur Calvin estoit ung vindicatifz', AEG/Consist.,
    vol. 4, fol. 46v (2 Aug 1548).
65 The ministers were not alone in refusing to work with the plague victims. Blanchet was
    authorised to make the last wills of the dying, a function which should have been
    performed by a notary. Grenus-Saladin, *Fragments*, p. 9.
66 AEG/RC/31, fol. 195 (13 Feb 1538).
67 AEG/RC/34, fol. 388 (20 Aug 1540). After Morand's departure, the Conseil ordered that
    'ung home scavant' should be found to replace him but there is no mention of Calvin
    until Marcourt's resignation a month later. Cf., AEG/RC/34, fol. 452v (21 Sep 1540).
68 CO, vol. 11, col. 430 (to Viret, 23 Aug 1542).
69 AEG/RC/37, fols. 226v–227 (24 Sep 1543).
70 AEG/RC/36, fol. 178 (27 Nov 1542).
71 AEG/RC/36, fols. 94 (14 Aug 1542), 184 (5 Dec 1542).
72 CO, vol. 11, col. 430ff. (to Viret, 23 Aug 1542).
73 AEG/RC/40, fol. 72 (6 Apr 1545).
74 AEG/RC/40, fol. 74v (7 Apr 1545).
75 AEG/RC/40, fol. 79 (11 Apr 1545).
76 AEG/RC/40, fol. 134v (1 Jun 1545).
77 AEG/RC/40, fol. 159 (23 Jun 1545).
78 AEG/RC/40, fol. 155 (19 Jun 1545).
79 AEG/RC/40, fol. 165v (29 Jun 1545).
80 AEG/RC/40, fol. 188 (20 Jul 1545).
81 AEG/Consist., vol. 2, fol. 23v (7 Jan 1546). The details of the case became apparent when
    the accusation was turned against Megret later. The ministers Champereau, Megret and
    Claude Veyron 'coucharent tous en une chambre que ledit Champereau avoyt
    commender les litz tous en une chambre. Toutefois qu'il (François, the witness) ne

pense pas estre pour mal et n'ont eut avoir mal faict.' This was in the company of Champereau's wife and two of her female relatives.

82 AEG/RC/40, fol. 188v (20 Jul 1545).

83 AEG/RC/40, fol. 219 (20 Aug 1545).

84 AEG/RC/40, fol. 233 (8 Sep 1545).

85 AEG/RC/40, fol. 272v (26 Oct 1545).

86 CO, vol. 12, col. 144f. (to Farel, 24 Aug 1545).

87 AEG/RC/40, fol. 286v (10 Nov 1545). See also, AEG/PC/1re Ser., 417 (Oct 1545) and PC/2e Ser., 648 (25 Jun 1545).

88 AEG/RC/40, fol. 299 (23 Nov 1545).

89 AEG/RC/40, fol. 299v (23 Nov 1545).

90 AEG/RC/40, fol. 345 (11 Jan 1546).

91 AEG/Consist., vol. 2, fol. 23v (7 Jan 1546); RC/40, fol. 351 (18 Jan 1546).

92 AEG/RC/40, fol. 364v (1 Feb 1546). See the discussion above where the case is seen to have begun much earlier and involved Champereau when he had been a Genevan minister. In the original action against Champereau the conclusion seems to have been that nothing bad happened, but more information may have come to light by January. Or perhaps the scandal was such that it was felt necessary to move against Megret in any case.

93 AEG/RC/33, fol. 146 (30 May 1539, 2nd ser. pagination). Cf., also, Bergier, 'Salaires', p. 168.

94 *RCP*, vol. 1, pp. 58–61 (Apr 1549).

95 Ninaud asked to go home about two months after his mother died. AEG/RC/39, fol. 86v (2 Jan 1545). Petit had served the Reformed community in Mérindol before fleeing to Geneva. Heyer, *L'Eglise*, p. 501.

96 Kingdon, *Wars of Religion*, p. 6, comments on the noble background of some of the ministers.

97 AEG/RC/48, fol. 72v (12 Jun 1554).

98 AEG/RC/41, fols. 123–131v (28 Jun 1546). For a fuller discussion of the problems in Geneva relating to the control of sermon content see pp. 153–62.

99 See *DBF*, vol. 6, col. 1500 (Bourgoing); vol. 8, col. 914f. (Chauvet); vol. 9, col. 555 (Cop); vol. 10, col. 1353 (Des Gallars).

100 AEG/RC/46, fol. 152 (11 Feb 1552).

101 Heyer, *L'Eglise*, p. 503.

102 Magisterial miserliness is most evident in the receipts of 1544 which show over 10,500ff collected from the former ecclesiastical benefices and lands but only around 4,500ff paid out to the ministers, including the school workers. Monter, *Government*, p, 17f.

103 Olson, *Bourse*, pp. 120–6. The beginnings of the *Bourse* are often traced to the bequest to the poor in Geneva of 1,000 écus in 1542 by David de Buzanton of Hannau recorded by Roset, p. 309, though there is little evidence of any clear connection.

104 See Bergier, 'Salaires', p. 168, where he showed that throughout the period 1542–56 annual salaries remained constant at 500ff for the chief minister (Marcourt then Calvin), 240ff for a city minister and 200ff for those working in rural parishes. Calvin's substantially higher wage was because of 'son grand savoir', cf., Grenus-Saladin, *Fragments*, p. 8.

105 For example, see *RCP*, vol. 1, pp. 19–21 (3 Jun 1547).

106 This refers to warnings given to the ministers for their behaviour.

107 This includes problems among the ministers as well as complaints about their wages and working conditions, etc.

108 These are all related the the ministers' refusal to work with the plague victims.

109 Related to the Ameaux affair and baptismal controversy.
110 Related to the Ameaux affair and baptismal controversy.
111 Debating of actual power of Consistory.
112 All related to conditions in the rural parishes.
113 Mostly about Ferron and Ecclesia.
114 All about Ecclesia.
115 This contrasts with Innes, *Social Concerns*, p. 287, who emphasises that these new men 'had sacrificed a potential life of ease in order to follow their convictions to provincial Geneva'. Possessing wealth and position above that of most Genevans, they may not have seemed to have lost too much.
116 There is a definite connection between education and wealth which must not be forgotten. J. Dewald, *The Formation of a Provincial Nobility* (Princeton: 1980), p. 133f, has shown the high costs which were incurred in education. From 1550–1568, Nicolas Romé spent around 24,000ff on his education before entering the Rouen Parliament and his younger brother, who became a secretaire du Roy, spent more. In 1520–30, Charles de Bourgeville spent over 350ff per annum on his education.
117 On average, less than half attended and there were usually more magistrates. Cf., R. Kingdon, 'Calvin and the Establishment of Consistory Discipline in Geneva: The Institution and the Men who directed it', in *NAK*, 70 (1990), pp. 162–6.
118 Indeed he was a senator from 1536 until his death in 1554.
119 AEG/Min/C. de Compois, vol 13, fol. 73 (15 Mar 1540). Bertillion owed 7 sols, Blandin, 30 sols.
120 AEG/Min/F. Vuarrier, vol. 5, fol. 92 (9 Jan 1554). He also sold some property that same day to Pierre Favre, AEG/Min/F. Vuarrier, vol. 5, fol. 94 (9 Jan 1554).
121 Geneva seems to have lacked any trained legal experts after the Revolution and was, therefore, dependent upon the expertise that these local Genevans had gained through their years on the bench. The only other source of legal wisdom was in the French immigrant community (e.g. Calvin).
122 Respectively, AEG/PC/2e Ser., 451 (31 May 1539) and 477 (15 Jan 1540).

Calvin and the magistrates: the first crisis

Jusque Lon le temps propre

By the end of 1546, Calvin had overseen the establishment of an organised, qualified, and united Company of Pastors. He had also been able to collect a group of Consistorial elders who would continue to work together and provide stability for the Genevan ecclesiastical structure for the next half-decade. After years of disunity and strife, Geneva finally possessed a stable Church. Unfortunately for the city, the political scene took a somewhat different route. In 1541, Geneva was governed by a unified body of men, the Guillermin faction. By 1546 this group was to show signs of disintegration, ushering in a new era of factionalism which would reach its culmination in the crisis of 1555. What is more, early signs that the international situation would improve for Geneva were dashed in 1546 by the outbreak of religious warfare in Germany and the subsequent increase of religious persecution in France. Thus, just as the city was about to enter into an unprecedented period of ecclesiastical stability and vigour, the political situation, both at home and abroad, became increasingly unsettled.

Although recalling Calvin seems not to have been a priority for Geneva, the city acted quickly to implement his programme for bringing order and stability to the city's fractured church structure. The very day he returned, 13 September 1541, the Petit Conseil constituted a committee to assist Calvin in drawing up the Ecclesiastical Ordinances for Geneva's Church. The men appointed to assist him were Claude Bonna (or Pertemps), Ami Perrin, Claude Roset, Jean Lambert, Ami Porral, and Jean Goulaz.[1] The political power of this committee is apparent in the fact that three of them, Roset, Porral and Bonna, were elected Syndics in 1542.[2] With the political backing of these men, it is little wonder that the Ordinances were accepted, although modified somewhat from Calvin's original. It is also understandable that harmony and co-operation between Calvin and the magistracy would be the hallmarks of the early years after Calvin's return. The disorganised and demoralised state of the Genevan Church meant that Calvin's initial tasks would have left little time and few opportunities for clashes with the state or Geneva's ruling elite. This does not imply that there was no popular discontent; rather, that other concerns faced Geneva's magisterial and ministerial leadership.

A number of difficulties confronted Geneva in the years after Calvin's return. The most serious problem was the need to resolve the situation which arose as a result of the Articulant defeat. The relationship between Geneva and Berne was in a very perilous condition, bordering on war. As a result of the expulsion of the Articulant leaders, Geneva had suffered the loss of some of its leading citizens. All these things together, coming so soon after the many changes accompanying the Revolution, meant that Geneva's situation and constitution were all in need of immediate attention. Not only was it necessary to restore Geneva's international alliances, centred on Berne, but the city's entire governmental and legal system desperately needed reforming. This latter problem was perhaps the easiest to solve. The city had to produce a code which would recognise and legitimise the changes which had occurred as a result of the Revolution and the subsequent crises. The task of rationalising Geneva's governmental and legal system was entrusted to Calvin. It is not surprising that Calvin, a well-trained lawyer, was asked to apply his learning and talents to this problem. The result made few if any substantive changes; Calvin's role was more that of redactor than legislator. Though his involvement is a clear demonstration of the high esteem which the city magistrates placed upon his abilities, it would be a mistake to read more than that into Calvin's role in this effort.[3]

The expulsion of the Articulants presented a more difficult problem for the city. The Genevan tendency to exact revenge and profit at the expense of the exiles is clearly evident. Claude Savoy claimed unspecified damages from the confiscated goods of Claude Richardet only months after the Articulant defeat.[4] Likewise, Jean Goulaz demanded 2,500ff in compensation from Aimé Chapeaurouge and Jean Lullin.[5] Nevertheless, the magistrates seem to have decided to follow the unusual course of forgiving and rehabilitating the exiles. This process began very quickly; Claude Chateauneuf, François Lullin, Estienne Chapeaurouge and François Chamois were pardoned in June 1543.[6] Jean Gabriel Monathon, Jean Lullin, François Rosset and Boniface Officier, as well as Claude and André Philippe, were allowed to return by March 1544.[7] The Philippe brothers, however, were forced to pay an indemnity of 2,500ff to the city.[8] The speedy rehabilitation of these men merely serves to underline the extent to which the Articulant–Guillermin crisis is best understood as a temporary political dispute and not a permanent split resulting from irreconcilable differences of principle.[9]

The Guillermins used the absence of the Articulants to purchase even more of the lands seized from the Church and the supporters of the Bishop and Duke of Savoy. Table 2 has demonstrated that the Guillermins were already the most active in this area; their purchases only increased in 1541 and 1542. Jean Ami Curtet bought, for about 250ff, a house on the Rue des Chanoines which had belonged to the Navis family, as well as revenues for 136ff.[10] Domaine d'Arlod joined Curtet in buying these revenues, though d'Arlod bought the larger share for 1,910ff.[11] Ami Bandière gained a garden, which had been a monastic holding, opposite the new hospital, for 170ff.[12] Ami Perrin also purchased some land for about 500ff.[13] A house attached to the Chapelle de Ste. Madeleine was sold to Pierre de Verney for 238ff.[14] Two other houses on the Rue des Chanoines were purchased for 300ff and 68ff by Aimé Chambouz.[15] Goods attached to the church holding at Rive were sold for about 500ff to François Vandel.[16] Pierre Jean Jessé and Michel Voisin collaborated in buying a house for 1,020ff[17] while, for 1,100ff, Jean Mollier bought another which had been confiscated from the Bienchona family.[18] The largest acquisition, though, was for certain rentals; Antoine Panissod bought them for 4,200ff.[19]

Such expenditures placed a heavy burden on the citizens involved. The city's dire financial situation forced it to sell these assets quickly and this could well account for the rush to buy up lands, houses, and rents. However, this frenzy of buying converted much of the elite's disposable cash into property. Thus it is not surprising to find that some citizens overextended themselves in the process. Ami Porral was forced to resign as a Syndic because of monies owed to the city.[20] A similar fate befell Claude Bonna (Pertemps) who was dismissed as Lieutenant for delinquent debts.[21] Michel Guillermet had a house and garden seized by the city to cover a debt of 400ff.[22] Guillermet's debt, though, could be paid only if the city found someone willing to redeem the confiscated goods. François Philibert Donzel expressed an interest but was unwilling, or unable, to purchase the property outright. Eventually, after strenuous negotiations, he agreed to cover the debt in return for control of the property for three years and right of refusal on the sale of the personal effects in the house.[23] François Favre also had some property seized to redeem debts of over 1,000ff owed to the city.[24] Finally, Baudichon de la Maisonneuve and Jaques des Arts were both threatened with jail for debts of around 10,000ff.[25]

This serves to highlight one of the most important considerations facing Geneva's magistrates in the aftermath of the Revolution and Articulant crisis. Threatened by Savoy and at odds with Berne, Geneva was in desperate need of cash to finance its own defences. This made it

TABLE 10   *Genevan public borrowing (Jul 1542-Apr 1546)*

Details	Borrowed (écus)[32]	Repaid (écus)	Reference (AEG)
From Geneva		2,000	RC/36, fol. 70v (16/17 Jul 1542)
From Basle	4,643		RC/36, fol. 120 (13 Sep 1542)
From Basle	1,500		RC/36, fol. 224 (29 Jan 1543)
Request to Basle	6,000-7,000		RC/37, fol. 72 (26 Apr 1543)
From Basle	3,300		RC/37, fol. 136v (25 Jun 1543)
Request to Basle	2,000		RC/37, fol. 270 (12 Nov 1543)
From Basle	537		RC/38, fol. 31 (14 Jan 1544)
Request to Basle	3,000-4,000		RC/40, fol. 309v (2 Dec 1545)
From Basle	1,000		RC/40, fol. 341 (5 Jan 1546)
Request to Basle	6,000		RC/41, fol. 56 (22 Mar 1546)
From Basle	1,835		RC/41, fol. 71 (12 Apr 1546)

Summary (*écus*)

Total repaid: 2,000
Total requested 17,000-19,000
Total loaned from Basle: 12,815

even more important to resolve the dispute with Berne. For these related problems the city looked to Basle for help. Just as Berne had been Geneva's military protector, so Basle was to serve as the city's greatest source of capital and its mediator in the discussions with Berne. Table 10 gives some idea of the extent of Geneva's indebtedness to Basle. In less than four years Geneva borrowed around 60,000ff, or about 15,000ff per year. Geneva's cash crisis is readily apparent when this sum is compared with the revenues which the city had available in the period. In 1544, Genevan receipts were only 29,437.5ff.[26] This does show the city in a better financial position than during the Revolutionary period, the decade before, when receipts roughly balanced expenditures of 17,500ff per year.[27] However, this need for cash, which could only increase along with the debt burden, placed the city in a financially precarious position and certainly increased the drain on the available capital of the citizens themselves.[28]

Geneva was beholden to Basle in other ways as well. After difficult negotiations Basle was able to mediate a settlement between Berne and Geneva. A full agreement was finally reached on 15 February 1544 solving the territorial dispute between the two cities. Both were forced to make concessions.[29] Geneva gained fourteen benefices which meant that the city needed to fill ten new ministerial posts.[30] In thanks, Geneva voted, a year later, to pay about 900ff to various Basle officials who had been involved in the mediation.[31] Most importantly, though, this treaty allowed Geneva to regain a certain degree of security in international affairs, which had been seriously endangered as a result of the Articulant débâcle.

A superficial examination would seem to imply that Geneva's position was very secure and stable by 1546. The crisis with Berne had been resolved and Geneva's financial problems had been momentarily eased by the large infusion of money from Basle. The Articulants were rehabilitated and the Genevan social fabric, riven by factionalism, largely repaired as a result. Finally, the ecclesiastical structure was entering upon a new era of stability and unity. However, closer examination shows the extent to which this harmonious façade concealed the latent fissures in Geneva which would give way as soon as external pressures abated. Further, such a peaceful exterior belies the substantial changes in the city which were the result of two years of plague. It is important to recall that the changes which were wrought by 1546 are visible only with hindsight. The city continued to boil with personal disputes. This was especially true among the ministers before 1546. In this context it is useful to recall the case of Sebastien Castellio, the regent of Geneva's school system. His public clashes with the ministers and Calvin, and other similar quarrels would have led to a popular perception that Geneva's leadership was still in a constant state of turmoil.

Castellio, an acquaintance of Calvin in Strasbourg, had been hired as school regent on 20 June 1541, prior to Calvin's return from exile; he served for a number of years in obscurity.[33] His next mention in the records is at the start of the plague in 1543 when it appears that he volunteered to work with the victims; either he withdrew the offer or was told he could not.[34] By the end of 1543 serious disputes erupted between him and Calvin. Traditionally the explanation has been that Castellio was angered because Calvin refused to accept him as a minister, a post to which he had aspired in an effort to supplement his meagre income.[35] It is quite true that Calvin reported that Castellio was unsuited for the ministry on 14 January 1544 because of opinions that Castellio held about the Song of Songs and the Apostles' Creed.[36] Moreover, Calvin did protest about the inadequacy of Castellio's wages which were raised from 400ff to 450ff per year.[37] However, this account overlooks an earlier ministerial report of 17 December 1543. This entry in the records strongly implies that the ministers, led by Calvin, were busily looking for a new regent and had even gone so far as to identify 'ung savant homme de montpellier'.[38]

There can be no doubt about Castellio's financial problems. His wages were 400ff a year from the city plus one sou a month from the wealthier parents for each child in school; a sum rarely paid.[39] With this money Castellio was supposed to support himself, his family and the two teachers, Pierre Mossard and Estienne Roph, who received only 82ff a year apiece.[40] His distress was real and contrasted sharply with Calvin's position. Calvin was paid 500ff a year cash and food as well.[41] He had had his house refurbished for 121ff and his ecclesiastical robe had been supplied by the State.[42] Castellio's financial problems, which had existed for his entire tenure in Geneva, must have been as nothing compared with his surprise when he discovered that he was to be replaced. Shocking though this treatment may have been, it was not to be the last such example. Castellio's successor, Charles Damont, was forced to ask what would become of him when the city decided, without warning, to replace him with one Cordenis; Damont also tried, unsuccessfully, to become a pastor.[43] This public clash, which continued in the midst of a plague epidemic and additional ministerial squabbles until Castellio was dismissed on 12 June 1544, must have presented to the public disturbing pictures of a miserly magistracy and a rather inconsiderate ministry, neither of which was edifying.[44]

Public disputes were not confined to the ministers. Geneva's magistrates and leading citizens continued to show their enthusiasm for squabbling. Appendix 5 gives some idea of the constant turmoil in the city. For the most part disputes arose over property or business disagreements. But the clashes in the Councils again stress the very volatile nature of Genevan political discourse as well as the high level of popular involvement in Geneva's government. Many of the cases relate to long-standing disputes, for example Claude Bonna (Pertemps) against Girardin de la Rive. Others, however, give evidence of debates amongst relatives; for example François Ramel against Pierre Ruffi and Antoine Lect versus Oddet Chenallat (see Appendixes 7 and 8).[45] There is no evidence here of a factional split; rather, these disputes simply emphasise the very unsettled nature of Genevan society. Personal disputes and political clashes continued unabated even without a major factional crisis. Thus, it would be an error to see the easing of external troubles and the end of turmoil in the ecclesiastical structure as proof of domestic harmony in Geneva.

There is a noticeable decline in the number of personal disputes after the middle of 1546. This will be discussed in greater detail below but suffice it to say that the outbreak of religious warfare in Germany had a profound impact on the Genevan domestic environment. Nevertheless, the prevalence of personal disputes, even in time of war or plague, should not come as a surprise. Geneva was a very small, crowded town in which people were very active, in every sense of the word, in the affairs of their neighbours. Appendix 8 highlights the more positive aspects of the inter-connected nature of Genevan society. Many of those involved in disputes are here seen actively to be in business with one another. For example, Antoine Lect and Oddet Chenallat, who were related by marriage through the Bonna family (see Appendix 8), were involved in a dispute on 2 June 1545, but signed an accord four days later. Geneva remained a volatile city, but its inhabitants showed no sign in this period of dividing into opposing factional camps. The inability to discern any pattern in these disputes is the clearest evidence of the relative lack of divisions in Geneva's govern-ment. However, it seems reasonable to suppose that when tensions pro-duced such a split in the 1550s these previous disputes would have taken on a new significance; Geneva's leaders had shown a definite tendency to remember the wrongs done them.

Finally, this early period after Calvin's return was marred by a very serious outbreak of plague.[46] The unwillingness of the ministers to work with the victims seems to have engendered a lasting sense of indignation among the magistrates for their ministers. The trouble arose when the magistrates ordered that a minister be sent to the Plague Hospital 'pour solager et console les povres infect de peste' at the first sign of the epidemic on 30 April 1543.[47] The Hospital Procureur was forced to report that 'les prédicants négligent le soin des malades'. The ministers declined as they feared for their lives and said they would prefer 'estre aux diables'.[48] By 17 May 1543 the plague was of such severity that the city ordered the separa-tion of all the victims or those suspected of carrying the infection.[49] By 1 June the plague had struck down the minister, Pierre Blanchet, who had been persuaded to volunteer to work with the victims.[50] This meant pressure was again brought to bear upon the ministers, who flatly refused.[51] The magistrates had specifically exempted Calvin and eventually Mathieu Geneston was selected.[52] The ministers' fears are understandable; even the magistrates ordered that a foreign doctor be found to work in the Hospital rather than recruiting a local Genevan.[53] This spectacle, in which foreign ministers refused to succour afflicted Genevans, must have left a very bad taste in the mouths of many citizens.

The severity of the plague put individual pressure on the general population as well as on the city's fragile social fabric. The most obvious example of this is the hysteria surrounding the suspected plague-spreaders. Monter has placed special emphasis on the wave of executions which accompanied this panic. According to Monter twenty-nine people were executed while Roget puts the number at thiry-one in four months alone.[54] In actuality the first execution, on 22 January 1545, began a string of deaths

TABLE 11   *Losses to Conseils,*[58] *1537-47*

Year	PC	LX	CC	Total
1537	8	15	52	75
1538	8 (2 dead)	13	21	52
1539	9	35	59	103
1540	7	unknown	unknown	unknown[132]
1541	12	5	69	86
1542	1	6	62	69
1543	3 (1 dead)	2	9	14
1544	0	3	28	31
1545	6 (2 dead)	2	22	30
1546	0	4	43	47
1547	3	3	11	17
1548	1	2	20	22
1549	2 (1 dead)	0	5	6
1550	2 (1 dead)	unknown	unknown	unknown
1551	2	10	20	31
1552	2	5	20	25
1553	3	2	21	23
1554	1	4	9	14
1555	3	7	20	29
1556	8	15	35	58
1557	7 (2 dead)	8	25	40
1558	4	6	19	29
1559	1	8	24	33
1560	1	7	31	40

which did not end until March 1546, by which time at least thirty-seven individuals had been executed.[55] In addition, another nine people were tried and, usually, banished; the final case, on 14 September 1546, resulted in an acquittal.[56] Perhaps the best example of the extent of the personal concern in Geneva about the plague, a concern which bordered on panic, is a rather humorous note in the city records on 3 August 1543. François Chappuis, a surgeon, had written a book on plague remedies. The Petit Conseil, in a unique move, donated money (10 écus) for the publication of the work and ordered that in return each member of the Conseil was to receive a copy.[57] There can little doubt that the plague occupied the full attention of the magistrates and ministers throughout the period 1543–45.

The most important political effect of the plague, though, was the extent to which it affected the ruling elite directly. Table 11 shows the extensive losses to the Councils in 1544–46. Prior to this period there were also losses, but these had represented permanent decreases in the size of the Councils which had become enlarged during the Revolution and Articulant crises. However, once a stable size (around 200 members to the Conseil des Deux Cents) had been attained, members who left (for example, in 1544–46) were always replaced. The lack of any other explanation for these losses seems to imply that they were the result of attrition caused by the plague. The large number of bourgeois admitted, predominantly from the Genevan countryside, in 1547 supports this view. In the light of Geneva's financial difficulties one might assume that these admissions were meant to raise additional revenue. The low average price suggests that this is probably not the best interpretation; it is much more likely that these men were admitted in a move to replenish an electorate seriously depleted by nearly four years of plague.

The plague struck specific leaders in Geneva as well as the general populace. Among the ministers, Blanchet, Geneston, and Jean Regalis died and Simon Moreau and Abel Poupin were infected.[60] The plague also struck down Jean Marchand; Henry Aubert's wife, Ettienna Gautier; and Laurent Meigret's wife, Ayma Warambert.[61] The list of Genevans infected is equally impressive: Wigand Köln, the printer, and Jaques Bernard's brother-in-law; François Philibert Donzel; Claude Curtet, Jean Ami's brother; Pierre Bonna and his brother, Jean Philibert; Claude Roset and Laurent Meigret.[62] In general, time and circumstances had conspired to remove many of the leading Guillermins. Michel Sept was dead by July 1541; Ami Porral died on 3 June 1542.[63] Both Ami Bandière and Claude Bonna (Pertemps) died in 1544.[64] Also, the Petit Conseil of 1541 had suffered additional losses by 1546. While it cannot be proven, it would appear that Louis Chabbod, Claude Salaz, and Antoine Gerbel had all passed away by 1546.[65] The result was that by 1546 the electorate and the political leadership of Geneva had changed substantially, not as the result of any spectacular crisis, but through natural wastage and epidemic disease.

On one level, then, one might view the few years between Calvin's return and 1546 as a period of stability. However, this would overlook the unsettled nature of these years. By 1546 the church structure had become organised, stable, and unified and would remain so for at least six years; but this stability would be apparent only in retrospect. At the time, most Genevans would have been acutely aware of the traumatic struggles which had beset the Company of Pastors since Calvin's return. They would also have noted the drastic change in the character, quality, and social status of the ministers. Alongside these changes in the ministerial cadre, the political stability of the triumphant Guillermin faction was being steadily eroded by attrition and death, with possible consequences for the co-operation between the foreign ministers and the magistrates. Geneva also faced, for much of this period, the threat of conflict with Berne, its sole defence against Savoyard revenge or French expansionism. Finally, the advent of plague at the end of this period would have served to distract and preoccupy the Genevans, and mask the impact of these longer-term structural changes. All these factors would have kept the Genevan situation tense while limiting large-scale factional disputes. Thus the many pressing concerns of the period served to focus the attention of Geneva's leaders, ministerial and magisterial, thereby producing a façade of stability, harmony, and co-operation which papered over many inherent weaknesses and problems.

With the removal of these prominent concerns in 1546–47, other internal tensions came to the fore. The settlement of the Bernese dispute and the end of the plague allowed the Genevan political leadership to turn its attention to more mundane concerns. The culmination of the process to purify the ecclesiastical structure had finally produced a group of ministers and elders able to work together effectively to implement Calvin's programme of church discipline, while the lack of pressing distractions meant that Geneva could devote itself to infighting and petty squabbling. The new, rising political elite, the heirs of the Guillermin triumph, and the newly improved aristocratic Company of Pastors seemed doomed to clash; minor disputes were sure to escalate into serious disagreements.

Before discussing the crises of 1546 it will be useful to consider the previous clashes between the ministers and citizens. The very paucity of cases will serve to highlight the abrupt change which occurred in Geneva during 1546. There are only three cases not connected with the care of plague victims in which Genevans expressed any reservations about their ministers. The first involved some youths, Petremand Pelloux, Jean Dorbaz, and Denys and François Hugues, who were arrested for deriding the ministers in song.[66] In the same year, 1542, André Piard, a notary and bourgeois, was accused of slander and disobedience towards the ministers and magistrates.[67] Finally, in 1545, François Locatel, the servant of Claude and André Philippe, was arrested for anti-French remarks aimed at the ministers.[68] As the Philippe brothers were associated with the pro-Bernese Articulant faction, Locatel's action is hardly surprising. What is noteworthy, though, is that none of these cases was important enough to warrant a mention in the Conseil records and only Piard seems to have been recalcitrant for long. In sum, problems between the ministers and local Genevans are noticeable by their near total absence before 1546.

However one additional case, which commenced in the summer of 1545, set the ministers on a collision course with many prominent local Genevans. The dispute started when Calvin abruptly refused to accept Jean Trolliet as a minister. Trolliet was a Genevan citizen who had left his monastery in Burgundy when he embraced Protestantism and returned to Geneva. The magistrates supported his attempt to fill one of the many vacant ministerial posts. Calvin refused out of hand, or so the magistrates felt, for they admonished Calvin and demanded that he present his reasons.[69] A fortnight later, on 29 June 1545, when François Bourgoing was hired, the city again tried to convince Calvin to accept Trolliet, but without success.[70] In August Calvin rejected Trolliet, although the magistrates were still not given any explanation.[71] A final unsuccessful attempt was made at month's end.[72] Trolliet became incensed by Calvin's treatment and by November Calvin was forced to include Trolliet with Champereau and Castellio when he complained about slanderous remarks being made against him.[73] Finally, on 26 January 1546, Trolliet despaired of the impasse and begged the city for some other employment and attestation of his good citizenship.[74]

It can hardly be coincidental that that very evening the first *cause célèbre* of 1546 began. On 26 January 1546, Pierre Ameaux launched a scathing attack upon Calvin, his theology, and the growing influence of the French in Geneva.[75] However, the roots of this attack go deeper than the Trolliet affair. Indeed, the historical tradition has overlooked any connection with Trolliet and instead emphasised Ameaux's personal dislike of Calvin.[76] Ameaux is seen to have had two complaints against Calvin. First, his livelihood as a cardmaker had been destroyed by the religious changes after the Revolution and he had had to beg the city for work.[77] This interpretation plays down the fact, discussed above, that these new regulations predated Calvin's arrival in Geneva and were the result of magisterial action. Also, nothing in Ameaux's appeals to the state for employment implied that he blamed Calvin.

A second explanation for the clash between Calvin and Ameaux is considerably easier to defend. In late 1543 a long-running domestic dispute between Ameaux and his wife, Benoîte Jaccon, erupted. He accused her of adultery; she retorted that he mistreated her.[78] For their part the magistrates accused her of unacceptable religious beliefs.[79] To Ameaux's great surprise and consternation, Calvin admonished him to take his wife back and be reconciled to her.[80] Under intense magisterial pressure Ameaux complied, though this proved to be only a brief hiatus in the quarrel.[81] The dispute simmered for over a year until Benoîte was arrested for adultery.[82] After this, Ameaux was finally granted a divorce and allowed to marry

Georgea Marchand.[83] There can be little doubt that this affair produced a lasting animosity between Calvin and Ameaux. Nevertheless, the specific comments made by Ameaux in 1546 are understandable only in the context of the Trolliet case. The marital dispute can explain the depth of feeling expressed by Ameaux, but the apparent concern at the heart of his attack was Calvin's consistent refusal, as he perceived it, to open the Company of Pastors to native Genevans and thereby dilute the growing influence of the French.

Ameaux's specific complaints are readily apparent from the court records. By 26 January 1546 Trolliet had abandoned any hope of gaining a ministerial post. Apparently Calvin's objections had stung him to the extent that when he asked for work he also insisted that the Petit Conseil attest to his character as a good citizen. That evening Ameaux gave a dinner party attended by Pierre Verna, Aimé des Arts, Jean Malbuisson, Amblard du Pain and Ameaux's servant, Jean Tanyer. After dinner he rose to address the gathering; the charges against him record his remarks.

> tu as dict, Que maistre Jehan Calvin ministre de Leglize de Geneve, avoit annonce faulse doctrine en ladt ville par Lespace de sept ans, et avoit empesche que les enfans dicelle ville, ne feussent instruictz en langue Latine, affin que sa faulse doctrine ne feust descouverte: Quil nestoit que ung picard meschant. Que messeigneurs de ladt ville ne faisoient rien en leur conseil sans le vouloir dudt seigneur Calvin, Et lon verroit que les francoys gouverneronent ladt ville. Et plusieurs aultres propos semblables.[84]

It is clear that Calvin is distrusted, in part, simply because he is foreign. Here is a Frenchman trying to conceal his sin and false doctrine from 'les enfans dicelle ville'. The very phrase recalled the epithet of the Revolutionary party. Lest there be any doubt, Ameaux declared that the Petit Conseil would not act without Calvin's express permission, which must have called to mind the former power of the Prince–Bishop and the Dukes of Savoy. Finally, Ameaux asserted that Geneva, which had escaped from the foreign rule of Savoy and barely avoided domination by France and Berne, was in danger of being overrun by the French.

The city reacted to this dispute with division and uncertainty. Part of the leadership wanted Ameaux to apologise, while others demanded that Ameaux, a citizen, be humiliated in public.[85] Initially the Petit Conseil, led by Claude Roset, tried to follow the moderate course.[86] Ameaux was unwilling to comply and the ministers were determined to see the harsher penalty applied.[87] Under intense pressure from Calvin and the new, articulate Company of Pastors, the Conseil gave way.[88] Popular reaction, especially in Ameaux's neighbourhood, St Gervais, was fierce.[89] The magistrates had to erect a gibbet in St Gervais as a warning to calm the enraged citizenry.[90] In the end Ameaux was forced to parade through town clad only in a shirt with a torch and beg pardon in the centre of Geneva.[91] He was ordered to give details, in an 'haulte et intelligible voix', of each charge he had made against Calvin, repudiate each criticism, and beg forgiveness from God, Calvin and the magistrates.[92]

The Ameaux and Trolliet affairs show the extent to which seemingly unrelated cases can be seen as interconnected when viewed in their full context. Because of the complexity of the events of 1546 it will be useful to study the events in a broadly chronological manner, essential if one is to appreciate the chaotic nature of the troubles. The large number of people involved in disputes in 1546 makes it nearly impossible to isolate individual quarrels. In effect, familial ties as well as the prevalant xenophobic undercurrents of the attacks against the ministers, tend to link all these events together. Thus it is possible to see the disputes of 1546 as part of a wider crisis which had its roots in the Trolliet affair and increased in intensity as the year lurched through succeeding crises.

In addition to the climax of the Ameaux affair, the first quarter of 1546 saw the start of direct clashes between the ministers and the large, powerful Favre clan. In January, the Consistory admonished Françoise Favre, Ami Perrin's wife and his mother, Pernette Grant for their constant bickering.[93] Perrin's father-in-law, François Favre, was ordered to present himself before the Consistory as he was suspected of fornication.[94] He simply ignored the summons.[95] When he finally deigned to attend he said 'ce consistoyre est une aultre juridiction dessus la justice de Geneve'.[96] His son, Gaspard, accused of disobedient and slanderous talk, expressed similar sentiments the following session. He felt that his father had been treated in an arrogant manner by the foreign ministers, which he resented. When Calvin attempted to question him Gaspard cut him short saying, 'qu'il ne respondroyt que à Monsieur le Sindique et non à aultre'. Asked to explain this remark, the young Favre said 'que doyt seulement responde à Monsieur le Sindique et ex Sieurs que sont bourgeois et citoyens de la ville aussi du Conseil' and 'qu'il ne cognyt point les ministres'.[97] Clearly these views simply echoed those expressed by Ameaux and seem to explain the animosity which the ministers faced from many of Geneva's ruling elite in 1546.

On 26 March 1546, near the climax of the Ameaux affair, a second dispute arose. Antoine Lect, a prominent Genevan and former member of the Petit Conseil, celebrated the wedding of his daughter, Jeanne, to Claude Philippe, son of Jean Philippe, the executed Articulant. During the course of the evening's festivities the partygoers danced,[98] and in the days which followed, a number of the guests were arrested for participating in this dancing. Appendix 9 presents a list of all those arrested,[99] and the prominence of those arrested is clear from the political and biographical information in the Appendix. Angered by the investigation, these people seem to have agreed that the best approach was to conspire to deny everything; Calvin was incensed by this apparently premeditated duplicity.[100] He attacked the Genevans from the pulpit as beasts and said that, 'les danceurs estoyent ruffians'. His sermon provoked a storm of protest which disrupted the service as Aimé Alliod, a member of the Conseil des Deux Cents, stood and vehemently repudiated Calvin's comments.[101]

When compared with Appendixes 7 and 8, Appendix 9 shows the extent to which much of this dispute revolved around two prominent families, the Favres and Bonnas. Antagonising these two interconnected clans risked creating a large, powerful bloc of prominent Genevans with personal reasons for disliking the ministers. Undoubtedly many of these Genevans, and their families by extension, suffered public humiliation at the hands of the French ministers in the course of the disputes in 1546. It is unlikely that these Genevan leaders soon forgot the treatment which was meted out to them. Such humiliation steeled many of them to resist any increase in the power and authority of the French ministers or their immigrant compatriots.

A wide cultural and ethnic gap is apparent in the information gathered in the investigations associated with this case. In addition to all those arrested, there was one other person mentioned in almost all the initial testimony who was never charged or questioned, Urbain Guisard, Sieur de Crans. He was a prominent figure from the Pays de Vaud near Celligny, in Bernese territory; his social position and nationality seem to have placed him outside Calvin's reach.[102] He was at the party because the Lect family, closely connected with the Favres and Bonnas, had extensive ties in Swiss lands. Antoine Lect's uncle, Jean, had married the sister of a Basle senator. Antoine's brother, also Jean, was a bourgeois of Fribourg, married to Pernette Dalwyt. The Lect family was of German extraction and relatively new to Geneva; his grandfather had emigrated there and received bourgeois status in 1473.[103] This provided the background for Lect's defence of the dancing. He pleaded that the dance had taken place because the Bernese nobleman, Guisard, had said, 'que la coustume est rire Messieurs de Berne est de dancer'.[104] Dancing was presented as the suggestion and request of a prominent Bernese guest; to Lect this appears to have been justification and explanation enough. That the ministers rejected this view may well explain the obstinacy of the Genevans involved.[105] Even the presiding Syndic of the Consistory, Amblard Corne, refused to repent for a fortnight. The ministers remained firm and eventually intimidation and imprisonment broke the resolve of the accused.[106] Slowly they repented and, for example, like Ami Perrin, 'humblement a remercier les bonnes admonitions'.[107] There is every reason to believe, though, that the humiliation these Genevans experienced at this time remained a factor in their subsequent relationship with the ministers.

At the height of the Lect affair and within a week of the culmination of the Ameaux case, two other disputes broke out. Once again, Françoise Favre and Pernette Grant were called before the Consistory; they were still at each other's throats. Françoise vexed the Consistory greatly as she was also angered over the treatment which her father had received, and obstinately refused to confess her part in the dancing at the Lect party.[108] One must read Calvin's letter of reconciliation to Perrin in this context. The letter appears to make a concerted attempt to drive a wedge between Perrin and his wife by studiously avoiding any direct attack on Perrin while laying the blame for the disagreement squarely on Ami's wife. Calvin even felt forced to deny that he was attempting to turn Perrin against his wife. Further, his letter overlooks any ethnic issues and never discusses whether native Genevans had any right to reject questions and admonitions from foreigners, mere habitants. In the midst of these disputes and the continuing squabble between Perrin's wife and mother, this letter appears more manipulative than conciliatory.[109]

A more serious clash was beginning to take shape at the same time. On 16 April, the city discussed the possibility of presenting a drama based on the Acts of the Apostles.[110] The play was submitted to Calvin and approved.[111] As the author was Abel Poupin, this can hardly be surprising.[112] Once accepted by Calvin, the city set about arranging its performance. They approved a date, 4 July, and ordered a place to be found and prepared.[113] There appeared to be no trouble with the play and the plans continued uneventfully until the end of June. On 28 June, a week before the performance and perhaps during rehearsals, Michel Cop preached a fiery sermon in which he equated the players with harlots. The reaction was so swift and violent that Cop was in danger of being dragged from his pulpit and beaten; Calvin even feared for his life. Cop was compelled to appear before the Petit Conseil; the other ministers were specifically ordered to stay away. The magistrates felt that this was solely a matter between them and Cop. Calvin argued that until some actual fault had been found the matter concerned all the ministers. Clearly, the magistrates had no desire to face the intimidating phalanx of the assembled ministers. The violent public reaction to Cop's sermon finally forced the magistrates to side with the law and good order. Cop was admonished by the Conseil and strongly rebuked by Calvin while the rioters were warned.[114] Much to Calvin's disgust, the Conseil decided to proceed with the performance of the play.[115]

In the midst of all the major clashes between the ministers and Genevans other minor squabbles grew out of these debates. Gaspard Favre, Jean Bergeron, Loup Tissot, François Daniel Berthelier, and Perrin's servant, Louis le Grand, were all arrested for gambling at an inn during the Easter Eucharist.[116] Three days later, on 29 April, under intense ministerial pressure, the magistrates agreed to close all taverns.[117] In their place the city proposed to open 'abbayes' where the Bible would be read and other spiritually edifying activities would take place in a social setting.[118] Needless to say this experiment did not prove successful; within a month the magistrates had to reconsider their decision and allow the taverns to re-open.[119] Throughout this diversion the clash between the ministers and the youths arrested for gambling continued unabated; only after magisterial threats did Gaspard relent and repent.[120]

In June, Reymond Chauvet became embroiled in a personal dispute with another Favre. The clash followed an investigation into an offensive sermon preached by Chauvet on 31 May.[121] Within weeks, Chauvet was in a public shouting match with Jean Favre, a bourgeois and clothmaker, François's brother, son-in-law of the former Syndic Aimé Plonjon. Chauvet heard Favre curse as they were passing along the street. The vigilant minister, newly arrived from France, strongly rebuked Jean and ordered him to kiss the ground and repent. Such a penalty could be imposed only by the Petit Conseil in normal circumstances. Stunned, Favre complied, though he was deeply offended. When Chauvet departed, Jean Pensabin, a criminal court judge and former elder, overheard Favre say that what he repented of was that he had not thrashed Chauvet. Brought before the Consistory and the courts, Favre was forced to repent and apologise.[122] Similar views are seen throughout the remainder of the year, although tensions lessened dramatically. From Calvin's viewpoint the problem remained the unwillingness of some Genevans, especially the Favre clan, to submit to good order and discipline.[123] Thus one sees that Perrin was ordered to control his family.[124] Pierre Tissot was admonished for refusing to take communion 'pour l'amour de Francoys Favre son beau-pere'.[125] Calvin was also troubled by the city's habit of dealing mildly with cases he thought important; Bonivard's wife, Amblard Corne's mother, was treated with great leniency because of her family connections when she was discovered to have attended a Mass.[126] Most annoying of all, a large number of youths were arrested in late November and December for fornicating, especially with Marie, daughter of Jean Mauris.[127]

The Genevans who were involved had an entirely different interpretation of the disputes. To these Genevans the problem was the arrogance of the French ministers who were acting above their station. For example, on 14 October, Loup Tissot and Jean Favre's wife were in trouble for remarks they made about the ministers and the French. Loup was reported to have said to Chauvet, 'voz ici venu pour nous gouverner, Item une aultre fois en derision dit audit ministre adieu mon amy. Se escuse et est rebelle et rigaux qu'il est homme de bien et qu'il est enfant de Geneva.'[128] Favre's wife, Jaquema, offended a foreign woman when she said, 's'il n'y a pas ung sien aussi bien en leur pays et le servir là aussi bien gue ici'.[129] In November, Jaques Nicolas Vulliet attacked the growing influence of the French.[130] The controversy over baptismal names, discussed below, began at this same time with the arrest of Ami Chappuis in August 1546.[131] The common thread in all the clashes in 1546 is a strong rejection by prominent Genevans of the power of the French ministers to humiliate them.[132] Undoubtedly Calvin considered that this was only a meaningless excuse on the part of the Genevans to hide their desire to live ungodly lives, but it would be unwise to discount the sincerity of the Genevan view.

These later cases were of short duration and seemed to have excited little local passion. This is largely because of the events of 12 July 1546. On that day the magistrates suspended the performance of the play 'jusque lon le temps propre'. What could have brought about such a drastic volte-face and cooled tempers so dramatically? The event which distracted Geneva's attention from these local concerns and galvanised the city into unity was the arrival of news that the Emperor was moving against the Protestant cities with 100,000 men.[133] The magistrates reacted swiftly by naming a secret council to oversee Geneva's preparations for war. The committee included the four Syndics for that year, Claude Roset, Jean Lambert, Amblard Corne, and Claude du Pan; the Capitaine Général, Ami Perrin; the treasurer, Pernet des Fosses; as well as Jean Coquet, Antoine Gerbel, Jaques des Arts and Pierre Tissot.[134]

It is impossible to overstate the calming effect the outbreak of war had on Geneva's domestic situation. For the next three months the city records report the waves of rumours which swept through Geneva. On 16 July, Bartholomie Foucher of Nice reported that the Pope was preparing 25,000 men to march against Geneva.[135] The next day a frantic letter arrived from Berne, discussing the need to prepare and be alert. The warning was heeded to the extent that the planned embassy by Claude du Pan and Jean Chautemps to Berne to discuss a minor matter was immediately cancelled.[136] Four days later Jean Arpeaux, a refugee, reported that 30,000 men were being gathered in Provence and Avignon to attack Geneva through

Savoy. The city acted that day to register all strangers and require them to swear a personal oath to the city.[137] Near-panic gripped Geneva when, on 27 July, 15,000 Spanish troops passed by the city on their way to aid the Emperor.[138] The magistrates ordered that provisions be collected and that arrangements be made to house all Geneva's rural inhabitants inside the city walls.[139] Tensions increased in August as the city received more details about the situation in Germany and the rest of Europe. On 2 August, reports reached Geneva that the Protestant forces were grouped in three camps of 30,000 troops each and that they were prepared to march on Rome after defeating the Emperor.[140] The full extent of the war was reported the following day. The magistrates were told that Charles, the former Duke of Savoy, was marching against Milan, while Buda was being besieged by 40,000 Tartars and 10,000 Turks. The Protestants were preparing, with their 90,000 men, to withstand the might of the Emperor and Pope. France was mobilising and had allied itself with the Ottomans.[141] In short, Geneva was a small, isolated city surrounded by war. In less than a fortnight reports arrived that 400 Italian cavalrymen were passing nearby.[142] Geneva's rulers expected that some passing Catholic army would eventually turn aside long enough to sack the city.

Finally, in September, Geneva received the first reports of battle. On 7 September, news arrived of an engagement between the Protestant and Imperial forces near Regensburg which left 40,000 dead.[143] George Virtenran, newly arrived from Germany, elaborated on this Protestant victory, saying that three Imperial captains had been captured, along with three large artillery pieces.[144] News of this victory was dampened by rumours that the Pope had dispatched spies, as well as soldiers, whose charge was the poisoning of wells in Protestant cities.[145] Fearful of Papal spies, the magistrates quickly assigned Jean Lambert the task of ridding the city of strangers who lacked proper attestations.[146] Within a week news arrived that the Imperial captains had been executed.[147] Tensions eased somewhat with the approach of winter and the necessary end of the campaigning. On 12 November, the Emperor was reported to have retired into his winter camp on the Danube near Tillinger.[148] The effect of the war was dramatic; prior to mid-July, Geneva was rushing headlong towards a full-scale confrontation between the ministers and leading Genevans. The months before had seen the continual exchange of charges, slanders and abuse accompanied by incessant protests by the ministers to the Petit Conseil. The clearest evidence of the effect of the outbreak of the war is seen in the fact that after the Cop affair on 28 June, the ministers made no additional complaints about local Genevans until 11 October when Calvin reported that Claude de la Pallud and François St Maistre's wife had committed adultery. Geneva's inhabitants were simply too busy to sustain the previous level of turmoil; their attention had turned elsewhere.[149]

It is essential, therefore, to set the events of 1541–46 in their proper context. After Calvin's return, Geneva was governed by a strong faction determined to withstand Berne and to bring order to Geneva's chaotic domestic situation. Calvin faced the immediate and pressing task of performing a similar miracle in the divided Company of Pastors. Before they were able to rest from these tasks the city was debilitated by plague. As the plague receded, Geneva found itself in a changed environment. Many leading Guillermins had died, the Articulants had returned and many of their lesser allies had taken posts on the Consistory. Together with a replenished, superior Company of Pastors, the Consistory was finally prepared to apply itself fully and vigorously to the control of Geneva's domestic life. When they are looked at in their entirety, one can see that these factors meant that prior to 1546 Geneva was too busy to focus on purely domestic, personal problems. Geneva's leadership had been much too occupied to appreciate the full effect of the changes taking place in the city. The magistrates were unable to grasp the complete implication of the stabilisation of their church structure around qualified foreign ministers until the process was complete.

By 1546, however, Geneva was free to turn its attention to an examination of what had taken place within the city since the defeat of the Articulants and Calvin's return. The end of the plague and drought, a fall in grain prices, and the removal of the threat of war with Berne eased the intense pressures under which the city had functioned for so long; for the first time in years it was safe and economically feasible to organise large festivities such as marriage feasts and dramas. With the external threats passed, Genevans showed a proclivity to turn their attention to the Genevan domestic scene. Finally, the loss of so many citizens to plague and the subsequent influx of bourgeois meant that much of the Genevan political structure was open to newcomers. The jockeying to fill this partial void in Geneva's government would have increased the tensions in the city as well.

After the outbreak of war, Geneva was distracted once again and the situation fell into a readily discernible pattern. Faced with the threat of imminent attack, the magistrates strove to control all internal turmoil. This course was adopted quickly; on 29 March 1547, Calvin, Favre and their supporters were called before the Petit Conseil and ordered to be reconciled.[150] The city was determined to present a united front to any and every foreign threat. Internal problems simply would not be allowed to endanger Geneva's security. Unable to remove the tensions which existed, the city strove to limit their effect so that none would have a chance to get out of hand. Just as the play was postponed 'jusque lon le temps propre', so every dispute, whenever possible, was brought to a speedy, pragmatic conclusion with mutual reconciliation.

International events of 1547 served only to justify the necessity of enforced internal harmony. On 8 April the city learned of the possible fall of Strasbourg, though the severity of this calamity was tempered by the news that Duke of Saxony had defeated the Emperor in a battle which killed 20,000 men.[151] This accelerated the long-standing Genevan debate about joining the Swiss Confederation, a move consistently blocked by Geneva's protector, Berne, which retained control of Geneva's foreign affairs.[152] Concern in Geneva had reached the point where the city finally closed its territory to all Catholics on 22 April 1547.[153] Events rushed on; the Saxon Duke raised another 30,000 foot and 5,000 horse.[154] He strove in vain, for Geneva received word on 6 June that the Duke of Saxony was the Emperor's prisoner and Wittenberg was besieged. Better news arrived the same day as the city learned that the King of Denmark and the German coastal towns had entered the war against the Emperor.[155] But the string of Imperial triumphs forced the Swiss to prepare for attack.[156] The new French King suggested that Geneva and Berne should join France in co-ordinating actions against the Emperor.[157]

The end of June 1547 saw the start of the first major clash in Geneva since the Cop affair the year before. Jaques Gruet, a former monk and one of the men arrested at Lect's party in 1546, seems to have been upset by the continued level of hostility which he felt was directed at the Favres by the ministers. In an attempt to intimidate the ministers, he attached a threatening note to the pulpit of St Pierre, the main church in Geneva. In the course of the investigation he tried to implicate Calvin as a French agent; it also became clear that he held a number of peculiar religious views and may well have been mentally unbalanced.[158] What is clear from this rather muddled affair is that Calvin was convinced that Gruet's actions were but one manifestation of the depravity and corruption which lurked in the city. In the end, the case was settled quickly by his execution on 26 July 1547. There was some popular protest against the sentence, but it never inflamed people to the same level of passion as had the Ameaux affair.[159] The investigations, which included the application of torture, did produce some interesting pieces of information. While in torment, Gruet implicated François Favre and his brother, Jean. Their opinions, as related by Gruet, emphasise yet again the xenophobic nature of the protests against the ministers. François was accused of saying 'que les prédicans volloyent tout gouverner et estoient meschans, qu'il falloit prendre garde que les estrangiers ne missent le pied sur la gorge des citoyens'. Gruet also reported that Jean Favre had declared that 'vous aultres enfans de Genève, ne vous laissés pas gouverner à ces prédicans; si on leur laisse fere, ils feront comment l'évesque et si les évesques du passé eussent fait cella que font, on ne l'eût pas tant enduré; mais le temps viendra que n'auront pas tant de babil'.[160] Such views provide the constant backdrop for all of the clashes throughout this period. Moreover, Gruet's attempt to tie Calvin to the French King may well have initiated the next major crisis to strike Geneva which followed fast on this case.

With the arrival of autumn 1547, the major Genevan domestic crisis of this period began. Apparently, the negotiations prompted by France's suggestion that action be co-ordinated against the Emperor had begun to excite suspicions about French intentions; Gruet's accusations probably increased these concerns. In this suspicious environment, Ami Perrin was arrested, on 22 September 1547, for conspiring with France.[161] Berne was sufficiently concerned to dispatch their ambassador, Naguely, to examine the matter. After an investigation, Naguely concluded that Perrin was innocent and pleaded on his behalf before the Petit Conseil.[162] At the same time he availed himself of the chance to speak for François Favre, who was in trouble again.[163] Suspicion began to fall on Laurent Meigret (called Le Magnifique). Geneva was not convinced by Naguely and decided to proceed against Meigret and Perrin at the same time.[164] On 9 October the city decided to depose Perrin as Capitaine Général.[165] Five days later a search of Meigret's house produced incriminating letters and he was jailed.[166]

The crisis became increasingly complicated after this and began to involve an array of other issues. Berne supported Perrin but was determined to see the case against Meigret prosecuted.[167] The ministers, on the other hand, were concerned to protect Meigret, a fellow French immigrant, though they demanded that the matter be settled before the Christmas Eucharist.[168] The city still suspected Perrin and expelled him from the Petit Conseil and then released him.[169] Meigret was freed as well but only after he was deprived of his bourgeois status, stripped of his state pension, and expelled from the Conseil des Deux Cents.[170] The city's tendency to promote reconciliation is obvious in this case; Meigret and Perrin had both behaved in a rather dubious fashion.[171] However, the magistrates preferred to limit the potential damage from this affair and contented themselves with removing the men from positions of authority while enforcing harmony on everyone involved. It is worth noting that the foreigner, Meigret, received the harsher treatment in being deprived of his civic rights. Berne also showed a strong inclination to support local Genevans while distrusting foreigners in the city. Bernese and Genevan rulers seemed to have feared the activities of the foreigners more than that of native Genevans.

The situation in Geneva remained calm for the next seven months. The disputes which arose were primarily related to business. Three cases, however, are worthy of note. On at least two occasions Calvin was cautioned for his sermons. On 21 May 1547 he was asked to explain his remarks; François Beguin, Ami Perrin and Hudriod du Molard brought additional complaints on 10 July 1547.[172] Finally, in March, Calvin's brother, Antoine, was involved in an argument with Philibert and François Daniel Berthelier over money which they said Antoine owed them.[173] Although the city's domestic state was relatively quiet, these few cases show that tensions continued to simmer. The external threat and the attendant need for internal harmony in Geneva dampened any disagreements.

The predominant concern in Geneva remained the progress of the Emperor against the German Protestants. In August, the city heard that Constance was besieged and Zürich threatened.[174] A week later, Perrin was reinstated as Capitaine Général because of the Imperial threat.[175] On 29 August 1548 the situation worsened as rumours swept Geneva that a treaty had been signed between the Emperor, the Pope and the French King.[176] The news, in late October, that Constance had fallen and Berne was in danger, brought Perrin's complete rehabilitation a fortnight later.[177] After the winter break, more bad news arrived as the city learned that the Emperor was raising an additional 4,000 cavalry.[178] By April 1549, Geneva expected an imminent attack.[179] However, the situation began to calm as the Interim, initially rejected by the Pope and French King, began to gain favour.[180] Thus by mid–1549 the Imperial threat had begun to recede. It is not surprising that the removal of the external threat coincided with the worst outbreak of public disorder since 1546. In July, a riot, involving Jean Baptiste Sept, Philibert and François Daniel Berthelier, Philippe de la Mar, and Tyven Patru, erupted after one of Calvin's sermons.[181] In October, André Philippe was charged with a similar offence.[182] These clashes coincided with an increase in xenophobic attacks on the French refugees who had begun to pour into Geneva in ever increasing numbers.

It is apparent that the domestic problems in Geneva throughout the decade after Calvin's return were directly related to the presence of external pressures on the city. Attrition slowly removed leading Guillermins and with them the cohesion of the faction began to crumble.

The nascent division among the Genevan leaders over how to handle the ministers, evident in 1546, was a sign of this evolution of the Genevan political situation. The threat from Berne and the devastation of the plague in the early years followed by the prospect of Imperial attack meant that for most of this period Geneva and its rulers were under constant pressure to limit the effect of internal problems. The end of the Imperial threat gave Geneva a chance to turn its attention to its internal affairs; the influx of substantial numbers of French refugees provided an immediate focus for many of the feelings which had been kept under control since they initially appeared in the interrelated disputes of 1546.

Calvin had a very different perception of the events of 1541–50. In his mind the period was marked by ever-increasing clashes between the forces of godliness and those who preferred to live sinful, wicked lives. He blamed all of the problems on the stubborn unwillingness of the Genevans to exchange their sinful lives and customs for true godliness. Throughout the period, Calvin complained of the lack of magisterial support in stamping out immorality.[183] He also reported that he faced constant opposition from 'intestinis malis' in Geneva.[184] In 1547, Calvin wrote to Viret that the situation had become so bad that, 'eo tamen prorupit improbatis, ut retineri qualemcunque ecclesiae statum diutius posse, meo praesertim ministerio, vix sperem'.[185] This interpretation has been substantially undermined by the foregoing discussion, but remains stubbornly influential in the secondary literature, particularily in those works which rely almost exclusively on Calvin's writings for their view of Genevan politics. Thus Parker has said that Calvin's opponents were 'a dissolute group ready for any mischief' and that they were correctly called 'Libertines' because 'they could not endure the yoke of discipline'.[186]

One way of probing whether Calvin's views have any objective validity is to examine briefly the business conducted in the Consistorial and criminal courts during the first decade of Calvin's ministry. Throughout the various crises after 1546, Calvin consistently raised the charge that his opponents favoured a looser control over morality, were themselves immoral, and were leading Geneva into greater wickedness. If his perceptions of the motives of the gathering opposition to his style and conduct were to be borne out, one might expect a marked increase in the moral cases. Certainly, one should find a clear disparity in the cases before the Consistory, in which the ministers exercised their most direct influence, and the criminal courts where the magistracy, including Calvin's opponents, still held sway. The following brief analysis demonstrates that neither of these expectations can be fulfilled.

Tables 12–14 present the data necessary for any discussion of this issue.

The criminal court records (Table 12) seem to support the contention that Geneva's domestic situation was affected by external factors. Six different crimes show abnormal peaks in the period. Plague-spreading, which accounted for twenty-four cases in 1545 and represents a majority of the executions in the period, is obviously the result of panic. Some increases in personal slander (1545, 1550) and domestic disputes (1550) can be noticed, but they are limited and may be the result of the vagaries related to the survival of cases. Greater variation can be seen in theft (peaks in 1545, 1546, 1550). These same years show increases in cases of attacks on the ministers and French immigrants. The most dramatic increases are in the area of sexual morality. From 1546, thirty-two cases survive and another forty-six from 1550. These also correspond to the years that saw the largest number of cases referred to the criminal courts by the Consistory. However, these data present certain difficulties. First, when studied as percentages many of these peaks become irrelevant; for example, theft averages around 14 per cent throughout the period with a high of 20 per cent in 1549 and a low of 0 per cent in 1544 (or 9.7 per cent in 1547). Moreover, except for 1545, 1546, and 1550 the total number of cases to survive is very limited; as a result, the statistical evidence is rather difficult to use. Of the three years with a significant number of extant cases 1545 must be viewed with caution as the large number of plague-related cases implies that this was an a typical year. Thus, for practical reason only 1546 and 1550 can be examined with any degree of confidence.

When one considers 1546 and 1550, one area of crime stands out, sexual immorality. Both these years present dramatic peaks in cases (where the crime is known) related to sexual immorality, 36.4 per cent for 1546 and 31.7 per cent for 1550. The averages drop somewhat when all the cases, known and unknown, are considered, 31.4 per cent and 28.2 per cent respectively. It appears, then, that these cases occupied slightly less than a third of the overall criminal processes for these years. There is no statistical increase in the frequency of these cases, although the total number of prosecutions climbs; indeed, the ratio actually shows a decline. The ministers could easily have seen the increase in total cases as a sign of growing immorality without appreciating the statistical decline in these cases in relation to overall crime. However, it would be difficult to conclude from these figures that the magistracy was not inclined to control immorality, a complaint often made by Calvin. Table 13 stresses the extent to which the magistrates attempted to avoid severe penalties. The punishments meted out show a decided preference to avoid harshness. If one overlooks the abnormality in the statistics related to executions caused by the cases of plague-spreading, the preferred punishments were short jail

TABLE 12   *Crimes in Geneva per year, 1541-50*[187]

Crime	Year										
	1541	42	43	44	45	46	47	48	49	50	Total
Sexual immorality	0	8	6	1	8	32	3	4	5	46	113
Theft	4	9	6	0	15	15	3	4	6	16	78
Slander magistrates	3	4	5	2	7	2	2	6	0	2	33
Plague-related	0	0	3	0	24	4	0	0	0	0	31
Domestic trouble	1	1	0	2	5	4	0	1	0	15	29
Attacks on ministers	1	3	2	1	2	7	5	1	0	5	27
Blasphemy	0	2	0	0	1	1	2	2	0	14	22
Treason	0	3	6	0	4	0	5	1	1	2	22
Personal slander	1	5	3	0	6	0	0	0	1	5	21
Assault	2	4	4	0	1	2	0	1	1	4	19
Public rioting	0	3	1	0	1	3	0	1	2	5	16
Catholic views	4	0	0	0	1	2	1	0	1	3	12
Anti-French acts	0	1	1	0	1	1	2	1	0	4	11
Counterfeiting	3	1	0	0	1	0	0	0	1	5	11
Disobey authority	1	2	2	0	2	1	0	0	0	3	11
Fraud	2	0	1	1	1	0	0	0	1	4	10
Murder	1	0	0	1	2	1	2	1	1	0	9
Official corruption	0	0	2	0	4	1	0	0	1	1	9
Duelling	0	0	2	0	1	2	1	0	0	2	8
Perjury	0	0	0	0	3	2	0	2	0	1	8
Religious violations	0	1	0	1	0	2	1	0	0	3	8
Witchcraft	0	1	1	1	1	0	2	1	0	1	8
Gambling	0	2	4	1	0	0	0	0	0	0	7
Kidnapping	0	0	0	0	1	3	0	1	0	0	5
Rape	0	0	0	1	2	0	1	0	0	1	5
Appeals out of city	0	0	0	0	2	0	0	0	0	2	4
Curfew violations	0	0	0	0	0	0	0	0	3	0	3
Dancing	0	0	0	0	0	1	0	0	1	1	3
Usury	0	0	0	1	0	0	1	1	0	0	3
Attempted murder	0	1	0	0	0	1	0	0	0	0	2
Business disputes	0	0	1	0	1	0	0	0	0	0	2
Suicide	0	0	0	0	2	0	0	0	0	0	2
Anabaptist views	0	0	0	0	1	0	0	0	0	0	1
Bribery	0	0	1	0	0	0	0	0	0	0	1
Drug related	0	0	0	0	0	1	0	0	0	0	1
Extortion	0	0	0	0	1	0	0	0	0	0	1
Hiring mercenaries	0	0	1	0	0	0	0	0	0	0	1
Immorality	0	0	1	0	0	0	0	0	0	0	1
Prison escape	0	0	0	0	1	0	0	0	0	0	1
Smuggling	1	0	0	0	0	0	0	0	0	0	1
Vandalism	0	0	0	0	0	1	0	0	0	0	1
Total cases known	24	51	53	13	101	88	31	28	25	145	559
Total cases unknown:	0	0	0	1	3	14	6	0	4	18	46
Total cases:	24	51	53	14	104	102	37	28	29	163	605
From Consistory:	0	3	0	3	7	22	0	2	0	79	116
Known cases (%) sent from Consistory	0	5.8	0	23.1	6.9	25.0	0	7.14	0	54.5	20.8

TABLE 13   *Punishments in Geneva per year, 1541-50*

Sentence[88]	Year										
	1541	42	43	44	45	46	47	48	49	50	Total[89]
Death	2	4	3	1	25	6	2	0	4	1	48[190]
Jail	3	6	4	1	2	10	6	1	0	12	45
Banishment	0	5	4	1	10	9	5	4	1	3	42
Beating	1	4	0	0	8	3	0	0	0	4	20
Fine	0	3	3	0	3	5	1	0	1	4	20
Public contrition	0	5	2	0	2	2	0	1	0	3	15
Warning	0	0	0	0	1	0	0	1	3	7	12
Release	1	1	0	1	0	0	3	1	2	2	11
Acquittal	0	0	0	1	0	0	1	0	0	0	2
Loss of office	0	0	0	0	1	0	0	0	1	0	2
Loss of rights	0	0	1	0	0	0	0	0	0	0	1
Summary[91]:											
Total known	7	28	17	5	52	35	18	8	12	36	218
Total unknown	17	23	36	8	49	53	13	20	13	109	341

TABLE 14   *Consistory cases per year, 1542, 1546, 1550*

Cases	1542 (no./%)		1546 (no./%)		1550 (no./%)	
Interpersonal disputes	98	30.7	170	40.5	238	40.3
Spouses	38	11.9	55	13.1	70	11.8
Other domestic disputes	20	6.3	36	8.6	30	5.1
Engagements	22	6.9	23	5.5	23	3.9
Slander	3	0.9	26	6.2	56	9.5
Other disputes	15	4.7	30	7.1	59	10.0
Public disputes	8	2.4	40	9.5	66	11.2
Riot	2	0.6	6	1.4	5	0.8
Disobedience to authority	3	0.9	15	3.6	23	3.9
Attacks on ministers/French	3	0.9	19	4.5	38	6.5
Morality violations	52	16.3	144	34.3	188	32.0
Sexual immorality	37	11.6	104	24.8	160	27.2
Gaming/dancing	15	4.7	40	9.5	28	4.8
Religious irregularities	161	50.2	58	13.8	86	14.6
Magical practices	5	1.6	8	1.9	5	0.8
Catholic practices	6	1.9	13	3.1	17	2.9
Missing sermons/catechism errors	149	46.7	37	8.8	64	10.9
Others	1	0.3	8	1.9	6	1.0
Business irregularities	1	0.3	7	1.7	6	1.0
Manslaughter	0	0.0	1	0.2	0	0.0
Persons involved:						
Men	196	52.4	338	63.4	553	62.3
Women	178	47.6	195	36.6	335	37.7
Total	374	100	533	100	888	100

terms of a few days on bread and water, and banishment, which for citizens was usually limited to a year.

A comparison of these years with the Consistory records (Table 14) shows a similar pattern. The Consistory's documents present a better overall picture as they contain the complete record of the cases for the years 1546 and 1550. The cases of sexual immorality and indeed all morality cases show the same pattern. They represent less than a third of the case-load of the Consistory and show a statistical decline as a percentage of all cases in 1546–50. Indeed, interpersonal and public disputes represent the majority of the cases in both 1546 and 1550 (50 per cent and 51.5 per cent, respectively). The total number of cases grew dramatically (420 cases in 1546 to 584 in 1550, a 39 per cent increase) in 1546–50; the change in the number of people involved is even greater (533 to 888, a 66 per cent increase). It is easy to see how the ministers could have perceived that there was a higher level of immorality and indeed, lawlessness in Geneva while native Genevans might have been more inclined to note the increased intrusion of the foreign ministers into domestic and private affairs.

However, the overall rise in the number of cases need not imply greater immorality. An examination of the Consistory's first year of operation is important. In 1542 the Consistory was occupied with the establishment of good religious habits in Geneva. Thus, cases involving sermon attendance, the correct recitation of the Creed and Lord's Prayer, and, especially, the eradication of latent Catholic superstitious practices represent the major-ity of the cases (50.2 per cent). By 1546 this area seems to have been effectively dealt with; such cases decrease to about 14 per cent for 1546 and 1550. The Consistory then turned its attention to other matters. One could conclude that the growth in the case-loads over this period is as much a result of the maturation of the Consistory as anything else. The net increase in cases would seem to imply that the Consistory became much more efficient at discovering, investigating, and admonishing disorder. It is hard to believe that there was such a substantial increase in the number of violations themselves. The extent to which the general pattern of criminal and Consistorial cases remained the same would seem to belie any such substantial increase. It is more reasonable to assume that by 1550 the Consistory, whose members had worked together since 1546 under the guidance of the enthusiastic French ministers, was better equipped to perform its tasks. Thus, a larger number of cases was prosecuted because the elders and ministers were better at their job and perhaps more zealous as a result of the qualitative improvements to the Company of Pastors. However, this increase could easily have been perceived by the members of the Consistory, and especially the ministers, as proof that Geneva was becoming increasingly immoral.

Finally, the change in the ratio of men to women examined by the Consistory (Table 14) must be discussed. The majority of the cases in 1542 related to sermon attendance and irregularities in religious practices. These cases tended to involve women who often said they found it difficult to attend sermons because they had to care for the children. Also, the use of the Consistorial examination to enforce the new beliefs affected women in larger numbers; they were less likely to know the Creed and Lord's Prayer in French and often recited the Ave Maria when examined. Once this problem had been corrected women became a much smaller percentage of those examined. With the growth in the number of men being examined, especially for personal disputes, the probability increased that the Consistory's activities would annoy more of Geneva's rulers. The opportunities for direct clashes between powerful, prominent Genevans and the foreign ministers multiplied as the Consistory began to confront more of the Genevan male electorate in areas which the Genevans might consider their own private concern. Thus, just as many of Geneva's rulers were worrying about the increasing French influence in Geneva, there was a greater likelihood that these same men might face examination and admonition by the French ministers.

The data from these sources seem to support the view that the crisis in 1546 and the increase in tensions which began to arise at the end of 1549 were the result of the lack of any serious external pressures on Geneva's rulers or society. Such distractions, when they had occurred, forced or allowed Geneva to avoid the deep-seated differences which existed in the city over the proper role and power of the French ministers. Further, the overwhelming number of cases, criminal and Consistorial, involved problems related to interpersonal disputes, not immorality as such. These cases put the Consistory in the position of being very intrusive in the private lives of many Genevans in an extremely public manner. The complaints of those Genevans who were examined supports this general interpretation; the source of contention is usually the perceived arrogance of the ministers. It is only in Calvin's view, found in his letters, that the locus of the trouble shifts to a desire to defend immoral behaviour. That Calvin and his fellow French ministers accepted this interpretation, while many Genevans did not, explains their inability to reach any compromise, or indeed even to understand one another's position. The major players in the crises simply did not see events in the same manner. For the Genevans the problem remained ministerial arrogance and the ever-increasing influence of the French immigrants.

NOTES

1 AEG/RC/35, fol. 324 (13 Sep 1541). Roget, *Histoire*, vol. 2, p. 3, lists Jean Balard rather than Jean Goulaz. He also states that all but Balard were staunch Guillermins. But if the Conseil records are correct, and there is no reason to doubt them, the presence of Goulaz would mean a committee comprised entirely of Guillermins.

2 AEG/RC/35, fols. 484v–485 (5 Feb 1542). Roset and Porral defeated Pierre Tissot and Jean Marchand while Bonna and Amblard Corne (the fourth Syndic that year) defeated Michel Morel and Lambert (the sole committee member unable to gain a post).

3 Cf., Roget, *Histoire*, vol. 2, pp. 65–8. Chenevière, *Pensée*, pp. 205–7, stressed that Calvin was perhaps rather more than just a redactor, as Roget argued, but certainly less than Geneva's Moses, as Fazy believed. Those slight changes Calvin made tended to strengthen the aristocratic elements of the Genevan constitution. Cf., p. 83, n. 121.

4 AEG/RC/35, fol. 194 (6 May 1541).

5 AEG/RC/35, fol. 204 (16 May 1541).

6 AEG/RC/37, fols. 134 (19 Jun 1543), 135 (22 Jun 1543). Cf., Roset, pp. 286f., and Bonivard, *Advis*, pp. 53f.

7 Roget, *Histoire*, vol. 2, pp. 112f.; Roset, pp. 302f.

8 AEG/RC/38, fol. 236 (3 Jun 1544). Lullin and Monathon were also presented with demands for reparations for over 1,000ff, AEG/RC/40, fol. 65 (26 Mar 1545). Chamois and Philippe, along with Jean Louis Ramel, had all been major subscribers to repay a debt to the Swiss in 1530; this second crisis must have cost them dearly. Babel, *Histoire Economique*, p. 43.

9 Cf., Roget, *Histoire*, vol. 2, p. 115.

10 AEG/RC/35, fol. 238 (17 Jun 1541).

11 AEG/RC/35, fol. 552v (7 Apr 1542).

12 AEG/RC/35, fol. 238 (17 Jun 1541).

13 AEG/RC/35, fol. 415v (29 Nov 1541).

14 AEG/RC/35, fol. 245v (27 Jun 1541).

15 AEG/RC/35, fol. 309 (3 Sep 1541).

16 AEG/RC/35, fol. 551 (30 Mar 1541). Vandel was embroiderer to Bezanson Hugues.

17 AEG/RC/35, fol. 322 (12 Sep 1541). Voisin, from Piedmont, had been admitted as a bourgeois on 20 September 1530. He was in the Conseil des Deux Cents in 1536. He was well connected, having married first Amanda, daughter of Lucien du Pan, and then Marguerite, daughter of Girardin Bergeron. *Bourg.*, p. 207.

18 AEG/RC/35, fol. 325v (16 Sep 1541).

19 AEG/RC/35, fol. 349 (1 Oct 1541).

20 AEG/RC/36, fol. 30 (5 Jun 1542).

21 AEG/RC/38, fol. 281v (9 Jul 1544).

22 AEG/RC/37, fol. 52 (6 Apr 1543).

23 AEG/RC/37, fols. 55 (9 Apr 1543), 58v (13 Apr 1543). François was related by marriage into a wealthy drapier family from Lyon. His daughter, Peronette, married Julien Bourdon (Conseil des Deux Cents 1541), Sieur de Compeys. Julien's brother François was also in the Conseil des Deux Cents, in 1544, and his sister, Gabrielle, married Jaques Blondel. Their father, Jean (died 1541), had become a bourgeois on 14 September 1512. *Bourg.*, p. 175.

24 AEG/RC/38, fol. 348v (2 Sep 1544).

25 AEG/RC/38, fol. 331v (21 Aug 1544).

26 Monter, *Government*, p. 17.

27 Monter, *Government*, p. 12.

28 The effect that this might have had on the city's willingness to accept wealthy

immigrants fleeing religious persecution in France will be discussed in the next chapter.

29 Roget, *Histoire*, vol. 2, p. 108. The concessions were resisted by nine unnamed men led by François Daniel Berthelier; Calvin had been one of the negotiators. Cf., Dunant, *Relations Politiques*, pp. 82f.

30 AEG/RC/38, fols. 131–131v (21 Mar 1544). The new posts were at Armoy, Draillans, Moën (with Collex and Gento), Troynex (Bossey, Évoides, Vessiez, Lancy, Onex), Neyden, Valliez (Chenex), Cartigny (Lacconex), Vandœuvre (Colligny), Russin (Malva, Dardagny), and Celligny.

31 AEG/RC/39, fol. 90 (5 Jan 1545). Sums were paid to the Burgermeister (20 écus), Bernard Meyer (30 écus), Theodore Bran (30 écus), Blaise Chesly (20 écus), Jaques Rueder (20 écus), the Falcemeister (20 écus) and the city secretary (40 écus).

32 In the period 1536–49 the écu was worth around 4ff–7s. (Geneva). Cf., Monter, *Government*, p. 157 and Bergier, *Genève et l'Economie Européene de la Renaissance* (Geneva: 1963), pp. 439ff. For purposes of convenience the écu has been accepted as worth 5ff (Geneva) for the entire period 1536–60 as it increased in value to 5ff 6s. (Geneva) by 1560. As exchange rates could fluctuate and were only partially regulated in any case it seemed best to adopt a simple, fixed exchange rate for sums in this work.

33 AEG/RC/35, fol. 240v (20 Jun 1541).

34 AEG/RC/37, fols. 80 (1 May 1543), 82 (2 May 1543). Cf., Roget, *Histoire*, vol. 2, p. 70; Roset, p. 298.

35 AEG/RC/38, fol. 36 (21 Jan 1544). Cf., R. H. Bainton, 'Sebastian Castellio, Champion of Religious Liberty', in *Castellioniana* (Leiden: 1951), p. 37. Beza, 'Calvin', p. 44, simplified the case by mentioning Castellio's levity and rejection of the Song of Songs. He overlooked the question of a ministerial post or of salary.

36 AEG/RC/38, fol. 45v (28 Jan 1544).

37 AEG/RC/38, fols. 30–30v (14 Jan 1544); Roset, pp. 305f.

38 AEG/RC/38, fol. 10v (17 Dec 1543).

39 AEG/RC/35, fol. 409v (22 Nov 1541).

40 AEG,/RC/35, fols. 438 (17 Dec 1541), 521v (9 Mar 1542). Thus, a substantial portion of Castellio's salary was siphoned off to support his colleagues.

41 AEG/RC/35, fol. 352 (4 Oct 1541). The payments in kind were '12 coppes de froment et 2 bosset des vin'. For details on Geneva's weights and measures see J. F. Bergier, *Genève et l'Economie Européene de la Renaissance* (Geneva: 1963), p. 440.

42 AEG/RC/35, fols. 328v (17 Sep 1541), 368 (24 Oct 1541). Jaques des Arts oversaw the repairs; the robe cost 8 écus.

43 Damont was hired on 11 July 1544 (AEG/RC/38, fol. 286). The city, on the advice of the ministers, moved to hire Cordenis on 20 March 1545 (AEG/RC/40, fol. 59) which led Damont to ask about his fate on 16 April 1545 (AEG/RC/40, fol. 84).

44 AEG/RC/38, fols. 160v (12 Apr 1544), 231 (31 May 1544), 246 (11 Jun 1544), 246v (12 Jun 1544). While it would be an error to overplay the importance of this clash, the dispute did occupy the ministers and magistrates for six months and sowed the seeds for the later animosity between Calvin and Castellio. It is inexplicable why McGrath, *Calvin*, p. 120, has overlooked this event and mentions Castellio only in the context of the Servetus affair as an opponent of Calvin without any reference to Castellio's previous relationship with Calvin or Geneva.

45 Chenellat, husband of Nycolarde Lect, was the brother-in-law of François Goula and Estienne Bon. His father, Estienne Chanellat, was a 'tondeur de draps' from Haute Savoye, admitted as a bourgeois on 1 March 1496. Cf., *Bourg.*, p. 127.

46 This was the only substantial outbreak of plague during Calvin's ministry in Geneva. Plague had occurred frequently from 1502 to 1530 but except for the 1542–46 outbreak

the city was spared until 1564, Perrenoud, *Population*, p. 446. This epidemic coincided with a period of drought and the deprivation and economies which resulted from wildly fluctuating grain prices; in 1544 a *coppe* (*c.* 79 litres) of grain varied in price from 2.5ff in January to 8.5ff in Dec. and back to 3ff by January 1546. Cf., Innes, *Social Concerns*, p. 194; Bergier, *l'Economie*, pp. 112f.

47 AEG/RC/37, fol. 77v (30 Apr 1543).
48 Cf., the ministers' comments on 1 May 1543 (AEG/RC/37, fol. 80) with the magisterial admonition on 5 June 1543 (AEG/RC/37, fol. 117) that not only 'en temps de prosperite mes en temps de guerre et de peste et aultres necessites est leur office de servyr leglise cristienne'. This attitude may lie behind the slanders of Paul Garet, hôte de StGervais, against the ministers and their countrymen, AEG, PC 2e Ser., 584 (2 Jun 1543).
49 AEG/RC/37, fol. 96 (17 Mar 1543).
50 Blanchet seems to have been inclined to work with the infected in any case as he had spent time at the Plague Hospital in October 1542 before the serious outbreak in 1543. AEG/RC/36, fol. 151v (23 Oct 1542).
51 AEG/RC/37, fols. 110 (1 Jun 1543), 112v–113 (1–2 Jun 1543),117–117v (5 Jun 1543). AEG/RC/37, fol. 93 (15 May 1543). Blanchet's meagre salary had been increased by 10ff per month, though he had scant time to enjoy it; a lesson not lost on his colleagues.
52 AEG/RC/37, fol. 110 (1 Jun 1543). Geneston died of plague on 11 April 1545. Cf., Heyer, *L'Eglise*, p. 469.
53 AEG/RC/37, fol. 124 (11 Jun 1543). J. Chautemps was deputed to locate a chirurgien at the salary of one écu per month. In three days he had located Hans of Zürich who was rejected because 'il ne scavoyt parler le francoys', only German. He was sent to the General Hospital but was allowed to work in the Plague Hospital after he appealed against the earlier decision, AEG/RC/37, fols. 127 (14 Jun 1543), 129 (15 Jun 1543). Later, Villiez Frans of Zeeland, chirurgien and barbier, was hired for about 360ff per year and given a house repaired at city expense near the Hospital, AEG/RC/40, fol. 83v (16 Apr 1545).
54 Monter, 'Witchcraft', p. 186; Roget, *Histoire*, vol. 2, p. 158. Cf., Roset, p. 307, which also gives a figure of 31.
55 AEG/PC/1re Ser., 388 (22 Jan 1545), 2e Ser., 679 (28 Dec 1545–Mar 1546).
56 AEG/PC/2e Ser., 720 (14 Sep 1546).
57 AEG/RC/37, fol. 168v (3 Aug 1543).
58 The Petit Conseil (PC) contained twenty-five men (four Syndics and twenty-one Senators), the Conseil des Soixante (LX) was made up of the PC and thirty-five additional men and the Conseil Deux Cents comprised the entire LX and another 140 members. These total numbers were only targets and the actual amounts fluctuated from year to year.
59 There is no list for the LX or CC preserved for 1540 or 1550.
60 Jean Regalis and his wife were reported dead on 1 June 1545 (AEG/RC/40, fol. 134v). Simon Moreau took ill on 6 October 1544 (AEG/RC/38, fol. 394v), Poupin on 25 November 1544 (AEG/RC/39, fol. 51).
61 Marchand became ill on 6 October 1544 (AEG/RC/38, fol. 398) and died at some point soon thereafter. Etienna Gautier died on 27 April 1545 (AEG/RC/49, fol. 96v) and Ayma Warambert on 16 August 1546 (AEG/RC/41, fol. 171v). Cf., A. François, *Le Magnifique Meigret* (Geneva: 1947), p. 166. Aubert's wife Ettienna was the daughter of Louis Gautier, an extremely wealthy merchant from Gex in Ain who had been ennobled by Charles V in 1524. Gautier became a bourgeois on 4 August 1508. His son, Claude Janin, married Louise, the daughter of another wealthy merchant, Legier Mestrezat. *Bourg.*, pp. 162f.

62 Köln took ill on 13 October 1544 (AEG/RC/39, fol. 4v); Donzel on 25 October 1544 (AEG/RC/39, fol. 19v); Curtet on 22 May 1545 (AEG/RC/40, fol. 125); the Bonna brothers on 10 August 1545 (AEG/RC/40, fol. 210); Roset on 29 September 1546 (AEG/RC/41, fol. 213v) and Meigret on 16 August 1546 (AEG/RC/41, fol. 171v).

63 Sept's widow is mentioned on 13 July 1541 (AEG/RC/35, fol. 262v). For Porral, see Roget, *Histoire*, vol. 2, pp. 38f.

64 Their deaths were noted on 11 February 1545 (AEG/RC/39, fol. 8v).

65 All their political careers ceased abruptly.

66 AEG/PC/2e Ser., 553 (17 Jul 1542).

67 AEG/PC/2e Ser., 561 (25 Aug 1542), 562 (27 Oct 1542); Consist., vol. 1, fols. 43v–44 (20 Jul 1542), 50v (17 Aug 1542). The original charge involved missing sermons.

68 AEG/PC/2e Ser., 650 (4 Jul 1545), 656 (6 Aug–17 Sep 1545).

69 AEG/RC/40, fol. 141 (8 Jun 1545). Cf., Roget, *Histoire*, vol. 2, pp. 171f. There is some confusion over Trolliet's given name, which was either Zeraphim or Jean. The former, which may well have been a name he took in the monastery, disappears quickly from the records.

70 AEG/RC/40, fol. 165v (29 Jun 1545). Roset, pp. 311ff., says the ministers objected because of 'sa vie & doctrine' but gives no other details. See, p. 201, n. 48.

71 AEG/RC/40, fol. 216v (17 Aug 1545). The city tried the next day, too, AEG/RC/40, fol. 217v (18 Aug 1545). Cf., Grenus-Saladin, *Fragments*, p. 12.

72 AEG/RC/40, fol. 227v (31 Aug 1545).

73 AEG/RC/40, fols. 299–299v (23 Nov 1545).

74 AEG/RC/40, fol. 358 (26 Jan 1546).

75 AEG/RC/40, fol. 359 (27 Jan 1546).

76 Cf., Gaberel, *Histoire*, vol. 1, pp. 374f. and Walker, *Calvin*, pp. 295f. McGrath, as in the Castellio affair, simply ignores Trolliet and Ameaux; in this he seems to be taking his lead from Beza, 'Calvin', p. 48ff, who also minimised the Castellio affair, dismissed Trolliet as a young sinner, and glanced over Ameaux with only a brief reference to the two ministers, given to drunkenness, who supported Ameaux. Beza's editing, and the subsequent omission of these cases provides a rather different picture of Calvin from the one gained by a careful examination of these cases. The best source for the documents of the case itself is Galiffe, *Ameaux*.

77 AEG/RC/37, fols. 144 (5 Jul 1543), 218v (11 Sep 1543). He was given charge of some of the city's gunpowder supply. He complained about his livelihood on 9 Feb 1543 (AEG/RC/37, fol. 8).

78 AEG/Consist., vol. 1, fols. 152v–153 (27 Dec 1543).

79 AEG/RC/38, fol. 24 (4 Jan 1544).

80 AEG/RC/38, fol. 29 (11 Jan 1544). Ameaux said that 'pour la ste Escripture ne la doys reprendre mes doys este separre delle'. See, AEG/Consist., vol. 1, fol. 157 17 Jan 1544), for Calvin's admonition.

81 Pressure was applied by Calvin and the magistrates throughout April. See, AEG/RC/38, fols. 163–163v (15Apr 1544),166 (17 Apr 1544), 178 (28 Apr 1544), 180v (29 Apr 1544). Success came on 1 May 1544 (AEG/RC/38, fol. 183v). It might be useful to recall that these events took place in the midst of the Castellio dispute, as this may well have coloured the ministers' perspective. The magistrates were the motive force behind the call for reconciliation.

82 AEG/RC/39, fols. 76v (22 Dec 1544), 93v (9 Jan 1545).

83 AEG/RC/40, fol. 133bv (2 Jun 1545).

84 AEG/PC 2e Ser., 684 (26 Jan–8 Apr 1546); RC/40, fol. 359 (27 Jan 1546).

85 AEG/RC/41, fol. 32v (27 Feb 1546). Cf., Gaberel, *Histoire*, vol. 1, pp. 375ff and Walker,

Calvin, pp. 296f. Roget, *Histoire*, vol. 2, pp. 209–23 gives a detailed account of the case.

86 The magistrates ordered reconciliation on 2 Mar 1546 (AEG/RC/41, fol. 34). Roset, who was leading the investigation, resigned in the face of the impasse and was replaced by Claude Du Pan on 9 Mar 1546 (AEG/RC/41, fol. 45). Cf., AEG/Consist., vol. 2, fol. 37 (4 Mar 1546).

87 AEG/RC/41, fols. 37v–38 (5 Mar 1546). The ministers refused to accept the lighter penalty even when ordered to do so by the Conseil des Deux Cents, AEG/RC/41, fols. 39v–40 (6 Mar 1546). Despite pressure, the ministers and elders held firm, AEG/RC/41, fols. 52v–53 (15 Mar 1546).

88 Not all the ministers supported this course, though. As discussed, this crisis led to the final break between De la Mare and the other ministers. AEG/RC/41, fols. 47 (11 Mar 1546), 52v (15 Mar 1546); PC/2e Ser., 702 (15 Apr 1546). Calvin expressed some surprise that he was seen as vengeful when he was really forgiving, CO, vol. 12, col. 284 (to Farel, 13 Feb 1546). See also, CO, vol. 12, col. 295 (to Farel, 20 Feb 1546) where Calvin again stresses his clemency and said that Ameaux doomed himself by attacking the magistrates.

89 Aimé Alliod even interrupted Calvin's sermon when Calvin accused the Genevans of being beasts, AEG/RC/41, fol. 59v (29 Mar 1546). For a fuller discussion of the impact of sermons in Genevan disputes see pp. 153–62. Alliod's disruption seems to have been closely connected with the dispute over dancing at Lect's marriage feast as well, see below.

90 AEG/RC/41, fol. 61v (30 Mar 1546). Cf., Gautier, *Histoire*, vol. 3, p. 268.

91 AEG/R/41, fol. 68 (8 Apr 1546).

92 AEG/PC/2e Ser., 684 (26 Jan–8 Apr 1546).

93 AEG/Consist., vol. 2, fol. 24 (7 Jan 1546).

94 AEG/Consist., vol. 2, fol. 30 (4 Feb 1546).

95 AEG/Consist., vol. 2, fol. 33v (18 Feb 1546).

96 AEG/Consist., vol. 2, fol. 34 (25 Feb 1546). Cf., Gautier, *Histoire*, vol. 3, p. 294 which reports that François Favre also said to Poupin 'je n'ai point affaire avec vous, je repondrai à M. le syndic'.

97 AEG/Consist., vol. 2, fol. 37v (4 Mar 1546); RC/41, fol. 36 (4 Mar 1546).

98 AEG/RC/41, fol. 58 (26 Mar 1546).

99 The case can be followed in AEG/RC/41, fols. 70v (12 Apr 1546), 73 (15 Apr 1546), 75 (16 Apr 1546), 76 (19 Apr 1546), 79 (22 Apr 1546) as well as, Consist., vol. 2, fols. 44v–45 (1 Apr 1546), 47v–48 (8 Apr 1546), 49v–50 (15 Apr 1546), 51v–52 (20 Apr 1546), 52bis–53v (23 Apr 1546), 56v and 58 (13 May 1546).

100 CO, vol. 12, col. 334–7 (to Farel, 16 Apr 1546). Calvin lays the blame on the desire of the Favre clan to live above the law; he omits to mention the strong ethnic undertones of the dispute.

101 AEG/PC/2e Ser., 695 (29 Mar 1546), 707 (31 Mar 1546); RC/41, fol. 59v (29 Mar 1546). Alliod was forced to apologise, AEG/RC/41, fol. 73 (15 Apr 1546); cf., Gautier, *Histoire*, vol. 3, p. 269. Treppereaux preached an offensive sermon as well, AEG/RC/41, fol. 73 (15 Apr 1546). Favre was also entangled in the dispute and charged with blasphemy and slander, AEG/RC/41, fol. 58 (26 Mar 1546); PC/1re Ser., 424 (27 Mar 1546).

102 He was also related to Ami Perrin. Cf., Vuilleumier, *Vaud*; CO, vol. 13, col. 26 (n. 11); and Grenus-Saladin, *Fragments*, p. 14. Another Guisard, Pierre, was married, in 1548, to Françoise, daughter of Domaine d'Arlod.

103 A. Choisy and L. Dufour-Vernes, *Recueil Généalogique Suisse* (Geneva: 1902), pp. 202–13. Louis Franc, arrested at the party, was also of German extraction; his mother, Nicolarde, was the daughter of Matthieu Manlich, from Augsburg, who had been

admitted as a bourgeois on 26 November 1538. *Bourg.*, p. 218.

104 AEG/Consist., vol. 2, fol. 44v (1 Apr 1546).

105 The ministers showed a continual inability to grasp the importance of the ties between the Genevans and the Swiss. In the weeks before the crisis over the Lect party, the ministers had insisted on the banning of certain Swiss symbols; 'barbe à la lansquenette' was banned on 12 March, 'chausses chapelées' on 2 April, Galiffe, *Ameaux*, p. 57. Beza, 'Calvin', considered these to be purely partisan symbols ignoring, or ignorant of, their Swiss connections. Gautier, *Histoire*, vol. 3, p. 355, saw this use of Swiss symbols by the Genevans as an attempt to link themselves with the earlier Eidgenots who had used similar devices (see p. 15).

106 Corne's confession was the first break in the conspiracy of silence, AEG/Consist., vol. 2, fol. 49v (15 Apr 1546).

107 AEG/Consist., vol. 2, fol. 56v (13 May 1546).

108 AEG/Consist., vol. 2, fols. 74 (12 Apr 1546), 83 (23 Apr 1546). The dispute between Françoise and Pernette continued throughout the year. Françoise made a point of mentioning that the ministers were all newly arrived in Geneva. Favre, *Libertins*, pp. 9f.

109 CO, vol. 12, col. 338f (to Perrin, Apr 1546). The letter which survives is a Latin copy of the lost French original. Presumably this copy was intended for a wider audience.

110 AEG/RC/41, fols. 74v (16 Apr 1546), 83 (29 Apr 1546).

111 AEG/RC/41, fols. 97v (24 May 1546), 104 (31 May 1546), 104v–105 (1 Jun 1546), 113v (14 Jun 1546).

112 AEG/RC/41, fol. 114v (15 Jun 1546). Along with Poupin's 'les actes des apostles', another play was also approved, 'la Chrétienté malade' promoted by Roz Monet, a later opponent of Calvin; cf., Galiffe, *Ameaux*, p. 73.

113 AEG/RC/41, fol. 119v (22 Jun 1546).

114 AEG/RC/41, fols. 123–131v (28 Jun 1546); CO, vol. 12, col. 356f (to Farel, 4 Jul 1546). It is worth noting that Cop was never brought before the Consistory. The ministers were always admonished first by their peers then the Conseil; a situation probably noted by many Genevans as well.

115 AEG/RC/41, fol. 135v (1 Jul 1546).

116 AEG/RC/41, fol. 80v (26 Apr 1546); Consist., vol. 2, fols. 55v (6 May 1546), 58 (13 May 1546), 65v (17 Jun 1546).

117 AEG/RC/41, fol. 82v (29 Apr 1546).

118 AEG/RC/41, fol. 83 (29 Apr 1546). In France, 'abbayes' often referred to youth societies, or 'sociétés joyeuses'. These groups were frequently supportive of the Reformation but were later stamped out because they were overly independent, for example at Lausanne in the 1540s. Lyon had about twenty 'abbayes'. Cf., Davis, 'Misrule', pp. 43f., 59, 71. See p. 15.

119 AEG/RC/41, fol. 119v (22 Jun 1546). Cf., Graham, *Calvin*, p. 112; Chenevière, *Pensée*, pp. 288f.

120 AEG/RC/41, fols. 116v (17 Jun 1546), 133v (28 Jun 1546). Because men often married late they frequently grouped themselves together in 'bachelleries' (as in Poitou, Berry, Angoumois, Vendée) or 'abbayes de la jeunesse' (as in Burgundy, Dauphiné, Savoie, Midi). Similar societies, which were often noted for their wilful behaviour, were to be found in Switzerland, especially in the Pays de Vaud. Cf., Davis, 'Misrule', pp. 50 and 56, n. 44.

121 AEG/RC/41, fols. 104 (31 May 1546), 104v–105 (1 Jun 1546). As the play was discussed at these sessions, it is tempting to connect the two events, but there is no supporting evidence. It is more likely that Chauvet's sermon contained general, offensive attacks on the Genevans.

122 AEG/PC/1re Ser., 429 (24 Jun 1546); Consist., vol. 2, fol. 67v (24 Jun 1546). Pensabin reported 'appres quel ledit ministre futz retirer ledit Favre ditz et principalement à ung mercier disant qu'il se repent qu'il ne ballat audit ministre deux sofflet et luy tordre le coul aussi au lieux de baiser terre luy arracher la barbe'.

123 AEG/Consist., vol. 2, fol. 81 (23 Sep 1546); CO, vol. 12, col. 377f (to Farel, 1 Sep 1546). The nadir of Geneva's decline, in Calvin's opinion, was the rioting which accompanied the marriage of a bastard Favre to another bastard, CO, vol. 12, col. 369f (to Viret, 11 Aug 1546).

124 AEG/Consist., vol. 2, fols. 83–83v (14 Oct 1546). Cf., CO, vol. 12, col. 391f (to Farel, 2 Oct 1546), Calvin wrote that a reconciliation of sorts had been effected between him and Perrin. Perrin had promised to make certain changes, which may refer to the control of his family, though Calvin remained convinced that Françoise was incorrigible.

125 AEG/Consist., vol. 2, fol. 80v (23 Sep 1546).

126 Grenus-Saladin, *Fragments*, p. 14.

127 AEG/PC/2e Ser., 726 (24 Nov 1546), 730 (9 Dec 1546), 731 (10 Dec 1546); Consist., vol. 2, fol. 92v (25 Nov 1546); RC/41, fols. 262 (14 Dec 1546), 265v (20 Dec 1546),269v (24 Dec 1546), 270v (25 Dec 1546). Those arrested were Jean François Ramel, Jean Bergeron, Amyed Andrion (Andrion was in the Deux Cents in 1552 and died in 1559; his father, Ami, was an apothecaire from Piedmont, who was admitted a bourgeois on 15 February 1513, cf., *Bourg.*, p. 176), Jean Curtet, Claude Gerbel, Nycolas Bramet, Louis de la Tour (his father, Lucien, an apothecaire from Piedmont, became a bourgeois on 25 April 1514; *Bourg.*, p. 178), Jean Furjod, Nycod Anse (Jean Robin's servant), Aimé Aubert, Jean Bandière, Estienne Chautemps, André Falquet, Jean Tissot, Jean Maurys, Pierre Mestrezat, Antoine Mugnier, Pierre Navet, Claude Jaquemoz, Jaques du Crest, François Forel.

128 AEG/RC/41, fol. 229v (26 Oct 1546); Consist., vol. 2, fol. 93v (14 Oct 1546). In Rouen, a Protestant French nobleman, Jumelles, complained to the Catholic authorities that Catholic commoners had insulted him by being too familiar and calling him 'buddy' or 'mate'. K. Neuschel, *Word of Honor, Interpreting Noble Culture in Sixteenth-Century France* (London: 1989), p. 65. Chauvet's complaint provides evidence of his opinion that he was socially superior to the Genevan ruling families.

129 AEG/Consist., vol. 2, fol. 84 (14 Oct 1546).

130 AEG/PC/1re Ser., 435 (15–22 Nov 1546); Consist., vol. 2, fol. 93v (25 Nov 1546).

131 AEG/PC/1re Ser., 431 (28 Aug 1546). Chapter 6 contains a fuller account of this controversy.

132 For example Peut d'Argent protested against being publicly admonished, AEG/Consist., vol. 5, fol. 63v (5 Sep 1550). The impact of the French on Geneva is treated in Chapter 5, while the specific effect of the ministers is dealt with in Chapter 6.

133 AEG/RC/41, fol. 142 (12 Jul 1546).

134 AEG/RC/41, fol. 142v (12 Jul 1546).

135 AEG/RC/41, fol. 146v (16 Jul 1546).

136 AEG/RC/41, fol. 147v (17 Jul 1546).

137 AEG/RC/41, fol. 151 (21 Jul 1546).

138 AEG/RC/41, fol. 159 (27 Jul 1546).

139 AEG/RC/41, fol. 159 (28 Jul 1546). The De la Mar brothers reported that they had supplies of grain which could be brought into the city if storage space could be found at Rive. Jean Lambert was ordered to find room for the grain.

140 AEG/RC/41, fol. 162v (2 Aug 1546).

141 AEG/RC/41, fol. 164 (3 Aug 1546).

142 AEG/RC/41, fol. 173v (16 Aug 1546).
143 AEG/RC/41, fol. 193 (7 Sep 1546).
144 AEG/RC/41, fol. 195 (9 Sep 1546).
145 AEG/RC/41, fol. 198 (13 Sep 1546).
146 AEG/RC/41, fol. 203 (20 Sep 1546).
147 AEG/RC/41, fol. 208v (28 Sep 1546).
148 AEG/RC/41, fol. 239v (12 Nov 1546).
149 AEG/RC/41, fol. 215v (11 Oct 1546).
150 AEG/RC/42, fols. 70v–71 (29 Mar 1547).
151 AEG/RC/42, fol. 81 (8 Apr 1547).
152 AEG/RC/42, fol. 85v (14 Apr 1547).
153 AEG/RC/42, fol. 92v (22 Apr 1547).
154 AEG/RC/42, fol. 123 (28 May 1547).
155 AEG/RC/42, fols. 133–133v (6 Jun 1547).
156 AEG/RC/42, fol. 185 (25 Jul 1547).
157 AEG/RC/42, fols. 188v–189 (28 Jul 1547).
158 Roget, *Histoire*, vol. 2, p. 295.
159 AEG/PC/1re Ser., 446 (30 Jun 1547); RC/42, fol. 164 (30 Jun 1547). See also, Roset, p. 320. Roget, *Histoire*, vol. 2, p. 303, n. 1, stresses that this case never came before the Consistory but was a purely secular affair. This contrasts with Gaberel, *Histoire*, vol. 1, pp. 388–93, which treats the whole case as another example of the religious and personal libertinism of Calvin's opponents.
160 Roget, *Histoire*, vol. 2, p. 302.
161 AEG/RC/42, fols. 252v–253 (22 Sep 1547).
162 AEG/RC/42, fol. 270v (7 Oct 1547). Any Genevan move towards France upset Berne. Cf., Roget, *Histoire*, vol. 3, pp. 8f.
163 AEG/RC/42, fols. 265v–266 (5 Oct 1547). Favre was released after posting a 1,000-écu bond. He resigned his bourgeoisie.
164 AEG/RC/42, fol. 270v (7 Oct 1547). A full account of these cases can be found in François, *Meigret*, pp. 112–23. See also, Roset, pp. 322–5 and *Advis*, pp. 75–89. Beza, 'Calvin', p. 51, mentions the action against Perrin but edits out any reference to Meigret.
165 AEG/RC/42, fol. 272v (9 Oct 1547).
166 AEG/RC/42, fols. 278 (11 Oct 1547), 284v (14 Oct 1547).
167 AEG/RC/42, fol. 288v (19 Oct 1547). Berne even demanded the right to question Meigret, which offended Genevan sovereignty. Cf., Roget, *Histoire*, vol. 3, pp. 16f.
168 AEG/RC/42, fol. 380 (22 Dec 1547). Cf., Roget, *Histoire*, vol. 3, p. 30.
169 AEG/RC/42, fols. 355v–356 (29 Nov 1547).
170 AEG/RC/42, fols. 388v (30 Dec 1547), 391v (2 Jan 1547). Meigret had been granted an annual pension of 400ff on 18 Feb 1541 (AEG/RC/35, fol. 80v). He retained his French pension which he had received throughout his ten years in Geneva. Cf., Roget, *Histoire*, vol. 3, p. 15.
171 Cf., Roget, *Histoire*, vol. 3, pp. 34f. Everyone was released in time for the 1548 elections, see also, vol. 3, pp. 38f where he stresses that the war situation 'détermine les citoyens à suspendre pour quelque temps leurs differends'.
172 AEG/RC/43, fols. 94v (21 May 1548), 132v–133 (10 Jul 1548).
173 AEG/RC/43, fol. 51v (27 Mar 1548).
174 AEG/RC/43, fol. 160 (13 Aug 1548).
175 AEG/RC/43, fol. 171 (21 Aug 1548).
176 AEG/RC/43, fol. 180 (29 Aug 1548).
177 AEG/RC/43, fols. 229v (30 Oct 1548), 243v (16 Nov 1548).

178 AEG/RC/44, fol. 14 (8 Feb 1549).

179 AEG/RC/44, fol. 74 (22 Apr 1549).

180 AEG/RC/43, fol. 270v (22 Dec 1548).

181 AEG/RC/44, fols. 171v (29 Jul 1549), 184 (8 Aug 1549).

182 AEG/RC/44, fol. 233 (7 Oct 1549).

183 For example see: CO, vol. 12, col. 32f (to Viret, 12 Feb 1545), col. 282–4 (to Farel, 13 Feb 1546), col. 355–7 (to Farel, 4 Jul 1546), col. 508f (to Viret, 27 Mar 1547), col. 531f (to Viret, 28 May 1547), col. 545–9 (to Viret, 2 Jul 1547), col. 559f (to Viret, 24 Jul 1547).

184 CO, vol. 12, col. 629 (to Farel, 14 Dec 1547).

185 CO, vol. 12, col. 629 (to Viret, 14 Dec 1547).

186 Parker, *Calvin*, p. 98.

187 Drawn from AEG/PC/1re and 2e Ser.

188 Some cases preserve multiple sentences. Only one has been counted following a ranking which considers beatings first, then banishment, jail, public repentance, fine, warning.

189 These numbers refer only to individual cases, not the number of people involved in each case. Thus the total number of people involved would be higher.

190 The total drops to twenty-six if the plague-related cases of 1545 are removed.

191 From those cases where the crime is known. See Table 16.

4 Geneva: hospitality and xenophobia

A la fin le Roi de France sera bourgeois de cette ville

Clearly these early disputes and confrontations were of importance for the later clashes in the 1550s. Nevertheless isolated cases cannot explain the consistent opposition which the ministers faced. It would seem reasonable to suppose that some basic problems lay behind this resistance to the ministers. As the discussion in the previous chapter has shown, there was one recurrent theme which appeared in a number of cases; opposition to the growing power and influence of the French in Geneva. Increasingly, many Genevans came to view the French refugees as a potential threat to their political power in the city. Also, the near total dominance of the Company of Pastors by French ministers was crucial; control of the pulpits must have been decisive in forming public perceptions and opinions in the decade before 1555. In this, one sees the importance of the aftermath of the period of transition and chaos from 1541 to 1546 when Calvin was able to collect around himself a stable and distinguished body of colleagues. Thus there were two aspects to the presence of the French in Geneva. The French ministers played an active role in the city while the refugees were more of a passive threat to Geneva's magistrates. As their numbers increased, however, they became a source of greater concern.

The previous chapter has already shown the extent to which political clashes in Geneva often involved, to some degree, opposition to the growing influence of the French religious refugees. Moreover, there can be little doubt that the single most common complaint in Geneva was this very issue. Especially after 1546, as will be shown, the question of the growing power of foreigners was to dominate Geneva. After 1549, the arrival of a number of very prominent and wealthy Frenchmen began to cause severe social and political problems in Geneva. But the basis for opposition to the foreign refugees predated this arrival and it would be a serious error to imagine that problems with foreigners date solely from 1549 or, in the previous period, involved only the ministers. It is best, therefore, to turn back to the origins of this issue.

Very soon after independence from Savoy and the adoption of the

Reformation, Geneva found itself burdened by large numbers of foreigners passing through the city. In 1540, a city guard was assigned the task of ridding the city of foreigners section by section because of the inability of the Hospital to meet their needs.[1] Unfortunately, the records contain no details of the number of refugees involved. However, it is fortunate that accurate records exist for the entire year which ended in October 1539, or just two months before this decree to clear the city. In the period from October 1538 to 1539, the city hospital assisted 10,657 poor strangers as they passed through Geneva.[2] This figure does not include those Genevans (estimated at about 5 per cent of the total population) who received regular assistance from the hospital.[3] Thus, when this order was issued, Geneva, a city of about 12,000 persons, was attempting to support 600 local poor people on a regular basis and an additional 10,000 in a one-year period.[4] It can hardly be surprising that Geneva found this too great of a strain on its resources. Nevertheless it is important to bear in mind that the actions of the city at the time seem to be the result of its inability to meet the needs of these foreigners rather than any ethnic bias against them.

It is not until December 1542 that the poor foreigners were next mentioned; another clearance was ordered. This time a Syndic was put in charge of the operation.[5] The reason for this action was that an outbreak of plague, which was to last until the end of 1545, had begun and the city could not meet the increased need which resulted.[6] But Geneva was not without compassion. Five months later the magistrates ordered that help should be given to all those regarded as being 'without suspicion'.[7] However, in the summer of 1543, when the plague worsened, the regulations became more restrictive.[8] Throughout the summer months the strangers were ordered to leave.[9] The second of the decrees gave them three days to vacate the city and threatened torture for those who remained.[10] Next, the city ordered an inspection to see that 'all without the means to live in Geneva' were indeed gone.[11] Later decrees, which appeared almost every fortnight, simply re-stated the previous decrees.[12] The same pattern continued into the autumn, which seems to have been necessary because the earlier orders had been unsuccessful. In the face of this failure the city moved to order the registration of all foreigners who had remained behind, whether they had the means to support themselves or not.[13]

Thus by the close of 1543 a clear pattern had begun to emerge in the relationship between the city and the foreigners. Geneva was willing to assist strangers on their way when it was able to do so. Only when local conditions, or the sheer scale of the refugee influx, strained its resources did the city take direct action, which was in most cases fairly ineffective. This compassion was extended to minor details as well. For example, the

Senate gave Calvin permission to lay on a special Eucharist for strangers who had arrived too late in the spring of 1544 to attend the Easter service.[14] Nevertheless, it is clear that throughout the plague years Geneva regularly tried to clear the overcrowded city of the refugees who filled its streets. Again these rulings seem to have sprung from a pragmatic decision that the strangers could not be cared for by the city rather than a specific dislike or fear of the foreigners.

This ambivalent response continued until 1546. Those who would not leave were threatened with beatings.[15] No one was allowed to rent even a room to a stranger without a licence and everybody was compelled to attend sermons, which would imply that the city more or less accepted its inability to rid Geneva of strangers entirely.[16] In a practical and generous gesture, though, the magistrates ordered that the fines for illegally renting to a foreigner were to be paid to the hospital to assist the poor.[17] In an apparent effort to stop the problem at its source, a Syndic was sent to one of the French areas hardest hit by persecution, Mérindol in Provence, with money for the Protestant minister there and his flock.[18] Geneva's enthusiasm to stop the flow of refugees from Provence is understandable when one realises that over 4,000 strangers arrived that year from Mérindol and Cabrières alone.[19] Further, even as the poor were cleared, Geneva ordered its guards to provide them with bread for the journey.[20] In another attempt to regulate the situation, the city ordered that houses be provided for the strangers, which would, of course, make control and eventual expulsion easier.[21] This was coupled with another decree to register all the foreigners.[22]

In the years which followed the end of 1545, there was a decided shift in the public response to refugees. Until 1546 the Genevan treatment of foreigners revolved around meeting their basic needs and sending them on their way. After 1546, there is a marked increase in anti-refugee sentiment and a greater incidence of trouble relating to the care of the poor strangers as well as the assimilation of those intent upon staying in Geneva. It seems possible to identify three explanations for this shift. First, the very fact that an increasing number of refugees showed no sign of leaving Geneva placed an added burden on the city. Second, as will be shown in the following chapter, the co-operation between the magistrates, who were all local Genevans, and the French ministers deteriorated rapidly. The troubles between the magistrates and ministers became, very quickly, tinged with anti-French rhetoric. Finally, as seen in the previous chapter, the unsettled state of European affairs and the danger presented to Geneva by the successes of the Emperor against the German Protestants seemed to have made the Genevans suspicious of all foreigners.

This is not to imply that the previous pattern of hospitality and moving the poor strangers on disappeared. Indeed, that is not the case. But the city records do display much less concern with this aspect of the foreign influx. Thus one sees the city attempting to meet the needs of the Hospital to aid the poor strangers.²³ Regular clearances and registrations are ordered, though much less frequently.²⁴ It is clear that the press of refugees continued to be an enormous strain on Genevan resources and society as, for example, when 500 French poor arrived from Strasbourg in June 1547.²⁵ But the references are fewer and the older pattern is broken. A new issue began to dominate Geneva, which was not how many refugees were passing through the city but how many seemed bent on remaining and gaining both power and influence. Attempts to control the integration of foreigners proceeded along two lines. The first was to limit the ability of foreign merchants to undercut local Genevan businessmen. The second was to bring these strangers into a more regular relationship with the structure of the city by administering oaths to them and, in the end, by allowing the more prominent foreigners to purchase civic rights as bourgeois. The latter method was designed primarily to ensure the loyalty and obedience of the foreign residents to Geneva and its government. It also had the added benefit of providing the city with a useful source of revenue. This was a matter of no small concern in the face of the enormous burden of debt under which Geneva had struggled since the Revolution.

Such methods for assimilating foreigners were not, however, unique to the period after 1546. Attempts to control resident aliens began to appear very soon after the successful revolt against Savoy and the triumph of the Reformation. In 1537, the city hastened to ensure that strangers were obliged to obey Genevan laws and were aware that they were subject only to Genevan justice and had no right of appeal to any foreign jurisdiction.²⁶ This would have been of obvious concern because of the territorial disputes with France and Berne. As one will recall, these disputes sprang, for the most part, from the confusion caused by overlapping legal jurisdictions in the disputed areas. That same year, the city also limited the freedom of widows and young girls to marry foreigners.²⁷ Strict economic controls began to appear in 1539 when the magistrates decreed that all books printed in Geneva, a trade dominated by foreigners, were to be submitted to the State for approval prior to publication.²⁸ In 1540, Geneva forbade foreigners from buying grain before noon or from re-selling their purchases, which would seem to imply that the strangers were willing to offer a higher price than most Genevans would or could.²⁹ By 1542 Geneva decreed that all residents had to register with their area commanders, or dizeniers.³⁰ Finally in 1543 controls were put upon resident foreign merchants. They were limited to selling in a single market-place and then only on Wednesday, Friday, and Saturday.[31]

By examining this other area of foreign activity one can see two of the problems the strangers posed for Geneva. The poor foreigners produced overcrowding and threatened disease. Moreover, they strained the charitable resources of Geneva to breaking point. But wealthier, skilled foreigners presented other problems. They often introduced unwanted and excessive competition for resources and markets. The regulation on marriages hints at the stress which resulted from other forms of competition. For practical reasons the wealthier foreigners, should they decide to remain in Geneva, were more likely to arouse an ethnic backlash. However, these wealthier strangers were not universally disliked nor were they always perceived as a threat. For example, the printing trade mentioned above did not displace local merchants and as long as the content was controlled the printers were allowed to work freely and appear to have been welcomed. Moreover, individuals reacted differently as well. By 1543, the Senate was forced to discuss those local merchants who were serving as 'fronts' for the foreigners.[32] No decision on any action could be reached. The magistrates showed their ambivalence as well less than four months later when they agreed to help establish, with money and housing, two coopers in Geneva 'for the honour and profit of the city'.[33] In most cases the real concern of the magistrates seems to have been the protection of local merchants and the control of foreign activity. Thus, rent controls included the leasing of large houses to foreigners; a licence was still required.[34]

It may be useful to highlight one positive area of the refugee influx, the printing trade. Prior to 1550, Geneva only had two prominent printers, Jean Girard and Jean Michel, both apparently foreign. Girard was not to gain bourgeois status until 1541.[35] After 1550, however, the bourgeois and habitant lists show evidence of a substantial increase in the number of printers in Geneva. Only two printers, Jean Crespin and Conrad Badius, were made bourgeois but an additional sixteen were granted residency as habitants.[36] These figures must be seen as representing the lowest figure possible, as some men would have been granted some form of residency without any reference to their trade. Indeed, Crespin and Badius were originally granted habitant status without any mention of their trade.[37] Clearly, though, this immigration of refugees, in this instance, would have provided Geneva with a valuable, and ready-made industry.

The city was not so hospitable when faced with foreigners who posed a threat to established Genevan traders. In July 1544, the city tried to ban all foreign merchants from the city to protect hard-pressed local businessmen.[38] However, this may not have been what it seemed. That same month the city recommended that these very merchant strangers be asked about buying bourgeois status. Perhaps the earlier order was an attempt to coerce them into purchasing civic rights, which not only increased city revenues but also gave the magistrates greater control over the merchants.[39] The Senate further showed its interest in keeping the right sort of strangers when it permitted a French couple to operate a school for boys and girls in 1545.[40]

As in the treatment of the poor strangers, the situation changed after 1546. The emphasis shifted to attempts to control each and every resident and to tie them to the city. Thus in July 1546 and in early 1548 the Senate decreed that all resident strangers were to be bound to the city by oath.[41] By 1549, Geneva was witnessing the first significant arrival of wealthy, even aristocratic refugees.[42] This new influx was particularly notable for the number of educated and noble Frenchmen and Italians and it was domi-nated by members of the liberal professions.[43] It is not surprising to see that the city moved quickly to curtail the business activities of these new foreigners.[44] Anyone who wished to do business henceforth had to enrol personally with the Procureur Général.[45] This showed a much greater interest in controlling individuals than had been the case before. One can say that the foreigners were no longer perceived solely as a faceless mass of transient poor. Rather, Geneva began to be concerned about each indi-vidual refugee, especially those who were socially prominent.[46]

The importance of these new foreigners, as well as the external threat of an Imperial attack, encouraged Geneva to move quickly to integrate these strangers. All new foreigners were again asked to swear a personal oath to the magistrates.[47] This order was re-issued the next day when the Senate

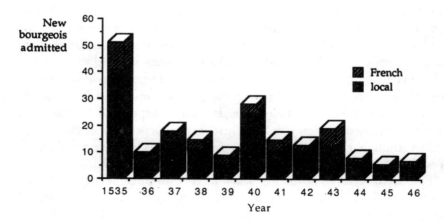

FIGURE 3 *Bourgeois origins, 1535–46*

heard rumours that 'two or three houses' contained traitors.[48] Two weeks later, in May 1549, the city records contained the first enrolment, as habitants, of 'ten French gentlemen, refugees because of the Word of God'.[49] So many strangers were beginning to settle that even the ministers began to be concerned about how to control the situation. In April 1550, Calvin and Poupin requested a visitation of 'all strangers, servants, and chambermaids to stop sexual immorality'.[50] By that August, the Consistory was expressing concern that there were so many new and unknown resident strangers that it was unsure whether they were all living with women to whom they were actually married, and that it needed assistance in finding out. The Senate ordered a city-wide investigation.[51]

As already mentioned, the situation in Geneva had begun to change in 1546. Many Genevans were becoming alienated from the French and the threat they presented by their numbers and prominence. By 1551, however, many in the city awoke to a greater danger; the threat presented by allowing so many strangers to settle in Geneva. Obviously, from the point of view of local Genevans, this is an entirely different issue from that posed by the waves of transient poor strangers (a problem largely solved by the effective establishment of the *Bourse Française* in the late 1540s). But in one sense, this was a much easier problem to solve. The main route of full assimilation open to the refugees was their ability to purchase bourgeois rights. This status gave a person the same rights as those held by a citizen except that of being able to serve in the Senate. Citizens were people born in Geneva to parents of citizen or bourgeois status. Thus, not only was it important to control the increase of bourgeois for its own sake, that is to limit the increase in the political power of the French refugees, but it was

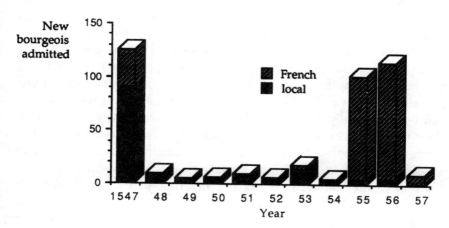

FIGURE 4 *Bourgeois origins, 1547–57*

also necessary to limit the number of new bourgeois because their children would be citizens and thus able to aspire to the highest offices in Geneva.

A number of problems faced those who wished to limit bourgeois admissions. The amount of revenue which could be raised by nearly unlimited admissions was substantial. In the period 1535–54 the city realised over 13,000ff from the sale of bourgeois rights. But in two and a half years from 1555 to 1557 the city raised an amount equal to that of the previous two decades. In fact in 1555 the amounts raised represented 20 per cent of the city's revenues for the year. To a cash-starved city like Geneva this was no small concern. In addition, this was an easy source of revenue since it made no extra financial demands on the citizenry. Also, as Figures 3 and 4 show in most cases Geneva was admitting locals. This large group of local bourgeois might respond well to calls for limiting the number of new French bourgeois, but was unlikely to support any moves by the Senate to curtail bourgeois civic rights. Thus, in 1551, when the Petit Conseil recommended that bourgeois be denied the vote for twenty-five years, they failed. While the action was obviously aimed at incoming refugee bourgeois, many of the older bourgeois must have resented any attempt to limit their rights.[52] This would also explain why not only were the proposals defeated but why they provoked heated exchanges in the General Assembly when debated.[53]

The desire to limit bourgeois admissions resulted from the growing fear that the new bourgeois could pose a political threat to Geneva's status quo. This fear, however, was not based on previous troubles related to bourgeois; the numbers admitted were usually small. And even in 1547, when 138 bourgeois were admitted, ninety-one of the men were of local origin. Nevertheless, in a foretaste of possible things to come thirty-five of the new bourgeois, considerably more than the normal total yearly average, were French. The increase in 1547 seems to have been motivated as much by a need to replace the electorate, seriously depleted by plague, as any attempt to raise money. Except for one other year, 1536, when many voters had been lost in the war and its aftermath, no year saw substantial admissions except 1555, when, for the first time, the admissions seem to have been politically motivated. The political nature of these admissions is obvious. The years 1535–54 saw an average admission of twenty-three but the period 1555–57 averaged 119 per year. Thus in the first twenty-year period around 250 were admitted while in the later three-year period over 460 were granted bourgeois rights. Initially, though, the perceived threat which some people felt seems to have been the result of the fear of the cumulative effect of regular admissions of refugees and the presence of so many of their countrymen in Geneva at the same time. One must not forget that the Genevans had no way of knowing at the time how many might actually try to remain in Geneva.

It seems, though, that by 1551 some local Genevans had become aware of the subtle political threat posed to their authority and freedom by the wealthier refugees who proposed settling in Geneva. Many scholars would hasten to point out that the actual numbers buying civic rights were small compared with the number of refugees in Geneva. On the whole they are quite right. Nearly 1,300 people were enrolled as habitants from 1549 to 1555, but relatively few remained in Geneva permanently. The delicate balance of forces politically, however, meant that only a few needed to remain and gain power to alter Geneva's domestic political landscape; nearly 300 would gain bourgeois rights during and after the 1555 crisis. It was of crucial importance that a much higher proportion of those who came before 1555 was inclined to stay than those who arrived afterwards. That 20 per cent of the earlier refugees were willing to purchase bourgeois status (compared with only 5 per cent of those arriving after 1555) presented Calvin and his local supporters with a large pool of men who could be used to sway Geneva's political balance of power.[54] Moreover, the obvious desire of so many of the initial refugees to remain in Geneva frightened many Genevans; they had no way of knowing that the demand for permanent residency would abate after 1555. The first group of refugees contained the wealthiest and most prestigious Frenchmen to flee to Geneva; they were less likely to be able to return and could better afford to settle in Geneva. Forced to contemplate permanent settlement in Geneva, they were more inclined to involve themselves in the city's domestic politics.

What must have disturbed the native Genevans was the extent to which these newcomers failed to mix. Of the 440 Frenchwomen who married in Geneva prior to 1557, only sixteen married local men.[55] The closed nature of the refugee community is readily apparent in the example of the Colladon and Budé families. Laurent de Normandie, Louis Guarin of Lyon and Jean Ragueau, the notary, were all sons-in-law of Leon Colladon and refugees as well. Leon Colladon's wife was Guinon, the daughter of Nicolas Bigot, Sieur de Fontaines. Likewise Christofle Favon, a very wealthy refugee, was married to a daughter of Germain Colladon. The Budé family showed the same tendency to unite with other prominent refugee families. Jean Budé married Marie, daughter of Magdelene Imbault, widow of Rogerin de Jouan, Sieur de Jonvilliers, while the wife of François Budé was Marguerite, sister of the minister François Morel, Sieur de Collonges. Two of Jean's sisters married Guillaume Try, Sieur de Varennes and Jean Anjorrant, former president of the Paris Parlement.[56]

TABLE 15   *Prominent French refugees after 1549*

Name (Title: Sieur de ... / Position)	Background
Laurent de Normandie (Lt du Roy, maire de Noyon)	ht 1549
Jean Budé (Verace)	ht 1549
Jean, Jaques & Ayme de St Martin (Garennes de Sens)	ht 1549
Jean du Mas (Lisle)	ht 1549
Antoine Popillon (Parey)	ht 1549
Guillaume Try (Varennes)	ht 1550
François du Pont (procureur/notaire du Roy)	ht 1550
Galeas Carraciola (Marquis de Vico)	ht 1550
Antoine Prevost (Vaneau)	ht 1550
François Prevost (Beaulieu)	?
Guillaume Prevost (St Germain)	?
Estienne Autour (Beauregarde)	ht 1550
Jean François Chastillon (Saillon en Vally)	bg. 1551
Jean de Grenas (Esquillez en Provence)	ht 1551
François Exchallad (Bolliée)	ht 1551
François Buynard (Touche) and brother, Maturin	ht 1551
Andrion de Percellet (Maillane)	ht 1551
Guillaume Maurisse (Compandie en Anjou)	ht 1552
Philippe de Caire (Rocqueboin de Lorraine)	ht 1552
Guillaume de Coincte (Bionville)	ht 1553
Nicolas de Coincte (Anguerville)	?
Claude d'Anduze (Veyrac en Languedoc)	ht 1553
Pierre, François, & Jean d'Aireboudouze, sons of Jean (Cevannes)	ht 1553
François Budé (Villeneuve)	bg. 1554
Antoine Budé (Trossy)	?
Regnault Anjorrant (Jolly)	ht 1554
Jean Anjorrant (president of the Paris Parliament)	?
Lucas de Berty (St Pere aux Espieux)	ht 1554
Antoine Disque (Verneul sur Marne en Champagne)	ht 1554
Claude de Rohauld (Grandval de Paris)	ht 1554
François de la Botiere (prevosté de la ville Muny)	ht 1554
Pierre Gorin/Gerin (Boisboissart de Poictu)	ht 1554
Bernard Hours (Calmac de Nîmes)	ht 1555
René de Billy (Maubinier)	bg. 1556
Charles de Brichanteau (St Laurent en Calabre)	?
François Bourgoing (Agnon)	minister
François Morel (Collonges)	minister
François Bouchard (Vicomte d'Aubeterre)	?
Etienne du Faye (La Tour)	?
Guy de Serignac (Tillac)	?
Pierre de Maldonnade (Maldonnade)	?

bg. = bourgeois
ht = habitant

Reference to the names in Table 15 will show the extent to which these two families thus united a large number of the more prominent refugees.

Nor were these the only ties which bound the refugee community together. Economically these refugees were united as well. Thus Jean Budé had business dealings with Jaques de St Martin, Sieur de Boursier, as well as Claude de St Pierre.[57] Likewise René de Billy, Sieur de Maubinier, loaned 100 écus to Conrad Badius, the printer.[58] Also, Jaques de Bourgogne, Sieur de Fallaix, served as an agent for Antoina de Versonnex when she purchased a house from Antoine Popillon, Sieur de Parey.[59] Nor were the refugees wholly cut off from their holdings in France. An excellent example of this is the sale of certain rights pertaining to lands at Bioly by Estienne Autour, Sieur de Beauregard to Christofle Favon.[60] One example in particular serves to highlight the level of interaction amongst the French in Geneva. In 1553, Pierre Gorin, Sieur de Boisboissart, signed an accord with Jean Vernon of Poitiers, an habitant, brother of Marguerite, wife of René Biennassis, to accept Vernon into his employ. The contract was agreed on the recommendation of Jean Calvin and Estienne du Faye, Sieur de la Tour, also an habitant. The transaction was witnessed at Calvin's house by Calvin, Du Faye, Germain Colladon and Nicolas de la Fontaine, all Frenchmen.[61]

Moreover, many prominent refugees served as donors to the *Bourse Française*, an institution established to assist poor refugees and alleviate the burden they imposed upon Geneva.[62] Together these examples show the extent to which the refugees, for obvious reasons, functioned as a somewhat insular group in Geneva. They had all shared the experience of going into exile for their religious beliefs. Further, they had strong social and ethnic ties with one another which just as effectively cut them off from the local Genevans. Clearly though, this situation, logical as it might have been, must have created a certain degree of unease amongst some Genevans even when, as in the case of the *Bourse*, they were designed to limit the areas of friction between the Genevans and the refugees. The overall economic impact of the refugees is of great importance as well. Indeed, the city was quick to exploit this source of revenue even as it allowed substantial admissions for political reasons. The average cost per person of bourgeois admissions from 1535 to 1554 was 32.5ff but this increased to 60ff in 1555–57.

A clearer source of data, though, would be a thorough examination of the notary records to see the sums of money involved in the various transactions. Such a study has produced some interesting results. In the period 1538–48, the average transaction, for the 332 cases examined, was worth 226ff. But the 204 transactions studied in the period 1549–57 averaged 367ff, an increase of over 62 per cent on the previous period.[63] Obviously these figures must be used with caution. First, it is nearly impossible to estimate the effect of inflation in the period. Nevertheless, the increase is substantial and in an age which did not understand inflation must have been perceived as such. In any event, the perception by Genevans that the refugees were often very rich is probably of greater importance than their actual relative wealth when inflation is taken into account. Also, these documents would naturally tend to preserve the dealings of the wealthier segments of Genevan society. But this is true of both samples and is therefore of little importance. Moreover, the local elite would be concerned primarily with the wealth of the more prominent refugees. The cumulative effect, though, would be that the native Genevans could well feel that the refugees were wealthy foreigners endowed with large sums of disposable income.[64]

Appendices 10 and 11 contain the ten largest transactions in each period. The average of these two samples, 2,830ff in the earlier period as opposed to 2,900ff in the later, shows almost no difference. But the type of individual involved speaks volumes for the situation in Geneva after the 1549 influx of refugees. All the earlier transactions involve at least one citizen. Indeed, at least six cases involve transactions only between citizens. But in the later sample, some eight of the cases involve refugees alone. The only citizens mentioned as direct participants were Jean Louis Ramel, Jean Moget and Jeffrey du Boys, of whom Ramel was the sole citizen of prominence. Thus it would appear that at the upper level of business dealings, the native Genevans had been supplanted by the free-spending foreigners. The overall increase in the value of single transactions in the period seems to point to a substantial increase in capital in Geneva.

It will also be useful to examine one refugee family in particular, the Trembleys. They provide an excellent example of the large amount of disposable income available to some refugees who did not actually appear to be overly wealthy through any single transaction. Loys Trembley does appear in Appendix 11 as the purchaser of a house from Jean Louis Ramel for 3,000ff. But this single transaction woefully underestimates the position of this family. Loys's brother, Estienne, appears as a major businessman on a number of occasions. He was involved in transactions with Loys Franc, a citizen, Loys Rebones, Jean Rey, a merchant, Pierre du Chable, Jean Rumille, François Besson, a bourgeois merchant, and Jean de la Maisonneuve, a citizen. In most of these cases he appears as a creditor and the sums he loaned totalled over 2,800ff in a period of only seven months (between September 1556 and March 1557).[65]

Such largesse must have had a profound economic, and more importantly, psychological impact upon Geneva. Obviously, the foreigners were in need of housing and services but their very ability to purchase so many things with such large sums must have caused many Genevans to worry. Genevans would have understood the fact, noted by Brady in discussing Strasbourg, that 'wealth, after all, whether old or new, honorable or tainted, from land or from trade, was the single *sine qua non* for the acquisition and maintenance of high status and access to power'.[66] Thus many locals might have concluded that the purchasing of so much property was a clear sign that the foreigners intended to settle in Geneva. In that circumstance, their wealth would soon bring them some measure of power and that could occur only through a diminution of the influence of the native ruling elite.

This still requires an explanation for the disappearance of the native Genevans from these larger transactions. It may be helpful to recall that the expulsion of the Savoyard supporters and the sale of ecclesiastical holdings would have provided wealthy Genevans with many opportunities to increase their holdings. This would necessarily have consumed much of the available capital in Geneva. Thus by 1549, many wealthy Genevans may have found themselves enriched in lands and buildings but exhausted of liquid capital. The refugees, on the other hand, would have had little else except ready cash. A supporting example for this interpretation can be found in the case of François Favre. He made substantial purchases of seized properties after 1536 but found that he had overextended himself, and was forced to petition the Senate to reduce the agreed price of one of his latest purchases as he was unable to raise the necessary cash.[67] If this interpretation is correct, one can well understand the perceived threat of these refugees as well as their attractiveness. On one hand they were a substantial group of foreigners able to spend large sums of capital. Moreover they represented a great increase in the wealthier segment of the society generally. Undoubtedly, and understandably, this would have been a concern to many. But if the wealthy elite was short of cash then these refugees would have represented an ideal source of new money. Moreover, their spending would certainly have invigorated the local economy at every level.

Thus far, though, the discussion has emphasised the economic aspect of the refugee influx. It is also essential to examine the issue of social status. Tables 15, 16, and 17 show the results of an examination of the notary records to discover all those in Geneva who could lay some claim to a title. Obviously this gives no real idea of the relative importance of the titles and is certainly not an exhaustive list. Nevertheless, it does present results consistent with the findings of the economic impact of the refugees. Those

TABLE 16 *Genevan nobility before 1549*

Name (Title: Sieur de…)	Background
Bezanson Hugues (Perolles)	Geneva
Claude Baud (Troches)	Geneva (expelled with bishop)
Pierre Vandel (Sacconex)	father bg. from Lyon, 1487
Jean Chrestien (Rogemont)	Geneva
Jean Lect (Matignin)	father bg. from Germany, 1479
Antoine Lect (Cointrin)	father bg. from Germany, 1479
Perrin de la Mar (Vanzier)	? (Articulant, left Geneva)
Estienne de la Mar (Vanser & Boys)	Savoy (?)
Ayme Plonjon (Bellerue)	? (Articulant, left Geneva)
Michel Guilliet (Monthoux)	? (Mammeluc, left Geneva)
Jean François Bernard (Dardagny)	Geneva
Michel Roset (Marvel)	Geneva, grandfather bg. 1442
Julien Bourdan (Compeys)	father bg. from Lyon, 1512
Michel Varro (Brassu)	father bg. from Piedmont, 1539
Ami Varro (Chollex)	father bg. from Piedmont, 1521
François Dalinge (Montfort)	Savoy (?)
Philibert Dalinge (Coudrée)	Savoy (?)
François de la Valeyse (Brens)	?
Michel de Vorsière (Sererier)	?
François Bonivard (St Victor)	bg. 1537
Amblard Bonivard (Luynes & Grollier)	? (brother of François above)
Olivier de la Pomeraye (Montigny & Vergier près Laval, France)	France (?)
Bernardin de Navaselle (Vernier)	?
Charles de St Joire (Chapelle)	?
Jean Felix Hallemand (Vossrier)	German (?)
Louis Franc (Crest)	father bg. from Piedmont, 1511
Louis de Choudens (Aire-la-Ville)	father ducal/imperial notary from Ain
Pierre de la Thoit (Beaumont)	?
Antoine de St Michel (Avully)	Geneva (?)
? de Bonvillars (Mesieres)	Savoy (?)
François de Langin/Landin (Veygiez & Auteville)	Geneva/Savoy (?)
George de Langin/Landin (Auteville)	Geneva/Savoy (?)
François Champion (Battie-Beauregard)	?
Gabriel de Viry (Viry)	?
Loys de Mandallaz (Crois)	Savoy (?)
Jean de Serre (Chateauvieux de Nîmes)	France (?)
Louise, dua. of Antoine de Cusinens (Challes/Baron de Cursenod)	Geneva/Savoy (?)
Clauda, dau. of Robert de Montvuagnard (Boêge) widow of Boniface de St Michel (Avully)	Savoy (?) Geneva (?)
Louis Du Four (Bossey)	Ain
Michel de Vossenex (Eysierier)	?
Urbain Guisard (Crans)	Pays de Vaud

bg. = bourgeois

TABLE 17 *Nobles of indeterminate origin or date*

Presumed after 1549

Name (Title: Sieur de...)
Françoise, dau. of Sabin Yserand (Chevalle de Vienne)
François Depreztavel (Granges)
Jaques Bourgogne (Fallaix & Bredans)
Jean Arpaud (Troches de Lyon)
Bernardine, dau. of François de Senarclens (Dulich)
Adrien de Prignault (Villenougys & Tournay près Genève)
Magdelene Imbault, widow of Rogerin de Jouan (Jonvillars de Chartres)
Claude Gallatin (Granges)
François du Val (Colenes)
Françoise Brachet, widow of Guillaume Aubelin (La Bruyere)
Claude Ramus (Mirat)

Unknown Date

Name (Title: Sieur de...)	Background
Jeanne de Pesme (Dame Brandis), wife of François de Montmayeuz	?
Jean de Verdon (Etambieres)	Geneva/Savoy
Claude Dallier (Rosey)	?
Charles de Sellenove (Baron de Gailliard)	Savoy (?)
Gabriel de Villette (Songer)	Savoy (?)
Maryn Rossillyon (St Genys)	Ain
Mathieu Girbard (Farges)	Ain
Jean Darbier (Mondesirs) son-in-law of Amblard Rossillyon	Jura (?)
Claude Chastillyon (Chastillyon) brother-in-law of Maryn Rossillyon	Ain

people with titles who arrived after 1549 nearly double the pre-existent list. Also the *Bourse* donor list clearly implies a connection between the bourgeois with titles and those with money as do the results of the examination of the notary transactions.[68]

Moreover, those men with titles before 1549 were not always of political importance. Only Hugues, the Lects, the De la Mares, Plonjon, Bernard, Roset, the Varros, the Bonivards, Franc, and Du Four can safely be identified as magistrates.[69] Also, many in Table 16 were only first generation Genevans themselves, for example, Chrestien, the Lects and the

Varros.[70] At least five (the De la Mares, Baud, Plonjon, Guilliet) had already left the city as a result of previous political turmoil. Thus, while this group may have had some social prominence, its members were not necessarily politically active. It is apparent, though, that while this pre-existent titled group may not have been very active politically, they were just as likely to function as a group as the incoming prominent French refugees. A number of examples should suffice. Pierre de la Thoit was owed money by George de Langin, a debt witnessed by Urbain Guisard.[71] Guisard himself was involved in a transaction with Jaques, son of Claude Dallier, Sieur de Rosey.[72] Bernardin de Navasselle signed an accord with Pierre Vandel.[73] Also, Claude, daughter of Robert de Montvuagard married Boniface de St Michel, Sieur d'Avully.[74] Antoine de St Michel and Loys de Choudens were both tutors of Jean and François de Pesmes.[75] Finally, Claude de Chastillyon was given a receipt by Maryn de Rossillyon and his wife, Clauda de Chastillyon and Loys de Rossillyon, son and heir of Humberte de Chastillyon.[76] For the most part, Geneva's gentry confined their business affairs to the people living in the rural areas around their properties. On the few occasions, though, when they were involved in business dealings with prominent Genevans, these titled men tended to limit their activities to men of similar background.

The most interesting area of economic interaction, though, is that which involves native Genevans and the refugees. These can be divided into two groups, those involving local Genevan gentry and those involving other Genevans. A few examples need to be given of each, but it will be useful to comment upon the general results at the outset. First, for all practical purposes no transactions have been found involving French refugees and those local Genevans who would oppose Calvin in 1555. Also, those Genevans who do involve themselves in business with the refugees are often men who would prove to be the backbone of Calvin's local political supporters. Why this should be is obviously open to speculation, but there can be no doubt that the economic ties between Calvin's local supporters and the refugees gave the former group added incentive for defending the rights of the French against their local opponents.

The examples of contact between Genevan gentry and prominent refugees are few but illustrate the sort of relationship which existed. François de Valeyse sold the revenues of some of his holdings to Jaques de St Martin for three years. The contract was witnessed in the house of Jean Ami Curtet, a staunch supporter of Calvin, by Curtet, Charles de Brichanteau and Leon Colladon.[77] A similar sale of revenues was made by George de Landin to Jaques de Bourgogne.[78] It appears that the local gentry were willing to sell future revenues in return for the immediate cash which the refugees could offer. Also, the refugees seem to have been interested in acquiring a local source of income. The contacts between prominent refugees and politically important local Genevans are also relatively few. Claude du Pan owed money to Charles de Brichanteau.[79] Also, Jaques de Bourgogne, Sieur de Fallaix, gave a receipt of payment to François Ramel.[80] In addition, Louis Franc, a prominent Genevan and supporter of Calvin, signed a procuration with Estienne Trembley.[81] Appendix 11 has already shown the property sale between François Chevallier and Anthoine Lautrec. The house sale between Jean Louis Ramel and Loys Tembley has been mentioned as well.

In general, the refugees appear to have functioned in a very self-contained manner. When they did conduct business with local Genevans, they limited their activities for the most part to the purchase of revenues from Genevan gentry and business deals or property purchases from local persons who supported Calvin and the French. The limited nature of the transactions between Genevans and the French must have served to increase tensions to some extent, in that the French may have been perceived to be a separate community within Geneva.[82] At the same time the general increase in cash in the Genevan economy would have seemed a blessing to others. Together, these factors must have made the Genevan response to the refugees highly ambivalent.

It is hoped that this rather arcane and detailed economic analysis has demonstrated the extent to which the city found itself in a difficult situation. Hospitality and religious sympathy inclined the Genevans to assist the refugees, rich and poor, but their sheer numbers often alarmed and overwhelmed the city. The social and economic benefits of accepting the foreigners, especially the wealthy nobles, had to be balanced carefully against the political threat they posed to the citizens. One can see, then, how the assimilation of strangers into Geneva could easily become a contentious issue. Both sides realised that the French bourgeois would be inclined, for ethnic and religious reasons, to support Calvin. Thus they became entwined in the struggles between the ministers and the magistrates. Indeed, they often became the issue at the heart of the disputes.

It is not surprising, then, to see that 1551–52 was dominated by a debate over the proposed limitations to bourgeois rights.[83] Even while Geneva was unable to resolve this issue, the city was able to continue to work to control the new residents. The magistrates strove to enforce the decrees on registration. The regulations regarding merchant activity were re-stated.[84] As before, all new strangers were ordered to take personal oaths to the magistrates.[85] But in the end, those who favoured limits on bourgeois rights failed to convince their fellow-citizens. They were only able to get the bourgeois ministers banned from the General Assembly.[86] A desire to exclude these men, educated, respected, and trained as public speakers is understandable. But this provoked such heated debate that within a month, in April 1553, Berne was led to ask for a detailed explanation of the situation.[87] The city responded to this and the mounting pressure by re-issuing all previous legislation designed to control resident aliens.[88] Never-theless, those opposed to the French were forced to remain silent until the events of 1555 as they were wholly unsuccessful in their attempt to limit bourgeois rights.[89]

The issue of bourgeois admissions and rights seems to have died down before the first part of 1554. This may well be, as one can see from Figures 3 and 4, because the magistrates severely restricted the number of new bourgeois admissions. Nevertheless, another unsuccessful debate had been held in October 1554.[90] It is interesting to see, in the light of the concern over bourgeois rights, that Geneva was still willing, in May 1554, to grant settlement rights in a rural parish to 400 families from Provence.[91] Of course this did not require that they be given any civic rights but did increase city revenues through taxation. This again highlights the different responses the city had to poor strangers who posed no serious political threat and the wealthier, socially more prominent refugees. But in 1555, Calvin's supporters won the elections by a majority of one: they moved swiftly to consolidate their power. As has been discussed, the method they chose to consolidate their power was to admit a large number of French religious refugees as bourgeois. These could be relied upon to support Calvin and his local, political supporters. In an apparent attempt to allay suspicions the Senate decreed that all the money collected would go to repaying part of Geneva's onerous debt.[92]

It is true that a great deal of money was raised and that the price of civic rights was high. But no one, especially not Calvin's opponents, was fooled. They protested on 13 May 1555 and the matter was referred to the Conseil des Deux Cents.[93] On 16 May a riotous protest was used as an excuse to move against Calvin's opponents.[94] Many were arrested or fled. On 27 May a rump Conseil des Deux Cents voted to accept the Senate's actions in admitting so many bourgeois and confirmed the new men in their civic rights.[95] By July a depleted Senate, only thirteen of twenty-five members, voted to condemn Perrin, Calvin's chief opponent,[96] who had last been in the Senate on 24 May.[97] In September, the Conseil des Deux Cents, by now purged of many of those opposed to the French, even gave the Senate the right to arm individual habitants in emergency situations.[98] Two weeks later a new oath was administered binding the foreigners specifically to the city and the magistrates and all strangers, even those already sworn in Geneva, were compelled to take it.[99]

These events will need to be discussed in greater detail below, but there can be little doubt that the actions of Calvin's supporters in admitting these refugees was at its heart a blatant political attempt to pack the electorate. Even Calvin, in July 1555, acknowledged this when he wrote to Bullinger that his opponents had protested against the new bourgeois because 'the worthless felt how much more secure the party of the good would be rendered by this assistance'.[100] In the context of a discussion of the role of the French in Geneva this must be the important point. They represented an alien element in Genevan society and politics. Economically and socially they were very prominent and potentially they could be a political power base for any faction in Geneva willing to embrace them wholeheartedly.[101] It must be remembered that Calvin's local supporters could rely on these new French bourgeois, secure in the knowledge that, as citizens, they alone would command the highest offices.

Thus, one can trace the tumultuous record of Geneva's relations with its foreigners. The city faced difficulties on a number of levels. The large number of poor refugees strained the city's resources and charity. A significant number of talented foreign merchants placed many locals at an economic disadvantage and threatened the established business patterns of Geneva. Prominent strangers appeared to be a likely source of revenue but the power they gained as bourgeois was a worry to many. Finally, once the French ministers fell out with leading civic officials, they became a constant source of annoyance and convenient whipping-boys for anti-French sentiments.

The sheer scale of the problems faced by Geneva because of its foreigners, as well as the existence of an increasingly cohesive group of citizens who supported the French refugees and ministers for religious or economic reasons, meant that the xenophobic defenders of local Genevan rights stood little chance of stemming the tide. This became patently obvious when they failed to convince the Assembly to limit bourgeois rights in 1551. The comment of François Daniel Berthelier, made not long before his execution for his part in the riot of 16 May 1555, adequately summarises what must have been the opinion of many Genevans. This son of the martyr of Geneva's struggle for independence from Savoy said 'adieu Geneve, a la fin, le Roi de France sera bourgeois de cette ville'.[102] In view of the number of French immigrants admitted, one could forgive an alienated local inhabitant such elegant hyperbole.

NOTES

1   AEG/RC/34, fols. 3v–4 (6 Jan 1540).
2   The city also cared for seventy-two regular pensioners. Lescaze, *Sauver*, p. 24.
3   Innes, *Social Concerns*, p. 132.
4   By 1550 the population of Geneva had risen to between 12,400 and 13,893 but would balloon to around 21,400 by 1560. Perrenoud, *Population*, pp. 24, 30, 37.
5   AEG/RC/36, fol. 190 (12 Dec 1542). Roset, p. 297, dates the start of large-scale immigration to Geneva from France to this year.
6   Innes, *Social Concerns*, p. 133.
7   AEG/RC/37, fol. 83v (4 May 1543).
8   AEG/RC/37, fol. 187v (10 Aug 1543).
9   AEG/RC/37, fol. 111 (1 Jun 1543).
10 AEG/RC/37, fol. 138 (26 Jun 1543).
11 AEG/RC/37, fol. 148 (9 Jul 1543).
12 AEG/RC/37, fols. 171v (6 Aug 1543), 199 (21 Aug 1543).
13 AEG/RC/37, fols. 211v (3 Sep 1543), 234 (1 Oct 1543), 248v (22 Oct 1543).
14 AEG/RC/38, fol. 152v (7 Apr 1544).
15 AEG/RC/40, fol. 59v (20 Mar 1545); RC/39, fols. 37 (13 Nov 1544), 46 (18 Nov 1544).
16 AEG/RC/40, fols. 54v–55 (18–19 Mar 1545).
17 AEG/RC/40, fol. 66v (27 Mar 1545).
18 AEG/RC/40, fol. 114 (14 May 1545). The city sent 10 écus. This was not an isolated event; on 25 April 1543, an unspecified amount of money had been sent to aid those who were being persecuted in Mex in Lorraine (AEG/RC/37, fol. 71).
19 Innes, *Social Concerns*, p. 133.
20 AEG/RC/40, fol. 149 (15 Jun 1545).
21 AEG/RC/40, fol. 268 (20 Oct 1545).
22 AEG/RC/40, fol. 300v (23 Nov 1545).
23 AEG/RC/43, fol. 265v (17 Dec 1548); RC/47, fol. 50 (6 Apr 1553), RC/52, fol. 20v (25 Sep 1556).
24 AEG/RC/42, fol. 194 (1 Aug 1547); RC/44, fol. 45v (15 Mar 1549); RC/46, fol. 316 (1 Dec 1552); RC/48, fol. 153 (27 Nov 1554); RC/49, fols. 142v (26 Jul 1555), 179 (9 Sep 1555).
25 AEG/RC/42, fol. 128 (3 Jun 1547).
26 AEG/RC/30, fol. 199 (27 Mar 1537).
27 AEG/RC/30, fol. 248 (4 Jun 1537).
28 AEG/RC/33, fol. 122 (13 May 1539, 2nd ser.).
29 AEG/RC/34, fol. 547 (6 Dec 1540).
30 AEG/RC/36, fol. 88 (7 Aug 1542).
31 AEG/RC/37, fol. 22 (23 Feb 1543).
32 AEG/RC/37, fols. 286–286v (4 Dec 1543).
33 AEG/RC/38, fol. 152 v (7 Apr 1544). A similar ambivalence was apparent in Lyons's reception of foreign merchants, cf., N. Z. Davis, 'The Sacred and the Body Social in Sixteenth-Century Lyon', in *Past and Present*, 1981 (90), pp. 46f.
34 AEG/RC/38, fol. 259 v (20 Jun 1544).
35 *Bourg.*, p. 222 (27 May 1541).
36 *Bourg.*, p, 242 (Crespin, 2 May 1555); p. 244 (Badius, 17 Oct 1555).
37 *Habit.*, p. 5 (Baduis, 17 Jun 1550); p. 13 (Crespin, 25 Aug 1551). Monter, *Government*, pp. 24f., stresses the importance of the immigrant artisans, especially the printers, on Geneva's economy. See also, Perrenoud, *Population*, p. 189, and Babel, *Histoire Economique*, pp. 170f.

38 AEG/RC/38, fol. 274v (4 Jul 1544).

39 AEG/RC/38, fol. 293 (18 Jul 1544).

40 AEG/RC/40, fol. 28v (19 Feb 1545). The admission of the printers above is another example. Such behaviour was not new for Geneva. In the three decades before the Revolution there seems to have been a concerted attempt to attract goldsmiths to Geneva; eight were made bourgeois. Babel, *Histoire Economique*, p. 104.

41 AEG/RC/41, fols. 151 (21 Jul 1546), 153 (26 Jul 1546); RC/43, fol. 16v (13 Feb 1548).

42 Roget, *Histoire,* vol. 3, pp. 104f. They began to buy or rent many of the fifty-five large homes in the centre of Geneva (of ninety-one houses) which had remained vacant since 1537. E. W. Monter, 'De l'Evêché à la Rome Protestante', in P. Guichonnet, ed., *Histoire de Genève* (Lausanne: 1974), pp. 166f.

43 M. Sauty, 'Le Premier Refuge', in *La Tribune de Genève* (Geneva: 1942), pp. 10, 12. Later, English and Scottish exiles would arrive in Geneva. They were granted, along with the Italians, their own church. However, these groups were never large enough to constitute a threat to Geneva's ruling elite.

44 AEG/RC/44, fols. 35 (5 Mar 1549), 37 (8 Mar 1549).

45 AEG/RC/44, fol. 48v (19 Mar 1549).

46 Similar concerns troubled Lyon, where a few major Lyonnais families, allied with some prominent foreigners, provided the backbone of the Protestant movement which was led by a predominantly non-Lyonnais ministry. Davis, 'Lyon', pp. 48f.

47 AEG/RC/44, fols. 74–74v (22 Apr 1549).

48 AEG/RC/44, fol. 77 (23 Apr 1549). At other times rumours were spread that the French religious refugees were to receive a pardon if they handed Geneva over to the King. Gautier, *Histoire*, vol. 1, pp. 533f.

49 AEG/RC/44, fol. 87 (3 May 1549).

50 AEG/RC/44, fol. 352v (3 Apr 1550).

51 AEG/RC/44, fol. 352v (3 Apr 1550).

52 AEG/RC/45, fol. 184 (6 Feb 1551). It is unclear whether the initial proposal would have disenfranchised all bourgeois or just new ones. In either case, its acceptance would have established the precedent whereby the Petit Conseil, comprised wholly of citizens, felt competent to propose limitations on bourgeois rights.

53 AEG/RC/45, fols. 217v (7 Mar 1551), 221–222v (12 Mar 1551), 226v (17 Mar 1551).

54 Monter, 'Demography', p. 409.

55 Monter, 'Demography', p. 411.

56 These unions were of important financial value as well. For example the work of Dewald, *Nobility*, pp. 129ff., has suggested that under normal circumstances in France the dowries for the gentry would have been around £t 1,320 (livres tournois) (*c.* 9,240 ff.).

57 AEG/Min/J. L. Blecheret, vol. 2, fols. 357v (3 Sep 1555), 382 (25 Jan 1555) are contracts with St Martin while fol. 380 (26 Sep 1555) relates to St Pierre.

58 AEG/Min/J. Ragueau, vol. 1, fol. 34 (6 Apr 1557).

59 AEG/Min/C. Pyu, vol. 1, fol. 411 (8 Sep 1551).

60 AEG/Min/J. Ragueau, vol. 1, fol. 34 (6 Apr 1557).

61 AEG/Min/M. Try, vol. 7, fol. 312 (7 Jan 1553). Dewald, *Nobility*, pp. 238f., found that at Rouen borrowing and lending were very closely connected to family and sociopolitical ties. Brady, *Strasbourg*, p. 41, emphasises that 'family' can encompass ties of blood, marriage, and business.

62 Olson, *Bourse*, pp. 120–6. It has been possible to identify twenty-eight (of fifty-one) of the nobles from (or presumed) after 1549 with donors. Also at least five ministers (Bourgoing, Calvin, Cop, Morel, St André) also appear as donors. Of the people listed

before 1549 (or unknown) only Michel Varro can be identified with certainty as a donor. I am indebted to Karin Maag, who is researching Calvinist educational institutions, for pointing out AEG/Instruction Publique A1, Livre des Affaires du Collège, which shows that after the 1559 establishment of the Genevan Academy many of these same refugees were its benefactors.

63 For the purposes of these comparisons it has been assumed that 1 écu= 5 Genevan florins (ff), or 10 sols of a livre tournois (£t), or 4.5 testons. For fuller discussions (and to see how these approximations were arrived at) see J. Meuvret, 'Monetary Circulation and the Economic Utilization of Money in 16th- and 17th Century France', in R. Cameron, ed., *Essays in French Economic History* (Homewood, Ill.: 1970), p. 144; P. Chaunu and R. Gescon, *Histoire Economique et Sociale de la France* (Paris: 1977), p. 280. Also Frank Spooner, *The International Economy and Monetary Movements in France 1493–1725* (Cambridge, Mass.: 1972), pp. 130–8, and 'Monetary Disturbance and Inflation 1590– 1593: the case of Aix-en-Provence', in *Histoire Economique du Monde Méditerranéen Mélanges en l'Honneur de Fernand Braduel* (Toulouse: 1973), p. 588.

64 Perhaps a sign of how this wealth might have been brought to Geneva can be found in the earlier case of Jaques Lievre, dit Jacob, who was hoste de St Loup. He was arrested for forcing the wife of François Champion, Sieur of Batie-Beauregard, a local aristocrat, to open his safe which was full of jewellery and silver. AEG/PC/1re Ser., 358 (21 Jun 1541). B. Diefendorf, *Beneath the Cross: Catholics and Huguenots in Sixteenth-Century Paris* (Oxford: 1991), p. 101, recounts the search of a Protestant house to find a trunk rumoured to contain over 4,000 écus (20,000ff). If the wealthy refugees arrived with similar trunks they would have been wealthy indeed by Genevan standards.

65 AEG/Min/J. Ragueau, vol. 2, fol. 52 (28 Sep 1556, a procuration from Louis Franc); J. Ragueau, vol. 1, fols. 2v (10 Sep 1556, François Besson owed £t 306 11s 3d), 13 (21 Oct 1556, Loys Rebones owed 890ff 3s), 13v (24 Oct 1556, Jean Rey owed 448ff 10s 1d), 17 (14 Nov 1556, Pierre du Chable owed 612ff 8s 4d), 26v (Jean Rumillie, habitant, owed £t 89 3s 6d to Trembley and Germain Colladon); P. du Verney, vol. 2, fol. 42 (31 Oct 1553, accord with J. de la Maisonneuve).

66 Brady, *Strasbourg*, p. 96.

67 He purchased a house confiscated from a certain Leschacgnier for approximately 5,000ff which he was unable to pay. See AEG/RC/31, fols. 33v (19 Jun 1537), 78 (25 Oct 1537), 118 (26 Nov 1537).

68 Dewald, *Nobility*, pp. 115f., gives some idea of the wealth of French magistrates and nobles. In the 1540s a magistrate would have had an income of around £t. 2,000–3,000 (*c.* 14,000–21,000ff) and an estate worth around £t. 40,000 (*c.* 280,000ff).

69 Some were powerful through their very size. The three Varro brothers Pierre (bourgeois, 13 Dec 1521), Michel, the elder (bgs., 19 Sep 1530), and Louis (bgs., 10 Jun 1539) were very well connected (*Bourg.*, pp. 193, 206, 219). Pierre's daughter, Domaine, married Pierre Ruffi, the Petit Conseil's secretary. Michel's daughters, Anne and Sara, married Jean du Molard and Jean de l'Arche, respectively.

70 Louis du Four (died 1561) was not even a citizen. He was admitted as a bourgeois on 14 October 1524. He was a commissaire of the Duke of Savoy. *Bourg.*, p. 201.

71 AEG/Min/A. Babel, vol. 2, fol. 163 (11 May 1551).

72 AEG/Min/A. Babel, vol. 1, fol. 344 (2 Apr 1550).

73 AEG/Min/C. de Compois, vol. 13, fol. 13 (8 Aug 1540).

74 AEG/Min/C. Pyu, vol. 4, fol. 107 (her testament, 29 Mar 1554).

75 AEG/Min/C. Jaccon, fol. 29 (7 Feb 1557)

76 AEG/Min/J. L. Blecheret, vol. 2, fol. 289 (21 Apr 1555).

77 AEG/Min/M. Try, vol. 7, fol. 274 (6 May 1552).

78 AEG/Min/C. Pyu, vol. 1, fol. 368 (1550/51).

79 AEG/Min/P. Alliod, vol. 1, fol. 18v (1 Mar 1555).

80 AEG/Min/C. Pyu, vol. 4, fol. 11v (18 Apr 1552).

81 AEG/Min/J. Ragueau, vol. 2, fol. 52 (28 Sep 1556).

82 K. Neuschel, *Honor*, pp. 76f., stresses the tendency of groups to identify their community along rather exclusive lines whether of class, ethnicity or linguistic, especially among the French nobility. A. D. M. Pettegree, *Foreign Protestant Communities* (Oxford: 1986) found that the Dutch refugees in England were the object of hostility because they were perceived as trading only among themselves and thereby harming the local (i.e. English) merchants. A similar phenomenon is reported in H. Schilling, *Niederländische Exultanten im 16 Jahrhundert. Ihre Stellung im Socialgefüge und im religiösen Leben deutscher und englischer Städt* (Gütersloh: 1972).

83 AEG/RC/46, fols. 277 (26 Sep 1552), 293v (25 Oct 1552).

84 AEG/RC/46, fols. 42 (21 Aug 1551), 46v (27 Aug 1551).

85 AEG/RC/46, fols. 51v (4 Sep 1551), 57v (14 Sep 1551).

86 AEG/RC/47, fol. 37v (16 Mar 1553).

87 AEG/RC/47, fol. 52v (10 Apr 1553).88

88 AEG/RC/47, fols. 53v–54v (11 Apr 1553).

89 Roget, *Histoire*, vol. 4. p. 170, n. 1.

90 AEG/RC/48, fols. 138v–139v (25 Oct 1554).

91 Roget, *Histoire*, vol. 4, p. 170 (n. 1).

92 AEG/RC/49, fol. 63v (2 May 1555)

93 AEG/RC/49, fol. 74 (13 May 1555)

94 AEG/RC/49, fol. 78 (16 May 1555).

95 AEG/RC/49, fol. 88v (27 May 1555).

96 Roget, *Histoire*, vol. 4, p. 280, n. 1.

97 AEG/RC/49, fol. 84 (24 May 1555).

98 AEG/RC/49, fols. 180–180v (10 Sep 1555)

99 AEG/RC/49, fols. 188v–189v (23 Sep 1555).

100 CO, vol. 15, col. 683f (to Bullinger, 15 Jul 1555).

101 Cf., Monter, *Government*, p. 121.

102 Roget, *Histoire*, vol. 4, p. 235.

The Company of Pastors: ministers or masters?

Ces precheurs nous iniurient mais nous ne nen endurerons plus

Many causes have been offered as explanations for the opposition Calvin faced in Geneva. Calvin's detractors have emphasised a theocratic dictatorship and a moral reign of terror. His supporters have viewed Calvin's Genevan opponents as Libertines, men of loose morals and lacking in religious zeal. Recently, arguments have been put forth stressing the struggle between Calvin and some magistrates to control the power of excommunication. It has also been suggested that the trouble in Geneva was that legislation on morals, which was to be found on the statute-books of many other places too, was actually applied in Geneva and, to the dismay of some in Geneva's ruling class, was applied in an even-handed manner. However, a careful re-examination of the records of the Genevan councils, criminal courts and Consistory has produced some results which seem to call into question these prevalent views.

It is commonly accepted that Calvin was no theocratic totalitarian. Nor was he the last bastion against rampant immorality in Geneva. Also, though they may have been important, complaints against the rigorous application of morals legislation or disputes over excommunication are rarely articulated as separate issues. Rather, there were two complaints commonly voiced by the native Genevans. Most frequently they protested against the increasing size and influence of the French refugee community. Second, many Genevans registered their resentment of the ministers' attempt to ban certain traditional given names. The role and importance of the refugees has already been discussed above. But the question of baptismal names which previous scholars have repeatedly overlooked or downplayed is also worthy of examination.[1] Research in the Genevan manuscripts has shown that this issue was of much greater import than has been recognised. In addition, this controversy, as will be shown, became inseparably linked with the protest against the French.

Reaction against Geneva's baptismal policy was a constant issue in the city. But the debate has attracted the attention of historians only twice. The first outbreak of protest, in 1546, involving Ami Chappuis, is related

TABLE 18   *Genevan baptismal names (%)*

		Pre-Reform	1550–55	1560–70	1602–15
Boys' names	Saints	43.3	18.7	3.2	16.3
	New Testament	54.6	62.1	64.1	63.8
	Old Testament	2.1	19.2	32.7	19.9
	Total biblical	56.7	81.3	96.8	83.7
Girls' names	Saints	49.0	12.5	1.8	14.0
	New Testament	47.8	69.4	70.4	64.6
	Old Testament	3.2	18.1	27.8	21.4
	Total biblical	51.0	87.5	98.2	86.0

in most of the early secondary sources. The second coincides with Calvin's only mention of the problem in his letters. In 1552 he wrote to Dryander that a riot had erupted in church when he refused a name offered by a sponsor. In the midst of the tumult he proceeded with the baptism, supplying a name to his own liking. This riot involved Philibert Berthelier, one of Calvin's chief opponents.[2] Because the earlier historians were more interested in events which involved prominent persons, or the beginning of a problem, these two affairs are the ones usually highlighted. In some case the matter is not discussed at all.[3]

It appears that later historians have taken their lead from Calvin and the earlier scholars and assumed that an issue so rarely mentioned was of little import. Consequently, it is usually given the same space as the affair of the slashed breeches, another debate in the 1540s which is usually mentioned only because it involved Ami Perrin. But, while the latter event was indeed a singular affair, the resistance to the banning of certain names was persistent. Moreover, a number of other well-known cases have been found to have entailed, at their start, a dispute over this very issue. Thus, while Calvin and later historians may have considered this a minor matter, it will become apparent that many Genevans believed it was very serious indeed.

The ministers wanted to ban in Geneva certain given names which they considered to be vestiges of Catholic superstition. They hoped to eliminate names associated with the Godhead, such as Jesus, as well as names for feast-days, for example, Pentecost. They also suppressed names which they considered unbiblical such as Gaspard, Melchior and Balthazar, the names of the Wise Men. Finally, they wanted to prohibit names associated with local saints such as Claude and Martin.[4] They wanted to eradicate Claude especially, as the saint's shrine was near Geneva, although it was the third most common name for boys and girls in Geneva.[5] Table 18 shows the extent to which they were able, for a time, to change the pattern of given names in Geneva. Indeed Claude disappeared altogether.[6] The ministers hoped and demanded that only names approved by Scripture should be used.[7] The immediate result, though, was that many Genevans faced public humiliation at the hands of their foreign ministers during baptisms. They were told, before the whole church, that their names were proscribed symbols of sinful Catholic superstitions.[8] It is important to remember that the ministers who thought these traditional Genevan names were superstitious were not themselves Genevans but rather French immigrants.

The most striking element at the beginning of this controversy is that the ministers moved to implement their policy without the advice or consent of the magistrates. The crisis began on 26 August 1546. Ami Chappuis, a barber, presented his son for baptism. The unknown sponsor gave the child's name as 'Claude'. The minister, who is also unknown, promptly, and without warning, baptised the child 'Abraham'. The father then grabbed the child back and said that no true baptism had taken place and that he would let his son wait until he was fifteen years old and could pick his own name.[10] At the same time, the congregation was swept with a 'great and scandalous commotion' as people protested against this act of ministerial arrogance.[11] The next day the ministers were called to explain themselves before the Petit Conseil, Geneva's supreme governing body. After consultation, the magistrates agreed to ban 'Claude' because of the proximity of the saint's shrine.[12] It appears, though, that the magistrates had no idea of the far-reaching interpretation the ministers would put on this decision.

Less than three months later, in November 1546, another riot occurred. Once again a child was named despite the objections of the father and sponsor. On this occasion it is unclear whether the original name was Martin or Ayme.[13] In either case, within a week another conference was held with the magistrates. At this time the ministers expanded their list to include Ayme, Martin and Mama as well as Claude.[14] The magistrates accepted this, though they demanded that the ministers prepare a specific and detailed list of names to be proscribed before they would make any additional rulings.[15] They had no intention of giving the ministers *carte blanche* to refuse baptismal names. The magistrates must have realised that a list was necessary if there was to be any hope of avoiding a recurrence of the riotous disturbances.

February and March 1547 saw the first strong public reactions against this new policy.[16] The magistrates now started to show some hesitation over the matter. The problem was that the ministers wanted the same civil actions to be taken against those who opposed them on this issue as for those who broke other Genevan laws. Thus, they wanted excommunication and civil sanctions to be applied against those whom the ministers felt were guilty of rioting, disobedience and insolence. The magistrates were disturbed by the involvement of a number of prominent citizens in the debate. Likewise there was concern as the whole affair began to be associated with xenophobic resentment towards the French ministers. The specific case which sparked the magistrates' re-evaluation of the policy occurred in February when Martin du Molard, a member of one of Geneva's most prominent families, threatened a minister who had refused to use 'Martin' as a baptismal name.[17] A week later a certain Claude Piaget had his name rejected as well despite his strenuous protests.[18] Another Genevan, André Furby, was also charged as a result of his protest over the minister's action. It is perhaps significant that Furby does not appear to have been directly involved in the baptism itself.[19] The matter had reached the point at which bystanders from the general populace felt obliged to become involved.

This crisis then became entwined in the first clash between the ministers and magistrates over the use of excommunication. Some people may be surprised to hear that this issue was raised as early as 1547. Indeed, this very serious early debate is too often overlooked. The General Assembly was consulted over the proper role of the ministers.[20] As a result the ministers were told that they had exceeded their authority.[21] This appears to be directly related to the Consistory's attempt to punish those responsible for the disturbances at the baptisms. Three prominent members of the Petit Conseil, Girardin de la Rive, Amblard Corne and François Beguin, were deputed to admonish the ministers to keep their place and to obey the edicts.[22] The next day, 29 March 1547, the ministers objected and demanded the right to apply excommunication whenever they felt necessary.[23] They were told, though, that 'les ministres ne layct a dire synon bonnes admonitions joux la parolle de dieu'.[24] While this may have circumscribed ministerial power to some extent it certainly did nothing to limit the ministers' zeal for applying only biblical names at baptism. Thus, in June 1547 Calvin complained that someone in a rural parish had tried to use 'Claude'.[25] In September, a certain Claude de la Ravoyre was admonished by the Consistory for trying to name his child after himself. He begged forgiveness, saying that he had erred out of an ignorance of the new regulations.[26]

One must wonder why the magistrates supported this obviously divisive policy. In part it may be because the ministers had acted before consulting the magistrates. In consequence the Petit Conseil would have been forced either to support their ministers or to side with those who had caused a public riot. Also, by the start of this debate the Company of Pastors in Geneva had become a unified group of experienced, prestigious, forceful preachers such as François Bourgoing, Nicolas des Gallars, Michel Cop, Reymond Chauvet, and especially, Calvin. Thus Geneva's leaders would have had a certain unwillingness after so many years of turmoil in the Genevan Church to engage in a contest of strength with the ministers. Moreover, once the magistracy had conceded the right to forbid some names, from a list drawn up by the ministers, their ability to control ministerial action in this area was highly limited. Finally, many might well have accepted the logic of banning certain names associated with Catholic practices, and this too would have served to undermine magisterial objections.

In the summer of 1548, the dispute became more serious. For the first time very prominent Genevans, even magistrates, began to protest against this policy. On 31 May 1548, Michel Cop refused to baptise a child 'Balthazar'.[27] The father, one André, denied the validity of the baptism.[28] In anger he called the minister 'a thief who had stolen chalices from a monastery and a usurer'.[29] Nicolas Gentil, the châtelain, or Genevan-appointed magistrate of the rural parish of Jussy, declared that 'we will endure no more' and that 'the foreigners rule everything'.[30] The case also involved Jean Baptiste Sept, the sponsor.[31] His father, Michel Sept, had been one of the leaders of the Guillermin faction which had recalled Calvin from exile in 1541. The secretary of the Petit Conseil, Philibert Berthelier, also complained about Cop's action.[32] Jean Blanc, the father's brother-in-law, also joined the protest.[33] This list of participants shows the active involvement of prominent Genevans. The witnesses against them are also interesting. All were foreigners: Monsieur de Cre, Pierre Borrette, Jean du Nast, a French aristocrat, and Pierre Renault, a bookseller.[34] Calvin also joined this group by protesting to the Petit Conseil.[35] He specifically charged Jean Baptiste Sept with insolence.[36] Thus Calvin became embroiled in a personal dispute with these men as well as in the debate over the baptismal names.

Two more cases followed in quick succession. Jaques Pechaud, a pâtissier was not allowed to baptise his child 'Claude'.[37] He said he preferred to leave without the baptism. Indeed, he demanded that the minister, Des Gallars, hand the child back immediately. Des Gallars baptised the child anyway, supplying a name he considered more suitable.[38] When admonished before the Consistory Pechaud apologised and said that he had not been aware of the relevant edicts.[39] In some way not quite clear, Berthelier seems to have been involved in this case for Calvin had cause to complain about his conduct to the Petit Conseil.[40] The second case involved Jean Bandière, a member of another prominent family. As sponsor he put forward a name which the minister, Reymond Chauvet, refused.[41] The event remained a source of dispute for days afterwards. The words of the two Genevans admonished for their public complaints about the case display the strength of the reaction against the ministers. Guygonne Revenderessa was heard in the street telling Bandière that she would have given Chauvet 'two thumps' for refusing the name.[42] The other Genevan, Pierre Berthet, said that Bandière should have 'grabbed Chauvet by the hair and dragged him out of his pulpit chair'.[43] Instead, Berthet was dragged before the Consistory where he quickly confessed and apologised.[44] It was not until three weeks later, though, that Consistorial pressure was able to force Revenderessa to repent.[45]

What one sees is the blending of Genevan resentment of the French and their dislike of these baptismal edicts. For their part, the French ministers seem to have been unable or unwilling to appreciate the anger of many of the Genevans at the banning of traditional names. Without a doubt this served to increase the tensions between native Genevans and the religious refugees. This situation could only worsen as more French arrived and the local populace was placed under greater stress. As long as this baptismal policy continued it was also an obvious focal point for protests against the increase of French influence in the city.

The city records show that there was no serious recurrence of this problem until February 1550. However, one must not be tempted to conclude that the problem had been resolved. It seems that disruptions continued to occur and that tempers were still running high. Indeed, in June 1549, Calvin went so far as to say that if the situation did not improve it would be necessary to post guards at baptisms to keep order.[46] He made the same complaint six months later in January 1550.[47] These complaints, coupled with the lack of specific cases, seem to imply that no major riots had occurred but that the baptismal policy was still a very sensitive and divisive issue. In February 1550 the controversy broke out anew in the rural parish of Jussy. Claude Pitard wanted the minister, St André, to baptise his child 'Claude'. The minister admonished him, explaining that the magistrates had proscribed the name. Claude's insolent response resulted in his being called before the Consistory. There, whether from ignorance or pique, he said that if his 'name wasn't any good would it please messieurs to give him another one'. He was arrested for this comment and eventually forced to repent. This case illustrates the humiliation, frustration, and confusion felt by many Genevans when told, in public, that they had sinful, unacceptable names.[48]

In March 1550 the debate became explosive with the arrest of Louis

Bandière.[49] He was the son of Ami Bandière, a Syndic in 1535 and 1541 and a member of the Petit Conseil from 1536 until his death in 1544. Louis was a brother-in-law of François Daniel Berthelier, the son of the martyr of Genevan independence, who was later executed for his part in the riot against Calvin in 1555. Bandière was also related by marriage to the important Hugue and Chapeaurouge families. He was arrested for an anti-French outburst arising from the ongoing baptismal controversy. By this stage, it is hardly surprising to find that he was accused by Charles de St Marie, the servant of Charles de Brichanteau, Sieur de St Laurent, a prominent refugee.[50] This case is a clear example of how the dispute over baptismal names was becoming increasingly interlocked with the growing ethnic tensions between important native Genevans and the socially more prominent elements in the French refugee community. Once again an aggrieved Genevan had responded by attacking the French. Bandière was accused of saying, 'God take the preachers; they've consumed their goods and lands in France and want to take over here.'[51] Further, he said: 'The Devil can take all the foreigners; they can go and eat their God of paste elsewhere', and 'the foreigners want to rule over us.'[52] At this point he was admonished by Bertrand Roz, the servant of the former Syndic Henry Aubert. Roz said: 'The French are good people and haven't come to rule over us and they ought to be left in peace.' Bandière responded to this timely admonition by punching Roz.[53] But they were not the only participants. The wife of Mathieu Canard, a member of the lower council, said: 'Curse the French; let them go eat their God of paste in their own country.'[54] Eventually, Bandière was forced to apologise.[55]

This case exposes the crucial, underlying complaint. Many Genevans saw this baptismal policy as an attempt to force a foreign practice upon them. These were not citizens attached to Catholic superstitions but people who strongly resented being forbidden, by foreigners, from giving their children traditional, family names. The ministers, though, deemed these Genevans to be disobedient people who refused to be governed by the Church and God's Word. Since the vast majority of the knowledge one has about Geneva comes from ministerial sources, it is not surprising that Calvin's Genevan opponents have been portrayed as people unwilling to accept discipline and good order. It is doubtful whether the Genevans saw discipline and order as the issue at stake. Rather they feared and resented the attempt by the French, as they saw it, to usurp authority and dictate to them, the citizens and rightful masters of Geneva.

This division in Genevan society between some local Genevans and the French is even more apparent in the next major clash which occurred six months later in September 1550. Gaspard Favre, Perrin's brother-in-law, and Balthazar Sept were arrested for causing a disturbance at another baptism. This service involved the nephew of André Mailliard, a Genevan judge and former member of the Petit Conseil. Equally as significant as the involvement of these prominent Genevans is the list of the witnesses against them. All six were French.[56] Sept protested that he had done nothing, rather, 'maistre Jean Calvin avoir faict grand scandale et insolence et qu'il troublier l'eglise'. In his mind it was the behaviour of the ministers which was at fault.[57] The ministers, for their part, continued to demand that the magistrates act to prevent these disturbances.[58] The end of 1550 evidenced a hardening of the protests against the ministers and their baptismal policy. Jean Bandière was admonished because he refused to go to sermons.[59] Balthazar Sept and Jean Cugniet walked out during a baptismal service and were brought before the Consistory as a result.[60] Cugniet was also admonished for saying that he wanted to thrash the French.[61] Gaspard Favre refused to present any children for baptism. He said that 'since his name could not be given he would present no child for baptism'.[62] Ministerial complaints continued unabated.[63]

In the short term relative calm was restored as no other cases are recorded until the end of the following year. In December 1551 however, prominent Genevans were once again in trouble for protesting at a baptismal service. Jean Baptiste Sept, Balthazar's brother, proposed a name which was refused.[64] The ministers complained at what they must have considered to have been premeditated insolence and disobedience.[65] Jean Philibert Bonna was also admonished for his behaviour in the riot which accompanied the service.[66] Bonna's brother, Pierre, had been on the Petit Conseil since 1541 and a Syndic in 1550. Soon after, in February 1552, Balthazar Sept and Gaspard Favre made an official protest to the Petit Conseil, demanding to know whether their names were acceptable or not.[67] Calvin defended the policy, especially with regard to the name 'Claude'.[68] It might not be purely coincidental that soon after this exchange Calvin was reprimanded by the Petit Conseil for one of his sermons.[69]

The last major confrontation was in October 1552. Balthazar Sept presented a child which Calvin refused to baptise at all. Calvin's defence against Sept's complaints was that since Sept never recognised him as a minister, he saw no reason to perform the duties of a minister for him. The dispute also involved two other ministers, Poupin and Chauvet. Fortunately part of the exchange has been preserved. Upon leaving the church Sept and Philibert Berthelier approached Jean Philippin, a Syndic that year. They said that 'these preachers have insulted us and we will endure it no longer'. At this point they saw Chauvet as he made his way out of the church. Berthelier cried out, 'There's that dandy, there's that dandy.' Chauvet called all present to bear witness that he was being slandered. But Berthelier persisted, mocking the fact that Chauvet thought himself worthy to bear a sword, a right which normally pertained to citizens. Poupin then said to the Syndic, 'I beg you, do your duty.' Berthelier, incensed, shouted, 'It's not your place to order the Syndic about.' Poupin replied, 'I didn't order him, I'm not some prince to order him about.' Sept broke in, 'You're quite correct (you're not), rather I'm one of your princes' and threatened to strike him.[70] When Berthelier was hauled before the Consistory he attacked everyone, especially the Senatorial elders, for betraying Trolliet who was then on trial for attacks on Calvin and predestination.[71] As a result Sept, Berthelier, and another citizen, Pierre Bonna, were all jailed for three days.[72]

The growing anger in Geneva as these two contentious issues, the ministers' baptismal policy and resentment of French influence, coalesced into a strong xenophobic backlash produced an increasingly confrontational environment between the preachers with their local and immigrant supporters and many Genevan citizens. The list of witnesses in this case also illustrates a similar merger of French refugees and Calvin's local supporters. Of the nineteen additional witnesses, eleven were citizens and another four were bourgeois of local origin. Of the eleven citizens, four had served or were serving on the Consistory. Also, six of these eleven would attain membership on the Petit Conseil only after Calvin's triumph in 1555. Jaques Bernard, the sole native Genevan minister, also testified. The other four witnesses were prominent French refugees: Laurent de Normandie, Robert Estienne, the printer, Guillaume Try, Sieur des Valtennes, and the minister, Des Gallars, Sieur de Saules.[73]

This particular case continued for the next few months. In November, Sept and Gaspard Favre again made an official complaint to the Petit Conseil.[74] The Consistory excommunicated Sept, Berthelier, and Bonna and refused to allow them to present children for baptism.[75] In February 1553, a child presented by Sept was refused and Bonna complained to the Petit Conseil.[76] The Conseil ordered a general conference of all parties and demanded a reconciliation.[77] Moreover, they expressly commanded the ministers to baptise the child. This seems to have defused the issue for a while. The final clash came in August 1554 when a child presented by Berthelier was refused.[78] By this point, though, the whole issue had begun to disappear into the wider dispute between Calvin's supporters and opponents.

A number of important factors in understanding Calvin's troubles in Geneva is apparent from this discussion. First, the whole dispute over baptismal names, beginning from 1546, was a consistent element in the opposition to Calvin and the ministers. Many other clashes did occur but, other than attacks on the French, this is the single most recurring source of conflict. It is also apparent that this issue became a central rallying-point for opposition to the French and their growing social, economic, and political influence. Indeed, the start of the controversy over baptismal names coincided with a sharp increase in anti-French outbursts. It should also be clear that relying wholly on Calvin's version of Genevan events has allowed this affair to be overlooked almost totally. Thus the image of the ministers facing constant disobedience and immorality is in stark contrast to the provocative nature of the ministers' actions, which is apparent in the other primary sources. The Genevans appear to have been striving, unsuccessfully, to maintain their traditions and customs in the face of growing foreign influence. In any case it is clear that many Genevans viewed the actions of the ministers as an unacceptable infringement of their liberties as Genevan citizens. They showed as strong a desire as the ministers to oppose insolence. Most important of all, this policy set the ministers on a course which meant that they would have to admonish and humiliate members of Geneva's ruling elite in public on a regular basis. In the end this served only to prolong and indeed aggravate the tensions which already existed in Geneva as a result of the influx of so many French refugees. Many Genevans must have come to share Berthelier's view that the ministers were insulting them and that they could endure no more.

Nor was this the sole area of tension between the Genevans and their French ministers. The pastors showed an amazing ability to underestimate the effect of their actions. Indeed, they seem to have been unwilling to concede anything to the sensibilities of the native Genevans. This lack of compromise meant that many of Geneva's ruling elite had little choice but to fight what they perceived as ministerial arrogance by open resistance. In this way the Church became an arena for public debate and was constantly rocked by violent disturbances for, in practical terms, the single most important means available to Calvin for shaping Genevan minds and mores was not the Consistory, but the pulpit. Week in week out, and nearly every day, Calvin and his colleagues proclaimed the Word of God and their vision of a godly society. People grew to maturity and their ideas and beliefs took shape under the shadow of Calvin's pulpit. From this platform Calvin was able to direct his verbal assaults against any and all opposition. The magistrates did indeed have their councils and courts. However, they were, for the most part, closed to public scrutiny; Calvin and the other members of the Venerable Company of Pastors occupied the pulpits. This meant that Calvin controlled the only means of mass communication and public indoctrination. The catechism classes laid the foundation, and from the pulpit Calvin was free to build upon this structure as he saw fit.

To what extent was Calvin, a foreigner and a hireling, free to speak his mind? He had been expelled once for a sermon expressing his opinions. One might suppose that Calvin would subsequently have abstained from direct attacks upon the magistrates and ruling elite of Geneva. Verbal assaults on magistrates and their authority were under Genevan law at best slanderous and at worst seditious. One might find it difficult to imagine that a good lawyer like Calvin would have set such a bad example by publicly criticising Geneva's rulers. The sad truth is that nothing has ever really been said about this matter.[79] Calvin's sermons have languished mostly unpublished and almost wholly unused.[80] Popular reactions to Calvin's sermons have not been commented upon, although the record of public actions is preserved in Geneva. Thus there is almost total ignorance about the effect of Calvin's preaching. What is known comes from a few references in Calvin's letters and some comments in the works of a few nineteenth-century chroniclers. As discussed in the opening chapter the former are obviously biased and the latter much too selective to be of great use; both are far too brief. It is essential to examine the surviving sermons to see how Calvin used his unique position as chief minister. One must discover whether he spoke only on general themes or whether he involved his pulpit in the daily struggles of Geneva and its faction-ridden society.[81] Finally, the reaction of the magistrates and people of Geneva to Calvin's preaching must be examined. From what the historical literature has said heretofore one might assume that insufficient material exists to answer these questions. As will be shown, that is definitely not the case.

The remainder of this chapter, then, will be devoted to an examination of the content of Calvin's sermons. Calvin not only preached generally against immorality and unethical activities which might have upset Genevan leaders but he also voiced specific, personal attacks. It is to be hoped that the following examination will make apparent both the unrelenting nature of Calvin's attacks as well as their pointed, even personal, nature. Only when one comprehends the constancy and fierceness of Calvin's preaching can one appreciate the reactions which his sermons elicited. It is unfortunate that the bulk of the sermons which survive date from after 1549. Nevertheless, these sermons are of sufficient number to allow one to draw conclusions about Calvin's general preaching activities. One must compare the repeated complaints made against Calvin's sermons after 1549 with those from the earlier period. The constancy of the complaints in both periods seems to imply that Calvin's sermons were consistent in force and content.

However, before discussing the content or impact of Calvin's preaching, it is essential to examine the preliminary question of language. As noted in the opening chapter, there are contradictory evaluations of this issue.[82] Obviously if most Genevans could not understand Calvin or the other French preachers then an examination of the sermons would be of little value. The reality, though, is that the whole matter has been the subject of much conjecture but little research. Technical discussion of the linguistic problems involved would not be profitable in this context although certain salient points are worthy of mention. First, the official written language of Genevan government after 1535 was French. All documents, even wills and marriage contracts, were in French. Also, since 1387 the franchises of the city had stipulated that the 'lingua materna' was to be used in the Cour du Vidôme, the Bishop's court.[83] Since this refers to a written language it should be understood to mean a form of French, as the local dialect was never a written language. Of course, the French used would have been heavily influenced by the local dialect.[84] While this might be important for the literate ruling class it does not necessarily imply that most Genevans understood French. But the fact is that the Genevan dialect was actually a blend of French and Provençal. Moreover, it was a dialect which was influenced, for the most part, by French.[85] Also, French served as the common language for discourse among the speakers of the various regional dialects in the linguistic border between French and Provençal.[86] Finally, the Genevan schools used French as their language of instruction and after 1535 these schools were open to all boys.[87]

The argument from the documents is even more convincing. First, it should be emphasised again that all the Genevan records were in French, apart from diplomatic papers and a few contracts written by older notaries, which were in Latin. Also, no one ever made a complaint before the court or Petit Conseil about his or her inability to understand French.[88] If this had been a problem one would certainly expect to see some evidence of it. Most striking of all, though, is the evidence from the Consistory records. Many people of poor backgrounds, even rural peasants, came before this body: and yet none ever protested that they could not understand the ministers.[89] Moreover, as they were often asked to recall the last sermon they had heard, it is surprising that they never availed themselves of such a convenient defence. Instead people simply said that they did not know or they could not recall the message. In the first year of the Consistory, one sees references to 'la langue maternelle' or 'vulgayre' or 'roman'.[90] However, except for these early references all others mention that people gave their confessions in French or Latin.[91] Obviously, one questions the meaning of these former terms. The only clue is provided by Vuyclauda Aubertorz, the wife of Jaques Richard, a servant of the Duke of Savoy. During an explanation about her lack of attendance at sermons, she said that she had three small children to look after and could not come. She did add, though, 'qu'elle aprent le pater à son filz en latin et roman et parce qu'on dit qu'il le fault savoir en deux langages en latin et francoys'.[92] Whether these were her exact words or those of the secretary is of little importance. The implication that the two terms are so closely identified as to be interchangeable is clear.

Perhaps the strongest proof comes from the reactions which local Genevans had to Calvin's sermons, which will be examined in detail below. One would hardly expect to find that riots would erupt during a sermon which most of the people present could not understand. The opportunities for complaints about a lack of understanding were many; Calvin preached twice on Sundays and every weekday in alternating weeks, in addition to teaching catechisms and giving lectures.[93] It appears, however, that enough Genevans understood French to protest against what they were hearing. Thus it will be profitable to discuss Calvin's sermons as there is every reason to suppose that most of his listeners were fully able to comprehend the content.

From December 1550 until January 1551 Calvin preached a series of sermons on Micah which set forth his ideal understanding of the duties of magistrates and ministers, as well as broad attacks against what he perceived to be the failings of those same magistrates in Geneva. Calvin preached that the 'salvation of the city, of the countryside and of the people' required that the magistrates 'maintain the honour of God' and that 'they use the sword given to them in such a way that God is honoured and served'. Also, the magistracy must strive to 'maintain such honesty and equality amongst men that everyone has his due but without injury to another'. Finally, 'they should root out dissolute and scandalous living'. For their part the ministers 'should desire that God's glory be upheld everywhere'. They must insist that the Son of God 'reign supreme and that He be obeyed'. Finally, and perhaps most importantly, the preachers 'ought not to prevaricate, rather let them openly declare and harshly attack every vice'.[94]

This might be dismissed as the sort of exhortation one expects to find in sermons if it were not for the specific violations of these guidelines which Calvin claimed to have found in the behaviour of Geneva's rulers. 'Those who have power, those who ought to establish order, they no longer even report the iniquities of the sinful, and thus they show that they are become

like ice.'[94] Likewise, the next day he preached, 'Can't you see the blasphe-
mies and scandals and immorality everywhere? The whole world is de-
bauched and every day I see that Geneva's impiety is so great that the city
resembles, as it were, a sinking cesspool of hell.'[96] Less than a fortnight
later, in January 1551, Calvin turned his attacks upon the specific abuses of
the greedy merchants. 'On the streets of Geneva you can find more
honour and loyalty among the dogs. The shops are dens for thieves who
are ever ready to slit a poor man's throat.'[97] If one remembers that Geneva
was governed by its merchant class one can see just how stinging these
rebukes would have been. Further, everyone must have grasped that
Calvin was publicly saying that a great gulf existed between a truly godly
society, properly administered, and the Genevan reality.

Admittedly, one might consider these attacks to be the normal stock-in-
trade of ministers, mere homiletic devices. But the detail found in later
sermons belies this. Some of the most vitriolic comments date from 1554,
the year before Calvin's decisive triumph over his political opponents. In
the last half of 1554 Calvin preached on a text from Job. Calvin presented a
harsh picture of how he saw Geneva.

> Let us consider the position of the wicked. Men wink at their lewdness. Nor
> are they punished as they deserve. They have become so bold that they strut
> through the streets bragging about their conquests. Oh that God would
> preserve us from such visions here and now. But how is it? An honest man
> barely dares walk the streets. He will be shouted and scoffed at, harassed and
> abused. When attacked he can scarcely defend himself. And what happens to
> these evil men, gallowsbait? They ought to have been hanged a half a dozen
> years ago.[98]

Calvin followed up this attack a month later, in October 1554. 'Look at the
way those in authority, the way they deck themselves out. Look at the state
of Justice. All you see is arrogance. All that is evident is pomp and
overweening pride. They don't even think they are mortal men.'[99] Calvin
was also quite sure of the cause of this degeneration. These sinners 'have
grown so bold that they think they are a law unto themselves'. In addition
to outright theft they would 'deceive, beat and abuse the poor folk'. So
bold had they become that there was no wickedness for which they would
not strive. Calvin saved his contempt, though, for the magistrates, who
had become 'more fearful than women'. They lacked God's Spirit and
'they prefer to prevaricate and please men: and what is more they half
agree with the wicked. Even though they know that evil abounds nevertheless they have no zeal to repress it.'[100] Moreover, Calvin attacked,
indeed ridiculed, specific magistrates. The elections of 1553 and 1554 had

seen an advance in the fortunes of Calvin's opponents and the introduction of a number of new men to the magistracy. To Calvin, these 'newly promoted louts' were 'nothing at all' and yet 'when they attain any position at all think themselves demigods'. They were uncontrollable because of their arrogance, but most men simply heaped scorn on their feeble attempts to gain honour.[101] One must not forget that these magistrates were probably present, in the main cathedral church, surrounded by their families, neighbours, and prominent French refugees.

In most cases it is impossible to tell what had sparked such rebukes. But the series of attacks just mentioned, which began in September 1554 and continued through the end of the year, seems to have sprung from a specific incident which occurred in August. In three sermons preached over the period of a fortnight, Calvin gave the specific details of his complaint and the reactions of others to his accusations. His indignation is obvious and could well explain the strong series of attacks just discussed.

> We don't have to decipher things a little at a time to understand the situation. Men see clearly enough. Are we so stupid that we are not grieved to see God so ill obeyed among us? ... Not only is God dishonoured by whorings, by dissolute living, by blasphemy, by theft, and the like—which rule everywhere and aren't punished as they deserve—but also, even when retribution is ordered men devise in their hearts to mock God and His Justice. I'm talking about what I saw yesterday with my own eyes. When a whore is jailed (on bread and water) she must be supplied with sweets to feast upon. She is locked up for a show but meanwhile she is provided with great gâteaux. I ask you, what sort of Justice is this?[102]

Unfortunately, this episode is not mentioned in any other sources; but, it is clear from the next sermon that the reaction was swift and strong. However, Calvin was not about to be deterred.

> When I talked last Sunday about the shameful outrage at Coligny, they fell to justifying themselves, conspiring against God and among themselves about how to hide what everyone could see ... The sermon was the subject of complaints ... Some men want to pick a fight, as if they had been wronged. You wretched men .... I told you about that shameful disorder so that you'd be sorry for it ... but in a rage you do the opposite—you seek nothing but to fight openly against God.[103]

Later the same week he pursued the matter again, when he was accused of dishonouring the city. His detractors claimed to be 'zealous of the honour of Geneva'. Everyone knew whom he meant. Calvin felt no need 'to point them out with his finger or call out their names'.[104] One wonders, though, whether his finger strayed over the congregation and the assembled magistrates even as he spoke. While this is the only detailed account of popular reaction to be found in a sermon, other sources prove that Calvin often raised a storm by his sermons. Thus one must turn to an examination of the reaction, official and popular, to Calvin's impassioned preaching. It is in this area that one can perhaps conclude that Calvin's preaching was consistent because the complaints were as well.

In 1545, Pierre Tissot, a Senator, was charged with public rioting for his behaviour after a sermon. He claimed that he had been outraged because Calvin had called for the hanging of 700 to 800 'enfants' of the city. 'Enfant' was the term used by Calvin's opponents to describe themselves and had also been the party title of the patriotic faction which had overthrown the Savoyard Prince–Bishop in 1535. Little wonder, then, that a prominent citizen, a magistrate since the 1535 revolt, would have found the sermon offensive.[105] A year later, in 1546, seven people, all citizens, were arrested for interrupting a sermon. They had risen to shout Calvin down when he had said that many Genevans were like 'brute beasts'.[106] Three sermons, from a later date, 1549, survive and contain attacks similar in nature. Likewise, these sermons provoked a public riot after the service, led by Philibert Berthelier, one of Calvin's chief opponents and the son of the martyr of Genevan independence.[107] Calvin's comments on that occasion are worthy of examination. 'Let it be known that these who would be pillars of the Church are wanton like dogs chasing after dogs in heat. They are drunkards and when at table they resemble brute beasts.'[108] And again the next day he preached that 'those who once showed a zeal for God are those who now maintain a life more dissolute than that of brute beasts'.[109] Yet again the following day Calvin declared that these 'beasts' did not desire such preaching but wanted the ministers to confine themselves to preaching 'salvation and the remission of their sins'.[110] It is hardly surprising that such pronouncements from a hired foreigner provoked protest, even rioting, among Geneva's ruling class.[111]

But opposition to Calvin's preaching was not confined to the unofficial popular level. Nor was Calvin the only member of the Company of Pastors to be censured for his sermons, and (perhaps most interestingly) Calvin was not slow to realise the powerful and dangerous nature of this tool, the pulpit. On three separate occasions in 1546 alone other ministers were called before the Senate to explain comments which they had made in sermons. Treppereaux, in April, was warned for insulting the magistrates.[112] In May, Chauvet, and later, in June, Cop were made to account for their sermons against the morality plays which were to have been presented.[113] Indeed, Cop's sermon was so fierce that he was arrested and nearly deposed. Even Calvin had found the comments too severe.[114] Two years later Jaques Bernard, a citizen, was rebuked for his sermon in a rural parish. His flock had complained that he had insulted them by accusing them of various sins and of being evil. Bernard's defence was that he had called them evil only in the sense that all men are evil and guilty of those sins which he had laid at their feet. He was told to be more circumspect in the future.[115]

Nor was such sensitivity confined to Geneva and its magistrates. In 1552, Jean de St André was arrested and then banned from Bernese territory for a sermon he had preached in a rural parish on the border.[116] Even Farel was censured for a sermon which he preached in 1553 while visiting Geneva during the Servetus affair.[117] It is also worth noting that while Calvin was opposed to being told what he could preach about he had no such qualms about other ministers. He repeatedly demanded that Geneva ask the Bernese authorities to curb attacks on him by their ministers, especially those in the parishes near Geneva.[118] Obviously he accepted, when it suited him, magisterial control over sermon content. Further, Calvin clearly understood the important role the pulpit had as a propaganda tool for shaping and controlling public opinion.

Calvin himself came in for specific censure on two occasions, in 1548 and 1552. In each he was asked to explain his sermon and warned against attacks on the magistrates.[119] In the latter case it has been possible to identify a sermon which may have been the object of the complaint. One of the offending passages is worth quoting.

> I say this. Messieurs the Senators, Judges and Advocates not only attempt to argue against God, thereby hoping to gain for themselves the right to mock him but, rejecting all the Holy Scriptures, they vomit forth their blasphemies as supreme decrees. These gargoyle monkeys have become so proud ... that they allow no place for reason or truth.[120]

If this sermon is not the one which provoked the complaint, then the one which did must have been censorious indeed.

There are a several conclusions which can be drawn from this discussion. First, in general, Calvin's preaching was much more polemical and politically informed than one might have supposed. Also, Calvin appears as a man and a preacher deeply involved in the daily affairs of Geneva. For all the fame which Calvin rightly had, and has, as a major international figure, his sermons prove that he was also a determined, forceful local pastor as well as an astute politician and propagandist. Specifically, though, Calvin's sermons also reveal some detailed aspects of the tensions in Genevan society. Calvin's great complaint was, as far as he was concerned, that the rulers of Geneva refused to accept correction and behave as they were told. In the days around the decisive riot by Calvin's opponents in May 1555, Calvin called upon the people of Geneva to consider the state of Christianity in Geneva. 'The Gospel has been preached here for twenty years. The very walls ought to echo with the Good News. The paving stones themselves should bear witness to the passing of God's Truth.' But such was not the case: instead 'these wild animals still wallow in their gross and barbarous rebelliousness'.[121] Likewise, Calvin preached that 'what we see nowadays is that rather than assembling themselves together there are many who wish to scatter God's flock. To find them we need look no further than this place. We see that these louts serve the Devil these days as though he paid their wages or owned them as slaves.'[122] Calvin had all but despaired in the face of the unwillingness of the Genevans to obey him and the other ministers, and to keep their proper place.

For their part many native Genevans refused to accept any correction, especially in public, from foreigners. They seem to have felt that the control of Genevan society was a role which belonged to the citizen–magistrates, not to their paid, imported ministers. Because of the magistrates' desire to leave the control of Geneva's society in their own hands they wanted, or so Calvin claimed, sermons which differed from those he and the other ministers believed ought to be preached. Calvin said that 'they no longer want that sort of Gospel here'.[123] Calvin admitted that they were not saying 'I no longer want him preaching to me' but rather, the more subtle, 'does he think the promise of God ought to be preached thus? Should it not be proclaimed with sweetness? ... Some say we are too rude and therefore God's Word is not received.'[124]

The other documentary evidence shows that many Genevans were offended by the tone and content of Calvin's sermons. What they wanted were ministers who knew and kept their place. What they failed to realise was that Calvin's control of Geneva's pulpits put them at a complete disadvantage, and that Calvin's willingness to use his position consistently and forcefully meant that they had little hope of winning the battle for the hearts and minds of Geneva's populace. With no popular platform of their own, Genevans opposed to Calvin and his vision of Genevan society were reduced to shouting in the pews, rioting in the streets and complaining in the Councils; none of which could equal the obvious persuasive power of Calvin's pulpit ministry.

This discussion has made clear the extent to which much of the dissension in Genevan politics in the period after 1546 was the result of the actions and indeed the personalities of the ministers. They were faced by dislike first and foremost because they were prominent representatives of the increasingly threatening immigrant community. But they made the situation much worse by their insistence upon certain baptismal names and their rejection of others. Further, by using their pulpits as political platforms for promoting their vision of Geneva they were able to launch fierce attacks upon their political opponents, and this increased tension even more. Those who wished to resist the ministers had no comparable means of publicising their viewpoint. The presence of so many prominent foreigners, as well as the personal prominence of many of the ministers and their often abrasive manner, forced many loyal Genevans into the path of outright opposition.

NOTES

1   The effect of the policy is discussed in Monter, 'L'Evêché', p. 146.
2   CO, vol. 14, col. 434 (to Dryander, Dec 1552).
3   For example McGrath, *Calvin*.
4   Gaberel, *Histoire*, vol. 1, pp. 412f.
5   Roset, pp. 318f.
6   Monter, 'Demography', p. 412.
7   AEG/RC/41, fol. 186 (30 Aug 1546).
8   Gautier, *Histoire*, vol. 3, p. 459.
9   Monter, 'Demography', p. 413.
10 AEG/PC/1re Ser., 431 (28–30 Aug 1546). It appears that his wife, Boniface, had baptised the child Claude later at home. AEG/Consist., vol. 2, fol. 74 (12 Aug 1546).
11 AEG/Consist., vol. 2, fol. 76 (30 Aug 1546). Evidence was taken from a certain Polyte Ruet. Ruet had also been examined by the Consistory, AEG/Consist., vol. 2, fol. 76 (26 Aug 1546). Andriq Pirarde was also questioned for his protest in the church, AEG/Consist., vol. 2, fol. 75v (19 Aug 1546).
12 AEG/RC/41, fol. 185 (27 Aug 1546).
13 AEG/RC/41, fol. 238 (9 Nov 1546).
14 AEG/RC/41, fol. 242 (15 Nov 1546).
15 AEG/RC/41, fol. 242 (15 Nov 1546). The list seemed to expand constantly. In December, Hyppolite Rivet (of the Deux Cents) was jailed for three days when he tried to have a girl baptised as Hyppolita. AEG/Consist., vol. 2, fol. 101 (23 Dec 1546); Galiffe, *Ameaux*, p. 77.
16 Galiffe, *Ameaux*, p. 75, writing later expressed sentiments similar to those of the earlier Genevans when he described the new legislation as odious, ridiculous and absurd.
17 AEG/Consist., vol. 3, fol. 14 (3 Feb 1547).
18 AEG/Consist., vol. 3, fol. 17 (10 Feb 1547).
19 AEG/Consist., vol. 3, fol. 17 (10 Feb 1547). Furby appeared twice and denied the charges against him.
20 AEG/RC/42, fol. 51 (8 Mar 1547).
21 AEG/RC/42, fols. 63v–64 (21 Mar 1547).
22 AEG/RC/42, fol. 69v (28 Mar 1547).
23 AEG/RC/42, fols. 70v–71 (29 Mar 1547).
24 AEG/RC/42, fol. 72v (31 Mar 1547).

25 AEG/RC/42, fol. 159v (28 Jun 1547).
26 AEG/Consist., vol. 3, fol. 145 (22 Sep 1547).
27 AEG/Consist., vol. 4, fol. 31v (31 May 1548). He insisted on 'Jean' instead, cf., Galiffe, *Ameaux*, p. 78.
28 AEG/Consist., vol. 4, fol. 32 (31 May 1548).
29 AEG/Consist., vol. 4, fol. 32v (31 May 1548). A glance at Appendix 4 will show that at a later date Cop was indeed a creditor which in Geneva implied that he was charging the legally accepted 5 per cent interest. Des Gallars actually broke the law when he loaned 300ff in 1554 and collected 447ff in 1560; as simple interest he had charged 8 per cent (6.7 per cent if compounded), both above the legal limit. Graham, *Calvin*, p. 126. Geneva's legal rate had been set by decree in 1538 and 1544. Babel, *Histoire Economique*, p. 483.
30 AEG/Consist., vol. 4, fol. 32 (31 May 1548).
31 AEG/Consist., vol. 4, fol. 33 (31 May 1548).
32 AEG/Consist., vol. 4, fol. 33 (31 May 1548).
33 AEG/Consist., vol. 4, fol. 35 (7 Jun 1548).
31 AEG/Consist., vol. 4, fol. 33 (31 May 1548).
32 AEG/Consist., vol. 4, fol. 33 (31 May 1548).
33 AEG/Consist., vol. 4, fol. 35 (7 Jun 1548).
34 AEG/Consist., vol. 4, fol. 32 (31 May 1548).
35 AEG/RC/43, fols. 131–131v (9 Jul 1548).
36 AEG/RC/43, fol. 105v (4 Jun 1548).
37 AEG/Consist., vol. 4, fol. 55 (30 Aug 1548).
38 AEG/Consist., vol. 4, fol. 50v (16 Aug 1548).
39 AEG/Consist., vol. 4, fol. 60v (20 Sep 1548).
40 AEG/RC/43, fol. 181 (30 Aug 1548).
41 AEG/RC/43, fol. 200v (24 Sep 1548).
42 AEG/Consist., vol. 4, fol. 62 (27 Sep 1548).
43 AEG/Consist., vol. 4, fol. 64 (4 Oct 1548).
44 AEG/Consist., vol. 4, fol. 64v (4 Oct 1548).
45 AEG/Consist., vol. 4, fol. 65 (11 Oct 1548).
46 AEG/RC/44, fol. 145v (1 Jul 1549).
47 AEG/RC/44, fol. 306v (20 Jan 1550).
48 AEG/PC/2e Ser., 813 (6 Feb 1550).
49 AEG/RC/44, fol. 350v (31 Mar 1550). He had already been admonished by the Consistory, AEG/Consist., vol. 5, fol. 9 (13 Mar 1550).
50 AEG/PC/1re Ser., 462 (4–14 Mar 1550). The case also involved Claude Maurys and Bertrand Roz (see below), AEG/Consist., vol. 5, fols. 8v (13 Mar 1550), 12 (20 Mar 1550). It also corresponds to a case in which Berchoda, wife of Claude Becho, was admonished for encouraging the youths to disobey the ministers, AEG/Consist., vol. 5, fol. 17 (Mar 1550).
51 AEG/Consist., vol. 5, fol. 9 (13 Nov 1550).
52 AEG/Consist., vol. 5, fol. 12 (20 Mar 1550). The use of the insulting phrase 'God of paste' is well attested in this period; for example, it was used in the Netherlands, Rouen, Lyon and Paris. However, except in Geneva, it was always directed against the Catholics. Its appropriation by Calvin's Genevan opponents implies that the phrase had become a more general term of religious abuse. Cf., P. Benedict, *Rouen during the Wars of Religion* (Cambridge: 1981), p. 61; N. Davis, *Society and Culture in Early Modern France* (London: 1975), pp. 157, 171; Diefendorf, *Paris*, p. 149; and A. Duke, 'Noncomformity among the Kleyne Luyden in the Low Countries before the Revolt', in his *Reformation and Revolt in the Low Countries* (London: 1990), p. 121.

53 AEG/PC/1re Ser., 462 (4–14 Mar 1550).

54 AEG/PC/2e Ser., 826 (27 Mar 1550).

55 AEG/Consist., vol. 5, fol. 14v (27 Mar 1550).

56 AEG/PC/2e Ser., 883 (20 Sep 1550). Jean Berthier (Bruges); Antoine Dagon, Jaques Dergomme (Nantes); Hugue Jordon (Dauphiné); Jean Appinsest, Mathieu Martinoz (Langres).

57 AEG/PC/2e Ser., 602bis (26 Sep 1550).

58 AEG/RC/45, fols. 100v–101 (28 Sep 1550).

59 AEG/Consist., vol. 5, fol. 73 (16 Oct 1550).

60 AEG/Consist., vol. 5, fol. 85 (4 Dec 1550).

61 AEG/Consist., vol. 5, fol. 96 (16 Dec 1550).

62 AEG/Consist., vol. 5, fol. 74 (16 Oct 1550).

63 AEG/RC/45, fols. 125–125v (11 Nov 1550), 148 (15 Dec 1550).

64 AEG/RC/46, fol. 117v (17 Decc 1551).

65 AEG/RC/46, fol. 120 (21 Dec 1551).

66 AEG/RC/46, fols. 123–124 (25 Dec 1551). Philibert Genod was also warned.

67 AEG/RC/46, fol. 144v (4 Feb 1552). They seemed to have been successful in getting the Senate to allow the use of Melchior, Gaspard and Balthazar. Calvin protested and the matter was to be referred to the Conseil des Deux Cents but the entire matter had to be postponed because of the elections. Roget, *Histoire*, vol. 3, pp. 224f.

68 AEG/RC/46, fols. 145v–146 (5 Feb 1552).

69 AEG/RC/46, fol. 165v (28 Feb 1552); Roget, *Histoire*, vol. 3, p. 227.

70 AEG/PC/2e Ser., 1008 (28–29 Oct 1552). The nobility and gentry in France were noticeable by their specific manners and appearance. Cf., P. S. Lewis, *Later Medieval France* (London: 1968), pp. 174, 187–90, and Neuschel, *Honor*, p. 77.

71 AEG/PC/2e Ser., 1008 (28, 29 Oct 1552); RC/46, fols. 283–285 (7, 8 Oct 1552).

72 AEG/RC/46, fol. 297v (2 Nov 1552).

73 AEG/PC/2e Ser., 1008 (28–29 Oct 1552). The future senators were Fr. Chavallier, Louis Franc, J. Chappuis (Olivier), Gme. Chiccand, J. Pernet, and J. de la Maisonneuve. The members of the Consistory were Cl. de Lestra, J. Chappuis (Olivier), Gme. Chiccand, and J. Pernet. The others involved were Jaq. N. Vulliet, A. Alliod, and Jaques Bernard. Those bourgeois of local origin were J. Bocquetz, Mermet Pictet, P. Philippin, Nyc Druet.

74 AEG/RC/46, fol. 302v (11 Nov 1552).

75 AEG/RC/46, fol. 302v (11 Nov 1552).

76 AEG/RC/47, fol. 25v (23 Feb 1553).

77 AEG/RC/47, fol. 27 (24 Feb 1554).

78 AEG/RC/48, fol. 111 (30 Aug 1554).

79 An exception is W. Nijenhuis, 'Calvin's Life and Work in the Light of the Idea of Tolerance', in his *Ecclesia Reformata, Studies on the Reformation* (Leiden: 1972), pp. 115–29. He had a different focus, though he demonstrated that the sermons were a valuable source for understanding Calvin and his beliefs.

80 This problem, however, is in the process of being remedied. All of Calvin's surviving sermons are being transcribed, edited, and published in the volumes of the *Supplementa Calviniana*.

81 For a while Calvin preached twice on Sunday; this was changed, on 11 September 1542, to once on Sunday and every weekday service on alternating weeks (CO, vol. 21, col. 302). Three sermons were preached every Sunday in Geneva, at dawn, 9 a.m. and 3 p.m. Weekday sermons, originally on Mondays, Wednesdays and Fridays, were increased to every day in October 1549. Catechism lessons were held every Sunday at noon. Cf., T.

H. L. Parker, *Supplementa Calviniana* (London: 1962), p. 8, and *The Oracles of God* (London: 1947), pp. 33–9.

82 See pp. 3f.

83 Eduourd Mallet, ed., 'Franchis de Genève, promulguées par l'Evêque Adémar Fabri', in *MDG*, vol 2 (Geneva: 1843), pp. 314–17. French, never patois, began to replace Latin in documents as early as 1260. Cf., E. Ritter, 'Recherches sur le Patois de Genève', in *MDG*, vol. 19 (Geneva: 1877), p. 51.

84 J. Jeanjaquet, 'Les Patois Romands et leur Vicissitudes', in *Heimatschutz*, 41 (May 1946), p. 43.

85 E. Muret, *Les Patois de la Suisse Romande* (Lausanne: 1909), pp. 10, 16f.

86 Jeanjaquet, 'Patois', p. 43.

87 Jeanjaquet, 'Patois', p. 44. This prevalence of French attracted the religious refugees as they faced no serious language problems in Geneva. Cf., Sauty, 'Refuge', p. 10.

88 It is worth recalling that the Petit Conseil insisted that the men hired to work in the Plague Hospital in 1543 must be able to speak French. See p. 114, n. 53.

89 However, the issue of language did arise in one case. Jaques Adriens of Anvers said that his wife could not understand the language of the Consistory because she was Flemish. The Consistory asked Mlle de Parex to attend the next session to interpret for the court and the lady. AEG/Consist., vol. 5, fols. 61v (28 Aug 1550), 62 (4 Sep 1550).

90 For example, AEG/Consist., vol. 1, fol. 22v (27 Apr 1542), Claudaz, the wife of Michel Julliand, a sellier, could say her confession in Latin but 'az dit l'orayson dominical en la langue maternelle'. Also, AEG/Consist., vol. 1, fol. 23v (27 Apr 1542), Marguerite, a servant, the wife of Aymoz Vignon 'az dit son pater en langue vulgayre'. Finally, AEG/Consist., vol. 1, fol. 56 (7 Sep 1542), Jane, the wife of Jehan de Genevaz 'a dit l'orayson et confession en roman et latin'.

91 For example, AEG/Consist., vol. 1, fol. 26 (2 May 1542), Roletaz Falliadaz, the wife of George Bonagnie 'az dit son pater en français'.

92 AEG/Consist., vol. 1, fol. 132v (13 Sep 1543).

93 T. H. L. Parker, *Calvin's Preaching* (Edinburgh: 1992), pp. 59–62. Prior to October 1549 sermons had been delivered on only three weekdays. For a brief period Calvin preached only once on Sundays before renewing the early pattern.

94 SC, vol. 5, p. 99 (Micah 3:9; 9 Dec 1550).

95 SC, vol. 5, p. 151 (Micah 5: 1f.; 23 Dec 1550).

96 SC, vol. 5, p. 163 (Micah 5: 3f.; 24 Dec 1550).

97 SC, vol. 5, p. 198 (Micah 6: 9f.; 5 Jan 1551).

98 CO, vol. 34, col. 377 (Job 23: 1–9; 3rd week, Sep 1554).

99 CO, vol. 34, col. 563 (Job 29: 13–17; 4th week, Oct 1554).

100 CO, vol. 34, col. 672 (Job 31: 16–23; mid-Nov 1v54).

101 CO, vol. 34, col. 161 (Job 34: 16–20; 4th week, Dec 1554).

102 CO, vol. 34, col. 143f. (Job 20: 1–7; 2nd week, Aug 1554).

103 CO, vol. 34, col. 202f. (Job 20: 26–9; 3rd week, Aug 1554).

104 CO, vol. 34, col. 213f. (Job 21: 1–16; 3rd week, Aug 1554).

105 AEG/PC/2e Ser., 654 (3 Aug 1545). For a discussion of the earlier use of the term 'Enfant' see pp. 15f.

106 AEG/PC/2e Ser., 695, 707 (29 Mar 1546); RC/41, fol. 59v (29 Mar 1546).

107 AEG/PC/2e Ser., 801 (29 Jul 1549).

108 SC, vol. 6, p. 111 (Jer. 17: 9–11; 24 Jul 1549).

109 SC, vol. 6, p. 118 (Jer. 17: 11–14; 25 Jul 1549).

110 SC, vol. 6, p. 124 (Jer. 17: 13b, 15f.; 26 Jul 1549).

111 Diefendorf, *Paris*, pp. 145–58 also found that inflammatory preaching had a direct and

often violent impact upon the Parisian situation.

112 AEG/RC/41, fol. 73 (15 Apr 1546). See above p. 116, n. 101.

113 AEG/RC/41, fol. 104 (31 May 1546).

114 AEG/RC/41, fols. 123–131v (28 Jun 1546).

115 AEG/RC/41, fols. 234v–235 (5 Nov 1548).

116 AEG/RC/46, fol. 309v (21 Nov 1552); *RCP*, vol. 1, pp. 132–134 (Mar 1552). Chauvet suffered a similar fate. Cf., p. 73 above.

117 AEG/RC/47, fol. 174 (3 Nov 1553).

118 AEG/RC/47 fol. 73(11 May 1553).

119 AEG/RC/43, fol. 94v (29 Mar 1546); RC/46, fol. 165v (28 Feb 1552).

120 CO, vol. 8, col. 309 (Ps 16: 30; prior to 20 Sep 1552).

121 CO, vol. 8, col. 106 (Deut. 4: 1f.; 15 May 1555).

122 CO, vol. 8, col. 134 (Deut. 4: 6–10; 21 May 1555).

123 SC, vol 6, p. 19 (Jer. 15: 1–6; 24 Jun 1549).

124 SC, vol 6, p. 19 (Jer. 15: 10f., 14f.; 26 Jun 1549).

see 189

6   *Calvin and the magistrates:*
the final crisis

J'ay pour Geneve endure grandz ennuis

As the two previous chapters have shown, Geneva's fear of strangers and annoyance at the growing influence of the French ministers was beginning to coalesce into a single issue by 1550. Chapter 4 emphasised the accelerating collapse of the political coalition which came to power after the defeat of the Articulants. Thus, by 1550, Geneva found itself moving inexorably towards a new factional crisis. With the lessening of tensions in the international arena, Genevans again turned their attention to their domestic situation. The extremely well-qualified ministers and the elders, ably led by Calvin, had been able to work in harmony for four years. With the arrival of significant numbers of French religious refugees, who showed every sign of remaining in Geneva, the French-dominated ecclesiastical structure gained the support of a socially prominent, ethnically united local following. These factors began to destabilise the already unbalanced, fragmenting Genevan ruling elite. Yet it was some years before these tensions were manifested in the clear polarisation which ushered in the decisive confrontation of 1553–55. The early 1550s were rather a period of comparative calm, with no more than the usual level of interpersonal rivalries and violence.

The elections of 1550 demonstrate that no decisive factional split had yet occurred. Three Consistory members were defeated, though prominent supporters of Calvin did win some posts. Guillaume Beney and Jean Chautemps, who would later be strong proponents of Calvin, lost the Syndic elections to Amblard Corne and Claude du Pan, former elders and also Calvin's supporters. Another former elder, Pierre Bonna, and Michel de l'Arche became Syndics, defeating Jean Lambert and Pierre Jean Jessé. The third elder to fail to be elected was Jehanton Jenod, who was beaten by Pierre Sermod, who became the new Châtelain of Celligny. Hudriod du Molard, the sole elder to win election, became Châtelain of St Victor but was unopposed. The most important result of the election was the continuing dominance of the interconnected Favre, Bonna and Sept families. Only two members of this extended clan were not elected, Jean

Louis Favre and Martin Fiendaz, the former standing for Châtelain of the Chapter, the latter for Châtelain of Jussy. Favre was beaten by the younger Jean Balard, who was also associated with these families; his sister was arrested at Antoine Lect's party in 1546.[1] Fiendaz was defeated by Denys Hugues, a relative of the Favre's through his powerful brother-in-law, Hudriod du Molard.[2] Four other members of these families who stood for election won: Pierre Bonna, Claude du Pan, Hudriod du Molard, and Jean Louis Ramel. Thus, of the four Syndics and five châtelains elected, two Syndics and three châtelains were connected with these interrelated families. Finally, the newly elected Lieutenant's secretary, Philibert Berthelier, was closely connected to the Sept brothers.[3] In this year, it is clear that political power in Geneva was concentrated, to a large degree, in the hands of a few families.[4]

In general, 1550 was a peaceful year for relations amongst the Genevans themselves, regardless of their problems with the ministers and the refugees.[5] Even these disputes were not yet able to produce too much ill will, as is shown by Calvin's performance of the marriage ceremony for Balthasar Sept and Andrienne de Livron in April 1550.[6] There are only three recorded cases of serious personal disputes. In February, Jean Collomb clashed with his son-in-law, Sivestre Mestral, while in July, Guido Malliet and Nicod du Chesne argued over the collection of the taille by Berne in certain territories connected with Geneva.[7] Balthasar Sept and Philibert Berthelier were involved in a clash with two unnamed persons later in September.[8] There were also only two prominent cases of fornication that year; Jean Lullin and Pierre d'Arlod were arrested for their immorality.[9] Youthful excess accounted for the final case involving prominent Genevans. As the year opened Baptiste Sept, Michel Sept, Gaspard Favre, Jean de la Mar and Philibert de la Mar had been admonished for disturbing the peace by riding a sleigh through the city late one night.[10]

The most important political dispute of 1550 occurred later in the year, in November. The city had followed the Bernese custom of allowing the celebration of the festivals associated with Christmas, Easter, and Pentecost. For some time, the ministers had sought, unsuccessfully, to break the close connection between these old feast days and the new Protestant Eucharistic celebrations. At the request of the ministers the Petit Conseil re-examined the issue and referred the matter to the Conseil des Deux Cents. After debate the council agreed to the change but insisted that the matter be ratified by the assembly of all Genevan voters, the Conseil Général. The matter was discussed and the assembly agreed to accept the ministers' recommendation and to ban the festivals. Any celebration would henceforth take place on the Sunday nearest the festival day. This change broke one of the few remaining ties between Genevan and Bernese church practices.[11] The speed with which this proposal was accepted—five days—implies a broad consensus in the city for this move. This debate, which occurred in the midst of problems related to baptismal names and rising xenophobia, is a testimony to the persuasive power and influence of the ministers.[12]

There is no doubt that the question about the position of the French in Geneva was increasingly important, though this concern was confined primarily to individuals rather than to a particular faction. Leading Genevans were much more concerned about the issue of baptismal names. For the most part Geneva's ruling elite did not fight among themselves about the French. The lone exception to this was the dispute between Louis Bandière and Bertrand Roz, Henri Aubert's servant; Roz defended the French, whom Bandière had slandered.[13] However, it was only a matter of time until this issue of French refugees began to exercise the minds of Geneva's rulers. The more French there were in Geneva, and the greater their integration into the political and social life of the city, the greater the likelihood that some of Geneva's magistrates would begin to feel politically threatened.

The refugee question exploded on Geneva's political scene in the elections of 1551. An attempt was made to limit the powers of the refugees granted bourgeois status. The proposal was that the bourgeois would be deprived of the vote for twenty-five years. It is not entirely clear whether this was meant to apply retrospectively but it appears that many were convinced that it would.[14] The Conseil Général refused to sanction the move.[15] Since at least 400 people had been made bourgeois after the Revolution it is understandable that any move which would establish a precedent limiting the privileges of the bourgeoisie would be resisted. This move, supported by the Petit Conseil, which by law contained only citizens, may well have made many bourgeois suspicious of the motives of Geneva's ruling magistracy. Though many might have wanted to control the access of the French to power, they may have wondered where such a move, sponsored by men drawn from the Favre, Bonna, and Sept families, would lead.[16]

This political dispute coincided with a clash over Geneva's finances as well as additional arguments between individuals about the influence of the French. The Berthelier brothers, Philibert and François Daniel, were involved in a dispute with Jean Goulaz, which raged through the election period, about his role in keeping the city accounts.[17] Ami Perrin and Jean de la Maisonneuve also argued over the city's records, the proposal on bourgeois rights, and the renewal of the treaty with Berne.[18] Clashes over the treaty produced a riot which pitted Philibert de la Mar, Balthasar Sept, Gaspard Favre, Louis Pecollat and Jean Malliard against Jaques Herauld and Laurent Meigret.[19] An unrelated riot resulted in the arrest of Jean Baptist Sept, Claude Vandel, Pierre Bonna, Loup Tissot, André Malliard, Gaspard Favre, Balthasar Sept, and Jean Philibert Bonna.[20] This disturbance seems to have been connected with the concurrent dispute between Calvin and Philibert Berthelier. Berthelier had complained that Calvin and the ministers refused to accept or acknowledge his repentance and apology; the Petit Conseil advised that he persevere in attempting a reconciliation.[21]

This string of disputes introduced a high level of sensitivity and combativeness into Genevan politics. For example, Jean Girard, a successful printer and bourgeois for many years, was jailed for printing a book without permission. Calvin was compelled to plead on his behalf; eventually Girard was admonished and freed.[22] The harshness of the magistrates' action is especially apparent when one realises that the book in question was 'le testament & mortz de la femme de pierre viretz'.[23] The magistrates may well have chosen to prosecute Girard as a warning to the ever-growing body of refugee printers in the city. At the same time François Dunant and François Chenallat were arrested for duelling. The duel may have been connected with the investigation of Bernardin Chenallat and the younger Pierre Ruffi for fornication; they were arrested two days later.[24] Nevertheless, the situation in Geneva, while volatile, had not yet resolved itself into an obviously factional dispute. The restoration of a pension for Meigret, one of Calvin's strongest allies who had been accused of spying for France, exemplified this best; in a period of factional fighting such a partisan move would have been greeted with vocal and violent protest.[25]

The next few months were marred by constant clashes between leading Genevans and the ministers. In late May, Pierre Ameaux was cautioned for refusing to attend sermons.[26] In June, Jean Philibert Bonna and Nicolas Gentil were admonished for arguing with the Consistory.[27] At the same time the Lieutenant, Pernet Desfosses, and his assistants, the two auditeurs, Jean Donzel and Jean de la Maisonneuve, clashed with the magistrates. They said that the magistrates had exceeded their authority in ordering the release of Jean Bandière who had insulted the Lieutenant and the auditeurs.[28] Troubles continued into July when Philibert Berthelier and Pierre Bonna protested about their treatment at the ministers' hands.[29] The situation was not helped by the refusal of Bonna's wife to appear before the Consistory; she claimed, in vain, that her pregnancy would not allow her to attend.[30] Jean Bergeron was also involved in a personal dispute with Jean Baptiste Sept and Jean Jourdon.[31] Jean Goulaz continued to be involved in conflicts throughout the year.[32] He had a business dispute with Collet Greloz in August. In October, he and Jean Philibert Bonna, a relative of the Berthelier brothers, were admonished for arguing.[33]

Events later in the summer and in the autumn demonstrate that the general situation in the city was becoming tense and contentious. All these troubles occurred before a backdrop of recurring disputes over bourgeois rights. However, this issue had not yet polarised Geneva's rulers into two opposing factions. For example, Jean Trolliet, who often argued with Calvin, proposed Pierre le Fort of Bordeaux for the bourgeoisie.[34] The granting of bourgeois status to Jean François Chevallier in September showed that the current debate was not an impediment to the admission of new bourgeois.[35] Moreover, the magistrates showed no preferential treatment when punishing citizens hostile to the French; for example, Philibert de la Mar was jailed for fornication in August.[36] Nevertheless, it is clear that the question of the French ministers and refugees was becoming an increasingly important and divisive issue in Geneva. The increase in personal disputes seems to reflect a gradual deterioration of the harmony imposed upon Geneva by the external threats which were felt to have receded in 1550 and 1551, culminating in the incorrect report, joyously received on 28 September 1551, that the Emperor had died.[37] Geneva's domestic situation was increasingly unsettled and the focal point for the subsequent tensions was the French presence in Geneva. Factionalism was returning to Genevan internal politics at the very time when the changing international situation removed any incentive for Geneva's rulers to impose harmony on their subjects.

The winter of 1551 was dominated by an altogether different sort of case. In October, Jerome Bolsec was arrested for attacking Calvin's views on predestination.[38] Bolsec was the doctor of Jaques de Bourgogne, Sieur de Fallais, one of Calvin's correspondents; Bourgogne spoke in Bolsec's defence.[39] The magistrates, unsure of the correct steps to take, sought the advice of the Swiss Protestant cities, Berne, Basle, and Zurich.[40] Their replies arrived and were given to a committee for translation appointed by the Petit Conseil: Loys Beljaquet, a doctor; Enoch, the school regent; and Jean Trolliet, a notary. The Swiss cities were unwilling to counsel harsh measures against Bolsec. To some extent as well, they were troubled by Calvin's predestinarian views and advised moderation.[41] Following their advice, the Genevan magistrates decided to banish Bolsec; he withdrew to Berne whence he continued to vex Calvin.[42]

It is essential that certain points relevant to the Bolsec affair be borne in mind. First, this prosecution was solely a secular affair; Bolsec never appeared before the Consistory.[43] Further, the lukewarm support which

Calvin's views received from the Swiss cities must have undermined his position somewhat. Their letters and Bolsec's opinions echoed the views expressed by Ameaux in 1546, one of the more violent clashes with the ministers and one in which Calvin appeared particularly harsh.[44] The dispatch of these letters showed the unwillingness of the Genevans to act alone on a contentious theological issue. Their relationship with Berne and desire for close ties with the Swiss also encouraged such co-operation with, and deference to, the Swiss cities. Calvin, however, saw the magistrates' actions as a blatant attempt to discredit him. Rather than caution, Calvin perceived a want of zeal for the true faith in the magisterial request for advice. This perception could not help but widen the gap which had begun to appear between the ministers and some elements in Geneva's ruling class; the Bolsec affair confirmed Calvin's worst fears about the opposition in Geneva.[45]

In the aftermath of the Bolsec affair, Calvin and the ministers were involved in the final stages of a lengthy debate with Jean Philibert Bonna over baptismal names.[46] The magistrates were clearly exasperated by all parties, for they warned everyone to reconcile and live in harmony.[47] The confused nature of Geneva's political situation and the still apparent desire to avoid open clashes is seen in other events as well. The ministers proposed that a defence of their views and actions in the Bolsec case be published in French and Latin. The magistrates responded by appointing a panel to act as censors for the work. Loys Beljaquet and Jean Trolliet were chosen to produce a politically balanced report on the book.[48] It would not have pleased the ministers that Trolliet, a man whom they had declared personally unfit to be a minister, was to sit in judgement over a defence of their theological views against Bolsec.

The remainder of 1551 saw prominent Genevans involved in personal disputes. However, the cases were few and no pattern exists to suggest a radical increase in factionalism. Jean Griffon and Aimé Plonjon were involved in a dispute which ended in a criminal investigation.[49] In a more serious case, Michel de Rages was charged with slandering Ami Gervais, a senator and former elder.[50] Finally, Denys Hugue was arrested for stealing wood from the state-controlled forest at Jussy.[51] As in 1550, discounting the Bolsec case, one sees an ever more troubled domestic situation in Geneva. The sole common theme is an increasing annoyance with the ministers, coupled with a distrust of their refugee compatriots. Nevertheless even this problem had not reached the stage at which it began to dominate Genevan politics. For the most part, Genevan disputes about the French continued to be personal clashes between specific Genevans and Frenchmen, whether ministers or refugees.

The elections of 1552 saw an increase in the power of those sceptical of the influence of Calvin and the French. In the Syndical contest, Hudriod du Molard and Jean Philippin defeated Estienne Chapeaurouge, a former Articulant, and Jean Chautemps. In the other Syndic's election, Jean Ami Curtet, the single Calvinist elected, and Pierre Vandel beat Jean Lambert and Pernet Desfosses, both supporters of Calvin.[52] This trend was to continue throughout the year. In November, Jean Lambert was again defeated, this time by Pierre Tissot, for the post of Lieutenant. The most shocking result came in the election of the Lieutenant's assistants, the auditeurs. Jean Louis Favre and Philibert Berthelier defeated Nicolas Gentil and Jehanton Genod. This election saw Berthelier elevated to a place in the justice system only three days after he had been released from jail for clashes with the ministers, while still excommunicated.[53]

The increase in the power of Calvin's critics was not the only setback which he faced in the February election period. At the instigation of the ministers, Jean de la Maisonneuve proposed harsh new edicts aimed at curbing behaviour of which the ministers disapproved. His suggestions were opposed vehemently by Jean Philibert Bonna, Philibert de la Mar and Philibert Berthelier; indeed a riot ensued.[54] The opponents of the proposed legislation articulated a view which was gaining credence throughout the city: 'vous voies comme ceste maison nous gouverne, avec ces edictz des Francoys & de Jehan Calvin'.[55] Ministerial pique at this rejection and accusation may explain why the magistrates had to admonish Calvin for the sermon he preached a week later.[56] Calvin may also have been provoked by an angry exchange between Michel Morel, five times an elder and the Consistory's presiding Syndic in 1551, and Jean Philibert Bonna, new appointee to the Genevan appeals court. They clashed over the proper scope of Consistorial authority, and Bonna claimed that a Consistory ruling could be appealed and overturned.[57]

The disputes moved beyond the political debate over the Consistory and the edicts and became very personal. Jean de la Maisonneuve, in the heat of the debate, loudly complained about the treatment which had been meted out to his father in 1544; the senior De la Maisonneuve had been arrested for debt.[58] He specifically attacked Hudriod du Molard, Antoine Chiccand, and François Beguin.[59] They had all been senators at the time and Du Molard and Chiccand were Syndics in 1543 when the case began. As in the earlier factional clash between the Articulants and the Guillermins, opposing groups were beginning to take sides over specific issues. As the battle-lines formed, previous personal disputes and slights began to take on a present and ominous significance.

From March till May there was a continuation of these clashes between

Genevans alone as well as ones involving the ministers. Calvin argued with André Philippe, De la Mar, Sept, and Bonna.[60] Chauvet disputed in the streets with Jean Fabri; the minister was supported by Jean Crestien, Sieur Rogemont. De la Mar, Berthelier and François Chenellat clashed with Chauvet as well.[61] The month before, in April, Chenellat had been arrested for violence.[62] Disputes continued about Geneva's financial situation; Jean Lambert and Claude Franc were questioned by the Petit Conseil as a result.[63] The city's desperate need for capital may explain why the magistrates, to Calvin's dismay, allowed the raising of a mercenary force in Geneva to fight in France.[64] All these clashes, including the continual complaints about the baptismal names and the refugees, ensured that Geneva remained in a constant state of internal turmoil.

In June a more serious case arose; the dispute was a direct continuation of the Bolsec affair but on a local level. Jean Trolliet, appointed by the Petit Conseil to review the ministers' defence against Bolsec, launched a full-scale assault on Calvin's predestinarian beliefs. Philibert Berthelier and Jean Philibert Bonna became involved as well on Trolliet's behalf.[65] The insults which accompanied this case were serious and highlighted the complete deterioration of the relations between the ministers and some leading Genevans. Beza, discussing the case later, reported that Trolliet was considered impudent and gained support from the wicked.[66] At the time, Calvin wrote that his opponents were 'tres perditi nebulones, ex primariis tamen familiis'.[67] Berthelier was particularily incensed because the Consistory refused to accept his apology, even though it was Poupin who had said, about Berthelier, that 'sescheroit sa tête en Champel'.[68] One can understand why a citizen would find it offensive, having apologised to a foreigner who had used such language, to be rebuffed.

As this case continued magistrates began to be involved on Calvin's behalf. Jean Ami Curtet insisted that Trolliet should not act as censor when he recommended the publication of a work by Calvin.[69] The dispute widened as attacks were levelled at the French and Calvin and Farel felt compelled to come to their aid. Numerous ministerial complaints were brought against Sept, Bonna, and Berthelier who were jailed as a result of their anti-French remarks.[70] Viret came to join Farel in an attempt to calm tensions and restore some semblance of harmony to Geneva.[71] This visit coincided with another outbreak of protest over the baptismal name policy.[72] The ministers also began to agitate for the removal of their colleague, Ecclesia, Trolliet's lone ministerial supporter and a personal friend.[73] The predominant goal of the magistrates in the midst of these serious and interrelated disputes was to enforce a general reconciliation.[74] In the end Trolliet apologised while the Petit Conseil declared that

Calvin's teachings were sound and, almost simultaneously, that Trolliet was a good citizen.[75]

The early years of the 1550s show a rapid increase in internal tensions in Geneva. Personal disputes remained a constant, as they had for so long. However, increasingly, clashes between local Genevans began to reflect the dominant issue of the day, the influence and power of the French in Geneva. The ministers continued to face animosity from the local Genevans, especially for their policy on baptismal names; this dispute intensified after 1550. The increase in attacks against the ministers directly reflected the growing xenophobia caused by the alarming increase of the number of French refugees in the city. For some Genevans, the two complaints coalesced into an intense dislike and distrust of all Frenchmen in the city. Eventually this issue, which had initially sparked individual clashes between specific Genevans and the French ministers and refugees, began to involve a wider audience. In this way the problem raised by the influence of the French in Geneva moved from one of sporadic personal complaints to a continuous political dispute pitting Geneva's rulers against one another.

Prior to the elections of 1553, this resentment of the French began to produce an even more marked shift in Genevan domestic politics. As noted above, Berthelier, fresh from jail and still excommunicate, had been elected an auditeur in November 1552. A few months before this election a committee had been appointed to examine bourgeois rights and privileges. The panel was politically balanced between Pierre Vandel and Pierre Tissot, who favoured strict new limits on the bourgeoisie, and Jaques Desarts and Jean Lambert, supporters of Calvin and the refugees.[76] After the election, the questions surrounding the French influence in Geneva became the most important political topic in the city. The position of a citizen or candidate, on this issue, began to have a direct impact on the elections.

The elections of 1553 produced a mixed result which serves yet again to highlight the division of the electorate into fairly balanced groups. Domaine d'Arlod, a moderate with Calvinist sympathies, and Pernet Desfosses, a Calvinist, defeated Jean Lambert and Claude Rigot, the former a Calvinist, the latter moderate, to become Syndics. The other two Syndics were Estienne Chapeaurouge, a former Articulant whose affiliation is unsure but who was probably a moderate, and Ami Perrin, leader of the anti-French group; they defeated Henry Aubert, a Calvinist, and Guillaume Beney, a moderate inclined to support the Calvinists. The Petit Conseil elections tended to favour Calvin's opponents more than the

TABLE 19 *New elders and senators added to the Consistory, 1544–58*

	1544	45	46	47	48	49	50	51	52	53	54	55	56	57	58
Elders only	3	3	2	1	0	0	0	0	1	7	2	1	4	4	3
Elders and senators	4	4	5	3	1	3	2	2	2	9	4	3	7	5	4

Syndic election. This was in spite of the failure of Perrin's supporters to modify the method of electing senators.

Traditionally, the Petit Conseil, to ensure continuity, included the previous four Syndics, the four new Syndics and around sixteen senators. These senators were elected by having the senators of the previous year's Petit Conseil stand for election with eight new nominees; the new Petit Conseil was elected from this group. It was suggested that the number of nominees be increased to sixteen, which, in theory, would allow for the defeat of every senator from the previous year. This could have resulted in the drastic alteration of the Petit Conseil at a stroke. After debate, this move was defeated even though those who proposed it did well in the election. Of the eight nominees, four became senators: two opposed to the French, Gaspard Favre and Jean Baptiste Sept; one moderate with Perrinist leanings, Claude Vandel; and one Calvinist, Michel de l'Arche.[77] The four defeated nominees illustrate the extent to which those who supported the French were out of step with their fellow Genevans. Pierre Bertillion and Jean Chappuis, elders since 1546, were defeated. François Lullin, one of Calvin's supporters also lost; the former Articulant had additional reasons for opposing the group gathered around Perrin, which was composed of many former Guillermins. The fourth person defeated was Claude Gerbel, whose position is not clear. His father, Antoine, had a number of clashes with the Consistory from which one might infer that he was either moderate or opposed to the French.[78] In any case the defeat of three definite supporters of the French was a clear repudiation of their position by the Genevans in 1553.

The most dramatic change was yet to come. An examination of Tables 19 and 20 shows the drastic alterations which were made to the body of elders on the Consistory. Of the twelve elders of 1552 only four were returned to the Consistory of 1553 (which had thirteen elders). It is clear, though, that this was not a total rejection of the men removed. Three of them, Jean Pierre Bonna, Jean du Molard and Pierre Dorsière, continued to serve in the criminal and civil courts of 1553 as they had in 1552. Three others retained their various council posts: Jean Philippin and Guillaume Beney in the Petit Conseil; Claude Delestra in the Conseil des Soixante. Only two elders, Mermet Blandin and François Syman, disappeared

TABLE 20 *Consistorial membership, 1552–57*

Person	1552	53	54	55	56	57	58
P. d'Orsieres	x						
J. du Molard	x						
M. Blondin	x						
J. Philippin	Synd						
P. Bertillion	x	x	x	x	x		
Fr. Symon/Sernavd	x						
J. Chappuis	x	Cons	x	x			
Gme. Chiccand	x	x	x	x	x	Synd	Cons
J. Genod	x	x	x				
Gme. Beney	Cons						
Cl. Deletra	Cons						
J.P. Bonna	x						
D. d'Arlod		Synd					
H. Aubert		Cons	Cons				
B. Lect		x	x	x			
J. Rosset		x	x	x			
G. Coste		x	x	x	x		
M. de l'Arche		x					
J. N. Vulliet		x					
T. Matellin		x	x	x	x	x	x
C. Maisonneuve		x					
C. du Pan			Synd				
P. J. Jessé			Cons	Synd			
F. Lullin			x	x	x		
P. Somareta			x	x			
J. Maisonnneuve				Cons			
J. Chautemps				Cons			
J. Chalamel				x	x	x	x
P. Migerand					Synd		
J. Donzel					Cons	Cons	Synd
A. Corne					Cons		
J. Collanda					x	x	x
A. Chasteauneuf					x		
A. Boulard					x	x	x
A. Vernay					x	x	
J. F. Bernard							Cons
G. Macard							x
C. Chiccand						x	x
D. Dentand						x	
F. Chasteauneuf						x	x
J. Porral							Cons
C. Testu							x
A. du Vernier							x
E. Chapeaurouge							x

Cons = Consistory   Synd= Syndic

altogether from Genevan politics (they may well have died). Moreover, this substantial change to the ecclesiastical court is in marked contrast to the situation in the criminal and civil courts. Of the nine men on the lower civil court, the Premières Appellations, only Domain d'Arlod, who was made a Syndic, was replaced. His position was taken by the new presiding Syndic of the court, Estienne Chapeaurouge. On the higher civil court, the Secondes Appellations, only two new men appeared to form the new court of thirteen judges. Since this body sat with the entire Petit Conseil, it was necessary to replace Jean Baptiste Sept, a new senator. Only Jean Louis Favre actually left this body; their places were taken by Pierre Fabri and Pierre Verna. In the criminal courts, the Procès Criminels, which also sat with the Petit Conseil when judging a case, Sept had to be replaced as well as the deceased Jean Pensabin. Michel Morel and the younger Jean Balard took their seats on the bench.[79]

The change to the Consistory could hardly have been more dramatic. From 1546 to 1552 the Consistory possessed an extremely stable collection of elders. In 1553 it is clear that this group became a political issue. However, it is impossible to view this move as an attempt to alter Geneva's system of crime and punishment. Had this been the case one would have expected equally dramatic changes to the other Genevan courts. An examination of the data relating to crime and punishment in Geneva (Tables 12–13 and 21–23) shows the stability and consistency of Geneva's justice system throughout the period after Calvin's return. It is over-whelmingly apparent that the clashes between the ministers and the magistrates produced no appreciable effect on the control or punishment of offences in Geneva. The change to the Consistory was clearly a political move designed to break the power and influence which a unified, promi-nent, sympathetic eldership gave to the ministers. It is conceivable that Perrin and his supporters wished to remove potential opponents, that is, the long-serving elders, from such a prominent, public position. In either case, this was a deliberate attempt to bring the ministers and their support-ers to heel by breaking apart the cosy, supportive group which had developed in the Consistory.[80]

Similar motives must underlie the move to ban bourgeois ministers from the Conseil Général. The magistrates ruled that the ministers could not speak or vote in the Assembly although their children were not to be affected by this ruling. Calvin's magisterial opponents must have feared the persuasive power and personal authority wielded by the ministers. These ministers were well-educated, articulate, socially prominent and widely respected figures. It must have been very intimidating indeed for a Genevan merchant to attempt to dispute with one of these ministers,

TABLE 21   *Crimes in Geneva per year, 1551–57*[83]

Crime	Year							
	1551	52	53	54	55	56	57	Total
Sexual immorality	26	8	7	14	7	12	76	150
Theft	19	8	6	7	6	13	23	82
Slander magistrates	3	7	0	0	2	5	6	23
Domestic trouble	8	0	4	11	5	5	35	68
Attacks on ministers	3	7	4	0	0	2	8	24
Blasphemy	5	0	0	0	1	8	16	30
Treason	0	1	0	0	23	5	10	39
Personal slander	5	0	0	4	2	2	6	19
Assault	6	2	5	1	3	2	2	21
Public rioting	1	0	0	0	2	6	6	15
Catholic views	3	0	2	1	0	0	22	28
Anti-French acts	2	0	0	0	1	1	1	5
Counterfeiting	4	3	2	3	3	2	0	17
Disobey authority	3	0	1	2	0	1	0	7
Fraud	0	0	0	1	0	3	2	6
Murder	2	1	3	2	0	5	7	20
Official corruption	0	0	0	1	0	0	1	2
Duelling	2	0	0	0	0	0	2	4
Perjury	2	0	0	2	1	1	4	10
Religious violations	4	1	4	5	0	1	13	28
Witchcraft	2	0	0	0	0	2	16	20
Gambling	0	0	0	1	0	0	4	5
Rape	1	0	0	0	0	1	2	4
Dancing	1	0	0	0	0	0	2	3
Usury	1	1	0	1	0	0	5	8
Attempted murder	1	1	0	0	0	0	1	3
Business disputes	1	0	1	2	2	7	4	17
Suicide	0	0	0	0	1	1	0	2
Anabaptist views	1	0	0	0	1	0	1	3
Drug-related	0	0	0	0	0	2	0	2
Hiring mercenaries	0	0	0	0	0	0	4	4
Immorality	4	0	1	0	0	0	10	15
Prison escape	0	1	0	0	0	1	3	5
Smuggling	0	0	0	0	1	0	0	1
Vandalism	0	0	0	0	0	1	2	3
Spying	1	1	0	0	1	0	0	3
Sodomy	0	0	0	1	1	1	0	3
Vagrancy	0	0	0	1	0	0	0	1
Total cases known	111	42	40	60	63	83	294	693
Total cases unknown	6	3	1	5	5	12	6	38
Total cases	117	45	41	65	68	95	300	731
From Consistory	38	0	18	30	4	2	206	298
Known cases (%) *referred by Consistory*	34.2	0.0	45.0	50.0	6.4	2.4	70.1	43.0

TABLE 22   *Punishments in Geneva per year, 1551–57*

Sentence[84]	Year							
	1551	52	53	54	55	56	57	Total[85]
Death	3	3	4	3	10	5	7	35
Jail	9	1	0	0	2	9	53	74
Banishment	9	4	7	10	10	17	39	96
Beating	3	3	3	4	3	7	5	28
Fine	4	2	0	3	5	5	9	28
Public contrition	1	2	0	0	3	7	13	26
Warning	2	0	2	4	7	4	17	36
Release	3	2	0	1	2	0	6	14
Acquittal	0	0	0	0	0	1	4	5
Loss of office	0	1	1	1	3	3	2	11
Loss of rights	0	0	0	0	2	4	2	8
Summary[86]:								
Total known	34	18	17	26	47	62	157	361
Total unknown	77	24	23	34	16	21	137	332

accustomed as they were to extemporaneous public speaking. The ministers protested strongly, but unsuccessfully, against their disenfranchisement.[81] These twin moves against the elders and the ministers were designed to limit the scope for political activity on the part of the ministers. This included the wilful disruption of the Consistory and the subsequent separation of the ministers from their closest local confidants, the elders who had served with them since 1546.[82]

February also saw heated disputes between the individual members of the two groups which were slowly forming into factions. The clashes now show a rather clear division of Geneva's rulers into two opposing blocs. Pernet Desfosses, who supported Calvin, was a central figure in a number of these clashes. He was involved in a dispute with Berthelier a week after the elections.[88] He also made unspecified complaints against Odet Jaquet and Jean d'Orbe.[89] Pierre Savoye was jailed for calling François Lullin an Articulant.[90] Finally, Philibert Berthelier was admonished for slandering Jean Louis Favre as 'ung meschant homme'.[91] By 1553 the disputes in Geneva began to involve more and more Genevans against one another; Calvin's local supporters came to treat his cause as though it were their own.

Claude Delestra clashed with Jean Philibert Bonna immediately after he was defeated by Jean Philibert Donzel for the office of Châtelain of St Victor.[92] The dispute was probably connected with the decision to post-

TABLE 23 *Major crimes as a percentage of total crimes, 1541–57*[87]

Crime	Year								
	1541	*42*	*43*	*44*	*45*	*46*	*47*	*48*	*49*
Sexual immorality	0.0	16.7	11.3	7.7	7.9	36.4	9.7	14.3	20.0
Theft	16.7	17.7	11.3	0.0	14.9	17.1	9.7	14.3	24.0
Slandering Magistrates	12.5	7.8	9.4	15.4	6.9	2.3	6.6	21.4	0.0
Domestic troubles	4.2	2.0	0.0	15.4	5.0	4.6	0.0	3.6	0.0
Treason	0.0	5.9	11.3	0.0	4.0	0.0	16.1	3.6	4.0
Attacks on ministers/French	4.2	7.9	5.7	7.7	3.0	9.1	22.7	7.2	0.0

Crime	*1550*	*51*	*52*	*53*	*54*	*55*	*56*	*57*
Sexual immorality	31.7	23.4	19.1	17.5	23.3	11.1	14.5	25.9
Theft	11.0	17.1	19.1	15.0	11.7	9.5	15.7	7.8
Slandering magistrates	1.4	2.7	16.7	0.0	0.0	3.2	6.0	2.0
Domestic troubles	10.3	7.2	0.0	10.0	18.3	7.9	6.0	11.9
Treason	1.4	0.0	2.4	0.0	0.0	36.5	6.0	3.4
Attacks on ministers/French	5.8	4.5	16.7	10.0	0.0	1.6	3.6	3.4

pone the other châtelain elections.[93] Normally the châtelains were elected every three years at the same time as the other elections in February. But after Donzel's victory the other elections were postponed and not held for a month. When the elections were held, adjustments had been made to the lists of candidates; these changes were designed to exclude Calvin's supporters. Originally, Jaques Blondel faced Paul Embler for the post at Peney. However, Blondel was elected for the position at the Chapter while Embler took the post at Peney. This move excluded the two Calvinists who were standing for the Chapter post, Pierre Dorsière and François Lullin. Also, the original nominees for Châtelain of Celigny, Pierre Verna and Pierre Savoye, were pushed aside when Louis Costel was elected. The one election which remained unchanged was at Jussy where Michel Morel defeated Jean Philibert Bonna.[94] In these moves, the 1553 Petit Conseil, with a majority opposed to Calvin, showed a willingness to tamper with the elections to affect a favourable result. That move, coupled with their banning of the ministers from the Conseil Général and their earlier attempt to limit bourgeois rights, must have raised in the minds of moderate Genevans serious suspicions about their goals. These doubts would have been especially strong among Geneva's substantial, local bourgeois population.

The same period saw other clashes between Genevans and the French ministers, and Genevans and refugees. The first surrounded the debates over baptismal names and excommunication.[95] The magistrates ordered

Sept, Bonna, and the Consistory to be reconciled. Also, they repealed the excommunication ban placed on Sept and Bonna. The magistrates specifically forbade the ministers from attempting to prohibit excommunicates from presenting children at the baptismal font.[96] The reprieve for Bonna proved to be short-lived as he was excommunicated again in June.[97] But the magistrates made an effort to control the refugees as well. Led by Perrin, they introduced legislation to confiscate all weapons in refugee hands except personal swords; these were no longer to be worn in public. Apparently, until this move some of the refugees had had access to various weapons and walked the streets armed.[98] Berne was especially supportive of this move, writing that Geneva 'se falloit garder de trahison, car lon en estoit en grandt danger, veu quil y havoit en la ville des estrangiers, en plus gros nombre que les citoiens et bourgeois anciens'.[99] The French, and their local supporters, protested against this action. Jean Lambert, whose brother had been burned for his faith at Chambery, argued violently with Perrin. He even went so far as to mention the earlier espionage charges against Perrin. He said that Perrin had been quite willing then to import armed Frenchmen into the city.[100] Beza later said that this was a move designed to deprive the godly of the right to defend themselves; fear of the French was only the pretext.[101]

Once again one sees that the two sides held widely divergent perceptions of each other's actions. Perrin and his supporters saw themselves as the true defenders of Geneva's independence. They styled themselves 'les Enfants de Genève', the epithet of the earlier Revolutionary party.[102] Their opponents and the French felt they were the sole champions of God's Word and godly living. The two factions held to their positions sincerely and were willing to consider and countenance almost any means useful for securing their power; compromise was a practical impossibility. Victory would be gained by the faction which managed to guarantee control of the various Councils over an extended period of time. Thus, behind the actions of the two factions, one finds motives aimed at securing political power rather than some desire to alter Geneva's enforcement of morality; control of the judiciary, secular and ecclesiastical, was simply one additional method of gaining political power and limiting the influence of the opposition.

In the latter half of 1553, two new cases started which would occupy and convulse Geneva for the remainder of the year and beyond. One, involving Michel Servetus, is undoubtedly the more famous today but of lesser importance in 1553. The premier case was Philibert Berthelier's attempt to have the Petit Conseil overturn the ban of excommunication placed on him. The magistrates co-operated with the ministers in prosecuting

Servetus while violently clashing with the ministers over the actual scope of Consistorial authority. The threat to ministerial power posed by Berthelier's appeal to the Petit Conseil was of much greater concern and, in Calvin's view, had the potential to end his ministry in Geneva, if not his life as well.[103]

However, there are some aspects of the Servetus case which merit examination. First, as in the Bolsec affair, the action against Servetus's was a wholly secular affair. Servetus did not appear before the Consistory and the ministers were brought into the case as theological specialists to dispute Servetus's opinions. It is also useful to recall that the Servetus case followed close on the heels of the Bolsec affair which had ended unsatisfactorily from Geneva's point of view; Bolsec had simply moved to Berne and continued his attacks of Calvin's doctrines from there.[104] The issues involved were also of much greater importance; Bolsec disagreed with Calvin on predestination while Servetus rejected traditional Trinitarianism and pædobaptism. Two other heresy trials had disturbed Geneva immediately before Servetus's arrest. In July, Robert le Moine, from Normandy, was banished for saying that prostitution and fornication were not prohibited by God's Word.[105] Three days before Servetus' arrest, Jean Baudin, of Lorraine, was banished for arguing that Jesus was a phantom and the Bible a book like any other.[106] These cases, and the magnitude of Servetus's errors, may have made Geneva especially sensitive to heresy and the Catholic charge that the city was a haven for every error.[107]

Servetus was arrested on 13 August 1553 after he was denounced by Nicolas de la Fontaine, Calvin's secretary.[108] After an initial investigation, the Lieutenant, Pierre Tissot, began the prosecution.[109] On 17 August, Germain Colladan appeared as a lawyer for De la Fontaine who was being held, according to Genevan law, until his accusations could be substantiated. At that point the Lieutenant stepped aside and gave the case to his assistant, Philibert Berthelier, who was still excommunicated.[110] The following day, for the first time, Calvin appeared as an expert witness to evaluate and refute Servetus's views.[111] As it became apparent that Servetus would probably become the first person to be executed for heresy in Geneva, the city decided to seek the advice of the other Swiss Protestant cities.[112] Geneva also appointed a Syndic, Ami Perrin, to assist Berthelier in the case. The replies which Geneva received from the Swiss were very harsh. In the Bolsec case the Swiss, led by Bullinger, had counselled moderation but no such advice was forthcoming for Servetus. The very day these replies arrived, the Petit Conseil condemned Servetus; he was burned as a heretic the next day.[113]

One of the more enduring reports surrounding this case is the assertion that Servetus was secretly being promised support by Calvin's opponents.[114] It is essential to realise that these reports spring solely from sources supportive of Calvin and desirous of discrediting Calvin's opponents. Calvin himself said that Perrin was working to assist Servetus; Roset, and later Beza reported the same charge.[115] Bonivard named Claude Geneve as the chief conduit of this encouragement to Servetus.[116] But this view is rather difficult to defend. The prompt condemnation of Servetus upon receipt of the Swiss letters would seem to imply that the Petit Conseil's delay was the result of a desire to share responsibility for the execution with the other cities rather than some Machiavellian plot to destroy Calvin.[117] An examination of the senators who condemned Servetus argues against this interpretation as well. If there was real support for Servetus it is hard to believe that two of the staunchest Calvinists, Desfosses and Jaques Desarts, and two of Calvin's fiercest critics, Gaspard Favre and Pierre Vandel, would have failed to attend. The eighteen senators who were present were evenly split between the two groups.[118] Finally, the lack of any disputes or public clashes in the course of the trial implies that the view of Calvin and his supporters was, at best, exaggerated. In any case Roset, Bonivard and Beza were all writing after the fact; Calvin's report is the only contemporaneous source for this charge. If Calvin felt that his opponents were capable of any excess, then he might well have assumed that any delay in the trial was a clear sign of collusion with Servetus; the evidence, however, makes this charge extremely suspect.[119]

The other important case of 1553, involving Berthelier, began a fortnight after Servetus's arrest. Berthelier launched a fierce assault on the Consistory's power to excommunicate. On 1 September, while excommunicated, he appealed to the Petit Conseil; he asserted that the magistrates had the authority to overturn the Consistory's ruling.[120] In reality he was reopening a debate which had been decisively settled, or so some thought, by the Petit Conseil in 1543. On 19 March 1543, the magistrates had ruled that 'le consistoyre ne aye nulle jurid(iti)on ny puyssance de deffendre synon seulement admonester et puỹs fere Relation en conseyl affin que le seyg(eu)re advise de juger sus les delinquans selon leur demerites'.[121] When the Conseil upheld its earlier ruling and supported Berthelier, Calvin's reaction was swift, uncompromising and guaranteed to provoke a hostile response from his opponents. He presented an ultimatum against the ruling on 2 September and denounced the decision from the pulpit the next day. By 7 September all the other ministers had rallied to Calvin's side, threatening the Council with a mass resignation. As the dispute raged, the magistrates and ministers lectured one another on the correct reading of the Ecclesiastical Ordinances and the subsequent edicts and precedents.[122] Calvin also ensured that his position reached a wider audience by giving his side of the debate in his letters.[123] The magistrates, faced with this impasse, resolved to solicit the opinions of the other Swiss Protestant cities; they wrote to the other magistracies, not the churches.[124] Calvin, however, wrote to the churches asking that the ministers in the other cities strive to convince their magistrates to support his position in Geneva.[125]

As the impasse continued, Farel made the situation even worse. He had been invited to preach because Calvin was indisposed. On 3 November, while the magistrates were demanding a reconciliation, Farel launched a scathing attack on Geneva's youth from the pulpit of St Pierre. He preached that 'la jeunesse de ceste cité sont pires que brigands, muertriers, larrons, luxurieux, athiéstes et aultres'. The Petit Conseil was quick to admonish him.[126] Afterwards, though, the magistrates sent notice to Neuchâtel, where Farel ministered, that they wished to prosecute Farel who had already left the city. Against the advice of the Neuchâtel magistrates who were concerned about his age and health, Farel decided to return to Geneva. In the end he was simply given a stronger warning by the Genevan authorities.[127]

Farel's zeal in supporting Calvin was not shared by the other Swiss Protestant cities. They clearly wished to avoid offending Calvin, but showed no desire to support his views on excommunication and ecclesiastical authority.[128] In any event, none of the other Swiss cities would have tolerated such a situation. The Church Ordinances of Basle (1530) clearly stated that excommunication was a civil affair. At the St Gall synod in 1530, Zwingli had told Fortenuller and Zulli that ecclesiastical discipline ought to be exercised by the civil authorities. In 1532 Bullinger, supporting Zwingli, argued against Leo Jud that excommunication was not a power reserved for the Church; it was a civil matter. In Berne, the Church and State agreed that the magistracy controlled excommunication. Unable and unwilling to support Calvin, the Swiss magistrates and ministers were primarily concerned that harmony be restored in Geneva.[129] A temporary, face-saving solution was found when the Petit Conseil insisted that Berthelier was free to receive communion but advised that he voluntarily refrain from doing so; the ministers would yield nothing.[130]

It is worth noting the extent to which bias enters into the accounts from the period, if only because these works have so often influenced later histories. In relating the end of the crisis, Beza attempted to downplay the power and popularity of Calvin's opposition. He insisted that the Petit Conseil was duped into supporting Berthelier. Beza also said that the advice not to receive was given to Berthelier privately by Perrin; there is no doubt, though, that this was the official recommendation of the Petit Conseil.[131] His interpretation of the events must serve as a warning of the dangers of too heavy a reliance on sources written by Calvin's supporters. The result of the case was that the issue remained unresolved. An artificial peace was procured by the public reconciliation of all the parties before the 1554 elections.[132] Faced with the impasse created by the determined opposition of the ministers, the magistrates had little choice but to climb down. Unless the Petit Conseil had been willing to expel the entire Company of Pastors its members had no other option; the issue itself could not be settled. The Perrinists were faced with the stark reality that there was a practical limit to their ability to control the ministers. Put simply, they had no effective means of forcing the preachers and their local supporters to give way; at best, they could only hope to maintain the stalemate.

The elections of 1554 produced no drastic changes to the political balance of power in Geneva. There appears to have been some movement in the direction of the Calvinists. In 1553, only one Syndic could be identified as a Calvinist; two were elected in 1554. Michel de l'Arche, a Calvinist, and Pierre Tissot defeated Jean Lambert and Claude Vandel while Amblard Corne, also a Calvinist, and Claude du Pan beat Pierre Bonna and Guillaume Beney. Henry Aubert was defeated in the election of Treasurer by Jaques Desarts; both were Calvinists.[133] But, as Calvin himself reported, the situation in the Petit Conseil did not change; the Perrinists' power remained intact, though somewhat reduced. Once again an election was marred by clashes between Perrin and Jean de la Maisonneuve.[134] The situation remained generally calm, though no one believed that the truce would hold; the factional groupings had become too well entrenched.[135]

The ties between Calvin and his supporters are obvious in his pastoral activities. In 1554, he was involved in the weddings of three pro-Calvinist Genevan families. In January, he performed the marriage service for Guillaume Chevallier, a prominent refugee, and Domaine d'Arlod, a senator.[136] Later in September, Calvin married Domaine's son, Pierre, and Marguerite, the daughter of the former Articulant, Claude Chasteauneuf.[137] He had blessed the engagement of his secretary, Servetus's accuser, Nicolas de la Fontaine, to Perrine, the daughter of Pierre Gorin.[138] Jaques, the son of Jean Ami Curtet, and Jehanne, the daughter of Jaques Desarts, were also married by Calvin.[139] These pastoral duties give some insight into the level of personal intimacy between the Calvinist Genevans, the French refugees, and Calvin. All the evidence of 1554 emphasises a definite factional split in the city. The ministers, allied with their supporters, were very much a part of the dynamics of this political crisis in marked contrast with their limited role in the earlier Articulant–Guillermin clash.

The harmony imposed by magisterial fiat before the elections began to collapse in March. Philibert Berthelier and his uncle, Pierre Bonna, clashed with the Consistory.[140] A few days later Berthelier was again excommunicated.[141] By 1 June, Berthelier was in trouble with the magistracy as well for striking a foreigner. Corne was so angered that he demanded that Berthelier be deposed as an *auditeur*.[142] Foreigners were a cause of continuing concern to others besides Berthelier. The Petit Conseil decided that the matter needed another examination because 'beaucoup des gens de la ville parlent sus les estrangiers'.[143] On 21 June, Calvin reported that anti-French sentiment had reached the point where he had received a death threat.[144] One dispute followed another as the situation worsened; Corne continued arguing with Berthelier, who was by then in jail.[145] Jean Baptiste Sept was also imprisoned on 25 August for striking André Vindret.[146] The Berthelier affair continued throughout September; by late October, the magistrates felt compelled to seek advice from the Swiss once again.[147] The ministers expressed concern about the increasing incidence of violence in the city, especially against the French.[148]

Many of the disputes became sufficiently troublesome to warrant criminal prosecutions. Claudine Pital and Philibert de la Mar were accused of fornication after a report from the Bernese Consistory at Gex.[149] Two of the *auditeurs*, Jean Louis Favre and Nicolas Gentil, clashed over the city's finances; they were of opposing factions.[150] At least one Frenchman lashed out at the xenophobia in the city; Jean Navet, of Tours, was banished for saying that the 'enfants de Genève' were 'gouliards'.[151] Later, in October, Gilles le Febvre, from Chartres, was also banished because he called the Genevans dogs.[152] One of the more spectacular cases occurred in July when André Vulliod, an elderly notary, was arrested for taking Communion while excommunicated. He pleaded that he had thought the Council's ruling on the Berthelier case the year before applied to all excommunicates; his tongue was pierced with a hot iron and he was banished, a particularly savage punishment.[153]

From the citizens' point of view it must have been obvious that Geneva was poised on the brink of a serious factional clash. Disputes were souring personal relations and polarising the populace throughout Geneva in a manner not seen since the Articulant débâcle in 1540. People were being presented with a choice between a defence of traditional Genevan rights and the ministerial vision of a godly society. The ministers were in a position to drive home their message that their opponents were godless lovers of disorder and immorality, opposed to God's Truth. Events in Geneva may well have served to validate this view in the minds of many Genevans troubled by the Republic's state of affairs. In a very real sense, all disorder and every act of immorality could easily be used against the Perrinists, proof that under their leadership Geneva was truly 'a sinking cesspool of hell'.[154] Calvin repeatedly stressed his view that his opponents were arrogant men who tolerated sin and delighted in wickedness.[155]

Just as 1545 was a year notable, and notorious, for a specific crime, plague-spreading, 1554 was marked by three notable cases involving sodomy. In March, Lambert le Blanc and others were accused. He and four others, on the advice of Calvin and the ministers, were burned at the stake for their crime.[156] This case and its very public result undoubtedly shocked the city; for many it must have been proof enough of Geneva's gross sin and wickedness. In September five youths were arrested for the same crime. Their age resulted in a lenient sentence; the two youngest were beaten privately by their parents while the three older boys were thrashed in front of the school students and burned in effigy as a warning.[157] The new year started with another case against Mathieu Durand, who was beheaded and burned.[158] The fact that these cases involved refugees might lead one to expect that they would have been used as an excuse for greater xenophobia. However, it is just as likely that these cases, *interpreted* by the ministers in their pulpits, could have produced an altogether different result. For many Genevans this 'outbreak of immorality' would have lent credence to the charges being made by the ministers: Geneva's rulers were allowing the Republic to slide down the slippery slope, the broad path to destruction. In such a situation the Calvinists may have seemed less the party of the French and more of moral decency, law and order.

This fear of increasing disorder would have been reinforced by the events which preceded the start of the election period. A group of youths was arrested for processing through the streets with candles and chanting the Psalms derisively. Those arrested were Michel Sept, Estienne Papaz, Pierre du Crest, Hudriod Levin, Geoffrey Levin, Jean Griffon, and Jean Jaques Dadaz.[159] In one example of their singing it was reported that where the Psalms said 'leve le cueur, preste laureille', the youths sang 'leve le cul, ouvre les cuisses'.[160] This was certainly no more than a case of drunken excess associated with a Christmastide party. Jaques Nicolas Vulliet had already been deposed as a guard for abandoning his post to attend one of Sept's feasts.[161] The procession was viewed more seriously when it became apparent that some of the youths had been carrying firearms. This affair, in the midst of so many others, might well have troubled many Genevans. The spectacle of armed drunkards roaming the streets, blaspheming, perfectly illustrated the dire predictions of the ministers.

Calvin drove home to the Genevans the extent of the debauchery which he alleged had infected the city's rulers. On 27 January 1555, as the elections approached, he launched a furious denunciation of Geneva's rulers and their ungodly behaviour: 'Et ceux qui ont voix d'elire, ce sont ceux qui frequentent moins les sermons. Il est vray qu'on ne les verra gueres non plus venir les autres iours au temple: cependant ils se presenteront les premiers au conseil general, et voudront avoir la plus haute voix, encores qu'ils n'ayent monstré en toute leur vie aucun signe de Chrestienté.'[162] The average Genevan was presented with a difficult choice. The ministers were predicting and bemoaning the collapse of all godly order and decency. They and their supporters offered stability and godliness to avert the impending and justified chastisement of God's Wrath. Their opponents, the Perrinists, held themselves to be the last bulwark of Genevan independence and civic rights against the threatening tidal wave of Frenchmen. The previous clash over excommunication in 1553 had shown the true extent, but also the limitations, of Perrinist power. They could not rid the city of the French refugees or control the actions and words of the French ministers. Thus, unable to gain an outright victory, the Perrinists could offer only continued strife and turmoil.

Nevertheless, the Lieutenant and auditeur elections in November 1554 had shown the enduring strength of the Perrinists. Hudriod du Molard defeated Pierre Bonna to become Lieutenant while Jean Philibert Bonna and Jaques Nicolas Vulliet were elected auditeurs over Jean François Bernard and Jehanton Genod; a sweep for the Perrinists.[163] This victory was to be the last success for the Perrinists. The high-water mark of their power had been the successful appeal by Berthelier; their inability to press, or even secure, this victory had shown the ultimate weakness of their position. The first dramatic sign of a shift in Geneva's political landscape came on 24 January 1555, a week after Durand's execution for sodomy and in the midst of the trial for the blasphemous procession. The Conseils des Soixante and Deux Cents overruled the Petit Conseil and accepted the ministerial interpretation of the Ecclesiastical Ordinances about excommunication; the Consistory's authority to discipline was secured.[164]

The elections of 1555 saw the Perrinist grip on political power finally broken. Unfortunately, the city records do not contain the names of the defeated candidates for that year. Nevertheless, the election of three committed Calvinists, Jean Lambert, Henri Aubert, and Jean Pierre Jessé, as well as a moderate with Calvinist sympathies, Pierre Bonna, is evidence of the decisive shift in Genevan politics. Antoine Chiccand's death and

Gaspard Favre's removal from the Petit Conseil meant that two new senators were elected. Chiccand, a moderate or Calvinist, and Favre, a staunch Perrinist, were replaced by two dedicated Calvinists, Jean Pernet and Jean de la Maisonneuve.[165] The turmoil in Geneva which followed meant that the deceased Michel Morel, a Calvinist, was not replaced as Châtelain of Jussy until the following year.[166] Additions to the Conseil des Deux Cents, elected by the new Petit Conseil, saw the inclusion of many new men with ties to the Calvinists: Jaques Curtet; Jean François Bernard; Charles Porral; Aimé and François Chasteauneuf; Guillaume Chevallier; Jean Chautemps, the younger; Pierre d'Arlod; Claude and François de la Maisonneuve; Jean Collanda; André and Jaques Furby; Estienne and Jean Bandière (or Amaury).[167] Also, Hudriod du Molard, who had served in the Petit Conseil every year but two since 1536 (when he was in the Conseil des Soixante), was relegated again to the lower council.[168]

Similar changes were seen at other levels of Geneva's government. The narrowness of the Calvinist majority is shown in their inability to eliminate the Perrinists from every office. In the lower civil court Jean Lambert, the new Syndic, and Hudriod du Molard were replaced by Claude Rigot, André Mailliard, and Pierre Savoye, none of whom was a staunch Calvinist. In the upper court, Jean Lambert, Pierre Verna, Jaques Nicolas Vulliet and Philibert Bonna made way for Jean François Bernard, Jean Rosset, Louis Franc, and Gaspard Favre; one Calvinist, Lambert, and three Perrinists were replaced by three Calvinists and one Perrinist, Favre. In the criminal court, the Procés Criminels, two Calvinists promoted to the Petit Conseil, were replaced by three new men, Pierre Dorsière, Jean Chautemps the younger, and Claude Gerbel. Dorsière and Chautemps were Calvinists but Gerbel's affiliation is not clear. Two more Calvinists, Pierre Jessé and Michel de l'Arche, were added to the all-Calvinist committee (Claude Delestra, Jean Ami Curtet, Pierre Dorsière) which oversaw the hospital's work.[169]

The election results of 1555 show a substantial if not overwhelming shift towards the Calvinists; the mixed results in the court appointments serve as a necessary caveat against any temptation to overestimate popular support for the Calvinists. It is not possible, however, to explain this change with complete assurance. Calvin's supporters at the time were unanimous in emphasising that the arrogance and clannishness of the Perrinists contributed to their defeat.[170] The earlier attempt to limit bourgeois rights and the exclusion of the bourgeois ministers from the Conseil Général may have made some Genevan bourgeois suspicious of the Perrinists; their close familial ties may have nourished these suspicions. The obvious inability of the Perrinists to defeat their opponents, control the ministers, or limit the influence of the refugees may have led some to swing to the Calvinists; voting for the Perrinists meant accepting continuous, inconclusive confrontation and disorder at the highest levels of Genevan government. These factors, along with Geneva's apparent slide into immorality, highlighted by the ministers, and the presence of a few French refugees with a vote, may have provided the rather slight shift in the electorate necessary to bring the Calvinists to power.

It is essential to stress the slim majority the Calvinists had. The 1555 Petit Conseil had twenty-seven members. Using all the available evidence it has been possible to identify twelve as staunch Calvinists: Jean Lambert, Jean Pierre Jessé, Jean Ami Curtet, Jean Pernet, François Chamois, Henri Aubert, Amblard Corne, Michel de l'Arche, Pernet Desfosses, Jaques Desarts, Jean Chautemps, and Jean de la Maisonneuve. Another five senators sided, to some extent, with these Calvinists in the critical votes against the Perrinists in the summer of 1555; no session against the Perrinists had more than thirteen senators in attendance, though.[171] Their subsequent careers imply that they were not zealous enough and were later moved aside as the Calvinists secured their hold on power; Claude Rigot left the Petit Conseil after that year, Domaine d'Arlod and Claude du Pan left after 1556, Pierre Bonna and Guillaume Beney after 1557.[172] Of the ten senators who failed to attend any session against the Perrinists, seven were clearly Perrinists: Pierre Tissot, Ami Perrin, Pierre Vandel, Pierre Mallagniod, Jean Baptiste Sept, Claude Roset, and François Beguin. Two more, Jean Philippin and Claude Vandel, were removed after the next year while Estienne Chapeaurouge left after 1557.

Such a slender majority suggests a shift in the balance of political power in Geneva without implying an overwhelming realignment of public opinion. Rather, it is reasonable to suppose that the Calvinists benefited from a rejection of the futile turmoil and confrontation which had marked the two years of Perrinist supremacy. The Calvinists were left with the problem of devising a means of securing and strengthening their position. The changes they made to the Councils and courts show that they tried to entrench their supporters at every level of Genevan government, as the Perrinists had done before them. Their greatest change was to the Conseil Général. The ambivalence of this body had raised the Perrinists to power and then replaced them with the Calvinists in a very short period of time. The Calvinists had no intention of risking such future changes. The obvious answer to this problem was to alter the character and composition of this body in such a way as to guarantee Calvinist majorities. The method which the Calvinists chose involved the admission of substantial numbers of French refugees to the bourgeoisie. While it is true that the numbers involved are not enormous, the finely balanced nature of the two factions, apparent in previous elections, was such that even a slight change to the electorate could have profound consequences. The enfranchisement of a dedicated bloc of pro-Calvin refugees, coupled with the fortuitous chance to exile many of their opponents, gave the Calvinists just the change they desired. Before the next election in 1556 around 130 new bourgeois were admitted and over fifty Perrinists faced judicial action ranging from warnings and disenfranchisement to exile or death. In a city of 12,000 persons with an evenly divided electorate, the addition of so many new voters and the expulsion of the opposition's leadership was sufficient to alter Geneva's entire magisterial structure.

There is no doubt that the admission of these bourgeois was a calculated political move to pack the Genevan electorate. The Petit Conseil did present its action as an attempt to raise revenues to repay some of Geneva's onerous foreign debt.[173] Bonivard's account highlights the danger of accepting this explanation without question. He stresses three reasons for granting so many Frenchmen bourgeois status: to control the elections; to increase the number of men available to fight in Geneva's militia; and to raise money to repay the debts.[174] Recent historical works have presented a very confused picture of the Calvinist victory and its aftermath. Bouwsma simply fails to give any explanation of the Calvinist triumph.[175] Parker accepts the blatant political nature of the bourgeois admissions but quickly passes over the affair.[176] McGrath presents a view which implies that the Perrinists, in control of Geneva's government, were somehow duped into admitting the Frenchmen to the bourgeoisie for financial reasons; realising the political implications of the admissions, they rioted.[177] The truth is that when the Calvinists decided to act they did so quickly, and the Perrinists responded with equal speed.

No action was taken until 18 April; in the next fortnight twenty-eight bourgeois were admitted. By 6 May another six were admitted; representations were then made to the Petit Conseil by citizens of the need to debate this new policy. Thus the Perrinists acted the minute they realised that these admissions were to continue. On 2 May the Petit Conseil announced that the move was to raise money; four days later the first official demands were made that the policy be put before the Conseil des Deux Cents. The Petit Conseil refused this request and admitted an additional sixteen bourgeois on 9 May.[178] More complaints were recorded on 13 May but were rebuffed by the senators.[179] At this point the policy had to be suspended while the city dealt with the problems associated with the convulsive riot which took place three days later on 16 May. The opportunity which the riot afforded the Calvinists to crush their opponents took clear priority over the admission of bourgeois. No new admissions took place until the last of the large trials of Perrinists was completed in August.

It would be a mistake to assume that the riot on 16 May was the first outbreak of trouble in 1555; clashes were more frequent than ever. Balthasar Sept had been jailed after disputes in January; he was not freed until 2 May, a fortnight before the riot.[180] He was re-arrested the next day.[181] Jaques Nicolas Vulliet argued with Thivent Furjod; Pierre Tissot clashed with Thivent's brother, Estienne.[182] Jean Baptiste Sept and Jean Cugnier were arrested for falsely accusing Jean Pernet and Jean de la Maisonneuve, the new senators, of treason.[183] Henri Aubert complained about the Sept brothers a few weeks later when Jean Baptiste was again in trouble.[184] Calvin argued with Perrin and others for attending a sermon in the Bernese church at Nyon in which he was attacked.[185] André Vulliod was arrested for blasphemy.[186] Finally, on 7 May, the day after the initial protests about the bourgeois admission, the senior François Comparet was accused of sedition; he was held throughout the troubles which followed and linked to the riot of 16 May, even though he was in jail. He was executed for treason on 21 June.[187]

Hudriod du Molard led the list of local Genevans who raised an official protest against this new policy on bourgeois admissions. He and the Perrinists recommended that the new bourgeois be denied arms and that the vote be withheld from them for ten years.[188] Jean Lambert, a frequent opponent of Perrin, spoke at length against this proposal. He argued that Perrin's ideas were contrary to the established customs of the city. Moreover, he could not understand Perrin's concern about armed foreigners. Lambert made an explicit reference to the sedition charges against Perrin in the late 1540s; he said Perrin was more than willing then to allow 200 French cavalrymen into Geneva. Finally, he rejected any infringement of bourgeois voting rights as inherently unfair and contrary to Genevan tradition.[189] The Petit Conseil, dominated by the Calvinists, refused to consider referring the issue to the larger Conseil des Deux Cents and pressed ahead with the admissions.

These internal problems were only exacerbated by Geneva's international situation. The treaty with Berne was due to lapse in March 1555 unless renewed. Negotiations dragged on inconclusively; there seems to have been an expectation and acceptance that they would fail. On 12 March, the Petit Conseil ordered that the army be put in order; the following day similar orders were issued for the city's fortifications, artillery, and munitions.[190] Geneva felt its position seriously threatened. Berne's antipathy to the growing influence of the French ministers and refugees was well known. With the Calvinist victory, the city could hardly expect a sympathetic hearing from the Bernese. The need, referred to by Bonivard, to increase the militia which the bourgeois paid for may have arisen out of a fear that the Bernese would react negatively to the Calvinist triumph; Berne would certainly be displeased once the admissions began. The threat of a clash with Berne and the chance to crush the Perrinists may have led the Calvinist magistrates to act quickly. It is worth noting that Calvin, Chauvet, and two senators, Henri Aubert and François Chamois, were sent to Berne to negotiate for Geneva on 28 March. They returned on 11 April empty-handed; within a week the magistrates began admitting the bourgeois.[191]

By 16 May it must have become apparent to the Perrinists that the changes being made at Geneva would keep them out of power for the foreseeable future. That evening, after dinner and drink, they took to the streets protesting against the actions of the Petit Conseil. The riot was no more than a drunken procession which became a disorderly brawl; such events had occurred on a number of previous occasions, as is obvious from the foregoing chapters.[192] Regardless of claims made later on, there is no evidence to support the assertion that this riot concealed a conspiracy to overthrow the State.[193] The magistrates acted to arrest some of the rioters, especially those of little political importance. In general the State was slow in moving against the more prominent men involved in the riot, which seems to imply that, at first, the riot was not regarded as too great a threat to Geneva. For example, Perrin was still attending Petit Conseil meetings on 24 May.[194] The slowness of the official reaction may have been an attempt to avoid antagonising Berne; Berne was greatly displeased with the subsequent actions taken in Geneva and linked the treaty's renewal with leniency for the Perrinists.[195] Likewise, the magistrates may not have realised immediately what a unique opportunity for destroying their opponents had been given them in the riot.

In time the magistrates began to move decisively against the Perrinists.[196] Throughout the summer Perrinists were fined, exiled or sentenced to death (see Tables 24 and 25).[197] On 6 June, Jean Baptiste Sept and Jaques Nicolas Vulliet were deposed as auditeurs and replaced by Jean Rosset, an elder, and Jean François Bernard, nephew of the minister Jaques Bernard.[198] On 19 June, the relatives of the fugitive Perrinists were disenfranchised and expelled from the Conseil Général; Nicolas Gentil was arrested when he protested against this move.[199] After the riot and the flight of many of the leading Perrinists, the Petit Conseil finally decided to consult the Conseil des Deux Cents over the bourgeois admissions; its actions were upheld.[200]

The actions of the Petit Conseil were attacked by a number of people, as

TABLE 24   *Individuals charged as Perrinists*

Person	Sentence
Bauffri, Jean	sentenced to death, fled
Bauffri, Pierre	sentenced to death, fled
Beguin, François	fled
Berthelier, Philibert	sentenced to death, fled
Berthelier, François Daniel	executed
Bornand, Jaques (Gallard)	warned, 100-écu bond
Bosson, Claude	fined, public humiliation
Chabod, François	sentenced to death, fled (?)
Cheneval, Jaques	banished for 10 years
Chenu, Michel	deposed from CC, 200-écu bond, released-
Comparet, François, jun.	executed
Comparet, François, sen.	executed
Cusin, Jaques	disenfranchised
Dadaz, Jean Jaques	?
Darbey, Antoine	deprived of rights, public humiliation
De la Rovina, Philibert	?
De Joux, Claude	sentenced to death, fled
De Joux, Pierre	sentenced to death, fled
De Joux, Rollin	warned
De Joux, Simon (Claudon)	sentenced to death, fled
Dolens, Pierre	public humiliation
Du Molard, Hudriod	fled
Foural, Jean	sentenced to death, fled
Franc, Claude	?
Furjod, Jean	warned
Gallois, Claude (Mermilliod)	public humiliation
Geneve, Ami	banished for 10 years
Geneve, Antoine	?
Geneve, Claude (le Bastard)	executed
Genod, Guillaume	banished for 3 years
Gentil, Nicolas	resigned from CC
Jaquemoz, Claude (le Fornier)	public humiliation
Mailliet, Janin	banished for 3 years
Mailliet, Jean	warned, 200-écu bond, released
Michallet, Jean	sentenced to death, fled
Paquet, François	fined, warned
Perrin, Ami	sentenced to death, fled
Savoye, Pierre	sentenced to death, fled
Sept Balthasar	sentenced to death, fled
Sept, Jean Baptiste	executed
Sept, Michel	sentenced to death, fled
Simon, Cary	?
Thomas, Girard	public humiliation
Tronchona, Louis	sentenced to death, fled
Vandel, Pierre	executed
Verna, Bezanson (Pierre's son)	warned
Verna, Pierre	sentenced to death, fled (?)

CC = Consel des Deux Cents

TABLE 25   *Individuals charged for contact with Perrinists*

Persons	Sentence
Arpeau, Jean (Sieur de Troches)	200-écu fine
Bisard, Jean	beaten
Bonna, Jaques	?
Bonna, Jean Philibert	?
Bonnet, Guillaume (Benoît's son)	executed
Chiccand, Jean (Antoine's son)	warned, 200 écus fine
Du Chesme, Nicod	executed
Favre, Jean	public humiliation
Freitag, Jaques (of Zürich, Fr. Clerc's servant)	jailed for 3 days
Hugue, Antoine (de Laval)	banished
Mestrazat, Louise (Gaspard Favre's widow)	public humiliation, 25 écus fine
Monetier, Mathieu (Pechod)	warned
Perrin, Madeleine (P. Vinaret's widow, Ami's sister)	warned
Pertemps, Clauda	warned
Pottu, Gabriel	?
Ramel, Jean Louis	?
Sept, Adrienne (F. Chabod's wife)	warned
Wife of A. Venerat	warned
Wife of P. Verna	warned

one might expect. Jean Baptiste Sept wrote to his brother-in-law, Pierre Bonna, the Syndic, to condemn the high-handed, authoritarian moves of 'votre demi-Conseil'.[201] Philibert Berthelier, angered by the execution of his brother, François Daniel, launched a scathing attack on the character of the senators. He called them variously thieves, murderers, Mamellus, Artichaux, sinners and perjurers.[202] Numerous anonymous placards were posted in Geneva denouncing the senators' actions.[203] The two contrasting epitaphs of the executed Perrinist, Claude Geneve, are worth examining. They give some idea of the vast difference between the perceptions of the State, led by the Calvinists, and the supporters of the defeated Perrinists. Bonivard recorded an epigram composed to justify Geneve's execution.

> Pour estre tumbe au meschef,
> Daimer plus un homme que Dieu,
> Claude de Geneve ha son chef
> Faict clouer en ce present lieu.[204]

A notice secretly posted at Cornavin, in the city, presented another view.

> Seur et loyal fus à ma Républicque,
> J'ay pour Genève enduré grandz ennuis,
> J'ay pour son heur, franchise et politicque

Submis mon corps aux dangiers jour et nuict.
O toy, passant, qui sabas te conduytz
Pour tous ces biens, tu vois mon sang espandre,
Mon chef cloé et mon corps en l'er pendre,
Indigne, hélas, de cest outrageux blasme.
Mays tien toy seur que de ce corps mourant,
Que maint amy va tristement plorant,
Le ciel joyeux a reçeu à soy l'asme.[205]

The Calvinists saw the Perrinists as sinners, lovers of wickedness, enemies of God; they were themselves God's champions, upholders of a godly society. The Perrinists considered themselves to be Geneva's truest, most faithful citizens; their opponents were the tools of Geneva's subversion to French domination.

Opposition to the Calvinist magistrates was not confined to Geneva. The mass expulsion of so many leading citizens may have left the local opposition leaderless and crippled, but it inflamed passions in the other Swiss Protestant cities. Bullinger received many letters attesting to the fury which the Calvinists had raised. Musculus wrote that in Berne Calvin was the object of an anger which increased daily.[206] Hotman wrote that Calvin was as popular in Basle as in Catholic Paris.[207] Haller, in Berne, reported that it was almost impossible to find anyone willing to speak well of Calvin.[208] Bullinger dutifully relayed these reports to Calvin and expressed his concern over the negative impact of the Perrinists' condemnation.[209] But the Calvinists were quite willing to risk the ire of their neighbours and supporters throughout Switzerland if it meant the defeat of their opponents; the Perrinists had shown an unwillingness to face such an adverse reaction on the part of the Swiss when presented with the threat of the ministers' mass resignation during the earlier excommunication debate.[210]

The Calvinists now put through a number of changes in Geneva. Women were separated from men in the churches.[211] The post of Capitaine Général was abolished and the bourgeois confirmed in their civic rights.[212] The Conseil Général voted to allow the Petit Conseil, at its own discretion, to arm even the habitants to defend Geneva.[213] These actions served only to anger the exiles. They took up posts on the Pont d'Arve and harangued passers-by.[214] Berthelier shouted to Claude Pilette, on 27 October, an excellent example of their opinions. 'Nous avions délibéré de n'avoir point d'escommunient, ni de Consistoire, ni de bourgeois françois; nous avons eu tant de peine de chasser le pape, la messe, les escommuniements, et ils nous les boutent plus grans que jamais.'[215] In the end, their complaints and those of the Swiss were of no avail; the Calvinists had triumphed and had no intention of relinquishing even a part of the field they had won.

Bonivard reported that the major cause of the Perrinists' defeat was their clannishness and arrogance. While it is not possible to prove their arrogance, there can be no doubt about the close family ties amongst the Perrinists. Of the sixty-six persons named as Perrinists, or their associates, twenty-six were directly related to the six prominent, interconnected families: Balard, Berthelier, Favre, Hugues, Sept and Vandel. Two of these families, Hugues and Berthelier, were long established in Geneva. The others dated from recent immigrations to Geneva no earlier than the end of the previous century: Balthasar Sept became a bourgeois in 1477; Bandissard Balard in 1486; Claude Vandel in 1487; Jean Favre in 1508. It may well be that these families, only recently established in Geneva, felt threatened by the new wave of wealthy immigrants seeking to gain political power for themselves and their children.

The notary records show a wider range of ties among the Perrinists. Jean Baptiste, Balthasar and Michel Sept were indebted to Gaspard Favre.[216] Denis Hugue was connected in a business deal with Jean du Molard, his brother-in-law.[217] Jean Favre, bought property from Jean and Thomas Dessires in a contract witnessed by Jaques Cheneval and Pierre Verna; the contract was signed in Verna's house.[218] Jean Griffon sold some property to Claude de Joux; Jean Jaques Dadaz was a witness.[219] Estienne Furjod, Jean's brother, was indebted to Claude Perrin, husband of Jeanne, Estienne's mother.[220] These records connect an additional six convicted Perrinists with those who were interrelated by blood or marriage. The familial and business ties added necessary cohesion to the Perrinist faction, the latter-day Enfants de Genève. These connections were the sinews which allowed the Perrinists to mould the Revolutionary motto into one of their own: 'que lo enfan de vella se devon manteni lun latro, & ne se laissi pas mastina a cesto françoes'.[221]

The most important issue related to the Perrinist defeat is not the admission of the French to the bourgeoisie. That was only a means of securing future election victories for the Calvinists. Nor can one look for the cause of the Perrinist rout in the riot of 16 May, which was a drunken, disorganised fiasco. After that riot was over the Calvinists used it as a convenient excuse to drive the leaders of the opposition from the city. If one is to explain or understand the defeat of the Perrinists, then one must explain their election defeat in February 1555. In November 1554 the Perrinists had swept the elections for Lieutenant and auditeur. In the interim enough public opinion was swayed to allow the Calvinists to persuade the Conseil des Deux Cents to elect a Calvinist majority to the Petit Conseil.[222]

By playing on their compatriots' fears about the French and annoyance at the ministers' actions, the Perrinists had been able to gain a workable majority in 1553. However, they were wholly unable to pass any of the reforms necessary to break the impasse which had developed in Geneva's ruling elite about the role of the French ministers and refugees. The Calvinist faction remained and could not be broken. Failing in their attempt to bring the ministers to heel, the Perrinists saw their hold on power weaken in the 1554 elections. Another year of futile confrontation may have been enough to convince some Genevans that it was time to give the Calvinists a chance to govern and break Geneva's factional deadlock. The immoral behaviour which erupted immediately before the 1555 elections may have swayed a few more people to support the Calvinists and their tough policies against corruption. Undoubtedly, the close family ties amongst the Perrinists, which helped secure their grip on power, would have worried some, and blocked the political ambitions of even more.

However, it is essential to recall that the margin of the Calvinist victory and the electoral swing which produced it were very slight. The Perrinists had been unwilling or unable to use their power to the point of expelling the ministers or the refugees; the Calvinists showed no such qualms or constraints. They were ruthlessly willing to alter the Genevan electorate to secure their grip on power: and when presented with the chance, they were able and willing to crush the opposition and expel a significant number of their fellow citizens.[223] As the next chapter will show, the Calvinists were not content with this singular victory; they used their new-found political power to sweep away much of Geneva's ruling elite.

NOTES

1 As was Amblard Corne, who had just managed to save his political career; he had been dismissed for his complaints about official corruption in 1545 only to become the new Syndic in 1546. Cf., Bergier, 'Corne', pp. 462–4. See Figures 7–9.

2 Fiendaz, who died before 14 August 1550, was a cousin to the Septs and husband of Antoine Froment's step-daughter. AEG/RC/45, fols. 67 (14 Aug 1550), 141 (5 Dec 1550).

3 Berthelier defeated Pierre Migerand, son-in-law of Jean Lect, Antoine's brother.

4 For the election results see AEG/RC/44, fols. 319v (7 Feb 1550), 323 (14 Feb 1550), 326 (18 Feb 1550).

5 These clashes involved an impressive list of Genevans: Louis Bandière, Claude Curtin, Michel Goudin, Pierre Lespinglier, Loup Tissot, Berthod du Molard, Roz Monet, Jaques Bonna, Gaspard Favre, Balthasar Sept, Michel Sept, Philibert de la Mar, Claude Pitard, Jaques Nicolas Vulliet, Louis le Grand (Perrin's servant), Roland Taccon, Nicolas Bramet, Amied d'Arnex.

6 CO, vol. 21, col. 463 (20 Apr 1550).

7 AEG/PC/1re Ser., 461 (24 Feb 1550), 2e Ser., 860 (14 Jul 1550). This coincided with an attempt to renegotiate the treaty with Berne mediated by Basle in 1544, cf., Roget, *Histoire*, vol. 3, pp. 128ff.

8 AEG/RC/45, fol. 102 (30 Sep 1550).

9 For Lullin see AEG/RC/45, fols. 36 (30 Jun 1550), 91v (15 Sep 1550) and, for d'Arlod, AEG/PC/2e Ser., 898bis (2 Dec 1550). Loys Blandin was also arrested on the Consistory's recommendation though the reason is unknown. AEG/RC/44, fol. 311 (27 Jan 1550).

10 AEG/RC/44, fol. 301 (3 Jan 1550); PC/2e Ser., 811 (9 Jan 1550).

11 Roget, *Histoire*, vol. 3, pp. 123f.

12 AEG/RC/45, fols. 125–125v (11 Nov 1550), 126v–127v (14 Nov 1550), 128v (16 Nov 1550).

13 See pp. 149f.

14 Gautier, *Histoire*, vol. 3, p. 416.

15 Roget, *Histoire*, vol. 3, p. 136.

16 AEG/RC/45, fol. 184 (6 Feb 1551); Roset, p. 336. This election marked the full rehabilitation of a leading Articulant, François Lullin, who was again allowed to stand for the Petit Conseil. Flournois, *Extraits*, p. 19.

17 AEG/RC/45, fols. 167 (16 Jan 1551), 210 (27 Feb 1551). See Roget, *Histoire*, vol. 3, pp. 211f. Geneva's financial predicament forced a reduction in magisterial salaries this year. Indeed, Chamois returned his entire 100ff per annum salary for overseeing the city's fortifications. The Conseil des Deux Cents discussed abolishing the châtelain posts and cancelling the restoration of Meigret's pension. The latter step was especially favoured by J. B. Sept, Pbt. Bonna, J. Fabri, and Nic. Gentil.

18 AEG/RC/45, fols. 217v (7 Mar 1551), 221–222v (12 Mar 1551), 226v (17 Mar 1551); PC/1re Ser., 468 (17 Apr 1551).

19 AEG/RC/45, fols. 217–217v (7 Mar 1551); PC/2e Ser., 930 (23 Mar 1551); *RCP*, vol. 1, p. 75 (8 Mar 1551). The treaty was eventually renewed for five years. Roget, *Histoire*, vol. 3, pp. 140–43.

20 AEG/RC/45, fols. 226 (17 Mar 1551), 236v (27 Mar 1551).

21 AEG/RC/45, fol. 236v (27 Mar 1551); PC/2e Ser., 933 (26, 27 Mar 1551). The dispute also involved Fran. Chabod, Jaq. Conte, Nic. Gentil. and Louis Pecolat, CO, vol. 21, col. 478 (27 Mar 1551). See, Roget, *Histoire*, vol. 3, pp. 145–8. Berthelier had been accused of fornication with Pierre Ruffi's widow. There were also two other minor clashes with the ministers. Louis Criblet slandered the French and Fran. Paquet, Geneva's regular ambassador to the French court, clashed with the minister Fabri. AEG/PC 2e Ser., 916 (1 Jan 1551), 927 (19 Feb 1551).

22 AEG/RC/45, fol. 272 (12 May 1551).

23 AEG/RC/45, fol. 271 (11 May 1551).

24 AEG/PC/2e Ser., 946 (16 May 1551); RC/45, fol. 275v (18 May 1551).

25 AEG/RC/45, fol. 287v (22 May 1551). The fluid state of the situation explains Calvin's distrust of the forced reconciliation of early 1551. See, CO, vol. 14, col. 133f (to Farel, 15 Jun 1551). Cf., also, François, *Meigret*.

26 AEG/RC/45, fol. 291v (25 May 1551).

27 AEG/RC/45, fols. 310v–311 (22 Jun 1551), 315v (29 Jun 1551); PC/2e Ser., 953 (29 Jun–6 Aug 1551). Bonna said to the elder Jehanton Genod that he 'maintenoit mieulx la loy des Francoys que de Geneve'. CO, vol. 21, col. 483 (18 Jun 1551).

28 AEG/PC/2e Ser., 952 (26 Jun 1551), 954 (29 Jun 1551). Roget, *Histoire*, vol. 3, pp. 152f. Cf., Roget, *Histoire*, vol. 3, pp. 131f, Desfosses was noted, and admonished, for his zeal in the pursuit of crimes. He questioned the servants of François Chamois, in Jan 1551, to see whether Chamois gambled. Chamois protested and Desfosses was told not to

continue with such methods of investigation.

29　AEG/RC/45, fol. 318 (3 Jul 1551); RC/46, fols. 1–1v (6 Jul 1551).

30　AEG/RC/46, fols. 32 (10 Aug 1551), 36 (14 Aug 1551). See, Roget, *Histoire*, vol. 3, p. 151. Bonna's wife was accused of dancing at Jaques Blondel's house. Bonna was also charged with arguing with a French apothecary, J. Decosterd, after a sermon.

31　AEG/PC/2e Ser., 955 (3 Jul 1551); RC/46, fols. 2v (6 Jul 1551), 4v (7 Jul 1551). Bergeron and Sept were often companions, both were arrested at Lect's party in 1546. Bergeron had also been admonished for complaints he made against the ministers' baptismal policy, AEG/Consist., vol. 5, fols. 44 (3 Jul 1550), 49v (30 Jul 1550). The factions had not formed to the extent that intra-factional disputes were laid aside.

32　AEG/PC/1re Ser., 470 (11 Aug 1551).

33　AEG/RC/46, fols. 68v–69 (5 Oct 1551).

34　AEG/RC/46, fol. 47v (28 Aug 1551).

35　AEG/RC/46, fol. 53 (14 Sep 1551).

36　AEG/PC/2e Ser., 959 (14–16 Aug 1551), 963 (Sep 1551).

37　AEG/RC/46, fol. 65v (28 Sep 1551). Hans Rey of Fribourg brought the news.

38　AEG/PC/1re Ser., 471 (16 Oct–23 Dec 1551). Cf., Roget, *Histoire*, vol. 3, pp. 182, and p. 182, n. 1. He was held in the custody of Pierre Tissot, Hudriod du Molard and Michel Voisin.

39　AEG/RC/46, fol. 89 (9 Nov 1551). Cf., Roget, *Histoire*, vol. 3, p. 180. Bolsec was also supported by a certain Jaques Goudard, AEG/PC/2e Ser., 970 (2 Dec 1551), 1000 (16 Jun 1552); Andrée, wife of Perrichon Andru, AEG/PC/2e Ser., 983 (1 Jan 1552); and François de Cassines, AEG/PC/2e Ser., 984 (11–27 Jan 1552).

40　AEG/RC/46, fol. 113 (9 Dec 1551).

41　AEG/RC/46, fol. 114 (11 Dec 1551). See, CO, vol. 14, col. 272f (to Farel, 27 Jan 1552), for Calvin's comments on the case. Also, cf., Roget, *Histoire*, vol. 3, pp. 188–97.

42　The case dominated sessions of the Petit Conseil for two months. AEG/RC/46, fols. 82v (27 Oct 1551), 84 (29 Oct 1551), 85 (30 Oct 1551), 86 (2 Nov 1551), 87v (5 Nov 1551),88 (6 Nov 1551), 90v–91 (12 Nov 1551), 95 (16 Nov 1551), 96–96v (19 Nov 1551), 104v (30 Nov 1551), 117 (15 Dec 1551), 118v (17 Dec 1551), 120 (21 Dec 1551), 121 (22 Dec 1551).

43　The case started at a Congregation meeting, or Biblical lecture. See *RCP*, vol. 1, p. 76 (15 May 1551), pp. 137f (16 Oct 1551). The initial witnesses were French refugees: L. de Normandie; R. Estienne; Php. Sarazin; J. Crespin; J. Bude; Ch. de Jonvillars; Ger., Leon, and Nic. Colladon; Gal. Caraciola, Marquis de Vico; and Enoch, the school regent. See, Roget, *Histoire*, vol. 3, pp. 161f, 179. Biographical information on the Estienne brothers, Robert, Henri and François, all famous printers can be found in F. Schreiber, *The Estiennes* (New York: 1982), especially, pp. 45f., 127f., 185 and E. Armstrong, *Royal Printer, Robert Estienne: An Historical Study of the Elder Stephanus* (Cambridge: 1954).

44　This connection may explain the virulently anti-ministerial placard found in St Pierre's pulpit during the case. AEG/RC/46, fol. 93 (15 Nov 1551).

45　CO, vol. 14, col. 200 (to Farel, 7 Nov 1551), col. 271f (to Farel, 27 Jan 1551). Some of Calvin's supporters expressed negative interpretations of the magistrates' actions. See., *Advis*, pp. 106ff. and Roset, pp. 343f.

46　AEG/RC/46, fols. 123–123v (25 Dec 1551), 128 (31 Dec 1551), 129 (1 Jan 1552).

47　AEG/RC/46, fol. 124v (25 Dec 1551).

48　AEG/RC/46, fol. 138v (21 Jan 1552). Calvin had already expressed displeasure at Trolliet's role as censor. Flournois, *Extraits*, p. 19 (19 Aug 1551). Geneva's ministers were not alone in their dislike for Trolliet. I am indebted to Penny Roberts of Warwick University for pointing out that Trolliet had also caused disturbances in the early 1540s in Troyes on his way back to Geneva from his monastery in Burgundy. Trolliet annoyed the Protestant ministers and the pharmicists by performing miracle cures; his attacks on clerical abuses brought down upon him the wrath of the Catholic clergy as well. However, he was extremely popular with the common people for his preaching. BN, Dupuy Ms. 698, Nicolas Pithou, *Histoire Ecclésiastique de l'Eglise de Troyes*, fols. 33–34v.

49 AEG/PC/2e Ser., 971 (9 Nov 1551).
50 AEG/PC/2e Ser., 979 (1 Dec 1551).
51 AEG/PC/2e Ser., 978 (1 Dec 1551).
52 AEG/RC/46, fols. 146 (5 Feb 1552), 148v (7 Feb 1552). Cf., Roget, *Histoire*, vol. 3, pp. 226f. Three others disinclined to Calvin gained office. Jean Philibert Bonna and Jean Baptiste Sept were made judges; Claude Rigot became Procureur Général replacing P. Vandel, elevated to the Syndic's post.
53 AEG/RC/46, fols. 300v (8 Nov 1552), 304 (13 Nov 1552). Roget, *Histoire*, vol. 3, p. 249.
54 AEG/RC/46, fols. 146v (5 Feb 1552), 147v (7 Feb 1552).
55 Roset, pp. 344f.
56 AEG/RC/46, fol. 165v (28 Feb 1552). Roget, *Histoire*, vol. 3, pp. 226f.
57 AEG/RC/46, fols. 162–162v (25 Feb 1552).
58 AEG/PC/2e Ser., 987 (12 Feb 1552). Cf., AEG/RC/38, fol. 331v (21 Aug 1544).
59 AEG/PC/2e Ser., 990 (16 Feb 1552).
60 AEG/RC/46, fols. 176 (21 Mar 1552), 181v (31 May 1552).
61 AEG/RC/46, fols. 207 (17 May 1552), 211 (24 May 1552).
62 AEG/PC/2e Ser., 995 (18 Apr 1552).
63 AEG/RC/46, fol. 185 (5 Apr 1552).
64 AEG/RC/46, fol. 183 (2 Apr 1552).
65 AEG/RC/46, fols. 222–223v (13, 14 Jun 1552), 225v–226 (20 Jun 1552). Roset, pp. 346f. Roget, *Histoire*, vol. 3, pp. 235f. François Daniel Berthelier stressed this same doctrine at his sedition trial in 1555. He said to Calvin that '(vous) n'êtes qu'un hérétique avec votre prédestination'. Gaberel, *Histoire*, vol. 1, p. 417.
66 Beza, 'Calvin', p. 60.
67 CO, vol. 14, col. 434 (to Dryander, Dec 1552).
68 Roget, *Histoire*, vol. 3, pp. 236f. Champel was Geneva's usual place of execution.
69 AEG/RC/46, fol. 258 (19 Aug 1552). François de la Rovina clashed in the Conseil des Deux Cents with Perrin, Trolliet, and P. Vandel, AEG/PC/1re Ser., 480 (3 Nov 1552–10 Jan 1553); PC/2e Ser., 1010 (3–10 Nov 1552); *RCP*, vol. 1, pp. 143f (7 Nov 1552). At least one refugee, Nicaise Bourgonville, supported Trolliet, albeit after the latter's recantation. AEG/PC/1re Ser., 481 (24 Dec 1552).
70 AEG/RC/46, fols. 248v (28 Jul 1552), 262v–263 (29 Aug 1552), 264 (30 Aug 1552), 265v (31 Aug 1552), 266v (1 Sep 1552), 280 (3 Oct 1552), 281v (6 Oct 1552), 283–285 (7, 8, 11 Oct 1552), 286 (13 Oct 1552).
71 AEG/RC/46, fols. 297v (2 Nov 1552), 305v (15 Nov 1552), 327v (23 Dec 1552), 336 (13 Jan 1553); PC/2e Ser., 1003 (13 Oct 1552), 1007 (Oct 1552), 1008 (28, 29 Oct 1552).
72 AEG/RC/46, fols. 299v (7 Nov 1552), 300v (8 Nov 1552).
73 The end of the Trolliet affair did not stop the ministers' quarrel with Ecclesia who was eventually forced out of Geneva. AEG/RC/46, fols. 333–333v (9 Jan 1553), 337v–338v (19, 20 Jan 1553), 339v (23 Jan 1553), 341v (30 Jan 1553); *RCP*, vol. 1, pp. 145–52 (14 Nov 1552–27 Jan 1553), 209–11 (20 Jan 1553). The ministers had had an earlier dispute with Ecclesia and seem never to have forgiven him. *RCP*, vol. 1, p. 47, 56–8 (15 Feb–13 Apr 1549).
74 The Petit Conseil deputed Jean Philippin, Claude Delestra and Guillaume Beney to enforce reconciliation. AEG/RC/46, fol. 327 (23 Dec 1552).
75 AEG/RC/46, fols. 301 (9 Nov 1552), 306 (15 Nov 1552).

76 AEG/RC/46, fol. 277 (26 Sep 1552). The panel could not reach agreement, AEG/RC/ 46, fols. 293v (25 Oct 1552), 294v (27 Oct 1552).

77 Roget, *Histoire*, vol. 3, pp. 275ff., sees Vandel as a definite supporter of Perrin. But he survived the 1555 débâcle and remained in the Petit Conseil in 1556 but dropped to the Conseil des Soixante in 1557. For this reason it seems resonable to classify him as moderate. Cf., *Advis*, pp. 115f.

78 AEG/RC/47, fols. 1 (5 Feb 1553), 3–5 (6–8 Feb 1553). Roset, pp. 349ff. saw this election as a clear victory for Perrin's group. Gaberel, *Histoire*, vol. 1, p. 416. who tends to belittle Perrin's power and appeal said that the result was balanced but that pressure and violence was used to sway the Petit Conseil against the ministers. The truth seems to lie somewhere in between these two views.

79 This material is gleaned from the *Registres du Conseil.* Election results were recorded every February.

80 Cf., Roset, pp. 350f.

81 AEG/RC/47, fol. 37v (16 Mar 1553).

82 Cf., Flournois, *Extraits*, p. 20.

83 Drawn from AEG/PC/1re and 2e Ser.

84 Some cases preserve multiple sentences. Only one has been counted following a ranking which considers beating first, then banishment, jail, public repentance, fine, warning.

85 These numbers refer only to individual cases, not the number of people involved in each case. Thus the total number of people involved would be higher.

86 From those cases where the crime is known. See Figure 16.

87 This figure charts all crimes which exceeded 10 per cent of the total in any two years.

88 AEG/RC/47, fol. 15 (16 Feb 1553).

89 D'Orbe was François Favre's illegitimate son. Roget, *Histoire*, vol. 3, p. 229.

90 AEG/RC/47, fol. 21v (20 Feb 1553).

91 AEG/RC/47, fol. 20 (17 Feb 1553).

92 AEG/RC/47, fol. 20v (17 Feb 1553). Cf., Roget, *Histoire*, vol. 3, pp. 278ff.

93 Delestra was normally a supporter of the ministers but he did argue with Poupin over the treatment of D'Ecclesia and thought the ministers ought to be elected every three years. Roget, *Histoire*, vol. 3, p. 239.

94 AEG/RC/47, fols. 10 (10 Feb 1553), 39 (17 Mar 1553).

95 AEG/RC/47, fols. 28v (27 Feb 1553), 32 (6 Mar 1553).

96 AEG/RC/47, fol. 27 (24 Feb 1553).

97 AEG/RC/47, fol. 88v (5 Jun 1553).

98 AEG/RC/47, fols. 107–107v (6 Jul 1553). Cf., Gaberel, *Histoire*, vol. 1, pp. 429f.

99 *Advis*, pp. 111f; Roset, pp. 351f.

100 Gaberel, *Histoire*, vol. 1, pp. 430f; Roget, *Histoire*, vol. 3, pp. 289f. Lambert was not the only Genevan touched by the French persecution. Philibert Berthelier, one of Calvin's fiercest opponents, had been imprisoned for his faith in France. J. B. G. Galiffe, *Les Procès Criminels Intentés à Genève, en 1547* (Geneva: 1862), p. 94.

101 Beza, 'Calvin', p. 60.

102 Monter, *Geneva*, p. 149 uses the title 'Enfant' when referring to this faction. 'Perrinists', a term favoured by their opponents, is used frequently in the historical literature (e.g., McGrath, *Calvin*, p. 114). Their opponents were called 'Calvinists', a term of derision, which is used in the historical literature as well. The terms Perrinists and Calvinists have the advantage of emphasising the personalities involved while avoiding the bias found in 'Enfants' and 'the party of the good', used by Calvin's supporters of themselves. The pejorative labelling of the Perrinists as 'Libertines', which still occurs (e.g., Parker, *Calvin*, p. 98; Innes, *Social Concerns*, p. 211), was never used at the time. Galiffe, *Procès*

Criminels, p. 75, n. 1, traces the term to Gaberel.

103 Calvin's pessimistic, if not apocalyptic, attitude to the Berthelier affair is apparent in his letters. For example see CO, vol. 14, col. 605f (to Viret, 4 Sep 1553).

104 *Advis*, pp. 107ff.

105 AEG/PC/1re Ser., 489 (24–27 Jul 1553).

106 AEG/PC/1re Ser., 491 (11 Aug 1553).

107 Beza, 'Calvin', p. 59 refers to these frequent accusations of heresy in Geneva by the Catholics.

108 AEG/RC/47, fol. 133 (14 Aug 1553); PC/1re Ser., 429 (14Aug–27 Oct 1553); CO, vol. 14, col. 589f (to Farel, 20 Aug 1553); *RCP*, vol. 2, pp. 3–46 (Aug 1553), 52 (27 Oct 1553).

109 Roget, *Histoire*, vol. 4, pp. 43, 45.

110 Roget, *Histoire*, vol. 4, p. 49.

111 Roget, *Histoire*, vol. 4, p. 50.

112 Roget, *Histoire*, vol. 4, p. 62.

113 AEG/RC/47, fols. 169v–170 (26, 27 Oct 1553). Roget, *Histoire*, vol. 4, pp. 85–91.

114 Parker, *Calvin*, p. 122, is perhaps the most recent proponent of this view. He said, 'the Libertines were using the trial to harass Calvin'.

115 CO, vol. 14, col. 418 (to Farel, 26 Oct 1553); Roset, pp. 352–5; Beza, 'Calvin', p. 61. Interestingly enough, McGrath, *Calvin*, p. 119, attaches this charge to Musculus alone.

116 *Advis*, pp. 107f.

117 Cf., Roget, *Histoire*, vol. 4, p. 54.

118 Roget, *Histoire*, vol. 4, p. 98, n. 1.

119 The case can be followed throughout the Council records. AEG/RC/47, fols. 134 (15 Aug 1553), 135 (17 Aug 1553), 137v (21 Aug 1553; the dispatch of the requests to the Swiss), 139 (24 Aug 1553), 143 (31 Aug 1553; letter from Catholic Vienne whence Servetus had fled a sentence of death), 154 (18 Sep 1553), 155v (19 Sep 1553), 162 (10 Oct 1553).

120 The dispute was protracted and time-consuming. AEG/RC/47, fols. 145 (2 Sep 1553), 146 (4 Sep 1553), 147v (7 Sep 1553), 151v (12 Sep 1553), 153v (15 Sep 1553), 155 (18 Sep 1553), 156v (22 Sep 1553), 175–177v (7, 9 Sep 1553), 179v–180 (13 Nov 1553), 197 (19 Dec 1553). Cf., *RCP*, vol. 2, pp. 48–51 (Sep 1553), and Roset, pp. 355f.

121 AEG/RC/37, fol. 37v (19 Mar 1543).

122 Roget, *Histoire*, vol. 4, pp. 64–70.

123 For example, CO, vol. 14, col. 655f (to Bullinger, 25 Oct 1553).

124 The ministers refused any compromise or reconciliation. AEG/RC/47, fol. 174v (3 Nov 1553); *RCP*, vol. 2, p. 52 (7 Nov 1553).

125 For example, CO, vol. 14, col. 673f (to Bullinger, 26 Nov 1553). Even Gaberel, *Histoire*, vol. 1, p. 420, who usually supports Calvin, said that the threat to Calvin was exaggerated. The Petit Conseil had no desire to lose the entire Company of Pastors and Calvin had the support of the Swiss cities which would have been scandalised at Calvin's removal.

126 AEG/RC/47, fol. 174 (3 Nov 1553); Roset, p. 356; *RCP*, vol. 2, p. 53 (1 Nov 1553). The complaint was brought by P. Verna, J. Balard, and Fr. Chabod, Roget, *Histoire*, vol. 4, pp. 133f.

127 AEG/RC/47, fols. 175–177v (7, 9 Nov 1553). And, Gaberel, *Histoire*, vol. 1, pp. 421ff.

128 Roget, *Histoire*, vol. 4, p. 148.

129 Bullinger's efforts on Calvin's behalf were crucial. Cf., J. W. Baker, 'Calvin's discipline and the Early Reformed Tradition: Bullinger and Calvin', in R. Schnucker, ed., *Calviniana. Ideas and Influence of Jean Calvin* in *Sixteenth Century Essays and Studies* (1988), 10, pp. 107–19.

130 Roget, *Histoire*, vol. 1, pp. 65f.; *RCP*, vol. 2, p. 54 (21 Dec 1553).

131 Beza, 'Calvin', pp. 62f.

132 Roset, p. 358. Roget, *Histoire*, vol. 4, pp. 152f. A public oath was administered. Calvin wrote that the reconciliation was private and probably only temporary, CO, vol. 15, col. 18f (to Viret, 6 Feb 1554).

133 AEG/RC/47, fol. 209 (4 Feb 1554).

134 AEG/RC/47, fol. 219 (5 Feb 1554).

135 CO, vol. 15, col. 39f (to Bullinger, 23 Feb 1554).

136 CO, vol. 21, col. (28 Jan 1554). Earlier, Calvin had married Jean Gabriel Magistri and Louise, the daughter of Ayme Couragel, CO, vol. 21, col. 510 (12 June 1552), and, in the lone action involving his opponents, Balthasar Sept and his wife (see p. 168). Later, he would baptise Jean Budé's daughter, CO, vol. 21, col. 614 (9 Sep 1555).

137 CO, vol. 21, col. 585 (9 Sep 1554).

138 CO, vol. 21, col. 569 (26 Feb 1554).

139 CO, vol. 21, col. 587 (21 Oct 1554).

140 *RCP*, vol. 2, pp. 54f. (8, 22 Mar 1554); AEG/RC/48, fol. 46 (30 Apr 1554). Calvin commented on the deteriorating situation a few weeks later, CO, vol. 15, col. 140f. (to Farel, 25 May 1554).

141 AEG/RC/48, fols. 47v–48 (3 May 1554).

142 AEG/RC/48, fol. 66v (1 Jun 1554). At this time the magistrates reformed consistorial practice so that it conformed to that in the other courts, AEG/RC/48, fol. 63 (28 May 1554).

143 AEG/RC/48, fol. 68 (4 Jun 1554).

144 AEG/RC/48, fol. 78 (21 Jun 1554).

145 AEG/RC/48, fol. 85 (6 Jul 1554).

146 AEG/RC/48, fols. 109 (28 Aug 1554), 110 (29 Aug 1554).

147 AEG/RC/48, fols. 113v–114v (6 Sep 1554), 118v–119 (13 Sep 1554), 138v–139v (25 Oct 1554). Magisterial anger towards the ministers did not stop them from warning the younger François Comparet for opening his shop during the Sunday sermon, AEG/PC/2e Ser., 1044 (25 Oct 1554).

148 AEG/RC/48, fol. 142v (5 Nov 1554). The ministers also resented the constant flow of attacks on them emanating from Berne; these were seen as contributing to the sad state of affairs in Geneva, CO, vol. 15, col. 257f. (to Bernese Senate, 4 Oct 1554).

149 AEG/PC/2e Ser., 1032 (10 Mar 1554).

150 AEG/PC/2e Ser., 1035 (20 Apr 1554).

151 AEG/PC/1re Ser., 505 (17–30 May 1554).

152 AEG/PC/1re Ser., 514 (15–18 Oct 1554).

153 AEG/PC/1re Ser., 509 (3 Jul–29 Aug 1554); *RCP*, vol. 2, p. 56 (7 Jul 1554).

154 SC, vol. 5, p. 163 (Micah 5: 3f.; 24 Dec 1550).

155 CO, vol. 34, col. 377 (Job 23: 1–9; Sep 1554).

156 AEG/PC/1re Ser., 502 (7–16 Mar 1554). Le Blanc was from Paris, the son of the Comptrolleur des Finances. Cf., CO, vol. 15, col. 69f. (to Genevan Senate, Mar 1554), for the ministers' advice.

157 AEG/RC/48, fols. 169–169v (27 Sep 1554); Roset, pp. 363f.

158 AEG/RC/48, fol. 181v (23 Jan 1555); PC/1re Ser., 518 (7–23 Jan 1555). Durand, from Auvergne, worked for a printer.

159 AEG/PC/1re Ser., 518 (11 Jan–16 Feb 1555); RC/48, fols. 175 (10 Jan 1555), 176v (14 Jan 1555); RC/49, fol. 10 (12 Feb 1555). Also, Roset, pp. 363f.

160 *Advis*, p. 96.

161 AEG/PC/1re Ser., 523 (9–18 Feb 1555).

162 CO, vol. 53, col. 452 (1 Tim 5: 1f.; 27 Jan 1555). See also, Parker, *Preaching*, pp. 122f.

163 AEG/RC/48, fol. 149 (18 Nov 1554).

164 *RCP*, vol. 2, p. 59 (24 Jan 1555); Roset, pp. 364f.; Roget, *Histoire*, vol. 4, pp. 189ff.

165 AEG/RC/49, fol. 1 (3 Feb 1555); *Advis*, p. 126; Roset, pp. 368f. Cf., Roget, *Histoire*, vol. 4, pp. 197ff. Bonna, who is considered a Calvinist by Bonivard and Roget, disappeared from politics after 1557. He may have been pushed aside because of suspicions about his family ties with the Perrinists as well as anger over his views on later legislation (see pp. 214f.).

166 AEG/RC/49, fol. 8 (8 Feb 1555); RC/51, fol. 21v (21 Feb 1556).

167 AEG/RC/49, fol. 5v (6 Feb 1555). Only five other men, not clearly related to the Calvinists were elected: Gabriel Pottu, Jaques Conte, Jean Janin (or Colloquier), Michel Roset (the chronicler), and Pierre Vallefroz.

168 AEG/RC/49, fol. 1v (3 Feb 1555).

169 AEG/RC/49, fols. 6–7 (6 Feb 1555).

170 *Advis*, p. 125; Roget, *Histoire*, vol. 4, pp. 200ff.

171 Roget, *Histoire*, vol. 4, pp. 280, n. 1; 300, n. 1; 303, n. 1; 312, n. 1.

172 There is also some question about the morality of some of these men; Du Pan was in trouble for monies missing from city accounts he was in charge of, and Beney was removed for misconduct.

173 AEG/RC/49, fol. 63v (2 May 1555).

174 *Advis*, p. 128.

175 Bouwsma, *Calvin*, p. 27.

176 Parker, *Calvin*, p. 126.

177 McGrath, *Calvin*, pp. 122f. The whole chronology of the Perrinists' defeat, implied in McGrath, is incorrect. The Perrinists were already politically defeated, at least for that year, prior to the riot which led to their total rout that summer.

178 See, *Bourg.*, pp. 242–4; Roget, *Histoire*, vol. 4, pp. 230–2 (Roget says fourty-four were admitted by 6 May, not thirty-four as recorded in *Bourg.*); Galiffe, *Procès Criminels*, pp. 102f.

179 AEG/RC/49, fol. 74 (13 May 1555).

180 AEG/PC/2e Ser., 1055 (18 Jan–2 May 1555).

181 AEG/RC/49, fols. 66v (3 May 1555), 68v (6 May 1555).

182 AEG/RC/49, fols. 12v (15 Feb 1555), 14 (18 Feb 1555), 21 (1 Mar 1555).

183 AEG/PC/1re Ser., 527 (26 Mar–5 Apr 1555); RC/49, fol. 42 (5 Apr 1555).

184 AEG/RC/49, fols. 56v (23 Apr 1555), 62 (30 Apr 1555).

185 AEG/RC/49, fols. 34 (22 Mar 1555), 37 (27 Mar 1555).

186 AEG/RC/49, fol. 52 (19 Apr 1555).

187 AEG/PC/2e Ser., 1057 (7 May–21 Jun 1555).

188 The French protested against the attempt to deny them weapons. Roget, *Histoire*, vol. 3, pp. 289f.

189 *Advis*, pp. 129ff.

190 AEG/RC/49, fols. 26v (12 Mar 1555), 27v (13 Mar 1555), 29–29v (14 Mar 1555). Geneva's precarious international situation is detailed in Chapter 1, pp. 21ff.

191 CO, vol. 21, col. 599f (28 Mar–11 Apr 1555).

192 See, AEG/RC/49, fol. 78 (16 May 1555) for initial reports on the riot. Also, Roset, pp. 369–74 and *Advis*, pp. 136–48.

193 Beza, 'Calvin', p. 68. Calvin presented a similar interpretation. For example, CO, vol. 15, col. 676–84 (to Bullinger, 15 Jun 1555), col. 686f. (to Farel, 16 Jul 1555), col. 693f. (to Farle, 24 Jul 1555); *RCP*, vol. 2, p. 63 (26 May 1555).

194 AEG/RC/49, fol. 84 (24 May 1555).

195 Roget, *Histoire*, vol. 4, pp. 282f.

196 AEG/RC/49, fol. 86v (25 May 1555).
197 There is a large number of cases associated with the Perrinist debacle. AEG/PC/1re Ser.,
530 (19 May–4 Jun 1555), 531 (20–22 May 1555), 532 (29 May–21 Jun 1555), 533 (3–4 Jun
1555), 535 (11 Jun–27 Aug 1555), 537 (19 Jun–2 Jul 1555), 539 (22 Jul–2 Sep 55; the largest
case, against Perrin, Sept, Berthelier, *et al.*), 542 (1–2 Aug 1555), 543 (6–8 Aug 1555), 544
(6–8 Aug 1555), 546 (28 Aug–6 Sep 1555), 547 (30 Aug–5 Sep 1555), 548, 930 (Aug–12 Sep
1555); PC 2e Ser., 1061 (17 May 1555–3 Feb 1556), 1062 (25 May–1 Jul 1555), 1063 (29 May
1555), 1064 (Jun 1555), 1066 (11 Jun 1555), 1067 (8 Aug–15 Sep 1555), 1069 (4 Nov 1555–
24 Jan 1556, 4–14 Jan 1558).
198 Roget, *Histoire*, vol. 4, p. 282.
199 Roget, *Histoire*, vol. 4, p. 284.
200 AEG/RC/49, fol. 88v (27 May 1555).
201 Roget, *Histoire*, vol. 4, p. 297.
202 Roget, *Histoire*, vol. 4, p. 317.
203 CO, vol. 15, col. 790f. (Placards Séditieux).
204 *Advis*, p. 147.
205 Roget, *Histoire*, vol. 4, p. 304.
206 CO, vol. 15, col. 753 (Musculus to Bullinger, 1 Sep 1555)
207 CO, vol. 15, col. 803f. (Hotman to Bullinger, 29 Sep 1555).
208 CO, vol. 15, col. 808 (Haller to Bullinger, 7 Oct 1555).
209 CO, vol. 15, col. 797–801 (Bullinger to Calvin, 28 Sep 1555).
210 Beza gave a strong defence of Calvin and his supporters. CO, vol. 15, col. 836–41 (Beza
to Bullinger, 22 Oct 1555).
211 AEG/RC/49, fol. 163v (19 Aug 1555).
212 AEG/RC/49, fols. 176–177v (8 Sep 1555); Flournois, *Extraits*, p. 22.
213 AEG/RC/49, fols. 180–180v (10 Sep 1555).
214 Roset, pp. 394f.
215 Roget, *Histoire*, vol. 4, pp. 325f.
216 AEG/Min/A. Babel, vol. 2, fol. 211v (13 Aug 1552).
217 AEG/Min/P. du Verney, vol. 2, fol. 6 (2 Apr 1552).
218 AEG/Min/M. Try, vol. 7, fol. 99v (29 Jan 1550).
219 AEG/Min/M. Try, vol. 12, fol. 948v (4 Nov 1554).
220 AEG/Min/F. Vuarrier, vol. 5, fol. 55 (24 Sep 1550).
221 *Advis*, p. 97. Brady, *Strasbourg*, pp. 109f., stresses the importance of similar ties in the
ruling elite in Strasbourg.
222 Galiffe, *Procès Criminels*, p. 73.
223 Roget, *Histoire*, vol. 4, pp. 265ff., commented on the merciless nature of the Calvinists'
actions in the wake of the May riot. Perrenoud, *Population*, p. 42, called the demographic changes 'extraordinairement brutal'.

Calvin triumphant

Quanto monitior hoc praesidio futura esset bonorum manus

The defeat of the Perrinists in 1555 left Geneva firmly in the hands of Calvin's local supporters.[1] They contrived to secure their new power by two methods. First, they continued to admit French refugees to the bourgeoisie; 144 were admitted before the elections of 1557. Also, they began a process of purifying Geneva's government. As mentioned in the previous chapter, Calvin's supporters made some changes in 1555 and after the riot they specifically disenfranchised the Perrinists' relatives. The Calvinists moved to purge all those even remotely connected to their opponents. Also, they elevated their own supporters to positions of power. The changes were dramatic; a new ruling elite was coming into being. It remains necessary to examine both the specific effects of the Calvinist victory and those men who were to be Geneva's new political masters.

One of the more obvious changes is the number of new French bourgeois admitted to the Conseil des Soixante and Deux Cents. By 1560, Guillaume Colladon and Galazeo Caraciola had both been admitted to the Soixante, the highest body open to bourgeois. Other prominent bourgeois became members of the Conseil des Deux Cents in the years following the Calvinist victory. Guillaume Magistri and Guillaume Le Vet had joined the lower council by 1556. Antoine Calvin and Antoine Froment were admitted in 1558 and by 1559 Laurent de Normandie, Jean Budé, and Guillaume Try had joined them in the Deux Cents. Less prominent refugees also gained membership in the lower council; Pierre de la Mare, François de la Botiere, Nicolas Picot, and Adrian Priquemand became councillors in the Deux Cents. Alone, these admissions to the councils represented a substantial increase in the political power and influence of the French refugees in Geneva.[2] As Calvin had written to Bullinger soon after the Perrinist rout, the 'bonorum manus' had indeed been made secure by 'hoc præsidio', the introduction of the bourgeois.[3]

Another sign of the increased prominence of the French in the city can be found in the negotiations with Berne about the treaty renewal and the fugitive refugees. In the autumn of 1555 it became clear that Berne was annoyed by the Perrinist defeat and that this would adversely effect the renewal of the military alliance upon which Geneva relied.[4] In attempting to defuse the crisis Geneva took the perhaps tactless step of deputing to Berne as ambassadors François Chevallier, a citizen with no previous political experience, and two Frenchmen, Calvin and Guillaume Colladon.[5] The city also decided that leading habitants would be consulted over any new treaty. Eventually, in December, four politically prominent citizens were sent to assist and consult the previous delegation. But the efforts of Pierre Bonna, Jean Ami Curtet, Michel de l'Arche and Claude Roset did nothing to mollify the Bernese.[6] Berne allowed the treaty to lapse on 26 March 1556, thereby placing Geneva in a precarious position.[7] The Bernese and the other Swiss cities considered the Genevan treatment of the Perrinists of paramount concern and demanded leniency. The fugitives, for their part, continued to lobby for support among the Swiss, for example, in October at Baden. All thirteen cantons wrote on their behalf.[8] But the position of the refugees and their supporters in Geneva meant that the city was no longer as interested in deferring to the Swiss as before; Geneva was increasingly turning its attention to France and the religious situation there.[9]

The clearest evidence of the shift in Geneva's ruling class came with the elections of November 1555 and February 1556. In November, Claude du Pan was elected Lieutenant over Jean Chautemps while Jean Rosset, Pierre Somareta, and Jean François Bernard defeated André Embler, Jean Cuvat, and Bartholomie Lect as auditeurs. Three auditeurs were elected rather than the usual two because of mid-term vacancies which occurred after the Perrinist defeat. The striking fact is that all the candidates were either known Calvinists or people inclined to support the Calvinists.[10] A similar trend is evident in the major elections in February. As one might expect, four Calvinists were elected as Syndics from a field of eight; Jean Ami Curtet and Pierre Migerand defeated Pierre Dorsière and Claude Deletra, while Jean Chautemps and Jean de la Maisonneuve beat Jean Philippin and François Chamois. This did not represent the original field of candidates, however. François Beguin had been nominated but was replaced by Dorsière when Amblard Corne protested that Beguin was unfit to stand.[11] Eventually, Beguin, along with Pierre Mallagniod and Pierre Tissot, was removed from the Petit Conseil because of contacts they had with the Perrinists.[12]

Calvinists or moderates who supported them swept the châtelain elections as well. Jean Donzel beat François Lullin to become Châtelain of the Chapter. Pierre Costel was elected Châtelain of Jussy, defeating Antoine de Loermoz. Loup Tissot became Châtelain of Celligny over André du

Roveray.[13] The Calvinist lock on power is further seen in that another of their faction, Jean Pernet, took the Consistorial post vacated by Jean Donzel when he became a châtelain.[14] It is worth noting that many of these men who stood in the various elections of 1555 and 1556 had never been mentioned as candidates before. The promotion of new men to political prominence was another hallmark of the Calvinist victory. Of the extra thirty-five men who, with the Petit Conseil, comprised the Conseil des Soixante, eleven were new to the council in 1556. The Conseil des Deux Cents, which was the Soixante and about 140 other men, had an additional nineteen new men; over 15 per cent of the members of the Deux Cents were entirely new to office.[15]

The changes in the smaller but more important Petit Conseil in the years immediately after the Calvinist victory show the same trend to promote new men. The contrast between the councils of 1555 and 1557 illustrate the dramatic difference (see Table 26). In 1555 the senators had served in the Petit Conseil an average of over twelve years apiece. But the Petit Conseil of 1557 had an average of only seven years of experience per senator. In 1557, seventeen of the twenty-eight senators (60 per cent) had come to power after the Calvinist victory in 1555. But in the 1555 senate only four of the twenty-seven senators (15 per cent) had served for as few years. The Perrinists, in 1553, when they improved their control in the Senate, had added only a few new members; the Calvinists radically altered the Petit Conseil membership. By 1558 only a quarter of the senators had served in 1555 or before. Previously the electorate had shown an aversion to radical changes in the senate; they had rejected the Perrinist plan to alter the form of nomination and election to the Petit Conseil. The defeat of the Perrinists removed any constraints on the Calvinists to maintain the status quo. From 1551–54 only four new senators were elected; in 1555–58 eighteen new men were brought into the Petit Conseil.

Similar changes took place in the other lower councils. In 1555 the Calvinists brought five new men into the Conseil des Deux Cents. In 1556, where Roget mentions nineteen new men, there were in fact thirty new members. Another thirty men were added to the Deux Cents in 1557; by 1558 an additional nineteen new men had joined. Thus, by 1558 the new contingent to the Deux Cents equalled, at 60 per cent, the ratio of new men found in the Petit Conseil the year before. A similar change was apparent in the Soixante over the same period; by 1558, nearly 60 per cent of the members had served three years or less. There was also a marked increase in the role of former members of the Consistory. Table 26 shows the steady growth of the power of elders in Genevan politics at the senatorial level. By 1551 a plateau seems to have been reached; until 1555 the

TABLE 26   *Senatorial and Consistorial experience*

Petit Conseil 1555	Years served	Petit Conseil 1557	Years served
Syndics			
J. Lambert	15	P. des Fosses	20
H. Aubert	15	J. Pernet	3
P. Bonna	15	L. Franc	2
P. J. Jessé	10	G. Chiccand	1
Former Syndics			
A. Corne	18	J. A. Curtet	21
P. Tissot	18	J. Chautemps	17
C. du Pan	15	J. de la Maisonnueve	3
M de l'Arche	6	P. Migerand	2
Senators:			
A. Perrin	18	E. Chapeaurouge	16
E. Chapeaurouge	14	H. Aubert	17
D. d'Arlod	19	J. des Arts	15
P. des Fosses	18	P. Bonna	17
J. A. Curtet	19	P. J. Jessé	12
J. Philippin	19	C. Delestra	5
P. Vandel	14	J. Chappuis	2
C. Rigot	5	P. Bertillion	1
G. Beney	7	P. Dorsière	2
P. Mallagniod	15	J. Blondel	2
J. B. Sept	3	J. Donzel	2
J. Chautemps	15	P. Somareta	1
F. Chamois	7	J. Porral	1
J. de la Maisonneuve	1	J. F. Bernard	1
J. Pernet	1	F. Chevallier	1
C. Vandel	1	J. G. Magistri	1
J. des Arts	14	L. Bon	1
C. Roset	19	M. Roset	2
F. Beguin	12	M. de l'Arche	8
		A. Corne	20

Senators (Syndics[16]) with Consistorial experience, 1544–60

1544	4	*1550*	12 (3)	*1556*	19
1545	5	*1551*	14 (3)	*1557*	19
1546	7	*1552*	15	*1558*	17 (3)
1547	8	*1553*	14	*1559*	20 (4)
1548	9	*1554*	15 (4)	*1560*	18
1549	11	*1555*	15 (3)		

former elders comprised between 48 per cent and 56 per cent of the Petit Conseil. But in the next five-year period, 1556–60, the elders increased their control to between 68 per cent and 74 per cent of the senatorial posts.

The specific losses to the two upper councils also show the other side of these changes, the purge of former members. The men demoted were often relatives of the Perrinists in the immediate aftermath of their defeat. But soon men who had had any clashes with the French ministers or their supporters began to be removed; presumably they were deemed to be unreliable. In some cases one has to go back many years to find the event which might explain the fall from power. For example, Jean Balard, who had clashed with Farel in 1535, was finally removed from political power in 1556. The riotous actions of the Perrinists may have been as much a result of their fury at the changes being made to the Genevan political structure as a consequence of their protests against the bourgeois admissions. In addition to the removal of Hudriod du Molard and Gaspard Favre from the Petit Conseil, changes were made to the Soixante. Philibert Berthelier, Balthasar Sept, Pierre Verna, Michel Morel, Jean François Marchand, Jean Louis Ramel, and Jean Buctin all lost their seats on this council.

The Petit Conseil of 1556, obviously, lost the leading Perrinists, Ami Perrin, Pierre Tissot, Jean Baptiste Sept and Pierre Vandel. But others (Claude Rigot, Claude Roset, François Beguin) who were associated only loosely with the Perrinists disappeared from political office as well. Substantial changes were also made to the Conseil des Soixante. The list of the purged holds few surprises: Hudriod du Molard, Jaques Nicolas Vulliet, Jean Pierre Bonna, the senior Jean Balard, François Chabod, Pierre Symon, Jean Favre, and Pierre Buctin. The removal of Jean Donzel, Claude Deletra, and Pierre Dorsière may have happened because they had had clashes with the ministers in the past and may well have been seen as dubious supporters, though this is far from certain. Louis Beljaquet, who was also removed, had been associated with Jean Trolliet as a censor and may have gained the dislike of the ministers as a result.

The changes in 1557 seem to show the removal of the last vestiges of Perrinist supporters or moderate leaders. The Petit Conseil lost Jean Philippin, Guillaume Beney, Claude Vandel, and Claude du Pan who were demoted to the Soixante while Domaine d'Arlod disappeared altogether. François Pierre Donzel, the younger Jean Balard, Jean Symon, Henry Goula, Jean Louis Favre, Bernardin Perret, Guillaume Chiccand, and Claude de la Maisonneuve were all removed from the Soixante.[17] De la Maisonneuve's relationship with the Lects (he was arrested at Antoine's party in 1546) may explain his removal. There are aspects to these changes which suggest more was at work here than attempts to eradicate the

Perrinists. It is hard to avoid the conclusion that some men were being removed for events which had occurred well in the past; under cover of crushing the Perrinists and creating a godly magistracy, several old scores were being settled. Also, many experienced politicians who had helped oust the Perrinists, for example Rigot, now found their usefulness had passed and they were pushed aside for more enthusiastic Calvinists. The inexperience of the new magistrates may also have meant that they were easier to influence, thus increasing their attractiveness to the remaining, dominant Calvinists.

These political changes show that Calvin's local supporters felt more was needed to gain control in Geneva than the exile or execution of the leading Perrinists. In reality, the Calvinists found they were not entirely in control of the Genevan political situation until after 1557. This lack of total control would explain the continued purges; all dissent was to be stifled and a united magistracy created to complement the unified Company of Pastors and implement their vision for Geneva. However, the defeat of the Perrinists had removed the vocal leadership of those opposed to Calvin. A limited number of personal clashes occurred but they were no more that the dying gasps of the opposition. Calvin and Trolliet continued their war of words over predestination in April 1556.[18] Aimé Bramerel was charged with slandering a Syndic while being admonished for frequenting taverns.[19] In January 1556 a riot occurred at Longemalle involving Pierre Bonna, Colin and Pierre Roman, Pierre Espaula, and Antoine Coenoz.[20] The General Assembly was disturbed by another riot in April.[21]

A few other clashes centred on the fugitives. Pierre Bienvenu, a notary, was prosecuted for his role in Claude Bonna's will which favoured some Perrinists.[22] In late October 1556 Pierre Tissot, also a notary, was arrested for treason because of Gaspard Favre's will. Gaspard had left 500 écus to his brother-in-law Perrin. In the aftermath of the dispute, the state seized the entire estate, valued at over 3,000 écus, and drove Gaspard's brother, Domaine, and his widow, Louise Mestrezat, from Geneva because they had not reported the offence.[23] Philibert Berthelier, while in exile, accused another citizen, Jean Papillier, of slander.[24] Louis de la Joux, the sole De la Joux brother not prosecuted after the May riot, was jailed for three days because he assaulted a foreigner.[25] Two further events seemed to have involved fugitives and Swiss in Geneva. In November Jaques Freytag, servant to François Clerc, sided with the exiles in a riot against citizens at the Pont d'Arve.[26] A month later, soldiers from Zürich staying in Geneva were involved in a riotous clash with citizens.[27]

The most serious disturbances of the year occurred at a meeting of the Conseil Général in November 1556. This riot highlights the extent to which Calvin and his supporters were still unable to impose their will upon all Genevans. The Petit Conseil, at the ministers' insistence, had proposed new legislation with harsh, mandatory secular punishments for various violations of Geneva's moral code. When these were presented to the General Assembly, a riot ensued. Pierre Bonna, a Syndic in 1555, spoke against these new regulations and proclaimed that they were 'trop rudes'.[28] Michel Grangier, a new bourgeois, attacked him. In the argument which followed, Bonna accused Corne, Aubert, Roset, and Calvin of personally hating him.[29] Pierre Bernard, a relative of the minister Jaques and senator François, was jailed and stripped of his rights for a year because of the violent remarks he made against the proposal.[30] In the end Bonna won the debate and the new regulations were rejected. Bonna was able to be re-elected to the senate in 1557 but he disappeared from the magistracy thereafter.[31] This defeat undoubtedly reinforced the need for further changes to Geneva's magistracy and electorate. The debate itself shows the strength of feeling against the French ministers and refugees even after the public crushing of the Perrinists.

Nevertheless, the elections of November 1556 and February 1557 show the continued growth of Calvinist power. Amblard Corne became Lieutenant in November, defeating Henry Aubert. Jean Porral and Domaine Fabri were beaten by Claude de la Maisonneuve and Aimé Chasteauneuf to become auditeurs.[32] Pernet Desfosses and Guillaume Chiccand were elected Syndics over Pierre Dorsière and François Chevallier. Jean Pernet and Louis Franc became the other two Syndics when they defeated Jean Donzel and Estienne Chapeaurouge.[33] Pierre Migerand defeated Henry Aubert to become the new Treasurer.[34] The dominance of the Consistory continued; of the fifteen men standing for these posts, eleven had Consistorial experience. To a certain extent the Consistory seems to have become the proving ground for future magistrates; Chasteauneuf and Migerand had made their appearance in office the year before when they were appointed elders.

The new masters of Geneva faced more protests in 1557 but the opposition was disorganised, ineffectual, and composed of people of little or no political importance. Jean Balard was disenfranchised for a year because he tried to nominate ineligible individuals as Syndics and for the Conseil Général. The relevance to earlier disputes is clear in this case, in that reference was made to Balard's clashes with Farel in 1535.[35] A similar case found Claude Vulliermoz arrested for having once said, in 1549, that he preferred a dog yapping to Calvin preaching.[36] Jean Lullin and Henri Philippe were involved in a riot at the church of the Madeleine.[37] A few days after Vulliermoz's arrest Jean Louis Ramel was prosecuted for saying that the exiles were as good as any minister.[38]

In April, Pierre Pape was jailed for three days for saying that the ministers were too harsh and overlooked their own faults while reprimanding those of others.[39] Pernette, the widow of one of Calvin's earlier opponents, Roz Monet, quit the city in disgust at the situation.[40] Jaques Bonna and Gabriel Pottu were charged, in May, for dancing at Philibert Bonna's wedding at Thonon, in Bernese territory; leading exiles had attended the party.[41] Some problems also arose with the foreign visitors to the city. Jaques Fornier, of Paris, an associate of the Duke de Guise, attacked Calvin's Bible and said the translation of the Psalms used in Geneva was the work of a scoundrel.[42] Later in July, Jaques Nergaz, a Bernese subject with Genevan relations, made comments supportive of Bolsec. He refused to answer any of the charges, saying that Geneva had no jurisdiction over him. His Genevan cousins, François and Charles Nergaz, posted a 200-écu bond to secure his release and stood as surety for his good behaviour.[43]

There was only a handful of cases which were actually serious. In February, Philibert Berthelier and others brought suit against Geneva at the Bernese court in the Bailliage of Ternier. Geneva refused to recognise the court's competence in the case; the court sided with the fugitives and ordered reparations which Geneva also ignored. The court empowered the exiles to seize Genevan properties in Bernese lands in compensation but this appears not to have taken place.[44] In July, Berthelier was involved in a riot at the Pont d'Arve between the fugitives and some citizens.[45] Pierre Dolens, in November, was arrested for slander of some unknown person; a few years earlier he had slandered an unnamed minister.[46] The year closed with a small riot after the Christmas communion service. The obscurity of those arrested in the riot is futher evidence of the disarray in the ranks of those opposed to the new order, as well as the success of the Calvinist campaign in purging the magistracy of all opposition.[47] Claude Tapponier articulated the last gasp of the anti-French party a few days later when he said that all the French ought to be burned.[48] Opposition clearly continued at Geneva but a dramatic change had been wrought; none of those involved was a magistrate. Bereft of all political power, the remaining Perrinist sympathisers were easily dealt with individually by the authorities.

Events in the last half of 1557 showed the increasing importance of the French to the city. In September the Petit Conseil was able to make the first large debt repayment to Basle since 1542. The 2,360 écus sent represented almost all the money raised through bourgeois sales in 1555 and 1556 (see Table 27).[49] Also, after long negotiations, Berne was forced to accept that nothing could be done for the exiled Perrinists. The new treaty

TABLE 27   *Bourgeois admissions and revenues, 1535–56*

Year	Persons admitted[54]	Total revenue (écus)	Average per person (écus)[55]
1535	61	280	4.6
1536	11	112	14.0
1537	22	90	10.0
1538	23	111	6.5
1539	14	213	15.2
1540	31	171	6.1
1541	21	192	10.1
1542	17	66	5.0
1543	28	110	5.2
1544	8	71	11.8
1545	7	68	11.3
1546	9	36	6.0
1547	138	725	5.4
1548	10	42	6.0
1549	6	32	6.4
1550	8	42	6.0
1551	15	80	8.0
1552	10	113	12.5
1553	24	104	5.5
1554	6	30	6.0
1555	127	1592	13.1
1556	144	1014	8.0

between Berne and Geneva was sent to Geneva and the Petit Conseil established a committee of Calvinists, François Bonivard, François Lullin, and Jean Maurys, to translate it into French. A sign of the radical change in Geneva is the participation of Lullin, whose brother Jean was one of the negotiators of the infamous Articles of 1540, which destroyed the Articulants' grip on power.[50] A changed magisterial relationship with, and attitude towards, the ministers was also apparent by January 1558. City ministers saw their wages raised slightly to 250 per annum, rural wages went up somewhat more to 240 per annum; a supplement of wheat was also included in this new arrangement.[51]

The elections of late 1557 and early 1558 continued the string of Calvinist victories. Once again the increased importance of previously unremarkable citizens is apparent. The new Lieutenant was Henry Aubert, who defeated Jean Ami Curtet, both of whom were veteran politicians. Two new men, Dominique Dentand and Guillaume Macard, became auditeurs by beating Jean Chautemps and Aimé des Arts.[52] The new Syndics brought to prominence some other new men as well. François Chevallier, who had held no offices before 1555, and Michel de l'Arche, defeated Pierre Dorsière and Jean Porral. Likewise, Jean Donzel, who had become a senator only in 1556, and Amblard Corne, were also elected Syndics over Jaques Blondel and Louis Bon; Blondel had entered the Petit Conseil in 1556, Bon in 1557.[53] The elders maintained their dominance as before. Only two of the newly elected magistrates, Curtet and Chevallier, had no Consistorial experience while three of those defeated, Des Arts, Blondel, and Bon, had never been elders. As in 1557, two of the new men, Dentand and Macard, had gained positions after only one year in the Consistory. Prior to this they had languished in political obscurity but were now the Lieutenant's assistants. There is no doubt that Consistorial experience was fast becoming the *sine qua non* of political advancement.

There must have been little surprise at Aimé des Arts' defeat; in June 1556, he had been deposed as Gros Saultier, or provisioner of the Petit Conseil, and publicly humiliated for slandering some of the senators.[56] This draws attention to the fact that the Calvinist magistrates and their families were not, nor had they been, paragons of moral rectitude.[57] Calvin's brother, Antoine, had had to divorce his wife, Anne le Fert, for adultery with Pierre Daguet, Jean Calvin's servant.[58] Jean Chautemps's son, Othon, was arrested for robbing Louis Baud's house in 1557. The Petit Conseil wanted him beaten but the Conseil des Deux Cents remitted the sentence in consideration of his family, which hardly seems to show a Calvinist enthusiasm for applying the same law to everyone equally.[59] Jean Chapeaurouge and Aimé Chenu were arrested for duelling; Jean was jailed and fined.[60] Another Chapeaurouge, Pierre, was prosecuted for slandering the Petit Conseil.[61] In the most serious case, Jean Philippin, a former elder and four-time Syndic, was jailed and fined for theft from the Châtelain of Peney.[62]

The Calvinists were even less exemplary in the area of city finances. In 1555, Jean Lambert was found to owe the city 13,622ff in debts stretching over twenty years; a quarter of the amount was still unpaid in 1569. Jaques des Arts owed Geneva 7,300ff in 1558 and 120 écus (c. 600ff) of a debt of 550 écus (c. 2,750ff) for cathedral ornaments he had purchased in 1536. Nor had he paid the 354ff purchase price on a house on the Rue des Chanoines bought in 1542, 225ff of taxes from 1536, and 500ff (of an origianl 722ff) for some rural property bought from Geneva; he was arrested in 1560. An additional 12,251ff had been due to the city since 1544 from Claude du Pan. Henri Philippe and Aimé Plonjon were so in debt that Philippe's estate lost 12,078ff upon his death in 1560; Ami de Chambery's estate was reduced by 2,340ff because of debts when he died in 1561.[63]

If the Calvinists were not identifiable as the faction of men committed to a strict morality, then what factors contributed to their cohesion as a group? There is certainly no extensive network of family ties apparent in the faction, though Dorsière, Bon and Chapeaurouge were all related through the large Chapeaurouge family. Three prominent men were also connected through marriage to the daughters of Pierre Navis; Jean Chapeaurouge married Claudine, Michel de l'Arche married Louise in 1542, and Claude Roset married Françoise. They did share some social ties as well, in that a number of them, Estienne Chapeaurouge, Louis Franc (Sr du Crest), Michel Roset (Sr de Chasteauvieux), Jean Pernet, Jean Ami Curtet, and Pierre Migerand, had titles or were related to titled families by marriage. This however, in no way represents an overwhelming characteristic of the group.

The Perrinists, as noted above, were descended for the most part from men who had gained bourgeois status in the late fifteenth and very early sixteenth centuries. In general, the Calvinists show the same pattern, though they seem to have gained their bourgeois status somewhat later than the Perrinist families. Aubert's father became a bourgeois in 1493; De l'Arche's in 1483; Curtet's in 1492; Blondel's in 1501; Chevallier's in 1506; and Franc's in 1511: and yet some Calvinists were scions of prominent or long-established Genevan families. Pierre Dorsière's father had been a Syndic eight times and another forebear was a Syndic in 1403. Porral's father had been a Syndic in 1532, 1536, and 1542; however, his grandfather had been an immigrant from Germany. It might be possible to see a certain tendency in the Calvinists to be drawn from families which had arrived recently and were of a somewhat more elevated social status. There is a bias in this direction, but the evidence is so slight and varies so little from that of the Perrinists that it would be dangerous to attach great importance to these factors in explaining the ties which bound the Calvinists together.[64]

It is also true that a number of the Calvinists was associated with the former Articulant faction while the Perrinists were overwhelmingly drawn from the Guillermin group. The Chapeaurouge family was Articulant and Pernet Desfosses and Jean de la Maisonneuve had ties with the defeated faction. However, the Calvinists included leading Guillermins as well, for example, Jean Chautemps and Jean Lambert. Some of the Calvinists, Amblard Corne, Henri Aubert, and Jean de la Maisonneuve, had other long-standing personal disputes with individual Perrinists or had been noted for continual support for the French. But there were also disputes in the late 1540s between members of the later factions. In any case, the disputes between Calvinists and Perrinists before the clear formation of the factions may actually have been part of the creation of the factions rather than events separate from the faction-building process.

There is a much more obvious connection between the Calvinists when one examines the Consistory; many of the Calvinists had served as elders. Some were long-serving members: Dorsière, Jean Donzel, Jean Chappuis (Olivier), Guillaume Chiccand and Pierre Bertillion. Even more had been elders for shorter periods: Aubert, De l'Arche, Corne, Chautemps, Jean Pernet, Chapeaurouge, De la Maisonneuve, Des Arts, Pierre Migerand, Pierre Somareta, Jean Porral, and Jean François Bernard. However, some of the leading Calvinists had never been on the Consistory: Lambert, Desfosses, Curtet, Jaques Blondel, Louis Franc, Michel Roset, François Chevallier, Jean Gabriel Magistri and Louis Bon. There can be no doubt, though, that the Calvinists were much more closely associated with the Consistory than the Perrinists. The presence of so many long-serving Consistory members is especially of importance because of the extended contact they had had with the ministers and the fact that they were closely identified with the ministers' goals for changing Genevan society.

However, thus far no evidence has been presented that adequately explains the cohesion of the Calvinist faction, let alone their popular support. The best possible explanation may be negative in nature. The unity, size, and grip on political power held by the Perrinists may explain the Calvinist faction to some degree. The influence of the Perrinists was so pervasive that it effectively suffocated the political ambitions of almost everyone outside their own bloc.[65] Thus, many people, denied power by the Perrinists, had a vested interest in curbing or eradicating their power. This especially would explain the support of obvious moderates in 1555, for example, Pierre Bonna and Claude du Pan. This interpretation would also support Bonivard's view that the change in Genevan public opinion was more of a reaction against the arrogance of the triumphalist Perrinists than a vote of support for the Calvinists. In this view, the Calvinists benefited from a popular move to break a near stranglehold on political power by the Perrinists; but once in power, by however narrow a majority, the Calvinists acted swiftly and ruthlessly to secure their own political hegemony in Geneva.

Another marked difference between the two factions was their attitude towards the French. The Perrinists resented their increasing influence and worked to limit French power at every turn. It is understandable that , as the leaders of Geneva and the established power-bloc in the city, the Perrinists would feel threatened by any group capable of limiting their authority. It comes as no surprise that one cannot find any Perrinists who had business ties with the French. The one possible exception is the Ramel brothers, Jean Louis and Jean François. However, attempts to connect them to the Perrinists are tenuous; in 1557, Jean Louis said an exiled Perrinist was as good as a minister.[66] Evidence of their business dealings with the French is equally sparse; they were involved in property sales to Jean Beguin, of Orleans, in 1550, and Loys Trembley, in 1557.[67] These contracts represent the only known ties. Claude du Pan, who may have been a moderate rather than a committed Calvinist, was also involved with foreigners. He had business dealings with Charles de Brichanteau, in 1555, and with Jean Manten, a German, in 1557.[68]

Interestingly enough, the Calvinist did not show much more of an inclination to conduct business with the French refugees, and then only after their victory in 1555. A lone exception was the involvement of Jean de l'Arche, Michel's son, with Loys Beljaquet in 1554.[69] Moreover, these contracts are totally confined to the activities of the Franc family. Louis Franc conducted business with Etienne Trembley in 1556.[70] Louis and his brother, Claude, sold some property to Estienne de Faye and Lorin Guyet, bourgeois merchants.[71] In 1556, Claude and his wife, Jehanne Baud, confessed a debt of 300 écus to the bourgeois printer, Estienne Girard.[72] In general, the French tended to confine their activities to their own exile community. When they had contacts with the Genevans, other than those mentioned above, they dealt with persons of no political prominence. Geneva, as a city, profited economically from the influx of French refugees; it is not clear that individual Calvinists gained specific benefits from the refugee presence.

The notary records do supply some additional data on ties within the Calvinist faction, though these tend only to reinforce already identified familial ties. Jean Chapeaurouge, in a contract witnessed by Louis Bon, presented a receipt to Jean Bron, a bourgeois merchant of local origin, and his wife Pauline.[73] Earlier, Louis Bon had bought some property from Estienne Chapeaurouge.[74] François Bonivard was indebted to Jean Porral and others in 1553.[75] Later, in 1557, François Chasteauneuf, a relative by marriage to Pierre Dorsière, married Françoise, daughter of Pierre Migerand.[76] However, these ties, as the other factors discussed above, are simply too tenuous and inconclusive to explain the unity of the Calvinist faction. Family backgrounds and connections, business ties, and relations with the bourgeois might have inclined these men towards one another, but can scarcely be credited with more. Rather, two factors in the factions before 1555 seem to offer the most persuasive explanation of why this group came together: the predominance of elders among the Calvinists and the exclusivity of the Perrinists.

Through their work as elders many of the Calvinists had had extensive, personal contact with the French ministers. It is reasonable to assume that their outlook was shaped, in time, to coincide with that of the ministers. When one recalls the exceptional quality and ability of the ministers after 1546 it is easy to understand how they would have had a profound impact on the opinions of the Genevan elders. This would have been especially true in the case of the five native Genevans who had served on the Consistory for an extended period of time. As their respect and admiration for the ministers grew they could easily have come to disapprove of the views expressed by the ministers' opponents. Finally, the longer they served on the Consistory the more closely they might have come to identify themselves with the ministers. In time these elders could have viewed attacks on the ministers as attacks on themselves. While this interpretation cannot be proven conclusively, it might be thought to explain the increase in confrontations between Genevans over the ministers. Prior to 1550 most clashes which involved the ministry were between ministers and Genevans. As events progressed clashes began to occur about the ministers which involved only Genevans; defending the French ministers, and the refugees, became a personal concern of local Genevans. This change is understandable if one accepts that some Genevans, especially the elders, began to identify their opinions and goals with those of the French ministers and their refugee compatriots.

The exclusivity of the Perrinists must be stressed as well. The Perrinists were a much more natural faction than the Calvinists. Their familial and business ties encouraged them to think and act as a group. The actions of the Perrinists and their tendency to view an attack on one as an attack on all of them is understandable, given the many factors which naturally bound them together. The clan nature of this faction had many advantages in Genevan politics. As long as they acted as a group there was little chance that their grip on power would be seriously loosened. At various times their domination of Geneva might be curtailed but in general they were secure in their position as the premier force in Genevan politics. The only way in which they could be defeated, even temporarily, was if there was a substantial, permanent shift in public opinion and the electoral balance. Even then, a shift in public opinion did not threaten total defeat for the Perrinists unless their numbers were greatly depleted or their opponents' strength augmented. The size and natural unity of the Perrinists was their guarantee that their influence in the magistracy would remain secure.

Yet, in 1555, this grip on power was broken. The admission of French refugees in large numbers to the bourgeoisie revealed to the Perrinists that their opponents had devised a means of permanently removing them from power. The Calvinists were also politically astute enough to seize the opportunity presented to them in the May 1555 riot to break the back of the Perrinist faction. With the crucial shift in the electorate and the exile of the leading Perrinists, the Calvinists had effectively destroyed their opposition. During their period of ascendancy the Perrinists had been unable or unwilling to crush and expel their most outspoken critics, the French ministers; the Calvinists clearly had no such qualms or constraints.

The consolidation of the Reformation in Geneva along lines consistent with Calvin's ideas of a godly state was a long, difficult process. The result was never a foregone conclusion; it would have been much more reasonable to expect the Genevan Reformation to conform to the model found in the other Swiss Protestant cities. In these cities the magistrates maintained a firm control over the ecclesiastical structure both in discipline and ministerial behaviour. The Genevan ministers fought to gain clear control over discipline and enjoyed, indeed exploited, a unique degree of freedom in their pulpits. The character, determination and quality of the Genevan ministers, combined with various fortuitous events, provided Calvin with the factors necessary to consolidate successfully the Reformation in Geneva.

It is essential to recall that one cannot begin any real discussion of a consolidation of the Genevan Reformation under Calvin's direction prior to his return in 1541. It would be a serious mistake to view the crisis of 1538 as the first round of a dispute which ended in 1555. The ministers in no way played a major role in the 1538 events. They were simply caught up in a political dispute in Geneva which revolved around the issue of the Republic's relationship with its military protector, Berne. The importance of political concerns remained after Calvin's return. It is clear from the changes to Calvin's original proposals for the Ecclesiastical Ordinances and the later rulings on excommunication that the Guillermins had every intention of creating a state Church along Swiss lines.[77] From the start, though, Calvin had little or no intention of adhering to the Swiss model; his vision of the correct relationship between the Church and State in Geneva differed radically from that of the magistrates who recalled him. The picture sometimes presented when discussing Calvin's return does not coincide with that found in the original records. Geneva's delay in recalling Calvin after the Articulants' defeat hardly agrees with Parker's assertion that 'it was believed that there was one man who could put things to right, and that man Jean Calvin'.[78] However, it is equally incorrect to deny the Protestant sentiments of the Genevans. Bouwsma's statement that the Geneva lacked 'significant local sentiment' for evangelical reform 'and turned for support to the Anabaptists' is baffling.[79] The situation in Geneva was much more complex, and the ministers much less important, than either of these views supposes.

The first few years after Calvin's return found him occupied with effecting changes in the area most directly under his control, the personnel of the Church. Calvin embarked on a fairly consistent programme of pushing aside the earlier, less qualified, less pliant ministers and replacing them with educated, socially prominent, hand-picked foreigners who could be expected to give Calvin their wholehearted support. Any attempt to change Genevan society required a unified, articulate Company of Pastors. Calvin must have been fully aware that the Genevan magistrates had found it much easier to expel him and Farel, knowing that the other ministers would remain loyal to the State. The more ministers who stood shoulder to shoulder with Calvin, the more secure his position in Geneva became. The socially prominent, high-profile French refugee ministers who joined the Company of Pastors in the mid-1540s were inclined to give Calvin every support. They had no ties to local Genevans as had some of the local ministers, such as Bernard, a citizen. Once this group was collected Calvin was assured of the control of the only effective means of mass communication and propaganda in Geneva, the city's pulpits. The only fora of dissent which then remained to his opponents were the councils, the General Assembly, and the streets.

By 1546, Calvin had also succeeded in another essential step in imposing his vision on Geneva; he had gathered together a body of supportive elders. Prior to 1546, in the Consistory's initial years, that body had experienced constant changes in personnel. The lack of a settled body of elders would have hindered any consistent application of discipline whether through admonition or excommunication. Each change also meant the loss of valuable experience in dealing with the various cases which came before the Consistory. But after 1546 the Consistory became an increasingly experienced, and qualified body; its legal expertise is widely attested by the inclusion of many of the elders on other Genevan judicial bodies. The scope of Consistorial activity went through an important change in this era as well. Initially the elders were occupied with the examination and correction of the religious beliefs of the Genevans; this involved enforcing sermon and catechism attendance. By 1546, the Consistory seems to have moved on to a closer involvement in the personal affairs of the Genevans. This did not necessarily mean that the Consistory was focusing its attentions on correcting immorality alone; to a large extent the new work meant that the Consistory became increasingly involved in the business and domestic relations of many of Geneva's inhabitants. As time passed, the elders became increasingly efficient in identifying and examining their charges, with a consequent increase in the number of cases and individuals before the Consistory. As those examined were called against their will and were often ignorant of the accusations against them, one can understand the annoyance which many of them expressed. Moreover, although the elders were local men, when the Genevans stood before the Consistory they were normally questioned and examined by the French ministers. The humiliation many Genevans felt as a result of being questioned and censured about their personal affairs by foreigners in front of fellow-citizens increased tensions between many Genevans and the ministers.

If Calvin's goals had been confined to consolidating his hold on Geneva's ecclesiastical structure, then by 1546 he would have been successful. The ministers and elders gathered around him were dramatically different from the body of men who had comprised Geneva's religious establishment in the early years after his return. The city's religious settlement was in the hands of a unified, determined, qualified body of men. At their head stood Calvin, a figure increasingly famous throughout Europe; as Calvin increased in importance, Geneva gained international prominence.[80] This new-found fame may well have aided Geneva in fending off the intentions of neighbouring states desirous of controlling the city. But Calvin was no pliant tool of the hands of the Genevan magistracy. Bolstered by the solidarity in the religious establishment, Calvin was increasingly free to agitate for the imposition of his vision of a godly society and polity. The fame of the Company of Pastors may have brought renown on the city but it also made it difficult for the magistrates to control their hired servants, the preachers.

However, as long as the ministers lacked any realistic means of altering Geneva's domestic political situation they could only annoy their opponents and try to accomplish their goals by the slow means of persuasion and indoctrination. The homogeneity and unity of purpose among the ministers protected them from the assaults of their detractors, but the political realities of Geneva gave them scant hope of effecting any radical changes in the immediate future. For Calvin to complete his moves to change Geneva's society and internal political structure, it was necessary either to change the make-up of the electorate or to eliminate substantial numbers of those opposed to his views. Throughout the last half of the 1540s Calvin's opponents found themselves unable to secure absolute control over Genevan politics. The nadir of their power was the near-eradication of the influence of the Favre clan as a result of the events surrounding Perrin's trial as a French agent. Nevertheless, Calvin was unable to exploit this disaster as the political structure had not become so polarised as to provide him with a local faction committed to promoting his interests as their own. Actions by the ministers in this period were rather premature and seem to have been counter-productive in that the ministers angered many Genevans by their seemingly insensitive and arrogant behaviour, for example, in their stance on baptismal names. The growing tensions of this era disappeared into the more serious disputes which arose as a result of increased French immigration into the city.

This immigration finally provided Calvin with the large body of supporters which he needed in the city which could, in the right circumstances, transform the general Genevan population as their compatriots had changed the Company of Pastors. Many local Genevans were quick to grasp the potential political and social threat represented by these new arrivals; the magistrates gathered around Perrin made various attempts to limit any growth in French influence. First and foremost they wished to keep them out of the electorate; the magistrates also removed from the General Assembly the articulate French ministers who had become bourgeois. But they were unable to halt the changes wrought on Geneva's society and economy by these immigrants. Obviously there was little incentive to deter the immigration of prominent, skilled, wealthy Frenchmen although these were the greatest potential threat to the city's ruling elite. Poor refugees added little to the city save burdens and were no threat to the balance of political power. The shift in Geneva's records from discussing the mass of poor refugees to focusing on the impact of the prominent Frenchmen is further evidence of the importance of these men on Geneva's precariously balanced internal situation.

While difficult to quantify, there can be no doubt that attempts by Perrin and his supporters to limit bourgeois rights damaged their position in the city. There seems to have been no resistance to their policy of restricting bourgeois admissions. But clearly, they wished for the debt-burdened city to be able to profit from the sale of bourgeois rights without risking any consequent changes to Geneva's political power-structure. However, their proposals to bar bourgeois from gaining full political rights for twenty-five years would have set a dangerous precedent with regard to bourgeois rights. It is essential to recall that these changes were supported by the Petit Conseil, composed wholly of citizens, but strenuously resisted and rejected whenever the bourgeois were consulted; they had no intention of allowing their civic rights to be jeopardised. Thus, the Perrinists faced the reality that Geneva now contained a group of men capable, should they gain political power, of dramatically altering Geneva's politi-

cal landscape. Undoubtedly, the potential for change which the prominent refugees represented was not lost on Calvin and his supporters.
However, first they had to break the political hegemony of Perrin's
relatives and supporters.

It is worth noting before proceeding that the dire predictions of the
Perrinists about the danger posed by the French were proved to be true by
later events and well beyond that caused by the changes ushered in
immediately after 1555. The Perrinists warned that the French would gain
control of Geneva and through their native-born, citizen children would
create a new ruling elite which would displace Geneva's older, established
families. It is clear that French power in the city grew substantially after
1555 and in later years as well. In 1574, the Petit Conseil contained six
senators (24 per cent) who were connected by marriage to French refugee
families. But by 1605, this number had risen to at least ten senators (40 per
cent), half of whom were related to the French by marriage while the other
five senators were sons of French immigrant bourgeois.[81] The Perrinists'
predictions probably failed to convince their compatriots because their
arguments would have appeared to be a way for the Perrinists to retain
their hold on power. Any objections by the interrelated Perrinists about
new bourgeois and changes to Geneva's power structure would have
seemed (justifiably) self-serving. The political power and unity of the
Perrinist faction would have helped to undermine their warnings; by the
time the reality of the changes became apparent it was too late to stop
them.

Nevertheless, it is also true, that the Perrinists' homogeneity was their
greatest source of strength. Their familial and business ties provided them
with the internal cohesion necessary to dominate Genevan politics; their
position and exclusivity also made them an object of envy, a barrier to
promotion for everyone else. If their opponents were ever able to unite,
then they could be defeated; for although they were a large group, and
increasingly a faction by the early 1550s, they did not represent a majority
of the Genevans. They were able to maintain their power by mutual
support and through the lack of powerful, co-ordinated opposition. Their
moves to limit bourgeois rights seem to have undermined their position in
the city and inclined some people to the opposing faction which was then
emerging, the Calvinists. The success of the constant barrage of anti-
Perrinist propaganda from the pulpits in weakening their political base
must not be underestimated. The ministers' accusations that immorality
in Geneva was the fault of the Perrinist-dominated magistracy would have
been politically damaging, and almost wholly irrefutable. The natural
exclusivity of the Perrinists, their blunders in handling the bourgeois issue,

and years of unanswerable criticism from the French-controlled pulpits combined to shake the Perrinist grip on power.

The slight decrease in the Perrinists' power was not, in itself, sufficient to end their role in Genevan politics. The single factor which provided the Calvinists with their chance to crush their opponents was the presence in Geneva of so many prominent refugees who were willing to buy bourgeois rights. Without the wholesale admission of the refugees to the electorate, it is hard to imagine how the Calvinists could have defeated the Perrinists; the Calvinists were swift to use the means available. The new bourgeois, and the close balance in Genevan politics, meant that the refugees could be used to effect a radical change. The May riots gave the Calvinists an even better opportunity for breaking the Perrinist faction decisively. But the Calvinists had already begun to move against the Perrinists; changes to the councils and the arrests of Berthelier and Comparet were clear signs of the Calvinists' plans and methods. Without the refugees, though, there is every reason to believe that the events of 1555, including the Calvinist electoral victory in February 1555, would have become no more than another episode in the recurring factional strife that was Genevan politics.

When discussing Genevan factionalism, one can draw on the earlier Articulant crisis for general comparisons. The defeat of the Guillermins had curtailed their political power and activities but produced no lasting effect. The collapse of the Articulants after their politically disastrous treaty with Berne was possible because their opponents remained a potent political force in Geneva despite their defeat in 1538. The drunken riot which marked the Articulant decline was used as a pretext for breaking their last vestiges of power. The Guillermins triumphed because they were able to capitalise on the fatal mistakes of their opponents and because of the fickle nature of Geneva's electorate. But the Guillermins' policy of exiling prominent Genevans was not a politically or socially sustainable course of action; it was also opposed by their military protectors, the Bernese, who valued stability in Geneva. The city needed the social stability and financial security of the leading Articulants. Domestic realities and external pressures imposed certain limits on Geneva's volatile political situation.

A similar pattern is apparent in the later crisis in the early 1550s, though with some major differences. The most important factor added to the equation was the French refugees. The Perrinists had gained the upper hand in 1553–54, but their arrogance and mismanagement meant that they were not able to maintain their strong hold on power. This provided the Calvinists with a slim majority which they were determined to increase through bourgeois admissions. The Perrinist riot allowed the Calvinists to crush, in a single blow, their opposition. But the Perrinists were not to be allowed to return from exile; they were no longer needed by Geneva. The shock to Geneva's social and economic fabric occasioned by the expulsion of so many leading citizens could be borne because of the cushion provided by the wealthy refugees. The clearest proof of Geneva's ability to survive so traumatic a shock is apparent in the founding of the Academy in 1559. The city, debt-ridden for so long, was able to take 50,000ff of the 60,000ff raised by the sale of the exiles' goods and apply it to the establishment of the Academy.[82] In the earlier Articulant crisis Bernese pressure and domestic realities forced the triumphant Guillermins to realise that they could not afford the loss of the few Articulants. But after 1555 the city was able to discard a significant section of Geneva's economic and political elite. The large number of prominent, wealthy refugees had provided Geneva with an over-abundance of talent and money; the Perrinists were expendable, superfluous troublemakers.[83]

While the foregoing discussion may explain Calvin's success and the Perrinists' failure it is still necessary to address the question of the existence of Calvin's local supporters. In many ways this is the most difficult issue. There is no strong evidence of such familial or business ties between the Calvinists as one finds with the Perrinists. This may well have proved to be a source of strength for the Calvinists; they were not marked by the same exclusivity as the Perrinists. Supporting the Calvinists to break the Perrinists' power would not have been seen as a vote to replace one insular bloc with another. Nor were there significant ties between the Calvinists and the refugees. It is true that the Perrinists were noticeable for their lack of contact but there is insufficient evidence to link the refugees to the Calvinists; for the most part, the French seemed to have functioned as a closed group within Geneva. However, the economic advantages offered to the city by the refugees were obvious; recognising these advantages did not require that one consider them worth the mass expulsion of citizens.

Definite connections between the Calvinists can be found when one examines the role of the Consistory in their faction. Many of the leading Calvinists were drawn from the group of citizens, the elders, who had the most frequent and intimate contact with the ministers. It is reasonable to conclude that the elders were the dedicated core of the Calvinist faction. As for their wider support in the community, Monter identified three explanations for the Calvinists' success.[84] While the information presented in this work has added detailed conclusions on the Genevan situation, Monter's general suppositions about Calvin's support among the general populace remain valid.

Monter emphasised the lack of a qualified opposition, the control of the pulpits by Calvin and his supporters, and the indoctrination of the Genevans, especially the young, in the catechism. Once the Company of Pastors had been brought under Calvin's full control in 1546, there were few qualified men left in opposition. The Perrinists' inability to withstand the persuasive force of the ministers explains their move to ban the bourgeois ministers from the General Assembly. When one recalls that Geneva's leadership was dominated by merchants of limited education, it is clear that they were no match for the articulate, university-educated ministers.[85] It is hard to imagine that many Genevans would have cared to stand before a crowd to dispute with the likes of Calvin, Cop, Des Gallars, or Colladon. Since many of the clashes with the ministers involved a dispute over the proper relationship between the Church and the State, few Genevans would have found themselves intellectually capable of matching the ministers in the debate. The most effective assaults of this sort made on Calvin were the attacks by Bolsec and Trolliet on predestination. But the general inability of Calvin's opponents to overcome him in an argument is apparent in the failure of Calvin's opponents to embarrass him on this issue; even with the Swiss unwillingness to support Calvin, his detractors were unable to capitalise on the situation. Debate in Geneva was controlled and directed by Calvin and the other ministers; the opposition, while vocal, was woefully inarticulate and therefore largely ineffective.

The position of Calvin's opponents was also greatly damaged by the control of the mass media, the pulpits, by the ministers. Once the pastors became unified and stable, the pulpit ministry of the Company of Pastors was a formidable force in Genevan society. The recurring clashes between the ministers and the magistrates over sermons (see Chapter 6) give some idea of the use to which the pulpits were being put. Disagreements with the magistrates were being aired by the ministers from their pulpits, but only one side of the debate was heard. Faced with the unified ministerial front, the magistrates proved consistently unable to control the content of sermons. The continual pulpit pronouncements on the decline of Genevan society into ungodliness and the consequent risk of divine retribution must have made a profound impact on the average citizens and bourgeois of Geneva.[86] Given that the electoral balance was precarious, even a slight impact could have had results out of all proportion to its actual effect on specific individuals.

Finally, one must realise that Calvin had controlled the education and indoctrination of the Genevans for over a decade prior to 1555. The catechism consistently drove home the ministers' view of reality; their vision of a godly life and society was the official view presented to the populace, even when leading Genevan magistrates disagreed with the interpretations the ministers put on some ideas.[87] One can see the moves against the elders in 1553 as an attempt to break this stranglehold on indoctrination. But the school and churches continued to proclaim an ideology and vision for Geneva consistent with that of the ministers. The effect, though, of the ministers' teaching and preaching could never have produced the radical changes of 1555. Nevertheless, many of Calvin's supporters were so convinced of the importance of the sermons and catechisms that they gave much of the credit for the overthrow of the Perrinists to these tools of indoctrination. For example, Bonivard stressed that a new generation had arisen under Calvin:

> Gens de bien, craignants Dieu, & principallement un tas de ieunes gens daage, mais desprit meur & raffis, qui nestoient pas nez & nourris en siecle, doctrine & meurs barbares, comme la pluspart des anciens, ains estoient nez tant seullement un peu devant que lEvangile vinst, & quant & luy les bonnes lettres, ausquelles ils furent nourris & endoctrinez.[88]

It would be ludicrous to suppose that every Genevan who voted against the Perrinists and their hold on power was actually voting for the Calvinist agenda.[89] Nevertheless, years of indoctrination must have inclined many to view the Calvinists with greater favour.

One of the greatest problems facing any examination of the Genevan Reformation and Calvin's role therein is Calvin's international importance. Far too often the temptation has been to focus on Calvin and to treat Geneva as an addendum to his life. In some ways this is understandable and perhaps justifiable, but it wholly overlooks the fact that Calvin was first and foremost a local minister. The research for this volume has driven home the depth of Calvin's involvement in the local political situation in Geneva. It is also apparent that there is a serious danger in historical studies' relying wholly and uncritically on interpretations of Genevan events from the viewpoint of Calvin and his supporters. These pro-Calvin sources are not intentionally misleading; indeed, they provide crucial insight into Calvin's understanding of events which then directed his later actions. Nevertheless, as this book has demonstrated, Calvin's interpretations are not the only ones available, nor are they necessarily the most reliable.

It is also clear that there has been too great a reliance on the secondary sources written in the last century. It is unfair to these sources to use them as though they had approached Genevan history with the same historiographical methods and presuppositions as are used at present; manifestly they did not. These earlier works provide an immense amount of data and analysis but one must not use them uncritically; the authors focused almost exclusively on a few prominent men and events. Too often spectacular cases were treated outside their historical context and allowed to gain an importance and weight far beyond what they actually deserved; the Servetus case is the best example of this. Servetus is certainly of interest in studying Calvin's theology and later issues about freedom of conscience, but there is no basis for treating the case as though it were as important in the Genevan context as the Ameaux, Trolliet, Berthelier, or the Perrin-Meigret cases.[90]

The picture which emerges from this study of Geneva is that of a long struggle by Calvin to realise his vision of a godly state and society. In no sense was the outcome a foregone conclusion. The persistence of Calvin and the other ministers after 1546 in agitating for the acceptance of their views can be credited with the victory in many ways. Their determination and unity made it impossible for their magisterial opponents to impose on Geneva a religious settlement and structure such as existed throughout Protestant Switzerland. In the finely balanced struggle in Geneva which emerged in the early 1550s, neither side was able to gain a total victory nor did either flag in its efforts. In time the ministers' preaching and teaching began to mould Geneva's mentality into their own image. Eventually this might have wrought a profound, yet evolutionary, change in Geneva. However, the presence of the French provided Calvin's local supporters with an easier, more revolutionary option. Ruthlessly, Calvin's local supporters used a slim majority to overwhelm their opponents by tipping the balance of power in the electorate with foreigners. Then, when the May riot gave them another opportunity, the Calvinists acted to crush their opponents and to drive a substantial number of their countrymen from Geneva.[91]

The consolidation of the Reformation in Geneva in 1555–57 also marked the end of Geneva's Revolutionary period. Under Calvin and the Calvinist magistrates Geneva was to enter into a new era in which it ceased to be a troubled city vulnerable to external pressures and began to emerge as a stable state playing a major role in European affairs. Just as Calvin's consolidation of control in the Company of Pastors and the Consistory in 1545–56 had allowed him to expand his efforts to Geneva's society in general, once they had made their position in the city secure, Calvin and his supporters were able to turn their attention farther afield. Calvin's success, then, was the result of a dogged determination by himself and his supporters to transform Geneva combined with an unhesitating willingness to capitalise on any and every opportunity to confound his opponents. In the end this perserverance was rewarded when the Calvinists were able to use a slight shift in Geneva's political balance of power, the presence of the religious refugees, and their opponents' incompetence to secure a total and lasting victory.

NOTES

1   Roset, p. 377, commented that even the hypocrites found it expedient to attend the services regularly.
2   Election lists occur in the February entries of the Registres du Conseil every year.
3   CO, vol. 15, col. 683f. (to Bullinger, 15 Jul 1555).
4   Roget, *Histoire*, vol. 5, pp. 6, 13.
5   AEG/RC/50, fol. 29 (7 Nov 1555); CO, vol. 21, col. 618 (7 Nov 1555).
6   Flournois, *Extraits*, p. 22.
7   Roget, *Histoire*, vol. 5, p. 24.
8   AEG/RC/52, fols. 33 (6 Oct 1556), 59v (23 Oct 1556).
9   A full account of Geneva's increasing entanglement in French affairs can be found in Kingdon, *Wars of Religion*.
10 AEG/RC/50, fol. 37v (15 Nov 1555).
11 AEG/RC/50, fol. 143v (7 Feb 1556).
12 Roget, *Histoire*, vol. 4, pp. 334ff.
13 AEG/RC/51, fol. 21v (21 Feb 1556). André, a notary, would eventually become Procureur Général in 1562. His father, Henri, was a pâtissier from Ain who had become a bourgeois on 11 January 1513. *Bourg.*, p. 176.
14 AEG/RC/51, fol. 45 (12 Mar 1556).
15 Roget, *Histoire*, vol. 4, pp. 334f.
16 These Syndic figures do not include the Syndic who presided in the Consistory each year, only those who had served before.
17 Chiccand had been a prominent local donor to the *Bourse Française*. See Olson, *Bourse*, pp. 108f.
18 AEG/RC/51, fols. 79–79v (3 Apr 1556).
19 AEG/PC/1re Ser., 570 (24–30 Mar 1556).
20 AEG/PC/2e Ser., 1074 (Jan 1556), 1075 (16 Jan 1556).
21 AEG/PC/2e Ser., 1080 (23 Apr 1556).
22 AEG/PC/1re Ser., 575 (10 Apr–12 May 1556). Bienvenu was connected to the Perrinists' faction through his marriage to Rolette Lect. Earlier in 1550, Bienvenu and Jean Philibert Bonna had clashed with Calvin during the Bolsec affair when they referred to the 'ministres' as 'ménestriers'. Roget, *Histoire*, vol. 3, p. 177.
23 Roget, *Histoire*, vol. 5, p. 36, n. 1. Louise's father, Legier, was a very wealthy merchant from Haute Savoye who had become a bourgeois on 14 October 1524. He had two other daughters, Jeanne, who married Bartholemie Lect, and Janine, who married Claude Janin Gautier. *Bourg.*, p. 201.
24 AEG/PC/1re Ser., 580 (1 Jun 1556).
25 AEG/PC/2e Ser., 1098 (Aug 1556).
26 AEG/PC/1re Ser., 598 (25–27 Nov 1556).
27 AEG/PC/2e Ser., 1113 (11 Dec 1556).
28 Roget, *Histoire*, vol. 5, pp. 40ff.
29 Roget, *Histoire*, vol. 5, p. 43.
30 Roget, *Histoire*, vol. 5, p. 45.
31 AEG/RC/52, fols. 95 (13 Nov 1556), 96v (15 Nov 1556); PC 2e Ser., 1104 (18–20 Nov 1556).

32 AEG/RC/52, fol. 94v (13 Nov 1556).
33 AEG/RC/52, fol. 246v (5 Feb 1557).
34 AEG/RC/53, fol. 2 (7 Feb 1557).
35 AEG/PC/1re Ser., 624 (8–19 Mar 1557).
36 AEG/PC/1re Ser., 626 (10–18 Mar 1557).
37 AEG/PC/2e Ser., 1126 (8 Mar 1557).
38 AEG/PC/2e Ser., 1127 (11 Mar 1557).
39 AEG/PC/1re Ser., 635 (3–9 Apr 1557).
40 AEG/PC/2e Ser., 1135 (15 Apr 1557).
41 AEG/PC/2e Ser., 1144 (13 May 1557).
42 AEG/PC/1re Ser., 649 (11–12 May 1557).
43 AEG/PC/1re Ser., 660 (17 Jul–2 Nov 1557).
44 AEG/PC/1re Ser., 616 (19 Feb–5 Aug 1557).
45 AEG/PC/2e Ser., 1154 (10 Jul 1557).
46 AEG/PC/2e Ser 1178 (4 Nov 1557), 1024 (14 Sep 1543).
47 AEG/PC/2e Ser., 1179 (9 Dec 1557).
48 AEG/PC/1re Ser., 688 (13–16 Dec 1557).
49 AEG/RC/53, fol. 320v (7 Sep 1557).
50 AEG/RC/54, fol. 24 (27 Dec 1557). The articles refer to the treaty which brought about the downfall of the Articulants (see p. 38).
51 AEG/RC/54, fols. 53v (20 Jan 1558), 61 (27 Jan 1558). Galiffe, *Procès Criminels*, p. 88, n. 1 contains an excellent, concise discussion of the history of the ministerial pay structure. The monetary increase was small; previous salaries ranged from 200ff to 240ff per annum. The increase for the rural ministers and the supply of grain was probably of the most use.
52 AEG/RC/53, fols. 401–401v (12 Nov 1557), 404 (14 Nov 1557)
53 AEG/RC/54, fols. 74–74v (4, 6 Feb 1558).
54 Includes those admitted free of charge.
55 Excludes those admitted free of charge.
56 AEG/PC/1re Ser., 582 (3–11 Jun 1556).
57 Corruption, which certainly did not lessen after 1555, was never great in Geneva. Monter, *Government*, pp. 106f.
58 AEG/PC/1re Ser., 610 (7 Jan–16 Feb 1557).
59 AEG/PC/1re Ser., 628 (17 Mar 1557).
60 AEG/PC/1re Ser., 663 (27–30 Jul 1557). Aime's uncle, Michel, from Nantua in Ain, had been a monk; Michel became a bourgeois on 12 December 1536. *Bourg.*, p. 216.
61 AEG/PC/2e Ser., 1162 (19 Aug 1557).
62 AEG/PC/1re Ser., 674 (14–17 Sep 1557). Galiffe, *Procès Criminels*, pp. 73f., emphasises the corrupt, immoral behaviour which can be found in leading Calvinists.
63 Monter, *Government*, pp. 21f.
64 The inconclusiveness of the data is evident in that Galiffe, *Procès Criminels*, p. 74 drew the opposite conclusion, that the Calvinists, who were newer, were socially *inferior* to the *much* longer-established Perrinists. Some of the new, though less prominent, men were of a very recent origin. Jean Charvet (Deux Cents in 1558) was the nephew of a Jean from Savoy who had become a bourgeois on 2 October 1520 (*Bourg.*, p. 190); Pierre Dansse (Deux Cents 1557, auditeur 1559, hospitalier 1561–65) was the son of Dominique, from Haute Savoye, who was admitted a bourgeois on 22 January 1518 (*Bourg.*, p. 187).
65 This is the very interpretation put on the events by Roset, p. 366.
66 AEG/PC/2e Ser., 1127 (11 Mar 1557).
67 Beguin was an agent for his son-in-law, Jean Stample. Their contract was witnessed by

two Frenchmen, Jean Crespin, the printer, and Ambroise Petit, as well as a citizen, Siboet Grifferat. AEG/Min/M. Try, vol. 7, fol. 139v (4 Aug 1550). For the Trembley contract see, AEG/Min/J. Ragueau, vol. 2, p. 142 (Apr/May 1557).

68 AEG/Min/P. Alliod, vol. 1, fols. 18v (1 Mar 1555), 95v (6 Feb 1557).

69 AEG/Min/M. Try, vol. 12, fol. 116 (22 Dec 1554).

70 AEG/Min/J. Ragueau, vol. 1, fol. 5v; vol. 2, fol. 52 (28 Sep 1556).

71 AEG/Min/J. Ragueau, vol. 2, fol. 117 (2 Nov 1557).

72 AEG/Min/B. Neyrod, vol. 1, fol. 204 (1556).

73 AEG/Min/G. Messiez, vol. 4, fol. 278v (11 Aug 1551).

74 AEG/Min/M. Try, vol. 7, fol. 217 (20 May 1550).

75 AEG/Min/M. Try, vol. 11, fol. 74 (18 Dec 1553).

76 AEG/Min/F. du Pont, fol. 16 (24 Dec 1557).

77 Martin, *Histoire*, p. 239, stresses that the magistrates consistently argued for the State's control over excommunication prior to 1555.

78 Parker, *Calvin*, p. 79. Nor is it reasonable to accept Parker's implication (p. 80) that Calvin's return provides evidence of magisterial acceptance of Calvin's views on ecclesiastical freedom, especially in the area of discipline. Subsequent events show that Calvin may have believed that that was the case; the magistrates certainly did not.

79 Bouwsma, *Calvin*, pp. 19f.

80 Calvin had become a tourist attraction in many ways. Even Catholics were reported to have gone to Geneva for no other reason than to have a look at Calvin. Cf., the account by Florimond de Raemond in A. Duke, *et al.*, eds, *Calvinism in Europe 1540–1610* (Manchester: 1992), pp. 35–8.

81 This material has been compiled from data in Monter, *Government*, pp. 95, 101f., and the genealogical works, Galiffe, *Notices*, and Choisy, *Recueil*. The problems with Geneva's genealogical works are few and the records which survive are excellent. Cf., L. Henry, *Anciennes Familles Genevoises* (Paris: 1956), pp. 25–30.

82 Monter, *Government*, pp. 25, 113.

83 See Chapter 5 for a discussion of the impact of the refugees. Monter, *Government*, pp. 165–87 has an excellent general treatment of the subject.

84 Monter, *Government*, pp. 99ff.

85 Cf., Monter, *Government*, pp. 92f. Roget, *Etrennes* , vol. 1, p. 18, says that Calvin's opponents were therefore mostly merchants, drapers, apothecaries and hotel owners.

86 Diefendorf, *Paris*, pp. 37ff. stresses the importance of a fear of divine wrath directed against the actions of Parisians as well.

87 As early as 1537, the catechism was teaching that excommunication was a power which rightly belonged to the church alone. Cf., Chenevière, *Pensée*, p. 254.

88 *Advis*, p. 127.

89 This contrasts with the view expressed in H. D. Foster, 'Calvin and His Followers Championed Representative Democracy', in R. M. Kingdon and R. D. Linder, eds., *Calvin and Calvinism* (Lexington, Mass.: 1970), p. 39, that, 'in the Biblical Common-wealth of Geneva, citizen and refugee were profoundly convinced of the righteousness of the Calvinistic theories'.

90 The epitome of this is McGrath. He treats the Servetus case as the culmination of the excommunication crisis and devotes almost seven pages (McGrath, *Calvin*, pp. 114–20) to it in his chapter on Calvin's consolidation of power. Yet he totally ignores the Ameaux, Trolliet, Perrin–Meigret, and Castellio cases and reduces Bolsec and Berthelier to the briefest of mentions (pp. 16, 121, respectively). Cf., Monter, *Government*, p. 69 and his complaints about the reliance of some scholars on a few spectacular cases for discussing Calvin and Geneva.

91 The importance of the French and the methods imployed by Calvin's supporters must be stressed to counter the views of those who would undervalue the importance of the refugees. The best expression of this position can be found in J. T. McNeill, 'Calvin Preferred Representative Democracy', in Kingdon and Linder, eds., *Calvinism*, p. 35. McNeill, while arguing that Calvin supported republicanism, said that, 'Calvin was masterful, sometimes vindictive, and often harsh; but politically he used constitutional methods and won his way (when he got it) by the persuasion of his fervid oratory. Under his leadership Geneva became a firmly established republic; quite conceivably, if more had been left to the council of citizens, faction would have destroyed the stability of the government'.

APPENDICES

Guillermins/Farets

P. Ameaux	H. Aubert	J. Balard, jun.
A. Bandière	Cl. Bernard	L. Bernard
Fr. Beguin	Cl. Bonna, dit Pertemps	P. Bonna
L. Chabbod	H. Chamfort	J. Chautemps
A. Corne	J.-A. Curtet	D. d'Arlod
P. de Faignon	B. de la Maisonneuve	J. des Arts
J.-Phil. Donzel	P. Dorsière	Nic. Druet
Mich. du Bois	Jaq. Eyral	J. Fansonnet
Fr. Favre	J.-Jaq. Forel	J. Furjod
Cl. Geneve, le Bâtard	J. Goulaz	Gme. Guigonnet
J. Janin	P.-J. Jessé	J. Lambert
L. Meigret	M. Morel	Phil. Morel
Ant. Mugnier	J. Pecollat	L. Perret
A. Perrin	Oddet Poisson	A. Porral
Cl. Roset	Fr. Rosset	Cl. Savoy
M. Sept	Fr. Sevard	M. Varro
L. Veygier	A. Vulliens	A. Vulliermoz

Articulants/Artichaux

J. Balard, senr.	P. Bertillion	J. Biolley
L. Blondin	Fr. Chamaystre	Fr. Chamois
A. Chapeaurouge	Est. Chapeaurouge	J. Coquet
Bezanson Dadaz	Est. Dadaz	Gir. de la Rive
Gme. de Romagnia	P. Dunant	Fr. Forel
Phil. Guex	Cl. Hugo	J. Jordan
Rolet Julliard	Ant. Lect	J. Levet
Fr. Lullin	J. Lullin	A. Mailliard
Cl. Malbuisson	B. Messeri	J.-G. Monathon
Jaq. Mugnier	Boniface Officier	Jaq. Patru
Cl. Philippe	J. Philippe	Geo. Planton
A. Plonjon	J. Syman	P. Syman
Cl. Testu	P. Tissot	P. Vandel

APPENDIX 2   *Personal relationships 1535–45*

Persons (faction)	Type of Contract	Reference (AEG/Min. or RC)
Jean-Gabriel Monathon (A) and Jean Jaquier witnesses: Domaine Dentand (?), François du Villard (?)	sale	Cl.de Compois, vol. 13, fol. 4 (26 Feb 1540)
Estienne Dadz (A?) Hans Landsberger of Fribourg (N/A) witness: B. de la Maisonneuve (G)	150ff debt to	Cl. de Compois, vol. 13 , fol. 67 (10 Dec 1540)
François Paquet (?) dau. of Jean Balard, jun. (G) guardians: M. Sept (G), A. Perrin (G), B. de la Maisonneuve (G) witnesses: P. Verna (?), A. Darbey (?), L. du Four (?), A. Chambouz (G)	marriage	Cl. de Compois, vol. 13, fol. 104v (10 Jan 1540)
Estienne (A?) & Bizanson (A) Dadaz B. de la Maisonnueve (G) witnesses: J. Chautemps (G), A. Charvet (?)	sale	Cl. de Compois, vol. 13, fol. 118 (10 Apr 1540)
François Favre (G) H. du Mollard (G)	receipt (1,500ff)	Cl. de Compois, vol. 13, fol. 237 (5 Apr 1540)
D. Dentand (?) Pierre-Jean Jessé (G) witness: D. d'Arlod (G)	rental	Cl. de Compois, vol. 13, fol. 242 (9 Jan 1540)
Françoise, dau. of Jean Levet (A) witnesses: B. de la Maisonneuve (G), A. Perrin (G), Jaq. Cheneval (?), Cl. Jaquemoz (?), A. Charvet (?), Jaq. Chevrot (?), Jaq. des Arts (G), Mt. du Lac (?)	testament	Cl. de Compois, vol. 13, fol. 251 (4 Aug 1540)
Jean Fonsonnet (G) Jaq. Chevrot (?) & G. Fonsonnet his wife witness: Mt. du Lac (?)	donation	Cl. de Compois, vol. 13, fol. 266 (30 Mar 1540)
Jean Lect (A?) Antoine Favre (G?) witness: Antoine Lect (A)	receipt	Cl. de Compois, vol. 13, fol. 304 (19 May 1540)
Dom. Dentand (?) Gl., dau. of Pierre Rosset (G?)	marriage	Cl. de Compois, vol. 10, fol. 117 (9 Jul 1539)
Estienne (A?) & Bizanson (A) Dadaz B. de la Maisonneuve (G)	sale of house	Cl. de Compois, vol. 10, fol. 232v (4 Sep 1537)
François Favre (G) H. Aubert (G)	house rental	Cl. de Compois, vol. 11, fol. 160 (21 May 1538)
H. du Mollard (?) Michel Varro (G)	sale	Cl. de Compois, vol. 12, fol. 40v (18 Nov 1539)
A. Chapeaurouge (A) Jaq. Bessonet (?)	receipt	Cl. Bernard, fol. 18 (13 Jul 1538)
Amb. Corne (G) Varro brothers (G)	sale	Cl. Bernard, fol. 32v (Jul 1537)
Amb. Corne (G) M. Varro (G)	receipt	Cl. Bernard, fol. 31v (20 Jul 1537)
Jean Goulaz (G) Jean Rosset (G?)	debt of 500ff to	Cl. Bernard, fol. 48 (4 Feb 1539)
Domaine Franc (?) A. Chambouz (G)	accord	Cl. de Mirabel, vol. 2, fol. 81 (5 Aug 1542)
Ant. (A), Jean (A?), & Barth. (A?) Lect Philibert Berthelier (?)	acquereurs for	J. du Verney, vol. 4, fol. 128v (31 Mar 1542)
Est. (G?) & Jean (G) Furjod A. Chapeaurouge (A)	debt of 3ff to	J. du Verney, vol. 8, fol. 67v (5 Apr 1543)

Persons (faction)	Type of Contract	Reference (AEG/Min. or RC)
Aimé des Arts (G) Cl. Malbuisson (A)	debt of 50ff to	J. du Verney, vol. 8, fol. 104 (16 Jun 1543)
B. de la Maisonneuve (G) J. Goulaz (G)	debt of 2,500ff to	J. du Verney, vol. 8, fol. 439 (17 Nov 1544)
J. des Arts (G) Cl. Sala (?), Pierre Bertillion (A), and Jean Vectry (?)	3,300ff loan to	RC/30, fol. 51 (5 Sep 1536)
J. des Arts (G) and M. Varro (G) Cl. Bonna, alias Pertemps (G)	debt to	RC/30, fol. 57 (18 Sep 1536)

APPENDIX 3   *Economic activity of earlier ministers*

Name (role in contract)	Details of contract	Reference (AEG/Min)
Bernard (buyer)	property from J. Chappuis de Peylier	P. Bally, vol. 1, pt. 2, fol. 32v (19 Mar 1543)
Bernard (witness)	sale from Pontex associates to Mon. de Lautrec, for 6ff.	G. Messiez, vol. 6, fol. 187 (24 Dec 1556)
Ecclesia (debtor)	4ff owed to P. de Ville and A. Rivilliod	B. Neyrod, vol. 2, fol. 59. (6 Feb 1557)
Champereau (witness) Treppereaux (witness)	donation from S. Galla to Janne Recordin, his wife	G. Messiez, vol. 6, fol. 51v (18 Jul 1545)
Marcourt (associate)	remission to F. Moyenne	A. Babel, vol. 2, fol. 377 (3 Apr 1555)
Marcourt (witness)	sale from A. de Lonnex to L. Guichard	A. Babel, vol. 2, fol. 381v (8 Feb 1555)
Marcourt (witness)	sale from P. Brochierand to A. Babel, bgs.	A. Babel, vol. 2, fol. 131v (15 Mar 1553)
Marcourt (father of bride)	dau. married Jaq. de Lonnex, citoyen, escoffier	F. Vuarrier, vol. 5, fols. 82, 84 (1 May 1553)
Marcourt (creditor)	loaned 500ff to J. Chappon and E. P. Thorex	J. du Verney, vol. 8, fols. 405 (27 Sep 1544), 410v. (11 Oct 1544)
Mare (witness)	marriage of N. de Chambet and Jeanne Emettaz	C. Blecheret, vol. 2, fol. 1 (22 Mar 1552)
Mare (disputant)	his wife, Clauda, dau. of F. Deleamont and his brothers against P. Favre	J. du Verney, vol. 5, fol. 43 (23 Nov 1542)
Mare (witness) Megret (witness)	cession of J. Puthiod, notaire, to J. Gavoy	J. L. Blecheret, vol. 2, fol. 37 (10 May 1554)
Megret (witness)	donation from C. Clerc to his wife, Clauda, dau. of Marin Raymond	C. Blecheret, vol. 1, fol. 72 (3 Dec 1551)
Megret (witness)	association of L. Lossiez and P. Forion (?), cit., apoth.	J. L. Blecheret, vol. 2, fol. 409v (18 Sep 1555)
Megret (witness)	association of C. Roset, cit., and S.Girard of Cugniez	G. Malliet, fol. 50 (4 Mar 1542)
Megret (seller)	property to P. A. de la Rive	J. L. Blecheret, vol. 3, fol. 190 (17 Jun 1558)
Megret (husband)	will of Pernette, dau. of F. Roset, cit., and niece of C. Roset, cit.	G. Malliet, fol. 71 (2 Jan 1542)
Moreau (witness)	will of Jaques Mugnier, bgs.	J. du Verney, vol. 5, fol. 52 (24 Jul 1543)
Vandert (witness)	marriage of P. Servel and Janne, dau. of C. Bastard	G. Messiez, vol. 4, fol. 120 (129 by new pagination) (16 Jan 1548)

APPENDIX 4   *Economic activity of later ministers*

Name (role in contract)	Details of contract	Reference (AEG)
Bourgoing (buyer)	offered 1,000ff for his house, city refused	RC/46, fol. 191 (19 Apr 1552)
Chauvet (witness)	will of Françoise, widow of S. Yserand, Sr de Chevalle in Vienne, wife of A. Chabert, bgs.	Min/P. du Verney, vol. 1, fol. 16 (29 Oct 1557)
Cop (debtor)	to P. de Veyrier (20 Dec 1553)	Min/A Babel, vol. 2, fol. 129v
Cop (creditor)	loan to Brochier family 147, 149 (19 Jun 1552)	Min/A. Babel, vol. 2, fol. 145,
Cop (receipt)	for 22ff from P. Brochier	Min/A. Babel, vol. 2, fol. 145v 19 Jun 1552)
Cop (associate)	cession from J. Charvet, cit.	Min/A. Babel, vol. 2, fol. 147v (19 Jun 1552)
Cop (associate)	ratification from A. Charvet	Min/A. Babel, vol. 2, fol. 149 (22 Nov 1553)
Cop (leave of absence)	wanted to sell land in France, approved by city	RC/42, fol. 90 (21 Apr 1547)
Cop (buyer)	offered 1,500ff for his house, city wanted 2,000ff.	RC/48, fol. 141v (1 Nov 1554)
Cop (creditor)	loaned 100ff to A. de Lonnex	Min/A. Babel, vol. 2, fol. 272 (6 Nov 1552)
Cop (renter)	house to C. Chenault, bgs. for 50ff per annum	Min/J. Ragueau, vol. 1, fol. 41 (ca. 1557/58)
Cop (seller)	house sold to Anne de Renty	Min/J. Ragueau, vol. 2, pt. 2, p. 105 (29 Apr 1557)
Cop (receipt)	for 250ff from Clauda Vedelle, wife of C. Drohot, Sr de Grandval, bgs.	Min/J. Ragueau, vol. 2, pt. 2, p. 191 (7 Nov 1557)
Des Gallars (witness)	will of J. Chaperon of Normandy	Min/J. Ragueau, vol. 2, pt. 2, p. 22 (28 Jun 1557)
Petit (associate)	confession of T. Raymond	Min/G. Patru, vol. 1, fol. 7v (4 May 1551)
Petit (associate)	cession from J. Chenu, cit.	Min/C. Blecheret, vol. 1, fol. 176 (26 Apr 1550)
Petit (associate)	exchange with P. Estallaz	Min/C. Blecheret, vol. 2, fol. 101. (5 Dec 1552)
Petit (buyer)	property from T. Reymond	Min/C. Blecheret, vol. 3, fol. 24v (29 Mar 1553)
Petit (seller)	property to J. Marchand of Chancy	Min/C. Blecheret, vol. 1 fos. 176 (26 Apr 1550), 13v (24 Nov 1551).
Petit (witness)	to last wishes of J. Mallard who died intestate	Min/G. Messiez, vol. 6, fol. 41 (1 Dec 1545)

APPENDIX 5   *Personal disputes, 1541–49*

Individuals	Cause/Result	Reference (AEG)
P. Durant v. P. Desire	assault	PC/2e Ser., 515 (5 Apr 1541)
J. Goula v. Rd. Vellut	argument in Conseil	RC/35, fol. 173v (23 Apr 1541)
M. Morel v. C. Curtet	repairs to their house	RC/35, fol. 189 (3 May 1541)
C. Clement v. C. Curtet	mutual slander	RC/35, fol. 220 (30 May 1541)
J. Donzel v. P. Baud	?	RC/35, fol. 254v (5 Jul 1541)
Bd. Chenalat v. Baud. de la Maisonneuve	?	RC/35, fol. 256 (8 Jul 1541)
P. Bonna v. J. Pilliod	?	RC/35, fol. 330 (19 Sep 1541)
P. Bonna v. J. Coquet	?	RC/35, fol. 335 (23 Sep 1541)
C. Bonna v. Gir. de la Rive	?	RC/35, fol. 384 (8 Nov 1541)
C. Bonna v. Gir. de la Rive	ordered to reconcile	RC/35, fol. 398v (15 Nov 1541)
C. Bonna v. Gir. de la Rive	ordered to reconcile	RC/35, fol. 409 (22 Nov 1541)
Ptte. de la Rive v. Hud. du Molard	property dispute	RC/35, fol. 411v (25 Nov 1541)
C. Bonna v. Gir. de la Rive	?	RC/35, fol. 411v (25 Nov 1541)
C. Bonna v. Gir. de la Rive	?	RC/35, fol. 419 (5 Dec 1541)
A. Boulard v. P. Bonna	property dispute	RC/35, fol. 504v (21 Feb 1542)
A. Chapeaurouge v. Gir. Chabbod	mutual slander	PC/2e Ser., 537 (21 Mar 1542)
J. Lect, jn. v. N. Cornier	mutual slander	PC/2e Ser., 541 (12 Apr 1542)
A. Alliod v. Procureur Gén.	mutual slander	PC/2e Ser., 551 (31 May 1542)
J. Goula v. heirs of J. Lect, sr.	?	RC/36, fol. 29v (2 Jun 1542)
Eust. de Massier v. J. Blanc	mutual slander	PC/2e Ser., 552 (Jun 1542)
Thom. Vandel v. F. Bonivard	?	RC/36, fol. 155 (27 oct 1542)
F. Ramel v. P. Ruffi	?	RC/36, fol. 172 (17 Nov 1542)
C. Michalet v. Alex. de Davonens	rioting	PC/2e Ser., 593 (7 Aug 1543)
P. Bonna v. Martine, wife of F. de Lassine	assault	PC/2e Ser., 594 (11 Aug 1543)
J. Biolley v. F. Chabbod	duelling	PC/1re Ser., 376 (15 Aug 1543)
P. Bonna v. Ant. Gerbel	Bonna arrested for slander	RC/37, fol. 195v (17 Aug 1543)
Ant. Darbey, J. Girod, C. Serex, J. Damouz, L. de Veyrier, C. Franc, C. Serve, L. Girod, J. Lambert, J. Fontannaz, A. Embler, N. Porral, F. D. Berthelier, M. Fiendaz, P. Girod, J. Biolley, J. Marchand	disputes in Conseil	RC/37, fol. 197v (17 Sep 1543) RC/37, fol. 229 (26 Sep 1543) RC/37, fols. 232–232v (29 Sep 1543) RC/37, fol. 240v (12 Oct 1543)
C. Papaz v. A. Vulliet	?	PC/2e Ser., 600 (24 Oct 1543)
A. Gervais v. Thom. Bonnaz	?	RC/37, fol. 279 (23 Nov 1543)
J. Philippin v. heirs of J. Lect	?	RC/37, fol. 280v (26 Nov 1543)

Individuals	Cause/Result	Reference (AEG)
J. Vectier v. J. Chautemps and J. Lambert	?	RC/38, fol. 71 (12 Feb 1544)
J. Corrajod v. P. Vernaz	repairs to their house	RC/38, fol. 125 (14 Mar 1544)
M. du Puis v. H. Aubert	loan dispute	RC/39, fol. 118 (30 Jan 1545)
J. G. Monathon v. a Syndic	slander of a Syndic	PC/2e Ser., 621 (12 Feb 1545)
M. Fienda v. Bd. Servand	assault	PC/2e Ser., 622 (2 Mar 1545)
Ant. Lect v. O. Chenallat	property dispute	RC/40, fol. 133b v (2 Jun 1545)
C. Clement v. C. Curtet	duelling	PC/2e Ser., 666 (13 Oct 1545)
F. Mestral v. P. Vandel	?	PC/2e Ser., 670 (3 Nov 1545)
J. Fontanna v. P. Verna, R. Monet and A. des Arts	business dispute	RC/40, fol. 312v (4 Dec 1545)
Barth. Lect v. C. Griffon and O. Chenallat	?	RC/40, fol. 360v (28 Jan 1546)
Barth. Lect v. J. A. Curtet	dispute over payment	RC/41, fol. 63 (1 Apr 1546)
P. Biolley v. L. du Four	mutual slander	RC/41, fol. 244 (16 Nov 1546)
M. Brassard v. F. Collomb	duelling	PC/2e Ser., 723 (16 Nov 1546)
J. Lambert v. A. Perrin	arguing	RC/41, fol. 245 (18 Nov 1546)
J. des Arts v. J. Lambert and Bez. Dada	arguing	RC/41, fol. 256 (6 Dec 1546)
M. Malliet v. J. Binot	assault	PC/2e Ser., 733 (12 Dec 1546)
Est. Chapeaurouge v. N. Gentil	mutual slander	RC/42, fol. 159 (28 Jun 1547)
J. A. Curtet v. Barth. Lect	property dispute	RC/43, fol. 27 (24 Feb 1548)
G. and P. Planton v. son of Sieur de Vergier	duelling, manslaughter	PC/2e Ser., 743 (Mar 1547)
M. Try v. J. Vionet	manslaughter	PC/1re Ser., 443 (10 Jun 1547)
G. Villod v. magistrates	slander	PC/1re Ser, 444 (20 Jun 1547)
A. Honjon v. magistrates	slander	PC/1re Ser., 445 (27 Jun 1547)
M. Morel v. F. Beguin	Business dispute	RC/43, fos. 132v–133 (10 Jul 1548)
N. Druet v. H. du Molard	assault	PC/2e Ser., 759 (Oct 1547)
J. B. Sept v. J. Herard	assault	PC/2e Ser., 773 (25 Jun 1548)
P. Bonna v. F. Favre	mutual Slander	RC/43, fol. 259 (6 Dec 1548)
H. Aubert v. J. Lullin	property dispute	RC/44, fol. 151 (5 Jul 1549)
P. Vandel v. J. A. Curtet and P. Bonna	slander	RC/44, fol. 154v (8 Jul 1549)
A. Darbey v. J. Chapie	rioting	PC/2e Ser., 800 (12 Jul 1549)
R. Monet v. Phil. and F. D. Berthelier	slander of memory of the Bertheliers' father	RC/44, fos. 260, 261v (8, 11, Nov 1549)

APPENDIX 6   *François Favre family relations*

Individuals directly related[1]	Political career	Additional information
Jean Gentil	?	?
Bezanson Hugues	Syndic 1528	d. 1532, son: Denis (below)
Ami Perrin	Syndic 1545	father: Claude (below)
Pierre Tissot	Syndic 1544	
Claude Bonna (Pertemps)	Syndic 1542	d. 1542
Pierre de la Mar	CC 1548	
Jean Louis Ramel	CC 1546	hired Antoine Lect as cureur
Jaquema Plonjon		
Clauda de Fernex		
Nicolarde Manlich		
Marguerite Hugues		

Individuals indirectly related[2]

Jean Baptiste Sept	LX 1546	father: Michel, sen. (below) Claude
Bernard	LX 1538	d. *c* 1546
Jean François Bernard	LX 1556	uncle: Claude (above)
Jean de Fernex	?	bro.(?): Guillaume (CC '46) sister-in-law: Jeanne Chenallat, dau. of Estienne (below)
Louis Franc	?	brother-in-law: Amblard Corne (Syndic '46); father: Domaine (LX '46)
Jean du Mollard	CC 1546	bro.: Hudriod (Syndic '43)
Denis Hugues	?	father: Bezanson (above)
Mathieu Manlich	bourgeois 1538	
Michel Sept, sen.	Syndic 1534	d. *c.* 1541
Henry Embler	CC 1535	son: André (LX '46)
Jaques des Arts	Syndic 1545	son/neph.: Aimé (CC '46)
Pierre du Villars	?	?
Laurent Symon	CC 1546	father-in-law: Claude Perrin (below); brother-in-law: Ami Perrin (above)
Pierre Vindret	LX 1546	father-in-law: Claude Perrin (below); brother-in-law: Ami Perrin (above)
Jaques Emyn	LX 1544	?
Nicod Ruffi	?	son: Pierre (PC secr. '46)
Antoine Gentil	?	?
Jean Ferra, sen.	CC 1546	?
Pierre Bonna	PC 1546	bro.: Claude (above)
Jean Philibert Bonna	CC 1546	bro.: Claude (above)
Claude Perrin	CC 1546	son: Ami (above)
Sebastienne Lect		
Guillemette de la Rive		
Clauda Pollier		
Louise Philippe		
Andrea Gentil		

Notes
[1] This refers to people related by marriage or birth to François's immediate family.
[2] This refers to people directly related by marriage or birth to people in the first category.

APPENDIX 7   *Claude Bonna (Pertemps) family relations*

Individuals directly related[a]	Political career	Additional information
George Lect	bourgeois 1479	son: Antoine (below)
François Favre	PC 1537, LX 1546	(see Appendix 6)
Jean Ferra, sen.	(see Appendix 6)	
Pierre Bonna	(see Appendix 6)	
Jean Philibert Bonna	(see Appendix 6)	
Jean Baptiste Sept	(see Appendix 6)	
Antoina Sept		
Humberte Bienvenu		
Jaquema Bitry		
Clauda Bonna		

Individuals indirectly related[b]

Antoine Lect	PC 1534	father: George (above)
Michel Sept, sen.	(see Appendix 6)	
Balthazar Sept	CC 1546	father: Michel, sen. (above)
Estienne Chenalat	bourgeois 1496	(see Appendix 7)
Jean Bruslée	?	?
Jean du Molard	(see Appendix 6)	
Michel Sept, jun.	?	father: Michel sen. (above)
Sebastienne Lect		
Pernette Ramel		
Andrienne de Livron		
Perrine de la Rive		
Andrea Gentil		
Marie de la Maisonneuve		

Families related to both the Bonna and Favre clans:

Lect, Sept, Gentil, Ferrat, De la Rive, Du Molard, Ramel

Notes

[a] This refers to people directly related by marriage or birth ot Claude's immediate family.

[b] This refers to people directly related by marriage or birth to people in the first category.

APPENDIX 8 *Selected notary contracts 1540–49*

Individuals involved	Type of contract	Reference (AEG/Min)
D. Dentand to P. J. Jesse	rental for 3 yrs at 35ff/yr	C. de Compois, vol. 13, fol. 242 (9 Jan 1540)
Fr. Paquet and Louise, dau. of J. Balard	marriage	C. de Compois, vol. 13, fol. 102 (10 Jan 1540)
Fr. Favre and wife, Marg. to H. du Molard	quittance for 316 écus-16	C. de Compois, vol. 13, fol. 237 (5 Apr 1540)
Est. and Bez. Dada to Baud. de la Maisonneuve	sale of house	C. de Cmpois, vol. 13, fol. 118 (10 Apr 1540)
A. Perrin to P. Vachat	procuration	C. de Compois, vol. 13, fol. 63 (29 Apr 1540)
J. Lect to Ant. Favre	quittance	C. de Compois, vol. 13, fol. 129 (19 May 1540)
P. Symon and Bernd. Chenellat	partnership	C. de Compois, vol. 13, fol. 198 (19 May 1540)
J. L. Ramel to Jaq. Emyn	debt of 21 écus	C. de Compois, vol. 13, fol. 36 (6 Aug 1540)
Hans Landsburger, of Fribourg to Est. Dada	debt of 30 écus	C. de Compois, vol. 13, fol. 67 (10 Dec 1540)
J. L., Jean, Fr., and P. Ramel, bros. & Jean, Ant., P. and Phbt. de la Mar, bros.	transaction	C. de Compois, vol. 13, fol. 366 (12 Sep 1541)
P. Migerand and Bezansone, dau. J. Lect	marriage	J. du Verney, vol. 5, fos. 9, 11, 14 (1 Feb 1542)
F. de Langin to his dau., Ptte., wife of J. A. Curtet	donation	G. Malliet, fol. 7 (22 Feb 1542)
Lect brothers to L. Dufour for P. Berthelier	cessions	J. du Verney, vol. 5, fols. 22, 29 (19 May 1542)
S. Grifferat to C. Roset	sale (160ff)	G. Malliet, fol. 48 (1 Jun 1542)
Gme. Dentand, ht of Paris, to D. Dentand	sale	M. Try, vol. 5, fol. 16 (24 Aug 1542)
J. Phbt. Bonna to C. Rosset	admodiation	C. de Compois, vol. 13, fol. 416 (9 Nov 1543)
D. d'Arlod to C. Clement (Humbert)	cession	G. Malliet, fol. 162v (24 Nov 1543)
J. du Molard and Jeanne, dau. of Bez. Hugues	marriage	C. de Mirabel, vol. 2, fol. 35v (12 Feb 1544)
A. and C. Philippe to J. Bergeron	procuration	C. de Mirabel, vol. 2, fol. 39 (20 Apr 1544)
P. and Phbt. de la Mar to J. Bonna	sale (180 écus)	P. Fabry, vol. 1, fol. 145 (28 Dec 1546)
J. A Curtet to P. Bienvenu	procuration	G. Malliet, fol. 216 (29 Mar 1544)
J. F. Ramel to P. Vandel, elder	sale	M. Try, vol. 5, fol. 39 and vol. 6, fol. 42v (7 Aug 1544)

Individuals involved	Type of contract	Reference (AEG/Min)
Jean, P., Mich., Vandel, bros. to J. Trolliet	house rental at	J. du Verney, vol. 8, fol. 154 (20 Oct 1543)
C., Ls., Char. chasteauneuf to C. Malbuisson	debts (217ff)	J. du Verney, vol. 8, fol. 242 (8 Feb 1544)
C. Clement (Humbert) to M. Varro	debt (30ff)	J. du Verney, vol. 8, fol. 356 (6 Jun 1544)
Baud. de la Maisonneuve to J. Goula	debt (500 écus)	J. du Verney, vol. 8, fol. 439 (17 Nov 1544)
J. G. Monathon to J. Dunant	sale of land (34 écus)	M. Try, vol. 5, fol. 114 and vol. 6, fol. 114v (6 Mar 1545)
C. Bonnaz, widow of C. Pertemps and sons to J. Bergeron, *et al.*	sale	J. du Verney, vol. 5, fol. 96 (6 May 1545)
A. Lect, dau. of Jean, to L. du Pont and L. Mestrezat	Money owed on sale of house (435 écus)	J. du Verney, vol. 5, fol. 97 (11 May 1545)
Ant. Lect and O. Chenellat	accord	J. du Verney, vol. 5, fol. 103 (6 Jun 1545)
G. Lect to C. Destral	cession	M. Try, vol. 6, fol. 153 (10 Jul 1545)
Bezansone Hugue, wife of P. Symon to D. Dentand	sale	J. du Verney, vol. 9, fol. 108 (1 May 1545)
G. Favre, Dentand bros., F. Forel, J. Guigonet with moderation by J. de Mageniez, L. Mermet	partnership in buying tithes of Cortier and Agnières	C. A. Fodral, fol. 97v (29 Jun 1547)
P. Chapeaurouge to M. Manlich	sale	A. Prevost, fol. 22 (15 Mar 1546)
C. and P. Dorsière (cousins) to J. A. Curtet	sale of property	M. Try, vol. 5, fol. 188 (28 Mar 1547)
F. de Fernex to L. du Fort and L. Mestrezat by their servant J. Moget	sale	A. Prevost, fol. 87 (20 Jan 1547)
P. Chapeaurouge to U. Guisard	sale of house and land	M. Try, vol. 7, fol. 5v (14 Mar 1548)
B. Dadaz to O. Chenallat	sale	C. Blecheret, vol. 1, fol. 240 15 Mar 1548)
C. Hugues to P. Savoye	debt of 25 écus	G. Messiez, vol. 4, fol. 117 (13 Apr 1548)
J. F. Ramel to A. Embler	admodiation	G. Messiez, vol. 4, fol. 105 (9 Sep 1548)
Baud. de la Maisonneuve to C. d'Arquembourg, ht, and his wife, Michée, dau. of Baud.	sale of house	M. Try, vol. 7, fol. 26 (8 Oct 1548)
D. Dentand to D. d'Arlod	sale	M. Try, vol. 7, fol. 83 (27 Nov 1549)

APPENDIX 9 *Individuals arrested at Antoine Lect's marriage feast, 25 March 1546*

Individuals	Political career	Additional information
Antoine Lect	PC 1534	host, father of the bride
Rolette		husband: Antoine Lect
Jeanne Lect		bride
Claude Philippe	?	groom
Mya Philippe		bro.: Claude (groom); husband Jean Philibert Gay; father: Jean
Amblard Corne	Syndic 1546	wife: Jeanne, dau. of Domaine Franc and ? Philippe
Jeanne Franc		husband: Amblard Corne
Louis Franc	?	father: Domaine; brother-in-law: Claude Philippe (groom)
Pernette Franc		father: Domaine; husband: Claude de la Maisonneuve (Baudichon)
Ami Perrin	PC 1546	wife (1st): dau. of Jaques Emyn
Françoise Favre		husband: Ami Perrin
Denys Hugues	?	wife: Jeanne Exchaquet (below)
Jeanne Exchaquet		husband: Denys Hugues
Jean Malliard	?	?
Jean Bergeron	?	?
Loup Tissot	CC 1549	wife: Jeanne Bergeron
Jean Baptiste Sept	LX 1546	wife: Clauda Bonna
Balthazar Sept	CC 1546	bro.: Jean Baptiste
Jaques Gruet	?	executed for attacks on Calvin, 1547
Pierre Moche	CC 1547	?
Claude Moche	?	?
Françoise Emyn		father: Jaques; husband: Guydo Malliet (LX '39)
Françoise		husband: François Philibert Donzel (LX '46)
Jehanton des Bois	CC 1545	?
Claude de la Pallud	CC 1546	?
Martine Balard		husband: Mathieu Canard (LX '46)

APPENDIX 10   *Major Genevan transactions 1538–48*

Individuals	Type of Transaction	Value	Reference (AEG/Min)
Pierre Delaleaz, cit. to Loys du Four and Legier Mestrezat	debt	£t 276 16s 8d (7,000ff)	C. de Compois, vol. 13 fol. 112 (15 Oct 1540)
Jeanne de Pesme, Dame Brandis, wife of François de Montmayeuz to François du Villard, cit.	sale of Tour du Molard	1,100 écus (5,500ff)	C. de Compois, vol. 12, fol. 237 (4 Feb 1539)
François Daniel Berthelier to Jaques Blanc, merchant bg of Berne and Thomas intermediary	Debt	600 écus (3,000ff)	P. Fabry, vol. 1, fol. 128v (9 Jul 1545)
Baudichon de la Maisonneuve to Jean Goula	promise to pay	500 écus (2500ff)	J. du Verney, vol. 8, fol. 439 (17 Nov 1544)
Antoine Lect to Loys du Pont and Legier Mestresatz, bg.	debt	435 écus (2,175ff)	J du Verney, vol. 5, fol. 98 (11 May 1545)
Henry Aubert, citoyen to Estienna, dau. of Loys Gautier	quittance /receipt related to dowry	200 écus and 800ff (1,800ff)	J. du Verney, vol. 7, fol. 46v (26 Apr 1544)
Rolet Bonnouz, bg., and his son, Thomas to François Bienvenu, cit.	debt	335 écus (1,675ff)	C. de Compois, vol. 11, fol. 211 (12 Jun 1538)
François Favre and his wife Marguerite to Hudriod du Molard	quittance/ receipt	316 écus-16s (1,580ff)	C. de Compois, vol. 13, fol. 237 (5 Apr 1540)
Girard Girard, ht., printer to Baudichon de la Maisonneuve	payment associated with a marriage	300 écus (1,500ff)	M. Try, vol. 7, fol. 46v (8 Oct 1548)
Jean Louis Ramel to Jaques Emyn	debt	300 écus (1,500ff)	C. de Compois, vol. 13, fol. 36 (6 Aug 1540)

APPENDIX II   *Major Genevan transactions 1549–57*

Individuals	Type of Transaction	Value	Reference (AEG/Min)
Jean Bourgeoys de Fribourg to Jean Arpaud de Lyon	Sale of Seigneurie of Troches	1,170 écus (5,850ff)	C. Pyu, vol. 4, fols. 36, 39, 42 (22 Oct 1552)
François Chevallier and his wife, Anthoina Morgnense and his brother, Guillaume and his wife, Jeanne d'Arlod to Anthoine Lautrec, bg, and his wife, Anthoynette de Vabres	Sale of property	950 écus (4,750ff)	G. Messiez, vol. 6. fol. 177 (24 Dec 1556)
Two daughters of René Perollet to Denis Lasère, bg	Sale of a house	930 écus (4,650ff)	J. Ragueau, vol. 2, pt. 2, p. 43 (21 Aug 1556)
Nicolas de Coincte, son of Guillaume, Comte d'Anguerville to his wife, Catherine de Gounis	Quittance/Receipt	900 écus (4,500ff)	J. Ragueau, vol. 2, pt. 2, p. 92 (21 Oct 1557)
Jean Louis Ramel to Loys Trembley	Sale of a house	3,000ff	J. Ragueau, vol. 2, pt. 2, p. 142 (18 Dec 1557)
Françoise Brachet, widow of Guillaume Aubelin, Sr de La Bruyère to Anthoine and Thièrry Morel, habitants	Sale of a house previously belonging to Jean Ami Curtet	560 écus (2,800ff)	J. Ragueau, vol. 2, pt. 2, pp. 205 (31 Mar 1558), 347 (1 Nov 1558)
Jean Beguin, bg., drapier to his son-in-law, Jean Stample, ht, drapier	Quittance /Receipt	£t 1,250 (2,700ff)	M. Try, vol. 7, fol. 147 (4 Aug 1550)
Jean Moget and Jeffrey du Boys, citoyens, to Loys Guyuchet, maçon, from Vyen-en-Salla	Debt	1,800ff	M. Try, vol. 7, fol. 96 (6 Feb 1554)
Jaques de Bourgogne, Sr de Fallaix, acquéreur of Anthoyna de Versonnex, widow of François Viennoys to Anthoine Popillon, Sr de Parey	Cession of a house	350 écus (1,750ff)	C. Pyu, vol. 1, fol. 411 (8 Sep 1551)
William Whittingham, bg., of Chester, and his wife, Catherine Jacquemin to his brother-in-law, François Bernier, bg.	Quittance /Receipt	£t 800 (1,730ff)	J. Ragueau, vol. 2, pt. 2, p. 96 (27 Oct 1557)

bg. = bourgeois

SOURCES

PRIMARY SOURCES (MANUSCRIPTS)

Archives d'Etat de Genève

Instruction Publique A1
Livre des Affaires du Collège

Minutes des Notaires	volumes (dates)
Pierre Alliod	1 (1554–72)
Aimé Babel	1 (1537–50)
	2 (1545–60)
Pierre Bally	1 (1537–47)
Claude Bernard	single volume (1537–9)
Claude Blecheret	1 (1548–51)
	2 (1552–55)
	3 (1551–54)
Jean Louis Blecheret	2 (1547–56)
	3 (1556–59)
Claude de Compois	10 (1537–40)
	11 (1538)
	12 (1539)
	13 (1540–44)
Claude de Mirabel	2 (1542–44)
François du Pont	single volume (1556–61)
Jean du Verney	4 (1538–43)
	5 (1541–46)
	7 (1543–46)
	8 (1543–45)
	9 (1545–46)
Pierre du Verney	1 (1553–70)
	2 (1551–59)
Pierre Fabry	1 (1543–44)
Claude Amyed Fodral	single volume (1546–47)
Claude Jaccon	single volume (1556–57)
George Malliet	single volume (1541–44)
Guillaume Messiez	4 (1545–54)
	6 (1544–62)

Bernardin Neyrod	1 (1556)
	2 (1556–57)
Gabriel Patru	1 (1548–96)
Aimé Prevost	single volume (1546–49)
Claude Pyu	1 (1535–51)
	4 (1552–50)
Jean Ragueau	1 (1554–58)
	2 (1556–8)
Michel Try	5 (1539–48)
	6 (1543–45)
	7 (1545–53)
	11 (1544–55)
	12 (1553–44)
François Vuarrier	5 (1537–67)

Procès Criminels
  1re Série, 190–695 (16 Mar 1518–28 Dec 1557)
  2e Série, 372–1179 (1 Feb 1537–9 Dec 1557)

Registres de Consistoire
  vol. 1 (1542–44): transcribed by Robert M. Kingdon, Isabella Watt, Jeffrey R. Watt.
  vol. 2 (1545–46): transcribed by I. Watt and J. R. Watt.
  vol. 3 (1547–48): transcribed by I. Watt.
  vol. 4 (1548): transcribed by Glenn Sunshine and David Wegener.
  vol. 5 (1550–51): transcribed by I. Watt.

Registres du Conseil
  vols. 28–54 (7 Feb 1535–3 Feb 1559)

Bibliothèque Nationale, Paris:

  Dupuy Ms. 698, Nicolas Pithou, *Histoire Ecclésiastique de l'Eglise de Troyes.*

PRIMARY SOURCES (PUBLISHED)

Balard, Jean. *Journal,* J. J. Chaponnière, ed (Geneva: 1854).

Bergier, Jean F. Kingdon, Robert M. Dufour, Alain, eds. *Registres de la Compagnie des Pasteurs de Genève au Temps de Calvin* in *Travaux d'Humanisme et Renaissance,* LV (Geneva: 1962). 10 volumes; vol. 1 (1546–53), vol. 2 (1553–64) used.

Beza, Theodore. 'Life of Calvin', in H. Beveridge, trans. and ed., *Tracts Relating to the Reformation by Jean Calvin* (Edinburgh: 1844).

Bonivard, François. *Les Chroniques de Genève* (Geneva: 1831).

— *Advis et Devis sur l'Ancienne et Nouvelle Police de Genève* (Geneva: 1865), 2 volumes.

Calvin, Jean. *Letters,* J. Bonnet, trans. (Edinburgh: 1855), 5 volumes (vol. 1. used).

— *Calvini Opera*, in G. Baum, E. Cunitz, E Reuss, eds., *Corpus Reformatorum* (Brunswick and Berlin: 1863–1900).

— *Sermons sur les Livres de Jeremie et des Lamentations*, in R. Peter, ed., *Supplementa Calviniana* (Neukirchen-Vluy: 1971), vol. 6.

— *Sermons sur le Livre de Michée*, in J. D. Benoît, *Supplementa Calviniana* (Neukirchen-Vluyn: 1971), vol. 5.

— *Psalmpredigten, Passion-, Oster-, und Pfingstpredigten*, in E. Mülhaupt, ed, *Supplementa Calviniana* (Neukirchen-Vluyn: 1971), vol. 7.

Covelle, Alfred L. *Le Livre des Bourgeois* (Geneva: 1897).

Flournois, Jean. *Extraits Contenus de Tout ce qu'il y a d'Important dans les Registres Publics de Genève* (Geneva: 1832).

Froment, Antoine. *Les Actes et Gestes Merveilleux* [Geneva: J. Girard: 1554]. Modern edition (Geneva: 1854).

Galiffe, John B. G. *Matériaux pour l'Histoire de Genève* (Geneva: 1830), 2 volumes.

Grenus-Saladin, François T. L. *Fragments Biographiques et Historiques* (Geneva: 1815).

Geisendorf, Paul F. *Livre des Habitants* (Geneva: 1957–64). 2 volumes, vol. 1 (1549–60) used.

Roset, Michel. *Les Chroniques de Genève* (Geneva: 1894).

SECONDARY SOURCES

Ainsworth, Arthur D. *The Relations between the Church and State in the City and Canton of Geneva* (Atlanta: 1965).

Babel, Antoine. *Histoire Economique de Genève des Origines au Début du XVIe Siècle* (Geneva: 1963).

Bainton, Roland H. 'Sebatian Castellio, Champion of Religious Liberty', *Castellioniana* (Leiden: 1951).

Baker, J. Wayne. 'Calvin's Discipline and the Early Reformed Tradition: Bullinger and Calvin', in R. Schnucker, ed., *Calviniana. Ideas and Influence of Jean Calvin* in *Sixteenth Century Essays and Studies* (1988), 10: 107–19.

Balke, William. *Calvin and the Anabaptist Radicals* (Grand Rapids: 1981).

Benedict, Philip. *Rouen during the Wars of Religion* (Cambridge: 1981).

Bercé, Y. M. 'Aspects de la Criminalité au XVIIe Siècle', in *Revue Historique* (1968).

Bergier, Jean François. 'Marchands Italiens à Genève au Début du XVIe Siècle (1480–1540)', in *Studi in Onore di Armando Sapori* (Milan: 1957).

— 'Le Démission de Trésorier Amblard Corne', in *Mélanges offerts à M. Paul E. Martin*, in *MDG*, vol. 40 (Geneva: 1961).

— *Genève et l'Economie Européene de la Renaissance* (Geneva: 1963).

— 'Salaires des Pasteurs de Genève au XVIe Siècle', in *Mélanges d'Histoire du XVIe Siècle offerts à Henri Meylan*, in *Bibliothèque Historique Vaudoise*, vol. 43 (Lausanne: 1970).

Bieler, André. *Pensée Economique et Sociale de Calvin* (Geneva: 1961).

Binz, Louis. *Vie Religieuse et Réforme Ecclésiastique dans le Diocèse de Genève, 1378–1450* (Geneva: 1973).

Bohatec, Josef. *Calvin und das Recht* (Graz: 1934).

Bornert, René. *La Réforme Protestante du Culte à Strasbourg au XVIe Siècle* (Leiden: 1981).

Bourgeois, Louis. *Quand la Cour de France vivait à Lyon* (Paris: 1980).

Bouwsma, William J. *John Calvin: A Sixteenth-Century Portrait* (Oxford: 1988).

Brady, Thomas. *Ruling Class, Regime and Reformation at Strasbourg* (Leiden: 1978).

Breen, Quirinus. *John Calvin: A Study in French Humanism* (Hamden: 1968).

Cahier-Buccelli, Gabriella, 'Dans l'Ombre de la Réforme de l'Ancien Clergé demeurés à Genève (1536–1558)', in *Bulletin de la Société d'Histoire et d'Archéologie de Genève* (18: 4): 367–89.

Caswell, R. N. 'Calvin's View of Ecclesiastical Discipline', in E. Duffield, ed., *John Calvin* (Abingdon, Berkshire: 1966).

Charpenne, Pierre. *Histoire de le Réforme et des Réformateurs de Genève* (Paris: 1861).

Chaunu, Pierre and Gescon, Richard. *Histoire Economique et Sociale de la France* (Paris: 1977).

Chenevière, Marc E. *La Pensée Politique de Calvin* (Geneva: 1970).

Choisy, Albert and Dufour-Vernes, Louis. *Recueil Généalogique Suisse* (Geneva: 1902).

Claparède, Théodore. 'Les Collaborateurs de Calvin à Genève', in *Histoire de Genève Varia*, AEG, 2012 (14).

Clark, P. and Slack, P. *Crisis and Order in English Towns 1500–1700* (London: 1972).

Cockburn, J. S., ed., *Crime in England 1550–1800* (London: 1977).

Collins, Ross W. *Calvin and the Libertines* (Vancouver: 1968).

Davies, Joan. 'Persecution and Protestantism: Toulouse, 1562–1575', in *Historical Journal*, 1979, 22(I): 31–51.

Davis, Natalie Zemon. 'The Reasons of Misrule: Youth Groups and Charivaris in Sixteenth-Century France', in *Past and Present*, 1971 (50): 41–75.

— *Society and Culture in Early Modern France* (London: 1975).

— 'The Sacred and the Body Social in Sixteenth-Century Lyon', in *Past and Present*, 1981 (90): 40–70.

Delumeau, J. *Le Péché et la Peur. La Culpabilisation en Occident, XIIIe–XVIIIe Siècles* (Paris: 1983).

Demole, Eugène. *Histoire Monétaire de Genève de 1535 à 1848* (Geneva: 1978).

Dewald, Jonathon. *The Formation of a Provincial Nobility* (Princeton: 1980).

Dictionnaire Biographique Française, M. Prevost, *et al.*, eds. (Paris: 1933–91). Aa-Joncoux.

Diefendorf, Barbara B. *Beneath the Cross. Catholics and Huguenots in Sixteenth-Century Paris* (Oxford: 1991).

Doumergue, Emile. *Jean Calvin: Les Hommes et les Choses de son Temps* (Lausanne: 1899–1917). 7 volumes.

Duke, Alistair. 'Nonconformity among the Kleyne Luyden in the Low Countries before the Revolt', in *Reformation and Revolt in the Low Countries* (London: 1990).

Duke, Alistar. *et al.*, eds, *Calvinism in Europe 1540–1610* (Manchester: 1992).

Dunant, Emile. *Les Relations Politiques de Genève avec Berne et les Suisses* (Geneva: 1894).

Fleury, François. *Les Confréries de Genève* (Geneva: 1869).

Foster, Herbert. D. 'Calvin and His Followers Championed Representative Democracy', in R. M. Kingdon and R. D. Linder, eds., *Calvin and Calvinism* (Lexington, Mass.: 1970).

François, Alexis. *Le Magnifique Meigret* (Geneva: 1947).

Gaberel, Jean. *Histoire de l'Eglise de Genève* (Geneva: 1858). 3 volumes.

Galiffe, Jaques A. *Notices Généalogiques de Genève* (Paris: 1829–95). 7 volumes.

Galiffe, John B. G. 'Bezanson Hugues', in *MDG*, vol. 11 (Geneva: 1859).

— *Les Procès Criminels Intentés à Genève en 1547* (Geneva: 1862).

— *Le Procès de Pierre Ameaux*, in *Mémoires de l'Institut National Genevois* (Geneva: 1863), vol. 9.

Ganoczy, Alexandre. *The Young Calvin* (Philadelphia: 1987).

Gartrell, V. A. C., Lenman, B., and Parker, G. *Crime and the Law. The Social History of Crime in Western Europe since 1500* (London: 1980).

Gautier, J. Alfred. *Familles Genevoises d'Origine Italienne* (Bari: 1893).

— *Histoire de Genève* (Geneva: 1898). 9 volumes.

Geisendorf, Paul F. 'Les Annalistes', in *MDG*, vol. 37 (Geneva: 1942).

Geremek, B., 'Criminalité, Vagabondage, Paupérisme: la Marginalité à l'Aube des Temps Moderne', in *Revue d'Histoire Moderne et Contemporaine*, 21 (1974).

Graham, W. Fred. *The Constructive Revolutionary: John Calvin & his Socio-Economic Impact* (Atlanta: 1978).

Guerdan, René. *Histoire de Genève* (Paris: 1981).

Hancock, Ralph C. *Calvin and the Foundation of Modern Politics* (London: 1989).

Head-König, A. L. and Veyrasset-Herren, B. 'Les Revenus Décimaux à Genève de 1540 à 1783', in J. Goy and E. Ladurie, eds., *Les Fluctuations du Produit de la Dîme* (Paris: 1972).

Henry, Louis. *Anciennes Familles Genevoises* (Paris: 1956).

Heyer, Henri. *L'Eglise de Genève* (Geneva: 1909).

Höpfl, Harro. *The Christian Polity of John Calvin* (Cambridge: 1982).

Innes, William C. *Social Concerns in Calvin's Geneva* (Allison Park, Penn: 1983).

Jeanjaquet, Jules. 'Les Patois Romands et leur Vicissitudes', in *Heimatschutz*, 41 (May 1946): 41–45.

Junod, Louis. 'De la Ville Episcopale au Chef-Lieu de Bailliage', in Jean C. Biaudet, et al., eds., *Histoire de Lausanne* (Lausanne: 1982): 151–78.

Kamen, H. 'Public Authority and Popular Crime: Banditry in Valencia 1660–1714', in *Journal of European Economic History*, 3 (1974).

— *European Society 1500–1700* (London: 1984).

— *Inquisition and Society in Spain* (London: 1985).

Kampschulte, Franz W. *Johann Calvin, seine Kirche und sein Statt in Genf* (Leipzig: 1869–99). 2 volumes.

Kingdon, Robert M. *Geneva and the Coming of the Wars of Religion in France, 1555–1563* (Geneva: 1956).

— 'Calvin and "Presbytery": The Genevan Company of Pastors', in *Pacific Theological Review* 18:2 (Winter, 1985): 43–55.

— 'Calvin and the Establishment of Consistory Discipline in Geneva: The Institution and the Men who Directed it', in *NAK*, 70 (1990): 158–72.

— 'The Economic Behavior of Ministers in Geneva in the Middle of the Sixteenth Century', in *ARG* 50(1): 33–39.

Körner, Martin. 'Réformes, Ruptures, Croissances', in Jean C. Favez, *et al.*, eds., *Nouvelle Histoire de la Suisse et des Suisses* (Lausanne: 1983): 7–96.

Lescaze, Bernard. *Sauver l'Ame Nourrir le Corps* (Geneva: 1958).

Lewis, Peter S. *Later Medieval France* (London: 1968).

McGrath, Alistair. *A Life of John Calvin* (Oxford: 1990).

McNeill, John T. 'Calvin Preferred Representative Democracy', in R. M. Kingdon and R. D. Linder, eds., *Calvin and Calvinism* (Lexington, Mass.: 1970).

Major, J. Russell. *The Monarchy, the Estates and the Aristocracy in Renaissance France* (London: 1988).

Mariotte–Löber, Ruth. *Ville et Seigneurie, Les Chartes de Franchises des Comtes de Savoie* (Geneva: 1973).

Martin, Paul E. *Histoire de Genève des Origines à 1798* (Geneva: 1951).

— 'L'Emancipation Politique de Genève 1519-1536', in *Almanach Paroissial* (Geneva: 1925): 27–31.

Martin, William. *Histoire de la Suisse* (Lausanne: 1959).

Ménabréa, Henri. *Histoire de la Suisse* (Chambéry: 1960).

Meuvret, Jean. 'Monetary Circulation and the Economic Utilization of Money in 16th- and 17th Century France', in R. Cameron, ed., *Essays in French Economic History* (Homewood, Ill.: 1970).

Monter, E. William. *Studies in Genevan Government* (Geneva: 1964).

— *Calvin's Geneva* (London: 1967).

— 'Witchcraft in Geneva, 1537–1662', in *Journal of Modern History*, 43:2 (June 1971): 179–204.

— 'De l'Evêché à la Rome Protestante', in P. Guichonnet, ed., *Histoire de Genève* (Lausanne: 1974).

— 'Historical Demography and Religious History in Sixteenth Century Geneva', in *Journal of Interdisciplinary History* 9:3 (Winter 1979): 399–427.

— *Enforcing Morality in Early Modern Europe* (London: 1987).

Muret, Ernest. *Les Patois de la Suisse Romande* (Lausanne: 1909).

Naef, Henri. *Les Origines de la Réforme à Genève* (Geneva: 1936). 2 volumes.

Naphy, William G. 'The Renovation of the Genevan Ministry', in A. Pettegree,

The Reformation of the Parishes: The Ministry in Town and Country (Manchester: 1993).

— 'Baptisms, Church Riots and Social Unrest in Calvin's Geneva', in *Sixteenth Century Journal* (expected publication: 1995).

Neuschel, Kirsten B. *Word of Honour, Interpreting Noble Culture in Sixteenth-Century France* (London: 1989).

Nijenhuis, Willem. 'De Grenzen der Burgerlijke Gehoorzaamheid in Calvijns Laatstbekende Preken: Ontwikkeling van Zijn Opvaltingen het Verzetsrecht', in *Historisch Bewogen, Bundel opstellen voor Prof. dr. A. F. Mellink* (Groningen: 1984): 67–97.

— *Ecclesia Reformata: Studies on the Reformation* (Leiden: 1972).

Oechsli, Wilhelm. *History of Switzerland.* Eden and Cedar Paul, trans. (Cambridge: 1922).

Olson, Jeanine. *Calvin and Social Welfare: Deacons and the Bourse Française* (Sellingsgrove, Penn.: 1989).

Paquier, R. *Le Pays de Vaud des Origines à la Conquête Bernoise* (Lausanne: 1942).

Parker, Thomas H. L. *The Oracles of God* (London: 1947).

— *Supplementa Calviniana* (London: 1962).

— *John Calvin: A Biography* (London: 1975).

— *Calvin's Preaching* (Edinburgh: 1992).

Perrenoud, Alfred. *La Population de Genève* (Geneva: 1979).

Pettegree, Andrew D. M. *Foreign Protestant Communities* (Oxford: 1986).

Plath, Uwe. *Calvin und Basel in den Jahren 1552–1556* (Zürich: 1974).

Rivoire, Emil and Van Berchem, Victor. *Les Sources du Droit du Canton de Genève* (Aarau: 1927–1935). 4 volumes, vol. 2 (1461–1550) and vol. 3 (1551–1620) used.

Ritter, Eugène. 'Recherches sur le Patois de Genève', in *MDG*, vol. 19 (Geneva: 1877).

Roget, Amadée. *Les Suisses et Genève* (Geneva: 1864).

— *Histoire du Peuple de Genève* (Geneva: 1870–87). 7 volumes.

— *Etrennes Genevoises* (Geneva: 1877). 5 volumes.

Roth-Lochner, Barbara. *Messieurs de la Justice et leur Greffe* in *MDG*, 54 (Geneva: 1992).

Roulet, Louis E. 'L'Obstacle de la Montagne dans les Guerres de Bourgogne', in *Revue Internationale d'Histoire Militaire*, 1988 (65): 91–104.

Sauty, Maurice. 'Le Premier Refuge', in *La Tribune de Genève* (Geneva: 1942).

Schilling, Heinz. *Niederländische Exultanten im 16 Jahrhundert. Ihre Stellung im Socialgefüge und im religiösen Leben deutscher und englischer Städt* (Gütersloh: 1972).

Schreiber, Fred. *The Estiennes* (New York: 1982).

Sharpe, J. A. 'The History of Crime in Late Medieval and Early Modern England: A Review of the Field', in *Social History*, 7: 2 (1982).

Spooner, Frank. *The International Economy and Monetary Movements in France 1493–1725* (Cambridge, Mass.: 1972).

— 'Monetary Disturbance and Inflation 1590–1593: the Case of Aix-en-Provence', in *Histoire Economique du Monde Méditerranéen. Mélanges en l'Honneur de Fernand Braduel* (Toulouse: 1973).

Thürer, Georg. *Free and Swiss, the Story of Switzerland.* R. P. Heller and E. Long, trans. (London: 1970).

Tremey, l'Abbé. 'Obituaire des Cordeliers de Genève', in *Mémoires et Documents Publiés par l'Académie Salésienne*, vol. 28 (Annecy: 1904): 235–57.

Vaucher, Pierre. *Luttes de Genève contre la Savoie: 1517–1530* (Geneva: 1889).

Vuilleumier, Henri. *Histoire de l'Eglise Réformée du Pays de Vaud* (Lausanne: 1927).

Wackernagel, Hans G. *Die Politik der Stadt Basel während der Jahre 1524–1528* (Basel: 1922).

Walker, Williston. *John Calvin* (London: 1906).

Wendel, François. *John Calvin* (London: 1963).

Zeigler, Sabine de. 'L'Alliance Perpétuelle entre les Confédérés Suisses et le Roi de France', in *Revue des Deux Mondes*, 1984 (6): 553–61.

INDEX